How to Do *Everything* with Your

iBook

About the Author...

Todd Stauffer is the author or co-author of over 20 books on computing, including *How to Do Everything with Your iMac (1st and 2nd editions)*, *Macworld Mac Upgrade and Repair Bible*, and *The Complete Idiot's Guide to Mac OS 8.5*. He's a contributing editor for MacCentral.com and has written for a number of publications including *MacTech*, *MacAddict*, and CMP Online. He's the publisher of Mac-Upgrade.com as well as the writer and co-host of the Emmy-winning television program "Disk Doctors."

About the Reviewer

John Rizzo is an author of several books about Macs, a computer magazine columnist, consultant, and founder of the MacWindows.com Web site. He was an editor at *MacUser* magazine and a columnist for *MacWeek* magazine.

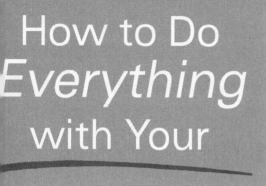

iBook

How to Do *Everything* with Your

Todd Stauffer

Osborne/McGraw-Hill

Berkeley   New York   St. Louis   San Francisco
Auckland   Bogotá   Hamburg   London   Madrid
Mexico City   Milan   Montreal   New Delhi
Panama City   Paris   São Paulo   Singapore
Sydney   Tokyo   Toronto

Osborne/**McGraw-Hill**
2600 Tenth Street
Berkeley, California 94710
U.S.A.

For information on translations or book distributors outside the U.S.A., or to arrange bulk purchase discounts for sales promotions, premiums, or fund-raisers, please contact Osborne/**McGraw-Hill** at the above address.

How to Do Everything with Your iBook

1234567890 VFM VFM 019876543210

ISBN 0-07-212419-9

Publisher: Brandon A. Nordin
Associate Publisher and Editor-in-Chief: Scott Rogers
Acquisitions Editor: Jane Brownlow
Project Editor: Mark Karmendy
Acquisitions Coordinator: Tara Davis
Technical Editor: John Rizzo
Copy Editor: Claire Splan
Proofreader: John Gildersleeve
Indexer: James Minkin
Computer Designers: Roberta Steele, Jani Beckwith, E.A. Pauw
Illustrators: Robert Hansen, Beth Young, Brian Wells
Series Design: Mickey Galicia
Cover Illustration: Cristina Deh-Lee

This book was composed with Corel VENTURA ™ Publisher.

Contents

Acknowledgments

A number of great folks helped me get the book together and in your hands so we could cover the exciting iBook computer as soon as possible. Apple is so secretive these days that publishing folks have to work quickly and intelligently to get books done about Apple's exciting new projects. Since I tend not to work either quickly or particularly intelligently by nature, it's nice to have good people to fall back on.

Jane Brownlow, acquisitions editor, has continued to pound the drum for the *How to Do Everything* series of books, including this iBook tome, after doing everything she could to make its uncle, *How to Do Everything with Your iMac* quite the success.

Mark Karmendy, project editor, was brave, helpful, thrifty, and cheerful throughout the process, even if he never quite did get my address correct on the overnight packages.

Claire Splan, copy editor, did the job flawlessly, making my creative use of the past presumptuous preterit tense something a bit more readable by, say, people fluent in English.

Tara Davis, acquisitions coordinator, kept the whole thing running smoothly, including covering up for hectic submissions gaffes and keeping us all on our toes, except when she took a sprawling and luxurious (though no doubt deserved) vacation. It's testament to her that we almost completely fell apart while she was out.

Very heartfelt thanks go to John Rizzo for his technical edits. The new technical information on AirPort, Mac OS 9, and this unique new iBook was enough to keep my head swimming. With John watching my back, I feel confident that you're getting great, accurate information in this book.

Thanks also the Rich Voelker and Voelker Research in Colorado for helping me get key Apple products when most people were still wondering if their backorders would ever ship. I'd also like the thank Leo Jakobson for keeping the Mac-Upgrade.com Letter going strong while he also provided a temporary roof over all of my test Macs and equipment.

Finally, my thanks to Donna Ladd, who put up with plenty of my late nights working on the project and who didn't object too strenuously on numerous occasions when I opted to order in Chinese food when I finally got home.

Introduction

After the warm welcome from readers that *How to Do Everything with Your iMac* received in the summer of 1999, it seemed only natural to cover the iBook as well, especially after the colorful little notebook's exciting Macworld Expo New York introduction. Before the show was over, we had plans to cover the iBook with the same thoroughness of spirit—over 600 pages worth. Thus, *How to Do Everything with Your iBook* was born.

The iBook may be cute, but it's a powerful, useful computer, made even more powerful by the fact that you can pick it up and take it with you. Bundled with some great applications, you can take the iBook right out of the box and start computing effectively. In fact, most iBooks even have a full battery charge straight from the factory!

In *How to Do Everything with Your iBook*, I'm able to discuss, in grand detail, how to accomplish important computing tasks with your iBook, from the first time you press the power button. Since the iBook comes bundled with powerful applications, I show you how to create documents, reports, memos, newsletters, spreadsheets, databases, and charts. And I mean how to *use* them in real-world situations like overseeing projects, turning in material to teachers, making presentations to your clients, or managing your hobbies.

You'll see how to create slide-show presentations. How to create a mail-merge form letter. How to use templates and assistants for all sorts of things. How to manage your calendar, task list, and contacts with aplomb. How to create databases to track just about anything—sports teams, weddings, recipes, projects, or classroom assignments.

The iBook is about creativity and fun, too. You'll draw, paint, and even create a newsletter or high-end report. You'll learn about QuickTime, digital audio, digital video, and even a little about creating your own movies. Plus, there's an entire chapter on games: How to play the iBook's games, how to add new games, and how to get the best gaming experience.

Beyond that, I'll talk about adding things to your iBook—print documents, add fonts, scan photos, backup data, add a removable drive, and customize your settings. You can even work with Microsoft Windows computers and network your iBook to a group of other Macs. Plus, you'll read about the exciting new

AirPort technology that allows you to create a connection between your iBook and other Macs or the Internet without any cables at all.

And, of course, I spend five whole chapters on the Internet, including e-mail, Web browsing, downloading files, reading the news, chatting in message groups, and exploring America Online.

The book communicates all this very simply. It has four major parts: Get Started, Get Things Done, Get Online, and Customize Your iBook. The book is both a reference and a tutorial. It's arranged so you can move quickly to an interesting topic you look up in the index, or you can just read straight through to get a complete understanding of a given topic. Plus, special elements help you along the way, including notes, tips, shortcuts, and cautions. And, every chapter includes at lease one special "How To" section that will explore one special feature to show you how to make the most of your iBook.

Want to reach me? You can, through my Web site for this book. It's **http://www.mac-upgrade.com/ibook/** on the Web. (You'll also find updates and news on the site, and even some bonus material that didn't make it into this book!)

Todd Stauffer
December, 1999

Part I

Get Started

Chapter 1

Welcome to iBook

How to...

- Prepare yourself for using your iBook
- Figure out all the parts of the iBook
- Set up and move your iBook
- Start, restart, and put your iBook to sleep
- Check battery power and recharge the battery
- Use the unique function keys on the iBook's keyboard

In the summer of 1999, Apple Computer introduced the iBook, marketing it as the "iMac to Go." The iBook is an interesting culmination of nearly two years of engineering on the part of Apple in an attempt to make an inexpensive, attractive, portable computer for education and consumer customers. Although the iBook uses some of the same parts as Apple's professional line of PowerBook portables, the iBook is certainly a unique machine.

Of course, one of the main differences is the look of the iBook. Designed to be simple and affordable, the iBook is also attractive—something that not many other computer manufacturers have accomplished. The idea of a portable computer as a fashion statement is one that the iBook embraces wholeheartedly, coming, in its first iteration, in brazen blueberry and tangerine colors.

Actually, there are tons of cool things about the iBook besides its looks, including:

- A new, curvy design that's lighter than many notebooks while being more rugged and offering a full-sized keyboard and trackpad area.

NOTE   *You'll hear the terms "notebook" and "laptop" used interchangeably. These terms generally refer to any computer that is very portable and can run exclusively from a battery, but still uses the same software that desktop computers use. The iBook is a notebook computer that runs the Mac OS and Mac OS applications (like AppleWorks and Microsoft Office), and is similar in many ways to an Apple PowerBook notebook.*

- Ports arranged on the side of the machine, instead of in the back, to make it easier to configure.

- An active LCD display that's brighter and crisper than most of its competitors, especially in its price range.

- Improved and simplified upgrading through the *Universal Serial Bus* (USB) port.

- Networking connections and a modem (for a telephone connection to the Internet or other online services) built in.

- Wireless networking using the optional AirPort card and AirPort Base Station. This technology (along with the antennas that are built into the iBook's case) allows you to share files or access the Internet without attaching any wires to the iBook.

■ An extended-life battery and energy-saving capabilities that afford up to six hours of battery life on a single charge.

■ A special recharging adapter that uses color to indicate whether or not the battery is fully charged.

■ A handle! Just close the iBook's lid and carry it by the handle, with less risk of it slipping through your fingers.

On top of all this, the iBook is great-looking. (The translucent, polycarbonate shell is actually the same plastic used to make bullet-proof shielding.) But don't let the fashionable looks fool you. The iBook is a complete portable computer, based on the Macintosh operating system (called *Mac OS*).

Your iBook can run just about any Macintosh program, read and edit just about any computer document, and certainly take full advantage of the Internet. In fact, it's designed to be just as functional in a school or small business as it is at home (or in a café).

As the title of this book suggests, if you have an iBook, you can do just about anything you can do with any other sort of computer. You're ready to go.

What Makes iBook Different and Cool

The iBook offers a number of distinguishing features beyond looks. The iBook is a powerful computer, based on the PowerPC G3 processor. It has at least 32MB of computer memory (which allows you to run more than one computer program at once) and at least a 3GB hard disk for storing programs and documents. It also has special features that make it a particularly good computer for gaming, graphics, or even running a small business.

Ease of use was important when Apple created iBook. The iBook is designed to help you get on the Internet, connect peripherals, and even attach to a network easily. It has all the important stuff built in—a modem, Ethernet port, graphics—plus the easiest, most modern way to add extras, the Universal Serial Bus. Plus, it comes with applications already installed that you can use for a variety of home or home-office tasks. And the iBook was designed specifically to be on the Internet—that's one reason it doesn't have a floppy disk drive. The idea is for you to be connected to the Internet most of the time, so you can transfer files to other computers using this global network.

The iBook is also designed to work collaboratively with other computers over the Internet or a local area network of Macs or PCs. It offers some special ways to transmit, share, and translate files that other computers use so you can share and edit them with others. And, as mentioned, it can even network and access the Internet wirelessly.

What Is the Internet?

It's obvious just from the iBook's name (The "i" suggests "Internet") that the Internet will be a huge focus of this book and your experience with the computer. So you'll need to know what it is. The Internet is the name given to a global system for connecting computers to one another using various sorts of cable and wire. Once connected, these computers can share documents and transfer files between one another. The result is electronic mail, message areas, and the World Wide Web.

The Internet began as a government project to move data over long distances with redundancies to survive some sort of wartime or natural disaster. Eventually, it became an important way to connect university computing centers and, later on, individuals. In the early 1990s the corporate world caught on, and electronic mail and messaging became one of the most popular ways to use a personal computer.

So what makes it the Internet? Any computer using a particular language called the Transmission Control Protocol/Internet Protocol (TCP/IP) can connect to the Internet. All you need is a modem or a network connection and an Internet connection through an Internet Service Provider (ISP). The ISP gives you an address on the Internet, called an IP address, which gives your computer a unique identity on this global network. Once you have an address, you're ready to send and receive Internet documents.

NOTE   *To learn more about using the iBook with the Internet, see the section "The Internet Setup Assistant" in this chapter as well as Chapters 16 through 20, in which I discuss the Internet in detail.*

iBook Is Still a Mac

The iBook, ultimately, is a Macintosh computer. It's been simplified, designed in very clever ways, and made to work well on the Internet. At the heart of the iBook, though, is a standard PowerPC G3 processor and the Mac OS.

Any of those Macintosh programs available in the store or through mail order will work with your iBook, as long as they're designed to run with your iBook's Mac OS version. Even new versions of the Mac OS available from stores support the iBook automatically—you don't have to buy special software that's only for

iBook. There are really only two things you need to look for when shopping
for software:

- **Does it run on or install from a CD-ROM?**   Remember, the iBook
  doesn't have a floppy drive.

- **Is it designed for PowerPC?**   Some older Macintosh programs aren't
  specifically designed for PowerPC processors like the powerful processor
  in an iBook. Those old programs should still run, but they might slow
  down the system.

The iBook does not run software specifically written for DOS, Windows,
Windows 95/98, or Windows NT/2000, although many programs are written in
both PC and Macintosh versions. Sometimes you'll even find both versions on
the same CD-ROM.

And that's not to say the iBook can't run PC software at all—it just can't run
PC software right out of the box. Special software programs, such as Connectix
Virtual PC and FWB Software's SoftWindows, allow you to run those programs
on your iBook. That software, called *emulation* software, can trick Windows
programs into believing that they're being run on a Windows-based machine,
even as they're being run on your iBook. It's a neat trick and it can be done
pretty inexpensively.

NOTE   *Computers that use Intel-compatible processors and DOS, Windows, or
Windows NT are often called "PCs" for the sake of convenience and to
differentiate them from computers that run the Mac OS. I'll follow that
convention despite the fact that your iBook is a "personal computer."
Also, Windows and DOS compatibility for your iBook is discussed in
greater detail in Chapter 26.*

iBook Uses USB

Soon after you've gotten your iBook, there's a decent chance that you'll want
external peripherals for it—you may want a printer, a document scanner, a digital
camera, or you may want to connect your iBook to other computers and copy files
between them. Part of the excitement of the iBook stems from its Universal Serial
Bus (USB) and Ethernet ports for upgrading. USB is incredibly easy to use—you
pretty much just plug things in and they work. Plus, it's a standard that the latest
Mac and PC computers can both use. That means your iBook is compatible with
most of the USB peripherals that are being made for computers these days.

When you shop for USB peripherals, have these two things in mind:

- **USB**   Make sure the peripheral offers a USB connector or adapter designed specifically for that item.

- **Mac Driver Software**   Many USB peripherals require special driver software for compatibility with the iBook. Some peripherals don't require driver software, including most keyboards, mice, trackballs, and USB *hubs* (devices that give you more USB ports). More sophisticated devices require the software, so read the box carefully, ask a salesperson, or just focus on USB devices that show up in the Mac section of the store. If it has a Mac, iMac, or iBook logo on the box, then it likely includes the software drivers you need.

You can also upgrade using the Ethernet port, which is a special port designed for high-speed networking connections for transferring files between computers. The Ethernet port doesn't *have* to be used for networking—there are actually some very clever peripherals and adapters that use the Ethernet port to make it easy to upgrade your iBook. Most of the time, though, you'll find the Ethernet port is used to connect your iBook to other computers. Devices like high-speed modems, cable-Internet access boxes, and high-speed printers use the Ethernet port.

You need to watch out for peripherals made for older Mac computers. These days, all of Apple's new products use USB ports, but older Mac printers and scanners may use either *serial* ports or *SCSI* ports for their connections. That's not the end of the world—actually, many of those other peripherals made for older Macintosh computers can still be used, but you'll need an adapter and some know-how. We'll discuss various peripherals in Chapter 23.

iBook: a Quick Tour

Before you get into the heart of setting up your iBook, let's take a quick look at it to get an idea what everything is and how things connect. You'll find that the iBook has some interesting and surprising nooks and crannies.

From the Front

Here you can get acquainted quickly with all the different ways you'll interact with your iBook on a daily basis. See Figure 1-1 for a look at your iBook from the front.

FIGURE 1-1   The iBook's keyboard, from the front

Here are some basic notes about the front of your iBook:

- Above the keyboard, iBook has a special POWER key (actually sort of a button, but we'll call it a key).

- You may also notice that the iBook has, in fact, a full-featured keyboard—it even includes ARROW keys. And, while it doesn't appear to have the number pad that you'll see on many desktop computers, you can use some of the letter keys as the number pad by holding down the special FN key located in the bottom-left corner of the keyboard.

Your iBook's Ports

The ports for your iBook's peripherals and Internet or network connections are on the side of the iBook. There is no special port door or enclosure—most of the available ports are in recessed holes on the left side of the iBook (that's the left side when you're facing the screen). Figure 1-2 shows those ports.

FIGURE 1-2   From left to right: the modem port, Ethernet port, USB port, and
headphone port

Here are some things to keep in mind about the left side of your iBook:

- The modem and Ethernet ports look similar, but accept different types of
  cable. The phone cable accepts a typical RJ-11 "modular" telephone cable
  connector. The Ethernet port accepts an RJ-45 10BaseT cable (also called
  "twisted-pair") connector. If your connector isn't fitting properly, examine
  the cable and the ports carefully.

- The USB port accepts USB cables in one direction only—if the USB
  connector doesn't fit easily, turn it over.

- The port for external speakers is a stereo miniplug port. The speaker port
  is a line-out source; it isn't amplified, so it will only work with powered
  speakers, a stereo receiver, or headphones.

The AC Adapter and CD-ROM Drive

On the right side of the iBook you'll find the CD-ROM drive and the AC adapter
port. Figure 1-3 shows these items.

FIGURE 1-3   On the left, the CD-ROM drive (note its button); on the right, the AC adapter port

Note that the AC adapter port is designed specifically to accept the AC adapter that's included with your iBook. It offers a special feature. When the AC adapter is plugged in (both to the iBook and the wall socket or your surge protector), the port glows either amber or green. Amber means the iBook's battery is currently being charged; green means the iBook's battery is fully charged.

The CD-ROM drive needs to be worked with carefully. If you don't have a CD in the drive already, you can open it by pressing the colored button on the drive. The drive pops open. (If you do have a CD in the drive, drag the CD icon on the iBook's desktop to the Trash icon. This is explained more in Chapter 2.) You'll need to pull the CD-ROM drive tray out with a finger. Then, place CDs as you would in any CD player and lightly push the tray back until it clicks shut. You'll hear the drive whir up to speed, and the CD's icon will appear on the iBook's desktop.

Clean Your iBook

Want to dust off the outside of your iBook or clean the screen? In most cases, you shouldn't use any liquids—a clean, dry, lint-free, non-abrasive cloth can be used to dust of the outside of the iBook or the LCD screen. (Shut down your iBook first.) Note that while the iBook's plastic shell is pretty rugged, it can still be scratched, and those scratches may mar the good looks. Likewise, the LCD screen's facing is plastic that can scratch as well, and it's an expensive component. So, stay away from abrasives or rough cloth.

If you need to clean the screen a little more thoroughly, you can find special cleaners for notebook computers' LCD screens at computer and electronics stores. You can also *lightly* dampen that same lint-free, non-abrasive cloth with water to wipe the screen. Under no circumstances should you spray or spill any liquid directly on your iBook—there are cracks and air ducts on the iBook that could let in the liquid, potentially damaging electronic components.

Before You Set Up Your iBook

If you've just gotten your iBook and you're waiting for me to tell you how to get started, this is your section. I'll also talk about some relevant issues for users who have their iBooks running—stuff not necessarily covered by the iBook manual from Apple. Let's take a quick look.

Get a Surge Protector

Not enough people get surge protectors for their computers, and I suggest you run out and buy one right now (or at least later today) if you plan to start or continue using your iBook. A surge protector is usually a power strip that plugs into the wall outlet, then allows you a number of plugs into which you can plug computer components. (This will be really important if you need to plug in a printer, scanner, camera, and so on as well as an iBook!)

The surge protector is designed to stop power surges from reaching your valuable equipment. It keeps your plugged-in iBook from getting fried, basically, when a power surge occurs thanks to a lightening strike, power outage, or problem with your (or your power company's) wiring.

You need to get the kind of surge protector that includes protection for the phone line, too. In my experience, extreme surges occur more frequently over phone lines than over power lines. Since your phone line will probably almost always be plugged into your iBook's modem port, it's possible for such a surge to go straight into the modem, causing it to cease functioning. In fact, this could affect your entire iBook.

A good surge protector costs at least $25, probably more depending on the features. Don't get an $8 protector and think you're done—often, those are just power strips (giving you more plug receptacles), not protectors. Check the box to see if the manufacturer offers a guarantee or equipment replacement insurance. If so, there's a decent chance the protector actually works well.

Keep Glare to a Minimum

Another important consideration before you set up your iBook is where the windows are. I mean actual windows—those things in the wall that let sunlight in.

Wherever you sit down with your iBook, avoid having a window or the sun, if you're outside, directly in front of the iBook (that is, when you sit at the iBook, the window is at your back). Likewise, avoid having a window or the sun directly behind the iBook (when you look at the iBook's screen, you can see the window behind it). The reason for this is simple—glare and eyestrain. If the window is directly behind you, then sunlight will glare off the screen and make it very difficult to see text and images on your iBook. If the window is directly behind the iBook, your eyes will have trouble adjusting to the varying levels of light, causing strain and fatigue.

Along those same lines, it's always a good idea to look away from your screen for a minute or more every fifteen minutes. That means looking out the window (which should be directly to your right or left if possible), reading a bit, or just letting yourself relax and perform eye exercises, raise a dumbbell, get up for some water, or do whatever you do to relax.

Don't Forget the Ergonomics

1

It's also important—especially if you plan to use your iBook for an extended period of time—to consider the ergonomic implications of your setup. While I'm not a doctor or physical therapist, I can pass on some general advice. You might want to consult an expert regarding your setup, especially if you're experiencing any pain or strain from repetitive movements.

Working with any notebook can cause more neck and back strain than working with most desktop computers, because notebook computers, by design, force most adults or teens to reach for the keyboard and look down at the display screen, especially while sitting at a table.

One thing to watch is how you hold your arms when you're working on the iBook. If you're sitting at a table, both your arms and legs should generally approach the table and chair that support you and your iBook at a 90-degree angle. That means elbows at 90 degrees and knees at 90 degrees with your feet flat on the floor, if possible. Adjust your table and/or chair if neither of these angles is correct.

If you use your iBook often in a reclining position or on your lap, you should at least attempt to keep your arms at right angles to the keyboard. Whether you use your iBook at a desk or on your lap, you should be aware of the way you hold your head and neck in relation to the screen. If you're looking up or looking way down at the screen (craning your neck), that's a great way to develop strain. Holding your neck or head at an awkward angle for any length of time could cause trouble.

You may also notice that placing the screen at different angles will give you a better look at the screen, making it brighter and crisper. The better the screen looks, the better the position you're in from the point of view of eyestrain and fatigue. If you adjust your sitting or reclining position, feel free to adjust the screen again to get it just right.

If you're traveling, moving from class to class or sitting in an outdoor café on a pleasant day, the iBook's screen and keyboard are both high-quality and should work fine. But if you have a desk or table where you'll be using your iBook in one place for a long time, then you might consider some additional tools.

For instance, a USB keyboard and mouse might be a good addition. You can plug them into the USB port on your iBook (or a USB hub, as described in Chapter 23) and use them when you're at your desk. That would also allow you to use a stand of some sort (all different types of computer stands are available from computer dealers and furniture stores) that will raise the iBook to eye level so that you don't have to look down at the screen. You should also avoid a desk or setup that requires you to twist your body in odd directions—sit with feet flat on the floor, looking straight ahead at your iBook. (Of course, the nice thing about the iBook is you can also flop on the bed, floor, or couch and continue using it, at least for a short while!)

 An external keyboard and mouse can use a little additional power from your iBook, so you'll probably want to use these somewhere where you can also plug your iBook's AC adapter in.

Also, don't let the iBook's wrist rest (or other wrist rests and mouse pads, if you have an external keyboard and mouse) let you get lazy. The ideal wrist position is actually over the keys slightly, not resting on the wrist pad—at least, according to most things I've heard and read. If you took piano class as a kid, then you know how you're supposed to hold your hands. Keep them aloft for a while. When you're tired, don't rest your wrists on the smooth plastic of the iBook's wrist rest or on little gel things—quit typing.

Don't forget to get up and move around. No matter how ergonomically perfect your setup, you should definitely leave your chair or switch positions every fifteen minutes or so. Get up, walk around, look at other things, smell the flowers, and so on.

Finally, the second you start to feel pain or strain, get ahold of your doctor. You may be able to get add-on keyboards, mice, or some other solution for working with your iBook. Or, your doctor may prescribe a vacation to the Bahamas for two weeks. Especially if you slip her five bucks or so.

Set Up Your iBook

Now for the moment of truth. When you've accounted for surges, glare, and ergonomics, the setup instructions that come with your iBook are perfectly acceptable.

1. Pull the iBook out of the box and place it on the table.

2. Plug the power cord into the power socket on the right side of the iBook, then plug it into your surge protector.

> NOTE
>
> *Actually, you don't have to plug in the iBook if you'd like to run on battery power. (Most iBooks come fully charged from the factory.) You'll probably want to plug it in though, just to make sure it gets a full charge after shipping and sitting on a shelf at the computer store for a while.*

3. If you'll be using the modem for your Internet connection and/or to send and receive faxes, you'll want to plug it into the phone line. Using the phone wire that came with the surge protector (or another that you have around the house), connect the phone wire from your wall socket to the Phone In socket on your surge protector. Use the phone cord that came with your iBook to stretch from the Phone Out socket on the surge protector to the modem socket on the iBook. (Note: you can use a small phone splitter from Radio Shack or a similar store if you want to place a telephone next to your iBook.)

4. Press the POWER key on the iBook's keyboard.

That's it. If all goes well, your iBook should fire up and be ready to go. You'll hear the startup tone, see the famous Happy Mac, followed by the "Welcome to Macintosh" (or the "Welcome to Mac OS 9") message. Soon, if this is the first time you've turned on your iBook, you'll be greeted by the Setup and Internet Assistants.

> NOTE
>
> *If you don't see anything on the screen, if you see something blinking, or if it's been, say, 20 minutes and nothing is happening and the small green sleep light isn't blinking or strobing, turn to Chapter 26 to troubleshoot your iBook.*

Get Online with the Assistants

Once the iBook has started up and loaded (all the little icons have traveled across the bottom of the screen, and the desktop appears), you'll be greeted by an Assistant. The Mac OS' Assistants are designed to walk you through some of the basic settings that your iBook needs to operate without making you dig too deep into all the configuration controls. The Assistant, instead, asks you plain questions and helps you enter the answers (see Figure 1-4).

Move Your iBook

Pretty soon after you get your iBook set up, you'll probably want to move it again. After all, that's the nature of the beast. There are a few quick things you should think about before moving your iBook:

■ **You might want to put it to sleep first.**   In many cases, this causes data to be saved to the hard disk, as an extra precaution just in case the iBook is dropped, shut down, runs out of battery power, and so on. To make sure this setting is on, consult the "Energy Saver" section of Chapter 21. Of course, you'll put it to sleep automatically if you close the iBook, as recommended next.

■ **Close the iBook and never lift or carry it by the screen.**   Your iBook is rugged, but it's best not to tempt fate. Close the iBook before moving it, and never pick up or move the iBook by grabbing its screen housing (the plastic that surrounds the screen). Always pick up the base of the iBook to transport it.

■ **Close the CD-ROM drive and make sure nothing else is attached.**   I can't tell you how often I get up and start walking with mine only to suddenly remember that the phone cable is plugged in.

■ **Use the handle or two hands.**   The iBook has a handy handle— use it! If you don't, then carry your iBook in two hands. While the rubberized exterior of the iBook may help your grip, slick hands can cause you to drop all six pounds of the iBook if you try to pick it up with just one hand and you're not using the handle.

The Mac OS Setup Assistant

The first Assistant you'll encounter is the Mac OS Setup Assistant. This little guy's job is to learn what it can about you and your iBook so it can make some basic settings. Run through the Setup Assistant and answer the questions. When you've answered a question, click the right arrow to continue. If you need to go back to a previous question, click the left arrow.

Mac OS Setup Assistant

Introduction

Welcome to the Mac OS Setup Assistant!

Based on your answers to a few questions, this assistant makes some basic settings on your computer and sets it up so that you can print documents and share files over a local network.

This assistant starts with some questions about yourself, where you are, and how you plan to use your computer.

Click the right arrow to continue.

◁ 1 ▷

FIGURE 1-4   The Setup Assistant, one of two you'll meet when you first fire up your iBook

A few notes about the Setup Assistant's questions:

1. The name, organization, date, and other questions should be fairly self-explanatory. Enter all this information, clicking the right arrow to move to the next screen.

2. When you're asked if you want to use the Simple Finder, the answer is No. Simple Finder just hides some of the basic commands for dealing with files. I'll discuss all that stuff thoroughly, so you'll want all those options available in the Finder.

3. On the next screen, the computer's name can be anything: "Todd's Computer," "Sleepy," "iBook 2079-34," "Fourth Graders' iBook," and so on. If you connect the iBook to a network, this is the name that will be used to represent your iBook to any other computers on the network. (This doesn't include the Internet—just networks in offices, schools, on university campuses, or in your house if you have two or more computers hooked up to one another.)

4. The password can be anything up to eight characters long, but it needs to be something you can both remember and keep private. You won't need it to get into your iBook and use its files—it's only for when you want to access your iBook from another computer, over a network connection.

5. On the next screen, you probably won't want a shared folder unless you're setting up a network in your office or organization. (See Chapter 24 for more on networking.)

6. If your printer is connected via a USB port, it's a Direct Connection. If it's connected via the Ethernet port (or if you print to a printer somewhere else on the network) it's a Network Connection. If you don't have a printer yet, choose Direct Connection.

7. Finally, choose the type of printer you have—if it's an Apple-brand printer. (Other printers need to be set up separately, as shown in Chapter 22.)

That's it. With all those decisions made, you can click the Go Ahead button and the settings are entered. Next up, it's the Internet Setup Assistant.

NOTE   *You can quit the Assistant at any time without causing undue harm to your iBook—just choose File / Quit or click the Close box. If necessary, you can start up the Assistant again. It's located in the Assistants folder on your iBook's hard disk.*

The Internet Setup Assistant

The first major decision you need to make regarding the Internet is how you plan to connect. There are four basic ways to do it. The first way is through a special deal that Apple has made with the Earthlink service. It's also the easiest one. The second way is through any different Internet Service Provider (or ISP). You'll find both national and local ISPs listed in your local newspaper, yellow pages, or a computer magazine if you'd prefer to go with a local service. The third way is using the America Online service, which can also act as an Internet Provider. The fourth way is to hook up to the Internet over a network instead of using your modem. Depending on which option you choose, you'll answer the Internet Setup Assistant differently.

■ **Earthlink or Other Apple-Recommended ISP**   If you choose to create a new Earthlink account, click Yes when asked if you want to set up Internet access. Then click No when you're asked if you already have an account.

Follow the onscreen and audio instructions for finding and creating a new Internet account.

NOTE   *In the top-right corner of the TotalAccess setup assistant, which walks you through creating an Earthlink connection, is a small QuickTime control that plays back the sound associated with each window. You can use the controls like a VCR's controls—click the play or pause button to stop and start the playback, or click the "X" icon to turn off the sound. You can click the musical note to listen to the sound again.*

- **Your Own ISP**   Choose Yes, you want to set up Internet access and Yes, you already have an account. You'll need to enter information about your ISP, all of which the service provider should be able to give you easily. (See Chapter 20 to learn more about the information required for an Internet account.)

- **America Online**   Tell the Assistant that No, you don't want to set up Internet access. Do it through the AOL service. (See Chapter 19 for more on America Online and the Internet.)

- **Over a Network**   If you have a LAN, cable modem, ADSL, or similar connection that uses Ethernet, tell the Assistant Yes, you want to set up Internet access and Yes, you already have an account. Then choose to connect via Network. This is discussed more in Chapter 20.

If all goes well, you'll end up with an Internet account. I briefly discuss how to connect to the Internet in Chapter 2, then you'll see all sorts of things you can do on the Internet in Chapters 16 through 20.

iBook: On, Off, Sleep, Info

Once you get past the Assistants, you're greeted with the desktop—the space that shows your hard drive icon, a few words across the top of the screen, and even a little Trash can. I'll discuss this in more depth in Chapters 2 through 5. For now, we need to talk about a few important commands.

Which Mac OS Do You Have?

The first one is the About This Computer command. Throughout this book, I'll be referring to different versions of the Mac OS. In order to know if a particular feature is available to you, you'll need to know if you have Mac OS 8.6, Mac OS 9, or a later version loaded on your iBook. To find out, move your mouse pointer to the top of the screen and point it at the little multicolored Apple picture. Click the trackpad button once. A menu appears.

Now, move the mouse pointer down the menu until it points at About This Computer. Click the trackpad button again. The About This Computer window appears:

This window tells you some other things about your iBook, including how much system RAM (random access memory) it has and how that RAM is being used.

Put iBook to Sleep

Unlike a lot of computers and most other appliances, you aren't necessarily encouraged to turn off your iBook when you're done using it. You may have already noticed that it takes a minute or so for your iBook to start up when it's completely off. Instead of powering down, you can choose to put the iBook to sleep instead, so that it wakes up more quickly and is ready to work. The best part is that the iBook is still using very little power, even though it's turned on and working. That means you'll use very little battery power, too.

In fact, you may have already noticed that your iBook will go to sleep automatically after only a few minutes if it's not connected to an AC outlet. That's because the iBook has special settings that help it conserve as much battery power as possible. These settings are made in the Energy Saver control panel, which is covered in Chapter 21.

For other times that you'd like to put the iBook to sleep, you just need to know the Sleep command. Click once on the Special menu, then click the Sleep command. Your iBook's screen blanks after a few seconds and the small sleep light at the bottom of the screen begins to strobe. (It looks a little like the iBook is snoring.) This tells you that iBook is in Sleep mode. You can also tap the POWER key while iBook is still awake to get that same window full of options. Click the Sleep button to put iBook into Sleep mode.

To wake up your iBook, just tap the POWER key or any other key. The screen will light back up and iBook will beep to acknowledge your command. You're ready to compute.

Want an even easier way to put your iBook to sleep? Shut the lid! The iBook is designed to go to sleep whenever you close the lid. You'll see the strobing sleep light on the back of the iBook. To wake it back up, open the iBook again. It should wake up automatically.

Make sure iBook is really asleep! If you close the lid to put your iBook to sleep, you should check after a minute or so to ensure that it's gone to sleep. (If the screen stays on for a long time while the iBook is closed, its possible for heat to build up and cause damage.) If the small sleep light isn't strobing or if the Apple logo on the back of the iBook is glowing a bit, that indicates that the screen may still be on. This can result from a system crash or some software problem that isn't letting the iBook go to sleep. Open your iBook back up and troubleshoot it to see if it has crashed or frozen. (Chapter 26 offers troubleshooting tips.)

Turn Off iBook

So say you don't want to use your iBook for a few days or longer. You can go ahead and shut it down to conserve battery power. There are a couple of different ways, and it's important to turn it off correctly.

Most of the time you'll choose the Shutdown command to power off your iBook gracefully. In the Finder, move the mouse pointer up to the Special menu. (If you don't see the Special menu, click once anywhere on the desktop background.) Click once on the Special menu item and the full menu appears. Now point to the Shut Down command and click the trackpad button again. Your iBook shuts down.

Another way to do this is to tap the POWER key on the keyboard or on the iBook's chassis once. A dialog box appears, allowing you to do a number of power-related things. To shut down, just click the Shut Down button.

You may notice that, after choosing Shut Down, your iBook goes through a few hoops. It will ask all open application programs if they need to save anything, then it tells them to quit. During that process, the application may ask *you* if you want to save something. Once all that business has been taken care of, the iBook quits all those programs, writes some last-minute things to the hard disk, and shuts itself down. To start up again, tap the POWER key.

Restart iBook

Sometimes you don't really want iBook to shut all the way down. Instead, you want it to simply restart—maybe you've just installed a new program or you're experiencing odd behavior because of an errant program or similar issue. In that case, you'll choose Restart from the Special menu. You can also tap the POWER key and choose Restart. Your iBook goes through the same procedure as when you issue the Shut Down command, except that it starts right back up again when it's finished.

 What's the difference between restarting and shutting down and turning iBook back on? With Restart, the power stays on and the Mac OS starts right back up again after shutting down and clearing out system memory.

Reset Your iBook When Frozen

Unfortunately, your iBook will sometimes "freeze" while you're working with it—things on the screen stop moving around and you can't move the mouse pointer and/or click on things. This can be the sign of a software or hardware problem—the sort of thing discussed in Chapter 26. But it also just sometimes happens when a minor error occurs. In that case, you should know how to quickly get your iBook working again.

First of all, make sure your iBook is really frozen. There are a few steps you can take to figure out if it's really time to restart your iBook:

■ **Is iBook waiting for you to do something?**   Sometimes you need to insert a particular CD-ROM, click a certain option, or otherwise follow the

1

instructions on your screen before iBook can continue. Make sure there isn't a dialog box or alert box in the middle of the screen telling you something you need to do before the iBook can continue working.

■ **Can you move the mouse pointer around?**   If you can move the mouse pointer around with the trackpad, but nothing else happens and there's no waiting message, iBook might just be thinking things through. Wait a few minutes (up to 15 minutes or more) to see if anything happens.

■ **Can you interrupt the current application?**   If you can move the mouse pointer but nothing else is happening, try to interrupt the current program. Press the ESC key or simultaneously press the ⌘-. (period) keys. You should also try pressing ⌘-Q to quit the application.

■ **Can you force the current application to quit?**   Sometimes an application encounters an error, but doesn't give control back to the iBook. In that case, you'll need to force quit the application. Press ⌘-OPTION-ESC. Then, click the Force Quit button. This should quit the application and return you to the Finder. Save work in your other applications and restart your iBook.

■ **Can you emergency recover?**   If nothing else is working, try pressing ⌘-POWER (that's the actual POWER key on the keyboard). If a text box appears on the window, type **G F** and press RETURN. That might return you to the Finder. Save your data and restart the iBook.

■ **Can you reset with the power button?**   If all else fails, hold down the POWER key on the iBook's keyboard until you see the screen go blank (about five seconds). That will turn off your iBook instantly (you'll lose data). Now press the POWER key again to start it up.

In some rare cases, none of these resets will work. If that's the case, you may need to straighten a paperclip and insert it in the reset button hole to restart your iBook. Do this gently, and press down until your iBook restarts. The reset button is located between the POWER key and the screen, hidden a bit among the grille openings. Figure 1-5 shows you how.

 Note that this procedure will cause you to lose data—it's only recommended as a last resort.

Resetting like this causes the iBook's internal clock to be reset, which is a pain. You'll need to update the current time and today's date in the Date & Time

FIGURE 1-5   Resetting your iBook using the reset button, located in the grille just above the POWER key

control panel. (Open the Apple menu, choose the Control Panels menu, then choose Date & Time. The Date & Time control panel is discussed in detail in Chapter 21.)

Check the Battery and Recharge

Your iBook is designed to run in two different modes—either connected to its AC adapter (which would then be plugged into an AC socket) or running on the internal battery. You can switch seamlessly between these two without doing anything special with the iBook—just plug its AC adapter in when you want to run off AC power and unplug it when you want to run from the battery.

Check Battery Consumption

While you're running your iBook from the battery, there's a countdown going on. The iBook monitors its battery carefully and tries to give you an accurate indication of how much time you have left on battery power. You're showed this

in two ways. At the top right of the screen, you'll see a small
icon that looks like a AA battery. If it's completely red, you're
fully charged. As you use the iBook on battery power, the indicator loses some
of its redness, indicating how much charge is left in the battery.

You can also use the control strip down at the bottom of the screen to monitor
battery life. The control strip is a small strip of controllers and indicators that you'll
find at the bottom-left of your screen (unless someone has moved it). Click the part
that looks like a tab, and you'll see the control strip spring open. Somewhere close
to the left edge of the control strip, you'll likely see the battery indicator (it can look
different in different configurations, but it probably shows at least one graphic that
looks like a car's fuel gauge.) Here you can find out how much time is left on the
battery, how full of charge it is, and so on. If you'd like to change the way the
indicator works, click it, then select the items you want to show or hide from the
menu that appears.

Recharge the Battery

The battery in the iBook is screwed in tight—it can be replaced, but Apple doesn't
encourage you to swap batteries while you're working with the iBook. (With past
PowerBooks and many other notebooks computers, users were encouraged to
swap batteries because of the short battery life of those models. The iBook,
according to Apple, can get up to six hours from a single charge!)

 You may need to swap the battery after many months or years of use,
though, which is discussed in Chapter 23.

Since it's locked into your iBook, the best way to recharge your iBook is to
simply plug in the AC adapter that came with it. (Don't use other adapters—if you
lose or break yours, get another Apple authorized iBook AC Adapter. They're
unique.) If you've plugged the iBook in correctly, you'll see a circle around the
AC port on the iBook start to glow. If it glows amber (orange-ish) then you know
that the iBook is recharging. Once it's fully charged, the color changes to green so
you know in an instant that you can unplug it again, if necessary.

NOTE *There are also onscreen clues that the iBook is recharging. The battery icon in the menu bar will have little lightning bolts to show it's being recharged, and the indicator in the control strip will also change to show you a recharging battery. Once the battery is fully charged, you'll see the indicator in the control strip change to an icon of a battery with a little AC plug to indicate that you have the AC adapter plugged in.*

If you're sitting somewhere near an AC socket, you can go ahead and leave your iBook plugged in, even if it's fully charged. You'll simply run off AC power (without using any battery capacity) until you decide to pick up the iBook and move on. Likewise, with the AC adapter plugged in, the iBook goes into a Better Performance mode, where it won't blank the screen, spin down the hard disk, and automatically sleep as quickly as it does when you're running on the battery.

TIP *You can change the power-saving settings that the iBook uses when it's plugged into the AC adapter or running from the battery. Check Chapter 21 for details on the Energy Saver control panel, where these settings are made.*

Explore the Special Keys

The keyboard on an iBook offers fewer keys than the typical desktop computer, but those keys can actually do more things that many larger keyboards. For instance, you can control the brightness of the screen or the volume of the speaker from the keyboard. You can also use some of the keys as a numeric keypad, and you can get some standard computer keys—like Page Up and Page Down—using the keyboard.

The FN Key

Look at your keyboard carefully and you'll see that many keys on the keyboard have two different labels. One label is black, the other matches the color of your iBook. For instance, on my blueberry iBook, the U key also has a small, blue 4 on it.

The colors offer a basic code. If a key has two different labels, the black label is active when you type normally. Press that U key in most cases and you'll get a "u" on the screen. (You'll get a capital "U" if you hold down the SHIFT key and press the U, just like back in typing class.)

If you hold down the small FN key in the bottom-left corner of the keyboard, suddenly the colorful labels become active. If you hold down FN and press U, then the result will be a 4.

1

That FN (it stands for "function") key makes your keyboard a lot more useful. You can turn the keys on the middle-right of the keyboard into a numeric keypad for number entry.

TIP
You can turn the number keys on so that you don't have to hold down the FN key. Just press the NUM LOCK key (also labeled F5) at the top of the keyboard near the middle. To get the letter keys back, press the NUM LOCK key again.

Now that you know the code, you can explore the different colorfully labeled keys while you hold down the FN key. For instance, the arrow keys turn into PG UP (page up) and PG DN (page down) keys for paging quickly through documents.

Control Keys

Up along the top of the iBook keyboard you'll see some other special keys. There are dual-purpose keys labeled with small icons (in black) and F1 through F6 (in color). When you're not pressing the FN key, these keys perform some special tasks:

- ■ F1 and F2 are the brightness keys. The icons in black look like the sun. Click the small sun (F1) to lower the brightness level of the screen; click the large sun (F2) to make the screen brighter.

- ■ F3 and F4 are the volume keys. The icons look like speakers with sound waves coming from them (or something like that.) To lower the volume, press the speaker that has fewer sound waves (F3); to raise the volume, click the speaker with more sound waves (F4).

- ■ F5 is the NUM LOCK key, which we've already discussed. Press it to activate the number keys on the keyboard for numeric entry.

- ■ F6 is the mute key. Press it to cut the sound to the speaker or sound-out port immediately.

So what about the F1-F12 labels on those keys? They're called *function keys,* and they're often activated within the applications you use for special commands. To use F1 through F6, hold down the FN key while you press them. F7 through F12 work whether or not you press the FN key.

Chapter 2

Get Acquainted with iBook

How to...

- ■ Figure out what the desktop is for
- ■ Learn how to use the trackpad and button
- ■ Click and drag on the screen
- ■ Get to know icons and windows
- ■ Change settings with the Control Strip
- ■ Get a quick start on the Internet

The iBook really is pretty easy to set up and power on, since everything is clearly labeled and there are only a few different cords to deal with. If you've worked your way through Chapter 1, then, hopefully, you've gotten past the Assistants, you have an Internet account, and all your settings are in order.

Now let's take a look at what you see once you've powered up your iBook. Your iBook is a combination of hardware—things on the outside that you touch and push like the CD-ROM drive, the trackpad, and the keyboard—and software—pictures and words on the screen like icons, menu items, and windows.

In this chapter you'll see how those things come together. You'll learn how to move around on the screen, work with the trackpad and keyboard, even how to insert CD-ROMs, work with the internal hard disk, and change things like the sound settings.

What Is the Desktop?

Let's begin at the beginning. After you've pressed the Power button and your iBook has started up, you'll see the desktop (assuming you've gotten past all that Assistant stuff discussed in Chapter 1). The *desktop*, for all practical purposes, is the background pattern or color you see on the main screen of your iBook when it first starts up. Think of it in terms of 3-D: The little hard disk picture, the Trash picture, and everything else is sitting *on top of* the desktop, as shown in Figure 2-1.

If it's called the desktop, then clearly this is supposed to have some relationship to a typical desk, right? Sort of. The desktop represents the top of a desk, but there's stuff on it that you wouldn't normally put on the top of your desk, like a trash can and a hard disk. But, for the most part, the metaphor holds up.

So what are you looking at? The desktop is comprised of three major components: icons, menus, and windows. Each represents a real-world idea you'd find near, or on, a desk.

What's an Icon?

Icons are the small pictures that represent parts of your iBook or files on your computer. The Macintosh HD icon, for instance, represents the hard disk that's inside your iBook's enclosure. A hard disk is used for storage—it's sort of a virtual filing cabinet. The icon, then, allows you to open that filing cabinet and root around in the file folders.

The Trash icon is similar—it's where you toss files that you no longer need in your filing cabinet. You put files in the Trash, then you empty it using a special command that deletes files from your iBook's hard disk.

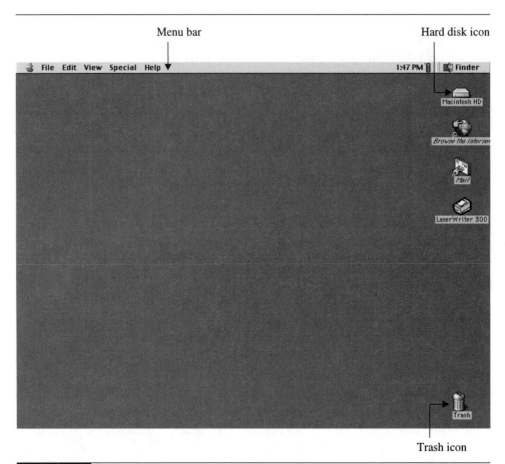

FIGURE 2-1   The iBook's desktop is similar to a real desktop, at least in some ways.

 If you've used Microsoft Windows 95 or Windows 98, you'll find that the Trash is very similar to the Recycle Bin in Windows. The major difference is that entire folders are stored, intact, in the iBook's Trash, while the Windows Recycle Bin will usually do away with folders.

What's a Menu?

The little words at the top of the iBook screen are called *menus*—they're situated in the long, white menu bar. Each of these menus holds related commands that allow you to accomplish things on your iBook, almost as if they were the drawers full of pencils, staplers, and scissors you'd find in a real desk. The menus that appear when you first start your iBook are part of an application called the Finder, which is started automatically whenever you turn on your iBook. The Finder is specially designed to help you manage your documents and file folders.

The menu bar offers two other distinct menus, shown in the following illustration. Both of these menus will appear no matter what application you're using on your iBook. One is the Apple menu; the other is the application menu (the icon in the top-right corner that changes to show the application you're currently using). Pull down the application menu and you can switch between programs that are currently open. Pull down the Apple menu and you can access a whole bunch of different applications and accessories to help make your computing tasks simpler. In a sense, the Apple menu is the "junk drawer" of your iBook desktop.

File   Edit   View   Special   Help   1:51 PM   Finder

NOTE   *If you're used to Windows 95 or 98, you'll notice that menus on the iBook work slightly differently. In Windows, each individual window has its own menu bar within that window. On the iBook, the menu bar is always at the top of the screen. Other than that, there really isn't much difference. It may seem like the iBook menus are always the same, but the menu bar actually changes every time you load or switch to a different application.*

What's a Window?

Our final element, the window, is sort of like a piece of paper you might find on your real-world desktop. It's in windows that you'll type things, read things, draw things, and so on. In fact, on the iBook, just about anything you do will take place in a window, like the ones shown in Figure 2-2. If you'd like to see a window, point your mouse pointer at the Macintosh HD icon and click the trackpad button twice quickly. (That's called a "double-click" and it almost always *opens* the item you double-clicked.) We'll talk about windows in greater depth later in this chapter.

FIGURE 2-2 Just about everything that happens on your iBook happens in a window.

Use the Trackpad and Keyboard

Unlike most computers you'll encounter, the iBook does not offer a mouse for controlling things on the screen. Instead, you use a trackpad—the small, silvery square in the middle of the wristrest on the iBook—which allows you to move the mouse pointer around on the screen.

The trackpad can take some getting used to. Instead of moving a mouse around on a mousepad, you slide your finger around on the trackpad. Your finger movements move the mouse pointer around on the screen. For some folks, this makes sense almost immediately; for others, the solution is to buy a mouse. (You can hook one up pretty easily using Universal Serial Bus, or USB for short. See Chapter 23 for details.)

There are a few things to watch out for with the trackpad. First, in some setups, the trackpad will also act as a mouse button, as mentioned in the next section. If you tap your finger on the trackpad, you may be selecting or even opening things, so watch out for that. Second, things can get wacky if you put more than one finger on the trackpad at a time. Figure out which finger is most comfortable for you, then try to stick with it. Some people use their pointer or middle finger while others can actually use the trackpad with their thumbs while leaving their hands on the keyboard. (Not a skill I've developed, despite my childhood piano lessons.)

Also, try not to get the trackpad wet or use your trackpad with sticky, wet, or overly sweaty fingers. You'll have to wait for the trackpad to dry out to be useful again, since it actually senses moisture from your finger to calculate movements.

Click with the Trackpad Button

The trackpad is used to point at, grab, carry, and activate items on the desktop. It'd be more convenient if you could just reach into your iBook screen to grab things, but that gets expensive really fast since you'd have to buy all those new iBooks. Instead, you use the trackpad and its button to point and grab for you.

When you move the trackpad, a little arrow on the screen moves around with you to indicate where the trackpad is currently pointing. That arrow is called the "mouse pointer," and it's something you'll get to know very well. (It's also sometimes called a "cursor," but mouse pointer is the correct name, even though you have a trackpad. iBook users are simply second-class citizens when it comes to the lingo.) No matter what you want to do with your iBook, you'll likely do it by fingering the mouse pointer over to an icon (or menu item or window) on your screen and clicking the trackpad button.

There are three basic actions that the mouse allows you to perform: selecting, opening, and dragging-and-dropping. Each of these is a combination of pointing with the trackpad and clicking the trackpad button:

- ■ **Selecting**   To select an item, move the mouse pointer until it's touching that item, then press and release the trackpad button once. A selected icon becomes highlighted, a selected window comes to the *foreground* (it appears "on top" of other windows), and a selected menu drops down to show you its contents. In the case of a menu, you move your mouse pointer down to the menu item and click again to select that menu item. You'll also find buttons and menus within applications. You'll select them in this same way.

■ **Opening** Icons like the Macintosh HD and the Trash are opened (to reveal their contents) by pointing the mouse pointer at the item and double-clicking the trackpad button. Other icons can be opened, too, like document and application icons.

NOTE *You can also open icons and folders in the Finder by selecting them (pointing at the icon and clicking once), pointing at the File menu and clicking once, then pointing at the Open command and clicking once.*

■ **Dragging-and-Dropping** On the desktop and in the Finder, you can drag icons around to move them from one place to another. Place the mouse pointer on an item, click and hold down the trackpad button, and move your finger across the trackpad. Now you're dragging. To drop the icon in its new location, let go of the trackpad button.

You'll also find that the mouse pointer changes sometimes to reflect different things that are happening. It'll turn into a little rotating beach ball, for instance, when the iBook is busy doing something that can't be interrupted. It'll turn into an *insertion point* (a capital "I", also called an *I-beam*) when the mouse pointer is hovering over a window (or sometimes a portion of a window, such as a part of an electronic form) where you can type, as shown in Figure 2-3. Click the trackpad button once while pointing at that window and the insertion point is placed in the document. Type with the keyboard and your words appear.

FIGURE 2-3 The insertion point shows you where typed text will appear.

Special Keyboard Keys

So you use the trackpad for selecting, opening, and moving things around on the screen. You use the keyboard, then, for getting text into your iBook. Most of the time, you'll find that typing on the iBook keyboard is like typing on any computer terminal, typewriter, or word processor. But there are special keys on the iBook's keyboard and special key combinations you'll use for various things.

The special keys are the CTRL (Control), OPTION (Option), and ⌘ (Command) keys, as shown in Figure 2-4. These keys, along with the more familiar SHIFT key, can be used in various combinations to perform special commands in your application or in the Finder.

You'll see these special keyboard commands throughout the text. In order to use them, you'll need to hold down all of the keys at once, then release them all together. For instance, ⌘-S can be used to save a document; press ⌘ first and then the S key, release them together, and the command will execute.

> NOTE   *Some of the most common keyboard commands are discussed in Chapter 8; others are discussed throughout the book.*

This brings up a fourth instance where you can use the trackpad to perform some interesting tasks. Hold down the CTRL key, click the trackpad button, and then release them both. Do this in the right place (usually when pointing at an object in the Finder or in an application) and you'll get a *contextual menu*—a special "pop-up" menu of options regarding that object, as shown in the

FIGURE 2-4   The special keys on your keyboard work together to create keyboard commands.

accompanying illustration. In essence, iBook is offering a special set of menu commands that are relevant to the object you've chosen.

 If you're used to Microsoft Windows, you'll notice that the iBook only has one trackpad button. This CONTROL-click scheme is sort of like "right-clicking" in Windows.

Work with Icons and Windows

I mentioned that icons are the small pictures on your iBook screen which represent parts of your iBook's internal filing system. And while icons represent different parts, *windows* are the way you view those parts. When you open a file folder or a document, you'll view its contents using a window. Let's look at icons and windows each in turn.

In Depth with Icons

You can often tell right away what a given item is based on the way its icon looks. There are about five different types of icons you'll encounter on your iBook, and each gives you an idea of what it does based on its general appearance.

■ **Hardware Icons**   These icons appear automatically on the desktop whenever the iBook recognizes certain types of hardware items, like a disk it can use for storage or a printer it can use to print. Whenever you start up your iBook, for instance, the internal hard disk is recognized and the Macintosh HD icon is placed on the desktop. Similarly, if you pop a CD-ROM into your iBook's CD-ROM drive, that CD's icon appears on

2

the desktop. Another major type of hardware icon is printer icons, which allow you to manage any printers you have attached (or networked) to the iBook. *Hardware icons generally look like the devices they're representing—the disk icons look like little disks and the printer icons look like little printers.*

■ **Folders**   Open your Macintosh HD and a window appears that shows you more icons—most of them will be folders. Folder icons are used by the Finder to help you manage your documents and applications. You can create a storage system by creating new folders that organize your documents and applications. *Folder icons look like file folders.*

■ **Programs**   Application programs like AppleWorks or Internet Explorer have their own icons, too. When you "open" an application (by pointing to its icon and double-clicking the trackpad button) you start up that application, loading all of its menu commands and, probably, a document window. You can then start creating. *Program icons are often the most creative—they tend to be unique icons designed by the application programmers.*

■ **Documents**   Document icons are created whenever you save a document from an application. If you create a report in AppleWorks, for instance, a new document is created when you invoke the Save command, and a new icon appears in the Finder. Just as with a document in a physical filing system, you can move that document icon to a folder where you want it stored. *Documents often, although not always, look like pieces of paper or some variation on that theme— a piece of paper with a special logo, for instance.*

■ **System Icons**   This is a catch-all category that we won't discuss too much right now. The Mac OS features many special little icons that perform certain tasks behind the scenes on your iBook. For instance, there are system icons that represent the fonts you use in your documents and the control panels you use to change settings on your iBook. You'll read a lot more about system icons in Parts 4 and 5 of this book.

■ **Aliases**   An alias is a special "empty" icon that doesn't really represent a file or a device—instead, it *points* to that file. For instance, an alias allows you to have a pointer to a document or application on your desktop while the actual document or application is stored deep in your hard disk's file folders. Instead of being an entire *copy* of a file, an alias is simply an icon that represents the file. *An alias looks like the document or application it points to, but it has a special arrow as part of the icon and its text is always italic.*

Icons will respond to the trackpad commands described early in this chapter. They can be selected, opened, and moved around the screen using drag-and-drop. In fact, you'll find that there's often reason to drag an icon over another icon and drop the first icon on the second icon. For instance, you can drop a document icon on top of a folder icon to store that document in that folder. Similarly, you can drop a document icon onto an application icon to start that application and view the document.

Rename Icons

Want to give an icon a new name? It's easy enough, as long as the icon isn't stored on a locked disk or on a CD-ROM. (You'll learn about read-only disks later in this chapter.) Here's what you do:

1. Find the icon you want to rename.

2. Point the mouse pointer at the name of the icon.

3. Press RETURN. The name portion of the icon changes and an insertion point appears.

4. Type the new name (or press DELETE to erase the current one).

5. Click elsewhere—on the desktop, away from the icon— when you're done editing.

Open Up Windows

So what do you do with these icons? In most cases, you open them. When you open them, a window appears. Double-click the Macintosh HD icon, for instance, and a window appears that reveals that disk's folders and other icons, as shown in Figure 2-5.

FIGURE 2-5   The Macintosh HD's window

Any window has standard parts that make it easy to deal with. All of these parts allow you to move things around, resize them, stack windows—do different things to make windows a little easier to work with. Here's what the different parts do:

- **Close Box**   Click this to close the window. If you're dealing with an application window, closing the window doesn't necessarily quit the application. You'll often have a different command to Quit (usually in the File menu).

- **Title Bar**   This part of the window tells you what the window represents. It's also used to drag the window around the screen: Click and drag on the title bar, then release the button to drop the window.

- **Size Box**   Click this box to resize the window to optimum (in many cases). Click it again to revert to the original size.

- **Windowshade Control**   Click this control to "roll up" the window so that only the title bar appears.

- **Scroll Bar**   This bar shows you that the window can be scrolled. If more information is in the window than can be shown at once, you'll be able to scroll to see it.

- ■ **Scroll Box** Click and drag the scroll box to scroll the window's contents up and down (or side to side, if you use the bottom scroll bar).

- ■ **Scroll Arrows** Click the arrows to scroll up and down or side to side within the window.

- ■ **Resize Box** Click and drag the resize box to make the window larger or smaller.

You'll also encounter some different sorts of windows, called *dialog boxes*. These windows are designed so that the Mac OS can ask you questions or get you to provide information. Usually, dialog boxes require you to click Cancel or OK after you've finished entering information. They don't always, though. As shown, some dialog boxes (sometimes called *modeless* dialog boxes) require you to click the Close box once you're done with them.

Close box

TIP   *If you have experience with Microsoft Windows 95 or 98, you'll notice some minor differences in the way Mac OS works with windows. In Microsoft Windows, the Close box is on the far right side; in Mac OS, the Close box is far left. It works the same way in both, except that the Close box in Mac OS doesn't usually quit the application (sometimes it does quit the application in Microsoft Windows). Also, Microsoft Windows doesn't offer a Windowshade control, whereas Mac OS doesn't have a Minimize button.*

Another type of dialog box is called an *Alert*. These messages appear when the Mac OS or an application needs to get your attention because something immediate is happening. This can range from something wrong with a printer or peripheral to a problem with a crashed or misbehaving application. You can usually dismiss an Alert by clicking the OK button. In some cases you may want to click the Cancel button if you don't want to perform the action.

 Your iBook may be set to read Alert text out loud using a technology called PlainTalk. This can be helpful if you're not sitting in front of your iBook's screen.

Hard Disks, CD-ROMs, and Peripherals

You've already seen that one of the major types of icon is the hardware icon—the type that allows you to deal with hardware items found inside or attached to your iBook. Your hard disk is where you'll store most of your documents and any new applications that you install on your iBook. The hard disk is a small box inside your iBook that uses magnetic technology to write down the ones and zeros that make up "digital data." Visually, this digital data is represented by folder, application, document, and system icons that are displayed when you double-click the disk icon in the Finder.

CD-ROMs are slightly different. CD-ROM is a read-only technology because you can't actually save any files to the CD, delete files stored on the CD, or move things to different folders on the CD. Instead, you can only copy from the CD to another disk, start up an application, or open a document directly from the CD. (CD-ROM stands for Compact Disc–Read-Only Memory.)

Storage vs. Memory

Storage disks are different from main memory in any computer. Main memory is called Random Access Memory (RAM) and is actually comprised of little computer chips—usually arranged on a special plug-in module—that hold digital information. RAM is sort of the short-term memory of your iBook. Anything currently on the screen, anything being printed, and some behind-the-scenes work goes on in RAM. (In Chapter 1 you saw how to get the About This Computer information, which tells you the current status of RAM.)

But your iBook can easily forget what's in RAM, since RAM is wiped clean whenever you power down your iBook. In fact, if a power surge or a removed battery cut power to your iBook, you'd also lose whatever was in RAM at that time. RAM needs power in order to remember things.

That's why you have storage disks. Hard disks and removable disks (like Iomega's Zip disks) are used for writing things down and saving them long term. Whenever you create a document using your iBook, you'll want to save it to a disk—that lets you keep the document over the long term. The same goes for applications. If you bought and wanted to use Microsoft Office, you'd need to install the application by copying it to your hard disk. That way it's easily accessible to your iBook—your iBook will remember, long term, how to run Microsoft Office.

The Hard Disk Icon

The hard disk icon is always there on the desktop. As the iBook starts up, it looks for the hard disk and other storage disks that are attached to the machine. Any disks found are mounted on the desktop. That is, the icon is made available for you to use. The Mac OS automatically places these icons in the top-right corner of the desktop as the iBook is starting up. If you insert a disk (like a CD) after startup, the Mac OS places the CD's icon as close to the top-right corner as it can get without covering up another icon.

To peer into the hard disk's contents, you can point the mouse pointer at the icon and double-click. This opens the main-level window that shows all of the folders used to store things on your iBook. The hard disk icon can be renamed— you can even change the look of the icon—but you can't throw the icon away or store it inside a folder or on another storage device.

If you're having trouble renaming your hard disk or another disk (aside from a CD, which can't be renamed), you may have File Sharing turned on. See Chapter 24 for more information on the File Sharing feature.

The Trash Icon

We'll talk about the Trash in more depth in Chapter 3. Basically, it's the one way you delete things from your hard disks, removable disks, or desktop. You simply drag-and-drop icons onto the Trash. When you've dropped something on the Trash icon, that icon changes to reflect the fact that the Trash is now "full."

That doesn't mean that items have been deleted yet, though. You can still double-click the Trash to open its window, and then drag files or folders out of the Trash and back onto the desktop or your hard disk.

You can't throw the Trash icon away (well, you could try, but good luck) and you can't easily change the name, appearance, or location of the Trash icon. (You can move it around the screen but you can't store it in a folder.) In that respect, it's probably the most stubborn of the desktop icons.

The Trash icon is also used for something else—ejecting CDs and other removable disks. It takes some getting used to, but after you've dragged a CD or removable disk icon to the Trash, it will pop out of its drive (or the CD-ROM drive will open up). Disks are not deleted or erased when dragged to the Trash. There's a special command that erases entire disks when it's necessary to do so.

 Erasing disks is discussed in Chapter 26.

CDs

CD icons appear when you insert a CD into the CD-ROM drive of your iBook. If you don't already have one inserted, press the colored button on the right side (when you're facing the screen) of your iBook. The CD-ROM tray pops out slightly—you can use a finger to pull it out the rest of the way. Now, place a CD in the tray, label up, just as you would with an audio CD player. Gently push the tray back into the iBook. Once it snaps shut, the iBook will go to work spinning the CD and taking a look at it.

When iBook has recognized the CD, it puts a new icon on the desktop to represent that CD. If the CD is a CD-ROM (also called a data CD, meaning that it's designed to store data files that your iBook can access in the form of icons), then you can double-click the CD icon to open it and view the files, as shown in Figure 2-6. If it's an audio CD, you'll see a special audio CD icon. In that case, double-clicking the CD icon will open up a window that shows you the different music tracks on the CD. Double-clicking one of the music tracks will play that track.

Since a CD-ROM is read-only, you can't drag an icon from the desktop or your hard disk to the CD's icon or window. You can drag icons the other way, though, causing the items on the CD to be copied to your hard disk or desktop. (Actually, stuff copied to your desktop is also stored on your hard disk. You just see it on the desktop.)

FIGURE 2-6   Double-click a CD icon and you'll open a window that reveals its contents.

To eject the CD-ROM or audio CD, you can do one of three things. You can select the CD icon with your mouse pointer, then choose File | Put Away in the Finder. That ejects the CD. You can also select the CD and choose Special | Eject. Or, as mentioned before, you can drag the CD icon to the Trash. That ejects the CD; it doesn't erase it.

You can invoke the Put Away and Eject commands using keyboard shortcuts. Put Away is ⌘-Y and Eject is ⌘-E. Just select the icon, then press ⌘ and the appropriate letter key at the same time.

After you eject the CD, the tray pops out of the front of the iBook (again, you'll pull it the rest of the way out with a finger). Now you can remove the CD and close the tray or replace the CD with another one and start again.

Removable Disks

If you have an Iomega Zip drive, a SuperDrive, or some other sort of external storage drive, those disks will appear on your desktop as well. Usually, you just pop the disk into the drive and, after a short delay, its icon appears on the desktop. It'll work just like a CD, with the exception that you'll be able to save files to removable storage disks.

To eject removable disks, you have the same options as ejecting a CD:

- Select the disk and choose File | Put Away.
- Select the disk and choose Special | Eject.
- Drag the disk's icon to the Trash.

Printer Icons

Once you've attached your printer and properly set it up in the Chooser (discussed in Chapter 22), you'll have a new icon on the desktop—a printer icon. The printer icon works a little like the Trash icon, although you can rename the printer icon or store it in a folder if you want.

You can also drag documents onto the printer icon. When you drop them, the document's application is automatically opened and told to print the document; then the document is in the printer queue. The printer icon can be double-clicked to show the items that are in the printer queue to be printed, as shown in Figure 2-7.

In fact, every time you choose the Print command from within an application you create a print job. Each job appears in the print queue, which shows you which jobs are planned and their order. You can drag jobs around in the print queue to change their order, or you can select a job and use the buttons in the print queue to pause, start, schedule, and delete jobs.

FIGURE 2-7   The printer icon can be double-clicked to reveal controls for current print jobs.

For more on printing and desktop printer icons, see Chapter 22.

Change Settings with the Control Strip

The easiest way to change settings is through the control strip. The control strip can be used to change many things about your iBook's behavior, including sound, monitor settings, file sharing settings, and even getting connected and disconnected from a modem connection to the Internet. We'll cover the different uses of the control strip throughout this book. For now, though, let's just get started using it.

First, if you don't see the control strip, you need to do the following:

1. Move your mouse pointer up to the Apple menu and click once to open the menu.

2. Move down to the Control Panels entry. Another menu opens to the side.

3. Slide the mouse pointer over and highlight Control Strip, and click your iBook's trackpad button. This opens the Control Strip control panel.

4. Choose Show Control Strip. This is a radio button—just click the button next to the option you want to make active.

5. Click the control panel's Close box.

Now the control strip should appear on your iBook screen. One of the first things you may need to do is adjust the sound on your iBook. To open the control strip, click once on the little tab that appears at the edge of the screen:

Click the tab

TIP   *Want to move the control strip around? Point the mouse to the tab and hold down the OPTION key. The mouse pointer turns into a little hand. Now you can drag the control strip up and down the side of the screen. If you want to switch sides of the screen, just drag the control strip over to the other side.*

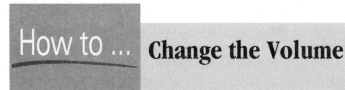

How to ... **Change the Volume**

Don't like your current sound level? With the control strip open, you can adjust the sound volume on your iBook. Here's how:

1. Move the mouse pointer to the small icon that looks like a speaker and click the trackpad button.

2. Now, move the mouse pointer up and down the slider bar to choose the volume level.

3. When you've chosen an acceptable level, click the trackpad button.

Your iBook reacts by beeping to show you how loud the sound is set. If you're happy with the level, you can click the tab again to close the control strip. We'll discuss all the other features of the control strip throughout the book. You'll learn how to customize it in Chapter 21.

Get a Quick Start on the Internet

This may seem like an odd place to discuss your first foray onto the Internet, but it so happens that this chapter (and Chapter 1) has covered all the tools necessary for you to get online. Plus, the Internet is just plain important when it comes to working with your iBook (remember, Internet is what the "i" in "iBook" stands for). I'll be discussing the Internet throughout this book (even before we get to a specific discussion of the Internet in Part 3). Let's get you online quickly so you can go exploring.

The tools we'll use are the control strip, the Browse the Internet icon, and the Mail icon. These last two should appear on your desktop by default.

Sign On to Your ISP (for Modem Connections)

If you used the Internet Setup Assistant to create a new Internet account or to enter information about an existing account, everything should be set up for you to dial your iBook's modem and connect to the Internet. Probably the easiest way to do so is through the control strip.

Open the control strip and you should see the Remote Access control—it looks like a little Mac and a telephone pole. This is the control you'll use to sign onto the Internet (if you're using a modem).

Here's how to connect to the Internet using a modem:

1. Click once on the control and the Remote Access control strip menu will appear.

2. Make sure your iBook's modem is connected to the phone line and make sure the phone line isn't currently in use. Click Connect.

3. You should hear your iBook pick up the phone and start dialing. (If you don't hear dialing, adjust the iBook's volume as discussed earlier in the "Change Settings with the Control Strip" section.)

4. Now iBook goes through the Internet sign-on phase. If all goes well, the Remote Access control will change and start to show a counting clock that shows the amount of time you've been connected. If things don't work out, you'll see an error message telling you why Remote Access can't sign on.

5. Once you're connected, you'll also see a blinking icon where the Apple menu's icon appears. The blinking continues for the entire time that you're connected to the Internet. You're ready to run Internet programs.

If you want a little more feedback while you're trying to get connected, choose the Remote Access control, then choose Open Remote Access from the menu. This opens the entire Remote Access control panel, where you can watch the connection and change settings according to instructions in Chapter 20.

Browse the Internet

Once you're connected to the Internet (whether you used a modem or another method), you can double-click the Browse the Internet icon in order to start up your Web browser and begin to explore the Internet. By default, this launches Internet Explorer (see Figure 2-8).

What you'll most often do on the Internet is read documents and click links to new documents. Sometimes you'll do other things, such as filling in forms and downloading files, which we'll discuss in depth in Chapter 17.

FIGURE 2-8   Internet Explorer can be used to browse the World Wide Web.

If you want to get a quick start, though, here are the basics:

- A *hyperlink* is text that appears underlined and in blue. (Images and buttons on the page can also be hyperlinks.) Click a hyperlink once to open a new Web page. Hyperlinks are the basic method for "browsing" on the Web—click a link you think is interesting to see the associated document.

- The Back and Forward buttons are used to move to a previous page, then forward again (if desired). If you click a hyperlink, for instance, read the page, then decide to go back to the previous page, click the Back button.

- The address box is used to enter direct Web page addresses and other sorts of addresses, as discussed in Part 3. It's in the address box that you'll type addresses (like **http://www.apple.com/**), then press RETURN to visit that address. You should enter addresses as precisely as possible including all the dots (.) and slashes (/).

Other than that, just experiment with the other buttons and settings. You'll notice that there are already some preprogrammed Favorites that allow you to visit interesting spots on the Internet, and there are buttons for changing preferences, changing the text size, or going directly to a "search" page where you can enter keywords and find new Web pages to visit.

To quit Internet Explorer, choose File | Quit from the menu. Once you've quit the browser, you might also want to sign off of the Internet so you don't keep the phone line tied up. That's discussed in the section "Sign Off Your ISP."

TIP
If you don't see the Browse the Internet icon on the desktop, it may have been thrown away. You can invoke the same command by clicking on the Apple menu, then clicking the Internet Access item. Now, click Browse the Internet.

Get Your Mail

We'll discuss this one really briefly. Double-click the Mail icon on the desktop and (by default) Outlook Express appears. If this is the first time you've run Outlook Express, you may see a dialog box with a bunch of settings. If you've already used the Internet Setup Assistant, you can just click OK in this settings dialog box.

Now, in the main Outlook Express window, you'll see the mail interface, as shown in Figure 2-9.

FIGURE 2-9   Outlook Express allows you to read your e-mail.

If your Internet connection is up and active, click the Send and Receive button. This causes Outlook Express to sign onto your e-mail server computer (which is at your Internet Service Provider's location) and get any e-mail you have waiting.

Once retrieved, new e-mail appears in the top-right window pane. All you'll see is the subject line and information about who sent the message and when. New mail is boldfaced. To read a message, click once on the name of the message. Its contents appear in the bottom-right pane of the window.

If you don't see your new messages, make sure you have the Inbox selected in the left pane of the Outlook Express window. If you have it selected and you still don't see any messages, it probably means you haven't received any new messages.

While you're reading the message, you can elect to reply to or forward the message by clicking the appropriate button in the toolbar. If you forward or create a new message, you'll need to make sure you've entered the recipient's e-mail

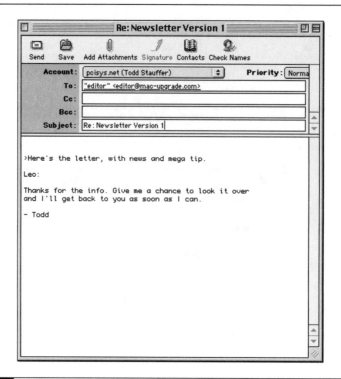

FIGURE 2-10   Sending an e-mail message

address in the To: line of the message (it's automatically placed there if you're replying), then enter your message in the body of the message window. When you're finished, click Send (see Figure 2-10).

Of course, there's a heck of a lot more you can do. If any of this is confusing or you need more information, Chapter 16 discusses e-mail in depth. To quit Outlook Express, choose File | Quit from the menu. Once you've quit the e-mail program, you might also want to sign off of the Internet so you don't keep the phone line tied up.

Sign Off of Your ISP (for Modem Connections)

When you're done with the Internet connection, you can select the Remote Access control in the control strip again. You'll have the option to Disconnect—click it. After a few seconds, you're disconnected and your phone line is ready to be used again.

Chapter 3

Manage Your Files with the Finder

How to...

- Dig through and organize Finder windows
- Select and move icons in the Finder
- Create folders, duplicate files, and deal with aliases
- Delete files and toss out the Trash
- Get information on your disks, folders, and files
- Organize your iBook with folders, aliases, and labels
- Change the way you view your folders

W hen you first start up your iBook, in addition to seeing the desktop, you also see the application that creates the desktop—the Finder. The Finder is a special application that's always active and can't easily be "quit." It's the Mac OS' built-in application for dealing with the files on your hard drive, CD-ROM drive, and removable media. It does some other important things, too.

3

The Finder 101: Windows

The Finder offers you the tools for a basic filing system on your iBook. It allows you to create and name folders, move documents around, store application programs where you want them, and delete icons of all sorts when necessary. In a way, it's convenient to think of the Finder as an icon management utility.

You've already seen that the Finder is also responsible for helping you manage the iBook itself. For instance, it offers you the commands to shut down, restart, or put your iBook to sleep. The Finder also provides the About this Computer command in the Apple menu, which allows you to view how system RAM is being used by applications.

Most of all, though, the Finder is about managing files.

In fact, the Finder works a little like a filing cabinet. Open the cabinet (that is, open a disk), root through folders, and create new ones when you need to file away documents for a new project. The only difference is that you have to do all this on your computer screen. (Oh, and you never have to run out for any of those smelly markers from the office supply store.)

NOTE   *If you're used to Microsoft Windows, you may be happy or unhappy to learn that the iBook really doesn't have an equivalent to the File Manager or Windows Explorer. Instead, you just use the Finder method of opening and closing folders to organize your files. Windows 95/98 has a similar capability, allowing you to open folders from the My Computer icon to view their contents. Since this is the only way to manage files on your iBook, though, the Finder's use of drag-and-drop is much more sophisticated.*

Dig Deep into Finder Windows

The Finder doesn't really help you *search* for things in an automated way—that's for Sherlock to do, as discussed in Chapter 6. Instead, the Finder helps you organize and look for things manually.

In a way, it's like comparing a library card catalog system to a computerized library search system. With the Finder, you'll be opening a lot of drawers and flipping through a lot of cards.

The most basic way to find something in the Finder is to dig for it. To do that, start out at the desktop and double-click the icon for your hard disk, CD-ROM, or a removable disk. This opens the window for that device so you can see its folders. Then, find the folder you want to look in next and double-click it. That folder's window opens. Keep double-clicking folders until you find the item you're looking for, as shown in Figure 3-1.

After a while, this can get tedious. Still, it's easier to find the icon you're looking for when your folders are subdivided.

FIGURE 3-1   Digging into your iBook's folders using the Finder

> TIP
>
> *There's a special trick to getting through many windows while keeping Finder clutter to a minimum: Hold down the OPTION key as you open new windows. Every time you open a new window, the previous one will close behind you if you're holding down OPTION as you double-click.*

Move Icons to Finder Windows

A big part of using the Finder is mastering drag-and-drop. You'll move files and folders around a lot in the Finder—from one folder to another, for instance. You do that by dragging the icon in question from one part of the Finder and dropping it on another part.

> TIP
>
> *Here's a neat trick. Say you have a window open but you want to view the window of the folder or drive that contains the folder you're looking at. (In computing parlance, we'd call that the "the parent folder.") Hold down the ⌘ key and click the name of the folder in the title bar. A little menu appears allowing you to open parent folders to view their contents.*

Spring-Loaded Folders

The Finder offers some interesting ways to accomplish your dragging and dropping. Consider this: What if you have a file on the desktop that needs to go into a subfolder—say, a folder named Memos inside the folder named Documents? If the file you're moving is on the desktop, you have two choices. First, you can open the Macintosh HD by double-clicking; then you open the Documents folder by double-clicking; then you open the Memos folder. With the Memos window open on the screen, you could drag your file into that window. But that's messy.

The better way to get that file into a particular folder is to use the spring-loaded folders feature in the Finder. Pick up the icon you want to move (point the mouse pointer at it and hold down the trackpad button) and drag it over to the Macintosh HD icon.

Now, leave it on top of the icon (so that the Macintosh HD icon is highlighted) for a few seconds. Keep holding down the trackpad button—don't drop the file yet. Suddenly, the Macintosh HD window springs open! Now, locate the Documents folder icon and do the same thing—keep holding down the trackpad button while hovering over the Documents icon. It'll spring open, too. You can keep doing that until you reach the folder you want to drop the icon in. When you get there, release the trackpad button and you've successfully moved the icon. In fact, this feature is so cool that the other windows will close as you open the next window, just to keep things neat and tidy.

Pop-Up Windows

Here's another cool feature of Finder windows. If you have a window open that you use a lot—like the Documents window—you can keep it open all the time, but out of the way. Just grab the window by its title bar and drag it to the bottom of the screen. Get far enough down and suddenly the window becomes anchored to the bottom and the title bar becomes a little tab, as shown in Figure 3-2.

 You can also select any open window in the Finder and choose View | As Pop-up Window from the Finder's menu to change it into a pop-up window.

To open the window and see its contents, just click the tab once. The window pops up. If you want to drag an item to a pop-up window, just hover over the tab itself (with the dragged item in tow) and the window pops up to reveal its contents.

FIGURE 3-2 Tabbed windows are a great way to store often-used windows accessibly, yet out of the way.

You can also resize the window using the little resize tools (the diagonal lines) on the side of each pop-up window.

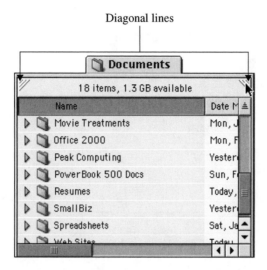

To turn a pop-up window back into a regular window, just drag the tab up until the outline turns into a normal window. Release the trackpad button and the window is back to normal. You can also select the pop-up window and choose View | As Window to change it into a regular window.

Select Items in the Finder

You already know how to select items and how to drag-and-drop. But what if you want to gather more than one icon at a time? There are two ways to do it.

First, you can select more than one icon at a time by dragging a box around the items. Here's how:

1. Place the mouse pointer just above and to the left of the first icon you want to select.

2. Hold down the trackpad button and drag the mouse pointer toward the icon you want to select.

3. Once the first icon is highlighted, keep dragging diagonally to expand the box you're creating. As you expand the box, every item inside the box becomes highlighted.

4. When you've highlighted everything you wanted to highlight, release the trackpad button (see Figure 3-3).

FIGURE 3-3   Drag a square around multiple icons that you want to highlight.

Now you have multiple items highlighted. Click and drag one of the items and they all come along—you can treat them all as if they were a single icon, moving them *en masse* to a different folder, to the printer icon, or to the Trash; opening them all using the File | Open command; and so on. To deselect them, just click anything else on the screen (such as part of the desktop or a different icon).

If you want to add icons that aren't grouped together on the screen, you can add them individually by holding down the SHIFT key as you select each icon. Now, each time you click another icon with the SHIFT key held down, it gets added to all the others that are highlighted, as shown in Figure 3-4.

Want to find a particular file in a folder? You can just begin typing its name. Type an S for instance, and "Sales Presentations" might be selected; type SI and "Simple Plan" might be selected; type SIZ and "Sizing Reports" might be highlighted. Keep typing letters in the name of the file or folder you want to select until it's highlighted.

Remember that these selections don't just work in Icon View windows— you can drag a rectangle around List View windows as well, and you can select

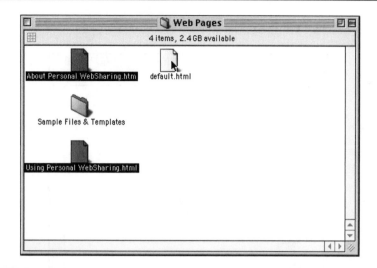

FIGURE 3-4   The SHIFT key lets you select icons that aren't physically close to
one another.

additional items in List View windows using the SHIFT key. (List View and other
views are discussed toward the end of this chapter in the section "Change How
Folders Are Displayed in the Finder.")

Get Information from Finder Windows

You can actually learn quite a bit about your iBook's hard disk and any other
drives you have attached to your iBook from their Finder windows. That's because
the Finder windows are usually doing a little math in the background for you.

One of the main concerns you may have as a computer owner is maintaining
your hard drive and making sure you have enough space to store new files. It's a
constant struggle that may keep you up nights. Often, the only answer is to delete
older files that you don't use anymore—at least once your drive gets a little closer
to full. But how can you tell if your drive is getting full?

Look at a Finder window. If you open the Macintosh HD window (or any
folder window) and take a look at the top of it, you'll see some information about
the Macintosh HD, as shown in Figure 3-5. Specifically, you'll see how many
items are in that folder and how much storage space is left on that particular disk.
This works just as well with a removable disk, too.

Storage space remaining

FIGURE 3-5   Finder windows show you how much storage space is remaining on that disk.

Finder 201: Create Folders, Copy Files, and Build Aliases

Before you get too busy moving things around, you'll need to create some folders you can move things into. You'll also find that it's often important to duplicate items or create aliases to those items. The Finder is designed to help you do just that.

Create a New Folder

You'll probably learn pretty quickly that it's a good idea to create folders of your own and store them on your hard drive or within other folders. For instance, I think it's a good idea to create a folder called Documents almost right away. We'll discuss a method for storing documents later in this chapter, but it's generally good to have a single Documents folder on your hard drive that contains subfolders where you organize all of your documents. That way, you always know where your documents are. It also makes it easier to back up your documents—copy them to a removable drive—for safekeeping.

3

To create a new folder, open and select the window where you'd like the folder to appear. (If you want it to appear on the desktop, you don't need to select a window.) Then, choose File | New Folder. (You can also just press ⌘-N.)

When the folder appears, its name is already highlighted. Just type to give the folder a new name. When you're done naming it, press RETURN. Now you have a new folder, as shown in Figure 3-6.

You'd think the next logical step would be creating a document, right? Well, you can't really create a document in the Finder—that's what applications like AppleWorks do. You'll be creating documents soon enough (in Chapter 5, to be precise). In the meantime, you can *duplicate* existing documents using the Finder.

Create a Duplicate

The Finder makes it easy to move files around, and it makes it simple to create a duplicate of an existing document, application, or folder. All you have to do is select the item and choose File | Duplicate. You could also select the item and press ⌘-D.

Duplicating creates an exact copy of the file, except that no two items can have the same name and be stored in the same folder, so the duplicate gets the appendage "copy" added to its name. Now, if you like, you can move that duplicate to another folder and rename it.

FIGURE 3-6   A new folder, created and named in the Finder

Remember, this is a duplicate of the original and it no longer has a relationship to the original file. For instance, if you had a memo document called *Memo to Bob* and you created a duplicate, you'd now have two memos. If you subsequently opened the duplicate memo in AppleWorks and edited it to say "Dear Sue," the original *Memo to Bob* would not be altered. Only the copy is affected.

Another note about duplicating—it takes up space. Every file you create takes up space on the hard disk in your iBook. If you create many duplicates, then you'll be filling up your hard disk. Instead, you might want to consider creating aliases.

SHORTCUT *Instead of duplicating the file, moving it, and then renaming it, how about duplicating the file "on the fly"? It's easy. Pick up the original icon you want to duplicate and drag it to the location where you want the duplicate to appear (you can use spring-loaded folders and all that jazz). Now, when you're in the final spot for the duplicate, hold down the OPTION key. Did you see the pointer turn into a plus sign? That means when you let go of the trackpad button, a duplicate will be created. Keep holding down the OPTION key and release the trackpad button. Your duplicate is made.*

Create an Alias

In Mac lingo, an *alias* is simply an icon that represents another file. For instance, when the desktop first appears on a brand new iBook, some aliases to Mail and Browse the Internet appear. These alias icons point toward real files buried deep in the Internet folder. The aliases are on the desktop for convenience.

There are a few advantages to creating aliases for your important files:

- ■ **Convenience**   Say you have the real AppleWorks icon buried three folders deep on your hard disk. If you like, you can create an alias icon for AppleWorks right on your desktop.

- ■ **Size**   Aliases are very small files—unlike a duplicate, an alias isn't a complete copy of the file. It's basically just an icon. So you can have many aliases in different folders on your iBook and still not be taking up too much storage space.

- ■ **Safety**   Why is it safer to create aliases? Because if you (or a co-worker, partner, or kid) throw away an alias, the original item doesn't get destroyed.

If I take that AppleWorks alias I created and trash it, for instance, then AppleWorks itself is unharmed back in the Applications folder. However, if I had dragged the actual program out to the desktop and trashed it, I'd be in trouble. The actual program would have been deleted.

Convinced? If so, get started creating aliases. In the Finder, select the file for which you'd like an alias. Then, choose File | Make Alias or press ⌘-M.

An alias appears, complete with italicized text and the word "alias" appended to the name. Now you can move the alias anywhere you want to and rename it, if desired.

 Want to create an alias that immediately appears in its final resting place? Here's how: Drag the original icon to the place where you want the alias to appear—you can use the spring-loaded folders or just drag it to the desktop. Now, instead of letting go, hold down the OPTION and ⌘ keys. See the pointer turn into a little curved arrow? That means when you drop the icon, it'll create an alias instead of moving the original. Keep holding down OPTION and ⌘, then let go of the trackpad button. Voilà! Your alias is ready.

Find the Alias' Original

Sometimes an alias just isn't good enough—you need to deal with the real file. If that's the case, you can select the alias' icon and choose File | Show Original (or press ⌘-R).

This will cause the folder containing the alias' original file to appear in the Finder.

Fix an Alias

Aliases can break sometimes—suddenly, the alias will no longer point to its original file. This happens for a variety of reasons, but mostly it happens because you move, delete, or otherwise mangle the original file. Perhaps you have an alias to Internet Explorer on your desktop, then you install a new version of Internet Explorer. The alias on your desktop points to the older version (which you've since deleted, let's say) and not the new one.

If an alias can't find its original, this dialog box appears:

If you don't need the alias anymore, you can click Delete Alias and the alias will trouble you no longer. (Actually, it's simply been moved to the Trash, not permanently deleted.) If you want to continue to use the alias, click Fix Alias... and the Fix Alias dialog box appears. Now, find the file you want the alias to point to, select it in the dialog box, and click Choose. Now the alias is pointing to the chosen file. (The Fix Alias dialog box works just like the Open dialog box, which is discussed in Chapter 5.)

Finder 301: Delete Icons

The Mac OS really only offers one way to delete Finder icons—by moving them to the Trash can. Actually, this is a good thing, because it makes you think carefully about what you're doing before you make a mistake and accidentally delete something. (Ask your Unix- or DOS-using friends if they've ever accidentally deleted something.) Plus, the Trash offers a way to recover files before they're permanently deleted, even if they've already been thrown away.

Toss Icons

If you're pretty sure you don't need a particular item anymore, you can drag it straight from its current location in the Finder to the Trash. Just drag the icon over the Trash until the Trash icon becomes highlighted, then release the trackpad button. The item is dropped and the Trash can becomes "full." (The Trash's icon changes so that the lid is off and you can see bits of "trash" inside.) You can throw out multiple files just as easily—select them all by dragging a box around them or holding down the SHIFT key, then drag the group to the Trash icon.

If this is all too much mousing (or, uh, *trackpadding*) for you, there are three other ways to move files to the Trash:

■ With the file(s) selected in the Finder, choose ⌘-DELETE to move items to the Trash.

■ Select the file(s) in the Finder and choose File | Move to Trash from the menu.

■ CTRL-click on a file, then choose Move to Trash from the contextual menu.

Retrieve Items from the Trash

Just because an item has been thrown in the Trash doesn't mean it's been deleted. If you have something in the Trash that you need to get back, just double-click the Trash icon. This opens the Trash window, allowing you to see everything that's been thrown away. When you find what you need, you can drag it back out of the Trash onto the desktop or into another window.

 Documents and applications can't be launched from the Trash—they must be dragged out to a folder or the desktop before they can be used.

Empty the Trash

The step that really gets rid of the items in the Trash is the process of emptying the Trash. Once it's been emptied, you can't get those items back. (Unfortunately, there's no "iBook Dumpster" to go rooting through.)

CAUTION *Think carefully before emptying the Trash. If you delete something accidentally, you'll probably have to buy a special utility program, like Norton Utilities, to get the item back.*

If you're sure you want to get rid of the items in the Trash can and reclaim the storage space that they're taking up, then choose Special | Empty Trash. The Finder will count up the items in the Trash and tell you how many items will be deleted and how much space you'll recover. If that all sounds good, click OK.

Once you click OK, the files are gone forever (at least, without a special recovery utility program). Say "Bye, bye!"

 Want to skip the alert box that tells you how much stuff will be thrown away? Hold down the OPTION key as you choose Special | Empty Trash. The Trash is emptied immediately.

What do you do if you really, really didn't want to delete a file and you've emptied the Trash? Well, there's a chance it can be recovered, especially if you haven't used the disk much after emptying the trash, but you'll need a special program like Norton Utilities. See Chapter 27 for tips on getting yourself out of trouble spots like an accidentally tossed file.

NOTE *If you do want to undelete files, the best plan is to stop using the iBook until you get your undelete utility program. That way, the iBook won't overwrite the area where the thrown-out files used to be on the disk. If the files are overwritten (usually by new, saved files you create) then they're almost impossible to recover.*

Finder 401: Get Information on Files

Another unique Finder responsibility is the Get Info command, which allows you to learn more about files in the Finder. The Get Info command can be used to tell you how much storage space an item takes up, who created the item, and any comments that have been stored about that item.

To get info, select the item in the Finder and choose File | Get Info. The Get Info dialog box appears, offering you information about the selected file, as shown in Figure 3-7. (Note that the Get Info dialog box's title bar name changes for the individual item you're getting info on.)

In the Get Info dialog box you'll see information based on the type of file selected—that is, an alias offers different information from a folder, which is different from an application. You may also see a special pop-up menu, which you can use to switch between General Information and information on Sharing (networking) and Memory, depending on the type of item you're getting information on.

To close the Get Info box, click its Close box.

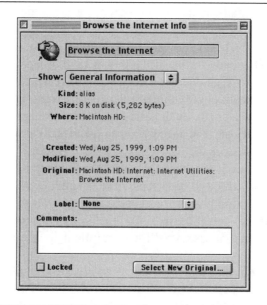

FIGURE 3-7   The Get Info box tells you basic information about your files.

Want to learn more about your hard drive or other storage device? Get info on it. There you'll see how much storage space the drive initially offered, how much is being used, and how much is left.

Finder Grad School: Get Organized

With all these Finder concepts under your belt, you're ready for the next step—getting your files organized. I realize you may not yet have a ton of documents and applications since you haven't gotten around to working with them much. Actually, that's a good thing. The earlier you implement a good organizational scheme, the better your entire experience with your iBook will be.

One of the main reasons to get organized is to make it easier to back up your data. *Backing up* is the process—automated or not—of systematically copying your documents and important files from your iBook's hard drive to some other storage facility—either removable media like SuperDisks or Zip disks, or to a network drive or an Internet backup area. You do that in case catastrophe strikes, such as your hard disk fails or an errant program (or virus) destroys data on your iBook. And that ultra-portable iBook is also somewhat steal-able. In most cases your data can be worth a lot to you, so you'll definitely want to back it up.

The best way to be ready for backing up is to store things in an organized fashion. You've already seen that it's a good idea to create a Documents folder and save all of your creative work in that folder—that way, you can easily back up all of the documents you create by dragging the folder to a removable media disk icon. (Your applications and the Mac OS don't necessarily have to be backed up, since you can always restore them from the CD-ROMs included with your iBook and subsequent application purchases. It's not a bad idea to back up your application *preferences*, though, as discussed in Chapter 26.)

Of course, organization goes beyond backup. Once you get a couple hundred files on your hard drive, you'll begin to find that you don't know immediately where everything is. In that case, you'll want a little help through organization.

> TIP
>
> *If you don't already have one, create a folder called Documents on your hard disk. Then, open the General Controls control panel (choose Apple | Control Panels | General Controls). In that control panel you can select the Documents Folder option down in the bottom-right corner of the control panel under the heading "When opening or saving a document, take me to…." Now, when you're working in an application, your Open or Save dialog box should open right to the Documents folder.*

Organize Documents Using Aliases

Should you save documents by type or by the project they relate to? If you want, you can use aliases to help you track your projects in their own folder. As a freelance writer, for example, I often send out invoices on projects I'm working on. I like to have all my invoices in the same folder (called Invoices) so I can see how many have gone out, what I numbered them, and so on. But what if I've created a folder called "Ergo County Consulting Project" and I want to store the invoices related to that project in that folder as well? Easy enough—I just create an alias to the invoice and put it in the project folder.

The best part about the alias is that I can double-click the alias to launch the document, but it's not a duplicate of the original—since it's an alias, I'm always changing the actual copy. And I can delete the alias without harming the original.

See how useful aliases can be? You can put them on the desktop, you can put them in project folders. One of my favorite uses of aliases is to create folders that are specifically for a given project. You can put any alias you want in the folder—even an alias to the applications you want to use or documents that are normally buried deep on your iBook's hard disk. Then, you can store the entire project folder on the desktop until you're done with the project (see Figure 3-8). At the end of the project you can either file away the project folder or delete all the aliases and leave the originals intact.

SHORTCUT *Create your project folder in the Documents folder itself—or wherever you eventually want the folder stored—then drag it out to the desktop. Now, when you're done with the project folder, you can choose File | Put Away in the Finder to automatically send the folder to its storage space in the Documents folder. Cool, huh?*

Use Labels to Organize

The Finder is capable of giving individual folders or items a special label that marks the folder with a particular priority and changes the color of the folder or icon. That may not seem immediately important, but it has some sophisticated implications.

To change the label on an item, choose the item in the Finder, then choose File | Label. A number of label options pop up in the Label menu. Choose one of those color labels and it's assigned to the selected icon, as shown in Figure 3-9.

FIGURE 3-8   Aliases allow you to create project folders that can be used to temporarily store aliases to documents and applications you plan to use frequently.

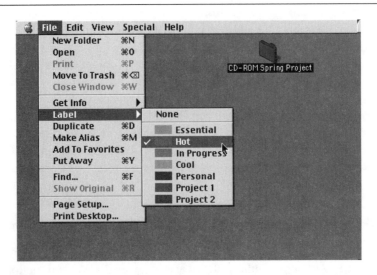

FIGURE 3-9 Assign a label to icons you want specifically flagged.

Why do this? First, a folder with a certain color may come to mean important things to you—that it needs immediate attention, that it's a project folder holding a bunch of aliases, or something along those lines. Perhaps more importantly, though, you'll often encounter applications and utilities that can read the label and do something accordingly—for instance, you might label a particular folder as "Hot" and have an automatic backup program choose to back up all Hot folders. You can even search your hard drive using Sherlock (discussed in Chapter 6) to find all the Hot folders or a similar label.

Fortunately, you can change the label names. Choose Edit | Preferences in the Finder and click the Labels tab. Now, click in the box where you see the name of each label and edit it to suit your needs. You could label things according to backup priority, according to the names of everyone who uses your iBook (Little Billy's file folders are all in Purple), or for whatever other reasons strike your fancy.

Change How Folders Are Displayed in the Finder

While we're on the topic of changing the way things look, managing the way your Finder windows appear can go a long way toward helping you find files. To change the way you view a Finder window, open that window and select it in the

Finder, then choose the appropriate view from the View menu. The Finder offers three basic options when it comes to how the Finder window displays its files:

- **As Icons**   In this view, the window is filled with icons that can be arranged any way you like. This is the default view in most cases.

- **As Buttons**   Buttons are like icons except they only require a single click to activate them. (To select, rename, and drag-and-drop a button, select its name instead of its icon, since a single click activates them.) Buttons are an odd way to arrange most windows, although not a bad idea for a quick pop-up window at the bottom of the Finder screen that could be filled with application aliases. That makes a quick mini-launcher that can be very convenient.

- **As List**   If you have a lot of items in a particular folder window, this is the way to go. Viewing as a list allows you to do two things. First, you get a whole lot of files on the screen at once in a very orderly manner, as shown in Figure 3-10. Second, you can use the little triangles to look inside subfolders without doing a lot of double-clicking.

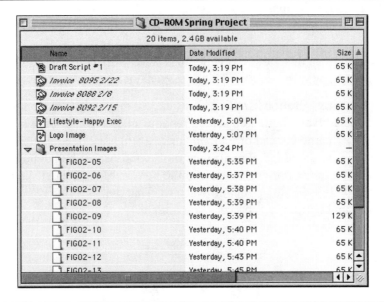

FIGURE 3-10   The List view makes it easy to see a lot of items quickly.

 ... **Drag to the Main Level of a List View Folder**

One peril of using the List view (and this occasionally happens in some other views as well) is that it can be tough to drop items in the open folder window, especially if you have a lot of subfolders in that window (or if you're trying to drag something *from* a subfolder in that same window). Here's the trick—if you want to drop something in the current folder, drag it to the little information bar at the top of the window, just below the title bar. Release the trackpad button to drop the item. This drops it in the main folder instead of in one of the subfolders.

Customize the List View

Once you have a folder in List view, you can do some other things to make that folder work better for you. At the top of the window, you'll find column listings for the different information that's offered about each file. Place the mouse pointer between two columns and it'll change to a little cursor with an arrow coming out of each side. That's your cue that you can drag the column divider to change the width of the column.

Want to change the order of List view columns? Go up to the column head name and click and hold the trackpad button. Now drag the mouse pointer to the left or right—the pointer changes to a hand and you're able to move the column to wherever you'd like it in the window. Let go of the trackpad button to drop the column in place.

To order the window according to a particular column, just click that column's heading name. To view your files organized by date created, for instance, just click the Date Modified column head. You can also change the order of that listing by clicking the direction control—now the listing switches from ascending to descending or vice-versa (see Figure 3-11).

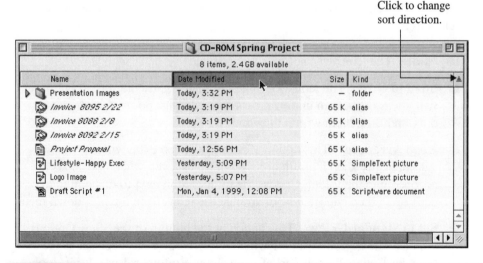

FIGURE 3-11   Click the sort direction control to change the ascending or descending order of a list.

Don't like what you've done? You can choose View | Reset Column Positions to put the columns back the way you found them.

Arrange Other Views

If you're not in List view, there's still some arranging you can do. In Icon and Button views, you can select the Finder window, then choose View | Arrange. That brings up a menu that lets you choose how you'd like your icons arranged.

If you want your Icon and Button views to appear a bit more uniform, you can select the window in the Finder, then choose View | Clean Up. This will move the icons or buttons around so that they're equally spaced and as many as possible fit in the open window.

    With any Finder window you can click the Size box to automatically reshape the window to display all or as many files as possible. Hold down the OPTION *key and click the Size box to maximize the window onscreen.*

Auto-arrange the View

Choosing View | Arrange re-arranges your Finder windows just that one time. Would you like it to be arranged all the time? That's easy enough. Select the window in the Finder, then choose View | View Options. In the View Options dialog box, you can choose to have the window automatically arrange icons. The choices are

- ■ **None**   The icons will not be auto-arranged.

- ■ **Snap to Grid**   The icons won't be put in any particular order, but they will always appear in uniform rows and columns, no matter where you drag-and-drop them within the window.

- ■ **Keep Arranged**   This option allows you to force the window to automatically keep icons in order at all times, even when new icons are dropped into the folder. Choose the radio button next to this option to activate it, then choose *how* to arrange the icons from the pull-down menu.

- ■ **Set to Standard View**   This button at the bottom of the View Options window allows you to set the window to whatever has been set as the "standard" view for this sort of view (Icon, Button, or List). It just looks up the setting in the Finder Preferences settings and applies it to the selected Finder window.

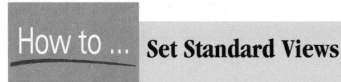

Set Standard Views

To set Standard views, choose Edit | Preferences in the Finder. In the Finder
Preferences dialog box, choose the Views tab. Now, choose the standard view
you'd like to edit from the menu (Icon, Button, or List), then use the check
box options to change the Standard view. Click the Close box to close Finder
Preferences—your changes are automatically applied to all Finder windows
that are set to Standard view.

3

Chapter 4

Pull Down the Apple Menu

How to...

- Use the Apple menu and its special qualities
- Explore the desktop accessories and other items on the Apple menu
- Quickly re-launch items, applications, and servers using the Recent folders
- Add Favorites to the Apple menu
- Add and arrange items on the Apple menu

As I've mentioned, the Apple menu is a sort of junk drawer of the Mac OS. It's where all those little things that might come in handy one day are stored. It's in the Apple menu where you'll find the virtual equivalents of solar-powered calculators, battery-tester packages, and fingernail clippers.

Actually, some of that is true. The Apple menu is a repository for a number of small programs called desk accessories, which allow you to quickly manage small tasks and deal with printers, networks, and other devices that are connected to your iBook. Plus, it's a great place to find shortcuts and other tools to help you use your iBook more efficiently.

What Is the Apple Menu?

The Apple menu is the menu on the far left of the iBook's menu bar that, instead of bearing a name, is represented by the six-color Apple logo. Pull down that menu and you'll gain access to all sorts of settings, small programs, and shortcut menus.

Here's an important tidbit about the Apple menu: It's always there. The Apple menu is always on the menu bar regardless of whether or not you're in the Finder. It's part of the overall Mac OS, a permanent fixture no matter what application you're currently using. That means you can access the Apple menu at any time, regardless of what you're doing. Plus, everything on the Apple menu stays the same when you move from menu to menu. So, you'll always be able to access everything that's on the Apple menu, even if you're working in different applications.

But the Apple menu is even more interesting than that. Unlike most menus, the Apple menu is completely customizable. In fact, all of its contents are stored in a regular folder that's in the System Folder on your iBook's hard disk. That means you can very easily add or remove anything you want to the menu.

And, the Apple menu is hierarchical. That means you can have menu items within the Apple menu that spawn submenus—they just keep traveling across the screen until you run out of menus or run out of room (or you reach five levels, whichever comes first).

By using a feature like Favorites, discussed later in this chapter, it's actually possible to gain access to every file on your hard drive through the Apple menu. This is one seriously high-tech junk drawer (see Figure 4-1).

Overall, the Apple menu works like any other menu—you move the mouse pointer up to the Apple icon, click the trackpad button, and the menu appears. Then, move the mouse pointer down the menu until you're pointing at the item you want to select. If it's a menu, it'll have a little arrowhead pointing to the right—another menu will appear directly to the right once the mouse reaches the arrowhead. You can then move to the right and choose something from the new

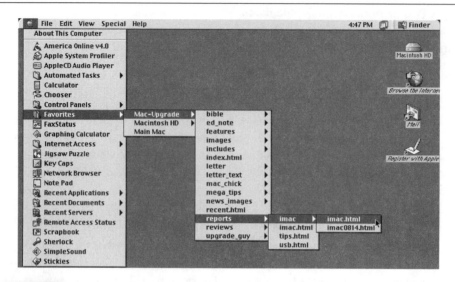

FIGURE 4-1   The Apple menu is sort of a junk drawer for your iBook.

menu. If there's anything that's remarkably different about the Apple menu, it's the simple fact that you're usually launching something—a desk accessory, a control panel, an alias—instead of choosing a command. Most commands in the Finder and in other applications are for performing a task—the Apple menu, on the other hand, is pretty much a quick-launcher.

You'll notice that, even visually, the Apple menu differs from most menus since it shows icons in the menu itself.

Items on the Apple Menu

So what's on this menu? Lots of things. Let's cover the different *types* of things you'll find on the menu, then we'll talk more specifically about what you can accomplish with the Apple menu. Here are the basics types of things that have the right stuff to make it on the Apple menu:

■ **Desk Accessories**   Desk accessories are little programs that usually have only one task, like allowing you to take notes or offering some basic calculator functions. They're sort of like the sticky notes and steno pads you might have hanging out on a regular desk.

■ **Control Panels**   The Mac OS has special programs called *control panels* that allow you to control various settings on your iBook. These are stored in the System folder, but the easiest way to get to them is here, through the

Apple menu. Just point at the Control Panels menu item to see a menu of all the control panels.

■ **Aliases**   You can actually put any sort of alias you want on the Apple menu. The Mac OS programmers have gotten you started by dropping aliases to popular utilities on the Apple menu. You may find that some other programs will drop aliases on there, too. America Online, for instance, put an alias to itself on my Apple menu when I installed it.

4

■ **Menus**   On the Apple menu you'll find a number of submenus that offer you a convenient path to applications, scripts, or aliases on your hard drive. For instance, the Mac OS includes a number of "recent" menus where documents and applications you've recently worked on will appear. (If you don't see any submenus, see the section "Customize the Recent Menus," later in this chapter.)

Let's look at each category in turn and see what you can do with all these items.

Desk Accessories

Originally, desk accessories were the only types of program that could multitask on the Macintosh. Very early Macs could only run one application—like a word processor—at a time. So, Apple had to create desk accessories to help out with important tasks that you need to perform while still using the application. That's why there are small, single-function programs like the Calculator or the Note Pad.

These days the line between full-fledged utility program and desk accessory is blurred somewhat. For the most part, desk accessories are stored in the Apple Menu Items folder (instead of being aliases) and they usually don't allow you to create and save documents; they either automatically save your work or they're designed to do something quickly on screen.

Most of the desk accessories are basic and useful—just choose the Calculator, Graphing Calculator, or Jigsaw Puzzle for some pretty self-explanatory fun. Here are the rest of the desk accessories and what they do:

■ **Apple System Profiler**   This utility is designed to tell you quite a bit about your iBook's hardware, system software configuration, and the devices that are connected to it. (This tool is also good for telling tech support representatives about your iBook when you're talking to them on the phone.)

■ **Apple CD Audio Player**   This accessory allows you to play audio CDs using your iBook's CD-ROM drive. You'll notice that the controls are just like a CD player in the real world, as shown in Figure 4-2—play, stop, pause, eject, move forward and backward between tracks, fast forward, and reverse. There's a volume slider control on the right-hand side. Click the Normal, Shuffle, and Prog buttons to choose how you listen to the CD. Click the small triangle and you can see each track individually—you can even click in the CD's title and the track titles and edit them to show the title of each song. The CD Audio Player will recognize the audio CD the next time you insert it and display the names again.

- **Chooser**   The Chooser is a special desk accessory that helps you select printers and connect to networked computers. You can read more about the Chooser in Chapters 22 and 24.

- **Key Caps**   This little program helps you figure out what key combinations you need to press in order to type certain characters. Launch it, then choose the font you want to use from the Font menu. Now, try different modifier keys—⌘, OPTION, CONTROL, SHIFT—in various configurations. The letter keys will change to show you the character that will appear when you press that same combination of modifier keys and that letter key.

FIGURE 4-2   The Apple CD Audio Player lets you groove to CD tunes while you work.

- **Network Browser**   If your iBook is attached to a network, especially a large one, the Network Browser makes it easy to see all the different machines and hard drives to which you have access. This accessory is discussed in detail in Chapter 24.

- **Note Pad**   The Note Pad is surprisingly handy. Select it and you're presented with a little window where you can type (or drag-and-drop) plain text on the pad. At the bottom-left corner of the page you'll see a little turned-up corner—click it to move to the next page or click the page below the turned-up corner to move back a page. By default, the Note Pad only has eight pages, but you can easily add pages at the end of the pad by selecting File | New Note. Another cool thing: You don't have to save your notes. Just click the Note Pad's close box when you're done with it and the notes will be there the next time you access the Note Pad from the Apple menu. Very handy. (I like to use the Note Pad for quickly pasting text I've found while surfing the World Wide Web, as shown in Figure 4-3.)

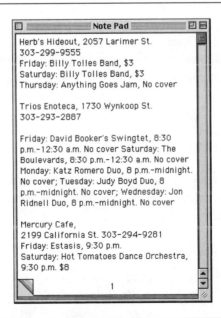

FIGURE 4-3   You can use Note Pad for quick notes or cut-and-paste text from other applications, like your Web browser.

- **Scrapbook** The Scrapbook is designed for cutting and pasting multimedia elements that you'd like to save for the future—stuff like pictures, drawings, audio clips, even QuickTime videos. All you have to do is highlight the desired item in an application, then choose Edit | Copy or Edit | Cut. Switch to the Scrapbook and choose Edit | Paste and your clipping is added at the end of the Scrapbook's pages. Now, when necessary, you can copy the multimedia clipping out of the Scrapbook and into some other applications. (Note: The Scrapbook is fully drag-and-drop aware, so you can drag-and-drop from applications to the Scrapbook, and vice versa, if you prefer.) To close the Scrapbook, click its close box. Anything you've pasted into the Scrapbook will be there the next time you launch it—it's saved automatically. To remove something from the Scrapbook, view it, then choose Edit | Clear from the menu.

- **Sherlock** Sherlock is the Mac OS' high-end search utility, which is discussed in Chapter 6.

- **Stickies** These ought to look familiar. Launch Stickies from the Apple menu and you've got little sticky notes you can add to your screen, sort of. Just type your message on a note, then position it on the screen; you can choose File | New Note if you need more little colorful opportunities to express yourself. (Choose the colors by selecting a note and then choosing the color from the Color menu.) Stickies don't need to be saved unless you want the note to no longer appear on the screen. In that case, click the note's close box and you'll be asked if you want to save the note as a text file. I personally leave Stickies open all the time. They can run in the background, then you can switch to them when you need to jot something down or read the notes. You can quit Stickies by choosing File | Quit in the Stickies menu.

 Some of these items may not appear if you have Mac OS 9 on your iBook. In that case, check the Applications and Apple Extras folders for the missing items.

Control Panels

Control panels are used to customize and make choices about your iBook. They can range from the droll, like setting the clock or deciding what sort of text the OS should use, to the fun, like the Appearance Manager, which allows you to change the colors and appearance of your iBook's interface.

Throughout this book I'll touch on most of these control panels; a lot of the appearance and customization panels are covered in Chapter 21. All you need to

4

know now is that they're there on the Apple menu, they'll pop right open when you select them in the Control Panels menu, and you can close them all by clicking the close box.

You might also be interested to know that control panels are stored in the System Folder on your iBook's hard disk in the folder called Control Panels. Any control panels in that folder will appear in the Control Panels menu on the Apple menu.

Aliases

In the Apple menu, you'll also find aliases to applications or utilities that are actually stored elsewhere on the hard drive. Most of these are added by non-Apple installation programs or by you. All you need to do is create the alias and put it in the Apple Menu Items folder in the System Folder. We'll get deeper into that later in this chapter.

Other aliases are added by installers—America Online and FaxSTF, for instance, both add aliases to the Apple menu to make it easier for you to start up an application conveniently or look into things like the status of your fax receiving.

Use the Recent Menus

If they're set up and working, the Recent menus make it easy for you to reload or relaunch a document, application, or network connection that you've used recently. You can set the number of recent items that are tracked and those that you're most interested in.

Select a Recent Menu

To use the Recent menus, just click the Apple menu, then point the mouse at one of the Recent menus: Recent Applications, Recent Documents, or Recent Servers (see Figure 4-4). Then, select the item you'd like to re-launch. Your iBook will switch back to the Finder (if necessary) and launch the application and/or open the document you've chosen.

If you choose a server (actually, a server's disk), you may need to log back into the server to access it. If you're not familiar with the process, consult Chapter 24.

NOTE   *A "server," in this context, is a computer that your iBook is connected to by networking cables or by wireless AirPort technology, if your iBook is so equipped. The server computer stores documents that are shared by everyone on your network. It may also allow you to print documents and store personal documents in a central location so they can be accessed from other computers.*

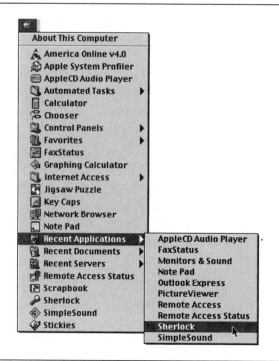

FIGURE 4-4 The Recent menus let you pick documents, applications, or servers that you've worked with recently.

Customize the Recent Menus

If you'd like to change the behavior of the Recent menus, you can do so through the Apple Menu Options control panel. Select the Apple menu, then point to the Control Panels. Select the Apple Menu Options control panel. In the control panel you can decide whether or not the Apple menu should have hierarchical menus by clicking the On or Off radio button. (It's probably a good idea to leave them on so that you have access to recent items, but they can slow things down a bit.)

Then you can decide if you want to use the Recent menus; if not, click to make sure there's no check mark in the check box next to the Remember Recently Used Items option. If you are using Recent menus, you can select how many items your iBook remembers—the default is 10. If you want to change that number, just click in the entry box and edit the number. (A reasonable number is probably 25-40. If the number is too large, it may slow down your iBook when you choose the Apple menu. A large number of entries may also be tough to wade through.) When you're done, click the close box in the Apple Menu Options control panel. Your changes are noted and put into action.

Want to delete entries from the Recent menus? Open the Apple Menu Items folder that's stored in your System Folder. Now, open the folder that corresponds to the Recent menu you want to clean out. In that folder, each alias corresponds to an entry on that Recent menu; drag any of the aliases to the Trash. Check the Recent menu in the Apple menu; those trashed items should be gone from the menu.

4

Create and Use Favorites

Favorites are really pretty cool. They allow you to choose parts of the Mac OS and sort of *bookmark* them for future use. If you've used a Web browser much, you might be familiar with this concept of electronic bookmarking. If you've used books much, you're probably also familiar with the concept of bookmarking. Haven't heard of either? Just read on...

The idea is this: Say you use a folder called Reports in your Documents folder all the time. To open that folder in the Finder, you usually have to double-click the Macintosh HD, then double-click your Documents folder, then double-click the Reports folder. What if, instead, you could just open directly to the folder using a menu in the Apple menu? That's one of the tasks that Favorites help you perform easily. Plus, these Favorites appear elsewhere, such as in the Open and Save dialog boxes and in system utilities like the Network Browser.

But Favorites do even more than that. First, Favorites actually allow you to create a menu. You do that by choosing a *folder* as a Favorite. The items in that folder become menu items in the associated menu! If you turn your Internet folder into a Favorite, for instance, you'll create an Internet menu under the Favorites menu on the Apple menu. What will show up on that Internet menu? The items that are in the Internet folder (see Figure 4-5).

Second, Favorites show up in the new, advanced Open and Save dialog boxes used by applications written (or re-written and upgraded) to recognize Mac OS 8.5 and higher. That means, in many cases, you'll be able to access your Favorites as you're trying to open or save documents. That's a nice time saver, as you'll see in Chapter 5.

FIGURE 4-5 Creating a Favorite makes that item appear in the Favorites menu on the Apple menu for easy access.

Create a Favorite

Before all this magic can happen for you personally, though, you're going to need to create a Favorite. Follow these steps:

1. Select an item in the Finder—it can be a file, a folder, or even a disk. It's probably best that it's a folder, though. (Select the folder icon, not an open folder window.)

2. Then choose File | Add to Favorites.

NOTE *You can select a disk icon and make it a Favorite, but that will likely slow down your iBook when you access the Apple menu. The iBook is forced to check all of those subfolders (four levels deep) so that it knows what to put on the menus. That can cause a little delay while the Apple menu is opening up.*

This creates an alias to that item and places it in the Favorites folder that's stored in the Apple Menu Items folder, which, in turn, is in the System Folder on your iBook's hard disk.

Use a Favorite

Once you've got a Favorite created, you can use it immediately:

1. Select the Apple menu and point to the Favorites item. If you have any Favorites created, they'll appear in a menu to the right.

2. Now, point to the Favorite you want to work with. If it's a folder, that folder's contents will appear in yet another menu. In fact, all of the subfolders become menus, too, allowing you to keep moving down the menu items and dig deeper into the subfolders on your iBook's hard disk (see Figure 4-6).

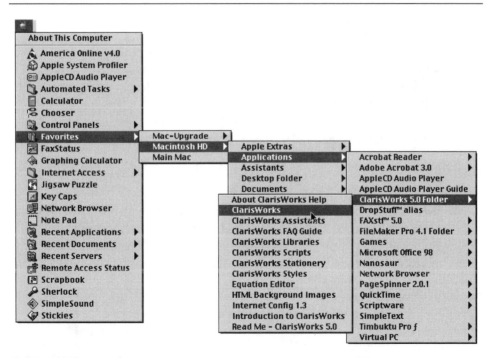

FIGURE 4-6   Select a Favorite from the Apple menu.

3. Once you find the item you want, you can select it. If you select a folder, it will appear in the Finder. If you select a file, it will be launched. If it's a document, its associated application will also be launched.

Put Your Own Aliases on the Menu

If you'd like to add items directly to the Apple menu instead of going through Favorites, you can do that easily. It works a lot like the Favorites discussed above, except it uses an AppleScript (assuming you want to do this the automatic way).

In some ways, adding an item directly to the Apple menu, instead of through Favorites, is more efficient. For instance, it allows you to see more levels of an entire drive if you add an alias of that drive to the Apple menu. Favorites, though, has its advantages, since it keeps your Apple menu a bit less cluttered and it allows those items to show up in other parts of the Mac OS—like the Open and Save dialog boxes and the Network Browser.

The Automatic Way

In this case, you'll use an AppleScript to place the item on the Apple menu. All this AppleScript does is make an alias of the selected item and place it in the Apple Menu Items folder, which is in the System Folder. Here's what you do to add an item to the Apple menu:

1. Select the item in the Finder. It can be a drive icon, a folder, or a file.

2. Select the Apple menu and point to the Automated Tasks menu. (This menu may not appear in Mac OS 9.)

3. Select Add Alias to Apple Menu. This is an AppleScript—a small program written in Mac OS' special automating language—that automatically creates an alias of the item and adds it to the Apple Menu Items folder. When it's done you'll see a message that says the alias has been added:

4. Check the Apple menu—you should see your item in the main level of the menu.

The Manual Way

You may have already caught on—if the AppleScript simply adds an alias of the selected icon to the Apple Menu Items folder in the System Folder, then you can do that on your own to the same effect, right? Select an item in the Finder, make an alias of it, and drag that alias to the Apple Menu Items folder in the System Folder. Rename the item if desired. Close the Apple Menu Items folder and check the Apple menu—the new item has been added.

You can also make an alias to a folder or a disk and put it in the Apple Menu Items folder. This creates a new menu on the Apple menu that allows you to access the contents of that folder. Don't forget that folders with many files and subfolders can slow down the Apple menu quite a bit.

TIP   *To remove items from the Apple menu, just remove them from the Apple Menu Items folder (drag them to the Trash or to a different folder). Once they've been removed from the Apple Menu Items folder, they'll no longer appear on the Apple menu.*

Shuffle the Order of Items

While you're in the Apple Menu Items folder, you might want to take advantage of the moment and reshuffle items in the Apple menu. As a rule, items are listed alphabetically. Changing the order of items is as simple as renaming them so that they show up in the alphabet where you want them on the menu.

In general, you'll probably want to move certain items either to the top of the menu or the bottom. If you don't feel like giving them new names, you can use this trick: Putting a blank space at the beginning of a menu item's name will put it at the top of the menu. Similarly, putting a bullet point (OPTION-8) at the beginning of an item's name will put it at the bottom of the menu. So, rename the items and aliases in the Apple Menu Items folder using these codes, and you can force items to the top or bottom easily (see Figure 4-7).

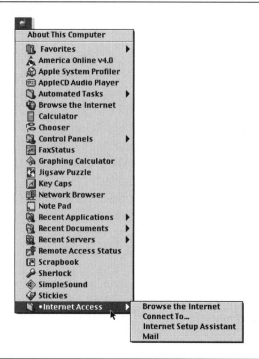

FIGURE 4-7   Apple menu items can be rearranged on the menu using special characters.

 Make Divider Lines in Your Apple Menu

This is a little advanced, but forge ahead if you're brave about your iBook's System Folder. (You probably won't mess anything up.) Go into the System Folder and make an alias of the Apple Menu Items folder. Rename that alias "---------------------------" or something similar to create a dividing line. Now, drag the alias into the Apple Menu Items folder. Next, check the Apple menu—any file that has a space as the first character in its name will appear over the dividing line. Plus, selecting the line opens the Apple Menu Items folder in the Finder for you to edit easily!

Chapter 5

Work with Applications and the Applications Menu

How to...

- ■ Learn what applications are and how to launch them
- ■ Create, open, and save documents
- ■ Perform basic tasks like printing, selecting text, cutting, copying, and pasting
- ■ Undo mistakes, close documents, and quit applications
- ■ Dig into the preferences settings of your applications
- ■ Multitask: switch between active applications

In Chapter 3, I outlined a good deal of the organizational tasks you can accomplish with the Finder. One thing I didn't mention much, though, is one of the Finder's primary functions—allowing you to launch programs. While the Finder itself is designed to help you manage documents you create in applications, you've got to get those applications started before you can create documents to work with.

That's what this chapter is about—getting started with any application and most other types of Macintosh programs. If you haven't used Macintosh applications in the past, get ready to learn a little bit about all of them.

What Are Applications?

A lot of times you'll hear the words "program" and "application" used interchangeably. That's usually OK, although I'm more inclined to say a *program* is any computer file that stores a series of instructions you run on a computer; an *application* is a large program that usually allows you to create a document of some sort. Its tools are *applied* toward some end goal.

One thing I can say about Macintosh applications is that they all have a number of things in common. One of the reasons that the Macintosh has been considered an easier-to-use computer for all these years is because Macintosh application developers are required to follow some pretty strict rules. The result: Every single Macintosh application will likely have things in common with other Macintosh applications. And all those elements make it easier for you to learn new tasks since they share common methods.

NOTE   *In this chapter I don't talk about any specific application, but if you'd like to follow along, most of the examples use SimpleText—a basic text editor that comes with the iBook. You should find its icon in the Applications folder.*

Start Up Applications

The first method common to most applications is how you start them up. Applications need to be opened, or "launched," before you can start working with them.

You can start up applications in a few different ways:

■ **Double-click the application icon.**   This launches right into the application and, in most cases, a default or blank document is loaded. (If the icon for the application is in the form of a button, you'll only click it once.)

■ **Select the application from the Recent Applications menu in the Apple menu.**   Pull down the Apple menu and you'll see an item called Recent Applications; highlight it and you'll see the last ten (or more) applications that were used. Your iBook keeps track of that for you, so you can get to often-used applications quickly.

NOTE   *The Recent folders are discussed at length in Chapter 4.*

■ **Double-click one of the application's document icons.**   When you do this, it launches the application and causes it to load the document you double-clicked. This works great when you're loading a document that has been saved by that same application previously (like when you double-click an AppleWorks document and you have AppleWorks installed on your iBook).

■ **Drag-and-drop a document onto the application's icon.**   This works well if you're trying to launch a document that was not originally saved by the application. In many cases, the application will launch and attempt to translate the document if necessary, so that you can work with it.

After you tell an application you want to use it, it starts up, asks the Macintosh for a certain amount of RAM (system memory), and warns the iBook's processor that it's going to have some tasks to assign it. Then the application loads computer code from the hard drive into RAM so that it's ready to be used. Next, it draws the screen, plants its menus on the menu bar and it may or may not open a document for you to edit. Once it's done with the preliminaries, it waits for you to do something.

Start-Up Trouble

If you double-click a document that your iBook hasn't properly associated with an application (maybe you copied the document over the Internet or over a network connection), then you'll see a special alert box. This tells you that the iBook doesn't know which application to use to load the document, so you'll need to tell it (see Figure 5-1).

In the list, select an application that can successfully load or translate the file. If it's a graphics file, you'll probably have success loading it into a program that includes QuickTime translation; a text document may be successfully translated by AppleWorks or, if you have it, Microsoft Word.

5

FIGURE 5-1   This alert allows you to choose the application you'll use to edit the document.

TIP

If you don't see an application that you know could open the document, try clicking the check box that says Show Only Recommended Choices. Then you'll see nearly every application on your iBook—hopefully, the one you want will show up now.

Once you've found the right application, select it in the window and click the Open button. Nothing really bad happens if you select the wrong application, by the way, so feel free to make a guess. If it doesn't work out, you'll just have to try again.

Create a New Document

Sometimes an application will create a blank document for you as it opens. Other times, it just launches and sits there. If that's the case (or if you're already working in the application and you want a new document), you can create a new document by choosing File | New. This works in *any* application that creates documents.

What happens next can vary. In some cases, a document just pops up. (That's what happens in a program like SimpleText.) In other cases, you may be greeted by a dialog box that requires you to make choices as to what sort of document you want to create, whether or not you want special help creating the document, and so on. We'll get more into those options as we create different documents in Part II of this book. You can also use ⌘-N to create a new document, by the way. For now, just remember File | New.

Open a Document

If you've already created a document you want to work on, the first thing you'll do after the application has started up is head to the File menu and choose Open. That brings up the Open dialog box, which may look something like Figure 5-2. If it doesn't look like Figure 5-2, it'll likely look more like Figure 5-3. If it still doesn't look like either of these, then you're probably working with a Microsoft application. They like to be different.

The Open dialog box offers a lot of different options to help you get to the document you're looking for, and its basic functions are easy to work with. In the file window, you can choose a document to open (if you see the one you want) or select a folder or storage device to dig into. Click Open to open the highlighted item. If you're digging deeper, you can repeat the process—keep opening folders until you find the document you're looking for. Once it's in the window, select it and click Open. That opens the document for editing in the application.

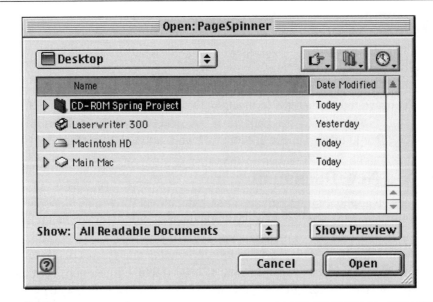

FIGURE 5-2   The new, improved Open dialog box appears when applications have been updated to use it.

FIGURE 5-3   The older Open dialog box still shows up in applications that haven't been updated.

SHORTCUT   *You can double-click folders and storage devices in the file window to open them more quickly.*

Not all programs' dialog boxes have a Show or Document Type menu, but when they do, you can use it to narrow down the number of files you're seeing in the dialog box. The application itself will offer suggestions like "AppleWorks Document" or "PageSpinner HTML" that you can choose if that's the sort of file you're looking for. If you choose something other than "All Documents" or "All Readable Documents," then be aware that you're not seeing every file in the folder. You're seeing a subset that matches the Document Type menu criteria.

In the newer dialog box, shown in Figure 5-2, you can use the Shortcuts, Favorites, and Recent buttons to move quickly to different parts of your iBook's storage system. Shortcuts point to the different drives and removable media currently mounted on your iBook's desktop, while the Recent button allows you to open a document or folder you've opened in the recent past.

The Favorites button lets you choose from Favorites that you set yourself through the Finder (see Chapter 4) or in the Open dialog box. If you're currently looking at a folder or item you want to make a Favorite, select it in the file window and choose Add To Favorites from the Favorite button. (These buttons work just like menus.) You can also select Remove From Favorites to edit the favorites you've created in the past.

These dialog boxes were brand new when Mac OS 8.5 was released and, at the time of writing, not all Mac applications have been updated to use them. Don't be surprised if you don't see many of these dialog boxes for a while. Eventually, updated applications will begin to use them more.

In the more traditional Open dialog box, you have the same basic tools for opening folders and finding files. This Open dialog box is a little more simple in its offerings—and is especially lax in its extras (like the Favorites and Recent buttons) for helping you move around quickly. Still, it gets the job done.

Save Your Document

Save quickly and save often. This is some of the best advice I can give you. When I'm writing a typical book chapter, I save that document just about every three sentences or so. That's right—every three *sentences.* Why? Because I don't want to type them again.

Whenever you're working in an application there's always a chance that the application could run into an error, something could go wrong in the Mac OS, or something could go wrong with your iBook. Whatever happens, losing a lot of data because you forgot to save regularly is no fun. So, learn to save.

The first time you save a document, you'll need to find a place to put it and you'll need to name it. To do that, become acquainted with another dialog box. Choose File | Save to bring up the Save dialog box and start the saving process. Figure 5-4 shows something that should look pretty familiar—this is the new Save dialog box that's very similar to the newer Open dialog box described earlier in this chapter.

This dialog box is fairly straightforward if you're used to the Open dialog box.

1. Select and open the folder you want to use to save the file. You can create a new folder for the file by clicking the New Folder button if you need to. Once that folder is open, you can enter a name for the file in the Name entry box.

2. With the name typed, you can choose the file format from the Format menu (if necessary) and then click Save.

3. The document is saved and you're returned to the document to continue working.

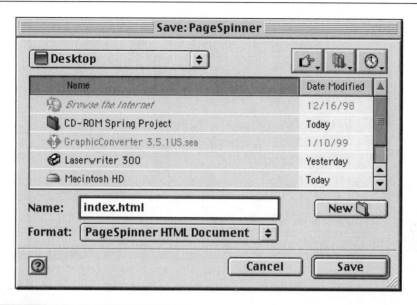

FIGURE 5-4   The newer Save dialog is similar to the new Open dialog box.

The older Save dialog box (see Figure 5-5) works the same way. The only difference is the absence of those Favorites, Shortcuts, and Recent buttons to play with.

Once you have the document saved, you can choose File | Save to save any changes to that same document—you won't see the Save dialog box, since the application already knows where to save the file and what to call it. In fact, for even faster saving you can just press ⌘-S to instantly save what you're working on. (That's what I do every three sentences.)

What if you want to save this file in a new place and/or with a new name? In that case, you use the Save As command in the File menu. That brings the Save dialog box back up, allowing you to save the document (and any unsaved changes) to a new document located in a new folder. This is sort of like duplicating the file in the Finder—you create an entirely new copy of the document, which you can give a different name and put in a different folder, if you like.

Plus, after you've invoked the Save As command, the document file on your screen is the new document you just created. This can be useful if you want to

FIGURE 5-5   The older Save dialog box. Boring.

keep the original file as it was, but you want to alter a copy of it to use for some other reason. Perhaps you're creating an invoice—you open last month's invoice, choose File | Save As to create a new copy with a new name, then edit the new copy for this month's invoice.

Basic Application Commands

Now that you've seen how to create, open, or save documents, you're ready to actually do something within those documents. Obviously, what you do depends somewhat on the application in question (I wouldn't try writing a novel in the Quicken financial management software, for instance), but there are some common commands that you'll find in nearly every application you encounter. Let's look at some of them.

Print

Open the File menu, choose the Print command, and the Print dialog box appears. This dialog box varies depending on the printer you use—in the examples here I'm using the LaserWriter 300 driver that's included with the Mac OS. Your printer will likely offer some of the same options and some different options that reflect the printer's capabilities (see the following illustration).

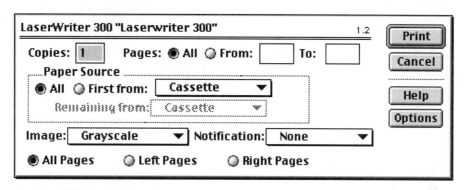

Common to all printers is the ability to print more than one copy by entering a number in the Copy entry box. You can also select which pages are to be printed. By default, the All radio button is selected. If you want to print a range of pages within the document (say, pages 6-12), you can click once to select the From radio button, then enter the page numbers for your range in the entry boxes. (If you want to print just one page, put its page number in both boxes, such as From: **6** To: **6**.)

Now you can make other choices in the dialog box. You may have the option to change the Quality setting, especially if you have an inkjet printer. In most cases, the lower the quality, the less ink the printer uses. You can choose to print in a lower-quality mode if you want to conserve ink and/or don't expect to distribute the document to friends or colleagues. You may also have options for managing color printing, choosing how images should be printed, and setting which paper tray the paper should come from for this printing. Make all those choices, then click the Print button to send the job to your printer.

After the application has finished sending the job to the printer, your printer icon (on the desktop) takes over. You can double-click the printer icon to watch or manage the print job as it happens. Or you can return to your application and continue working while the document is printed in the *background*, that is, while you're using the computer for another task.

NOTE   *If you have trouble, see Chapter 22 for help on setting up your printer.*

Selecting and Select All

You're familiar with selecting icons in the Finder with the trackpad. Selecting text (or objects like spreadsheet numbers or graphical images) in a document is similar, although it can vary a bit. For instance, if you're typing text in a text editor or word processor, you can't just point and click the mouse pointer once to select a word in that document. You can, however, point and *double-click* to select a word.

To select more than one word, hold down the trackpad button and drag the mouse pointer across the words you want to select. The words (or parts of words) become highlighted, just as if you were selecting multiple icons in the Finder (see Figure 5-6). You can drag the mouse pointer from left to right and/or up and down the page to select multiple words or lines of text.

There are a couple of tricks, too. In most text programs, triple-clicking will select an entire paragraph or a continuous line of text. In applications where triple-clicking doesn't select the entire paragraph, try clicking four times rapidly.

If you'd like to select everything in a given document, there's a command for that, too. Select the Edit menu and choose Select All. All the text (or objects) in

FIGURE 5-6   Highlighting text with the mouse pointer

the document will be highlighted. You can also invoke this command from the keyboard by pressing ⌘-A in nearly any application, including the Finder.

Cut, Copy, and Paste

These three are present in nearly every application ever written. The Cut, Copy, and Paste commands allow you to move text and objects within documents or from one document to another. In fact, you can cut and paste between applications in most cases.

The Cut and Copy commands are similar. Highlight text or objects in your document and select the Edit menu. Choose Cut if you'd like to delete the text or objects from the current document or current spot in the document; if you just want to copy the selection to use elsewhere, choose Copy. You can also use the keyboard: ⌘-C invokes Copy and ⌘-X invokes Cut.

Your selection is moved to something called the Clipboard—it's a file that's stored in the System Folder on your iBook's hard drive. Now, the contents of the Clipboard can be pasted into another section of the document or another document all together.

To paste, place the insertion point in the document where you'd like the text or objects to appear. (In some documents you don't place the insertion point; you just click the document window to make sure it's active.) Then, pull down the Edit menu and choose Paste. (Or, press ⌘-V on the keyboard.) The text or objects will appear in the document.

Want to do it another way? In many applications you can drag-and-drop text to different parts of the document, to a new document, or even to the Finder. Try this:

1. Using the mouse pointer, highlight some text you've typed into a SimpleText document.

2. Now, point the mouse pointer at the highlighted text, click the trackpad button, and hold it.

3. Drag the text to another part of the document, another document entirely, or to the desktop.

4. Release the trackpad button.

When you're finished, you've effectively cut and pasted the text, even though you didn't use the commands. Plus, if you dragged the text to the Finder, you've got a cool little text clipping that you can save, rename, or use to drop the text back into another document at some later date, as shown in Figure 5-7.

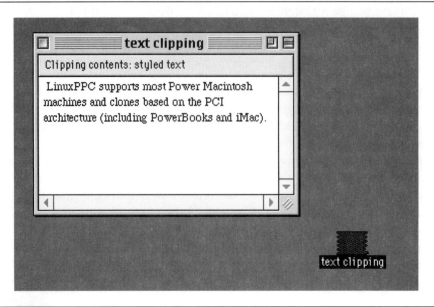

FIGURE 5-7   Create a text clipping by dragging text to the Finder.

> **NOTE**   *In the case of a desktop text clipping, the original highlighted text is left in the document, so that the process is more like a copy-and-paste operation.*

You can copy and paste much more than just text and objects like drawings and images. If you can select it in an application, there's a good chance you'll be able to copy and paste it. When in doubt, try the commands and see if they work.

Undo

Here's another perennial favorite of application programmers—the Undo command. This command is designed to immediately countermand the most recent action or command you've performed. For instance, if you just deleted an entire paragraph in AppleWorks, choose Edit | Undo to get that paragraph back. It usually works for formatting text or objects, pasting, deleting, typing, and so on. Most any activity can be taken back. You can usually undo immediately by pressing ⌘-Z on the keyboard.

Many programs will also have a Redo or similar command that is designed to undo an Undo command. If you undo something you didn't actually want to undo, head back to the Edit menu and look for the Redo command.

> TIP
>
> *Some applications have multiple undo capabilities. Basically, that means you can undo more than one command—keep choosing the Undo command and the program will keep working backward through your most recent actions. It's a convenient feature to have, but it's usually only implemented in higher-end, more expensive applications.*

Quit the Application

About done with that application? All applications have a Quit command that closes the application, hands the RAM memory space back to the Mac OS, and cleans up any open files. Usually, that command is in the File menu under Quit. You can also press ⌘-Q in almost any Mac application to quit.

When you quit a program, it should ask you to save any unsaved documents and may ask you to make other decisions—like hanging up the modem or waiting until a particular activity is finished. Of course, it depends on the program.

> NOTE
>
> *Most of the time, closing a window in a program does not actually quit the program. Many beginning Mac users make the mistake of closing a document window and believing the application is also closed. You can close a window by clicking its Close box, choosing File | Close, or pressing ⌘-W. But that rarely quits the program—it just closes the current window or document. You need to invoke the Quit command in applications; otherwise, they remain open, take up RAM, and make it more difficult for you to run other programs.*

Preferences

Most applications offer a dialog box that allows you to set your preferences for how the program behaves, what values it defaults to, and so on. The preferences are completely up to the individual application—there really isn't too much in the way of standardization, except for the location of the Preferences command. I discussed the Finder Preferences in Chapter 3; I'll talk about the preferences settings in AppleWorks, Quicken, Outlook Express, Internet Explorer, and your other iBook applications throughout the book.

To open the Preferences dialog box you'll usually invoke the Preferences command. In most applications it's under the Edit menu, since you're trying to "edit" the preferences. If you don't find it there, look under the File menu. If you don't see it in either of those two menus, then chances are good that you're using a Microsoft application. Look in the Tools menu for a command called Options or Preferences.

Other Interface Elements

You already know a lot about what to expect from applications. You'll see windows, menus, icons, pointers, and other little tidbits. But let's focus for a few moments on some elements you're likely to see pop up in various parts of the different applications you'll be working with. You'll want to be familiar with these parts of the interface so you can get your work done.

Buttons, Check Boxes, and Sliders

You'll find that many preferences settings, dialog boxes, and other components that make up applications—and even parts of the Mac OS—rely on some typical controls to help you make decisions. You've already seen some of these, but let me go ahead and define them formally. Here's what they do:

- **Radio Buttons**   This type of control allows you to make one selection among two or more different choices. Click the button next to the item you want to choose.

- **Check Boxes**   A check box allows you to choose each item individually—if you want the item active you'll click in the box next to the item and a check mark (sometimes it's an "x") will appear in the box.

- **Sliders**   A slider bar allows you to choose a range of values from low to high just as you might for a volume control on a home stereo system. In fact, slider bars are used most often for changing the volume level, brightness level, and so on. The volume control in the Control Strip (discussed in Chapter 2) is a slider control. You just drag the slider back and forth on the control to change the value.

Toolbars

While not required of Macintosh applications, toolbars are a popular addition. Toolbars put small *iconic* buttons in a special bar below the menu bar in an application, giving you quick access to the most popular commands in that program. An example is the following illustration, which shows the toolbar from AppleWorks.

It allows you to quickly access fonts, font styling, and many other commands that you might use frequently in the program.

Often, at least for me, the little icon buttons on toolbars make no sense whatsoever. In that case, the solution is usually to point at an icon with the mouse pointer and wait a few seconds. Most applications have a little pop-up window or other way of showing you what a particular icon is for. If you're still not getting any help, open the Help menu and choose Balloon Help, then go back and point at the icon in question. That may solve the problem and tell you what the icon is for. (Balloon Help is discussed in Chapter 7.)

The About Box

Want to know more about an application? All applications are required to have an About box, which you can access while the application is active. If you're currently working with the application, pull down the Apple menu. You'll see that the first menu item is About... followed by the name of the application. Choose that item and you'll see a little something about the application. Some applications will place help, tips, and other buttons in the About window that will, occasionally, give you help when using the application.

Multitasking: Use More Than One Application

Even though the iBook is cute, it is a very powerful computer. So powerful that you'll probably find very quickly that you want, need, and enjoy the idea of using more than one program or application at once. You may be downloading your e-mail messages while surfing the Web. When you find the article you're looking for, you might want to switch back to AppleWorks to type more into your report document. And so on.

There are good reasons to run more than one program at a time—so many good reasons that the process has a name: *multitasking*. Your iBook is able to do a perfectly good job of multitasking if you know the secrets.

The first secret is this: You'll need to start up more than one application if you want to use more than one application. You can do that by switching back to the Finder.

 Once you have more than one application running you can use the Cut, Copy, and Paste commands to move text and images between the applications. You can also often drag-and-drop from one application's window to another's, just like you can drag-and-drop text and images from applications to the Finder and back again.

The Application Menu

Up in the top-right corner of your iBook's screen you'll always find the Application menu, a menu dedicated to switching between your open applications. Which menu is it? It's the one with the name and icon of whatever applications you're currently running. Point to that icon and name, then click the trackpad button. As you can see from the illustration, it's a menu.

Switch Between Applications

If you have an application other than the Finder open, you can head up there right now, pull down the Application menu, and see all of your open applications. Choose one of those applications and it'll move to the *foreground*—you'll suddenly see that new application's menus and windows in front of you, ready to be worked on.

If you don't have any applications open, use the Application menu to switch to the Finder. (You can also just click the desktop to switch to the Finder.) Now, from the Finder, you can launch more applications. You could also, if you prefer, launch an application from the Apple menu if you've set things up correctly (see Chapter 4).

Once you have a couple of applications open, you can begin to see the power of the Application menu. Just pull it down and choose another application. It instantly comes to the front. Plus, your iBook is still multitasking—most of the time, programs in the background will continue working even if you switch away from them.

SHORTCUT *You can switch between applications with a keystroke, too. Press ⌘-TAB to switch from application to application. You can press ⌘-SHIFT-TAB to switch back in the opposite order.*

5

Hide and Show Applications

The Application menu has some other useful commands that help you when you switch between applications. If you've switched applications, and windows from another application are getting in your way or cluttering up the screen, you can pull down the Application menu and choose Hide Others, which hides all applications except the one you're currently working in. Now, the other applications' windows disappear. The applications are still running and you can still switch to them using the Application menu—only their windows are currently hidden.

You can also hide the application that you're working in—perhaps so you can see an open window in a background application. To do that, pull down the Application menu and choose Hide ... (the ellipse represents the name of the current application).

You'll probably use the Hide command the most when you switch to the Finder, since switching to the Finder doesn't automatically cause the windows of other applications to disappear. If you switch to the Finder and can't see parts of the desktop you need revealed, choose Hide Others from the Application menu; then you can work in the Finder.

The Show All command does exactly what you think it would—it reveals the windows of all hidden applications. You can also reveal individual applications by switching to them using the Application menu.

TIP *Want to hide an application as you switch away from it? If you're in AppleWorks and you want to switch to the Finder and hide AppleWorks at the same time, it can be done. Just hold down the OPTION key as you switch between applications. The application you're switching from gets hidden as you switch to the new application.*

Float the Application Menu

If you select the Application menu and hold down the trackpad button, then drag straight down the menu right off the bottom edge, you'll "tear away" the menu. Suddenly it becomes a floating window that includes the icons and names of the currently running applications.

The window will always float *on top* of all your other applications, so you'll always be able to see it. To switch to a different application, all you have to do is click once on that application's icon.

You can also customize the window somewhat. Do you want just icons and no words? Click the zoom box and the menu shrinks down to small icons. If you'd like the icons bigger, hold down OPTION and click the zoom box. If you'd like to change from vertical to horizontal, hold down SHIFT-OPTION and click the zoom box.

Still not happy? You can use some prewritten AppleScripts to change the menu more. From the Finder, choose Help | Mac OS Help. Search for the Help topic "Switching between open applications." In that topic you'll find links to AppleScripts that will help you customize the menu even further.

Need to get rid of the floating menu window? Click its Close box and it's gone. You can still, as always, use the Application menu the next time you need to switch applications.

Chapter 6

Search for Things

How to...

- Find anything with your iBook
- Search for files by filename
- Use a customized search to find a file
- Search within the contents of files
- Search the Internet
- Understand Sherlock 2's Channels
- Add search sites and channels to Sherlock

With the large hard disk included with an iBook—and the infinitely larger Internet your iBook is most likely attached to—you'll soon discover trackpadding around and double-clicking isn't always the most efficient way to find something. Instead, you'll probably wish you could figure out how to find things more directly and quickly. Fortunately, it's easy to do.

Plus, you'll find the Mac OS offers some advanced searching options that you might not have thought of—things like searching the Internet from your Mac's desktop. This can be a great timesaver for finding things on the Internet, with this added bonus: you don't have to learn special commands for using a Web browser. With the Mac OS, the searches happen right on your screen using familiar menus and commands.

6

You Can Find Anything with iBook

Although the iBook's basic interface—all those icons and windows—is called *the Finder,* it's not that good at automatically seeking out files and folders on your iBook. That sort of task is left to a program called Sherlock. *Sherlock* is a powerful program, capable of doing these three basic types of searches: Find File, Find by Content, and Search Internet.

Sherlock's Find File tool can search your iBook's own hard disk and any additional drives you have attached to it. It can even search hard disks on other computers if your iBook is attached to a network.

Sherlock's second tool, Find by Content, may be slower, but it's very cool—it enables you to search *inside* documents for phrases or keywords. You could search, for instance, for something like "Dear Grandma" to find documents on your hard disk that included those words.

Third, Sherlock can search the Internet. If you have any experience with the Internet, you know a big part of the process is searching for pages, usually at popular search sites like Yahoo! (**http://www.yahoo.com**), Excite (**http://www.excite.com**), or Infoseek (**http://www.infoseek.com/**). Well, Sherlock's Search Internet tool enables you to access the same sort of searches, but from within the Mac OS, inside Sherlock itself. This results in search listings from many of the most popular Internet search sites, including those just mentioned and others like Hotbot (**http://www.hotbot.com/**) and Lycos (**http://www.lycos.com**).

Meet Sherlock

The easiest way to launch Sherlock is from the Finder itself—click once on the desktop to switch to the Finder. Now, choose File | Find or press ⌘-F on your keyboard.

If you're not currently in the Finder and you don't feel like switching to it, you can also launch Sherlock from the Apple menu. Just pull down the Apple menu and select the entry for Sherlock.

When Sherlock launches, its searching dialog box appears (see the following illustration). Notice that the Sherlock interface includes tabs at the top of the dialog box that enable you to switch between the different types of searches. Each of these tabs represents one of the three types of search you can do: Find File, Find by Content, and Search Internet.

If your version of Sherlock doesn't look like the previous image, then you've probably got Sherlock 2, which comes with Mac OS 9. (Some earlier iBooks shipped with Mac 8.6, which includes the original Sherlock.) If that's the case, your version of Sherlock probably looks more like the following illustration.

Channels

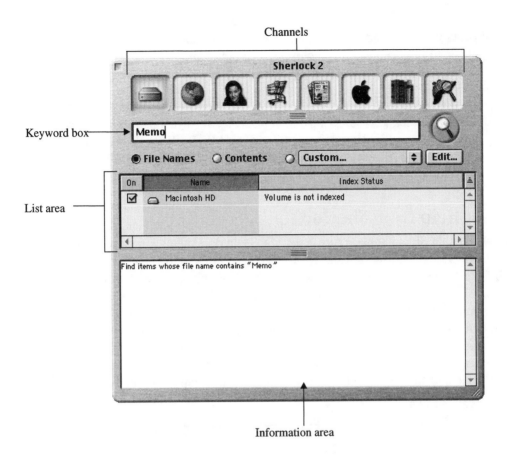

Keyword box

List area

Information area

6

> NOTE
>
> *In this chapter, I primarily cover the original Sherlock, but whenever something is different in Sherlock 2, I try to point that out.*

Sherlock is a complete program, but it acts like a *desk accessory,* which means it loads with its own menu bar and window, but the entire program quits if you close all its open windows. (This is different from most applications, which continue to run even when you close a document window.) Try it—close the Sherlock window by clicking its close box and Sherlock itself will quit. You can also choose File | Quit to close Sherlock.

 Are you a keyboard speed demon? You can switch between Sherlock's tabs using keyboard commands, if you like. With Sherlock open, use ⌘-F for Find File, ⌘-G for Find by Content, and ⌘-H for Search Internet. With Sherlock 2 and Mac OS 9, you can also use ⌘-G in the Finder.

Get Help from Sherlock

Notice that Sherlock has a full set of Mac Help documents associated with it. In the Sherlock window, you see a ? icon you can click to load the help pages; you can also choose the Help menu and the Mac OS Help command to search for help on Sherlock. (There's no ? in the Sherlock 2 window, but you can still get help from the Help menu.)

Balloon Help also works well for figuring out the Sherlock window (but not in Sherlock 2, alas). If you're curious to know what a particular menu, control, or other item is for, choose Balloon Help from the Help menu, and then point at the item in question and a small, cartoony balloon will pop up, telling you about that particular item.

Save Searches

No matter which sort of search you perform, remember you can always save what you've done and return to it at a later time. That goes for file, content, and Internet searches. To save your search criteria (after you've crafted a doozie of a search), choose File | Save Search Criteria. This opens a standard Save dialog box, enabling you to name the search and to save it to your iBook's hard disk. If you want to load the search again, choose File | Load Search Criteria.

Search for Files

The first tab in Sherlock's window is the Find File tab. With this selected, you can search for files on your iBook's hard disk, on disks attached to your iBook, or on disks attached over a network connection. You can also search the disk(s) in many different ways, including by the name (or part of the name) of the file, by the file's size, by the type of file it is, and by many other criteria. In fact, you can put a number of different criteria together to find a file with pinpoint accuracy.

6

> **NOTE** *In Sherlock 2, you accomplish this by clicking the File Names button in the Files channel. If you don't see a File Names button, first click the hard-disk icon at the top of the Sherlock 2 window.*

The Basic Search

Much of the time you search for a file, you probably do so using part of the file's name. After all, you may have a reasonably logical system (at least, it may seem logical to you) that you can use as the basis for naming your files. (If you don't, you might consider how this tactic could help you with file management.) Using even a few letters you think are in the name of the file, you can begin a search:

1. Make sure the Find File tab is selected. (In Sherlock 2, select the File Names button.)

2. In the Find Items menu, choose On Local Disks. This means only on drives connected directly to your iBook. (In Sherlock 2, you place a check mark next to each disk you want to search.)

> **TIP** *Sherlock 2 enables you to search only in a particular folder. To add a folder you'd like to search to the list, find it in the Finder and drag it to the list of drives. That folder now appears as a search volume—you can click to place a check mark next to it (or remove the check mark) just as you can with other disks. And, you can always add and select more than one folder at once, if you like.*

3. You can leave the other menus the same—you're searching for files whose names contain certain letters.

4. Enter the letters or part of the filename in the textbox. Examples might be "letter" if you're searching for business correspondence, "memo" or "invoice," or maybe "2000" or "March" if you tend to include dates in the names of your files.

5. Click Find.

That's it. After a few seconds, Sherlock pops up an Items Found window (see Figure 6-1) that tells you all the files it found that met your criteria. (In Sherlock 2, it doesn't open a new window; instead, you see the found files in the list area right below the box you typed the file name into.) You can then scroll through the list and click once on each result to see exactly where the file is located (the path to the file appears in the bottom pane of the Items Found window).

So what can you do in the Items Found window or the list area? Quite a lot, actually. You can double-click the resulting item in the top pane to open it in its associated application (or launch it if the result actually is an application). In the bottom pane (the *information area* in Sherlock 2), you can double-click the icon for the same result. Or, you can double-click any of the folders that appear in the bottom pane and that folder will open in Finder.

You can also select an item in the Items Found window or list area and choose File | Get Info (⌘-I) to get more information about the item. Or, select an item and choose File | Open Enclosing Folder (⌘-E). As the name implies, this opens the entire folder in which the selected file is stored.

Want to move the icon out to the desktop? You can do that, too. Just click-and-drag the icon from the top or bottom pane out to the desktop, and then release the trackpad button. You can also drag these icons to folders on the desktop, icons in the Application Switcher window, or even to the Trash, if you like. Likewise, you can drag items from a Sherlock window to a removable disk or network drive and the items will be copied to that disk.

You can watch the Items Found window in action by choosing Edit | Preferences and putting a check next to Show Current Search Status For Find File. This slows things down a bit, but it can be useful if you want to watch the search as it happens. There's no such preference in Sherlock 2.

FIGURE 6-1   In Sherlock (top), you see a new results window. In Sherlock 2 (bottom), you see results listed in the list area.

The Advanced Search

I promise you'll use basic search a lot—but it may not be the only type of search you conduct. The more hidden a file (especially if you've forgotten that *really clever* place you put the file or the *really clever* name you gave the file so you'd *definitely remember* where or what it was), the more advanced your search must be. And even if the file isn't particularly well hidden, an advanced search can be used for other reasons, too, like finding files created after a certain date or finding files that take up a certain amount of space. Both instances are helpful when you plan to back up your hard disk or conduct a little spring cleaning and delete files.

NOTE   *Sherlock 2 offers advanced searches, but not quite in this way. Instead, see the section "Custom Searches in Sherlock 2," later in this chapter.*

You may have already noticed that building a search in Sherlock is a whole lot like playing that old car-travel game, "Mad Libs." You choose from the different menu choices and enter keywords that completely change the search sentence. (The search sentence always says "Find items … whose …" but the rest can be changed.) The first item you can change is where you want Sherlock to look for the file(s) in question.

Search Locations

The first thing to tell Sherlock is where you want it to search. That's the menu right after Find Items that generally defaults to On Local Disks. Pull down that menu and you'll see other options.

If you search On All Disks, then Sherlock looks at every single disk—hard disk, CD-ROM, Zip, SuperDisk, network drive—to which the iBook has access. Local Disks means only disks physically attached to the iBook and On Local Disks, Except CD-ROMs means Sherlock will skip the iBook's CD-ROM drive, even if it has a CD in it. (Because you can't save files to a CD-ROM drive, this choice can be a timesaver when you're looking for a document file you created and saved yourself.) Choose On Mounted Servers and Sherlock will only look for files on network drives you've signed onto through the Chooser or the Network Browser. (If the network drive's icon appears on your desktop, then it's been mounted.)

The other two search locations are interesting: On The Desktop means what it says—it searches the desktop. In The Finder Selection searches in any windows or folders currently selected and frontmost in the Finder. And, at the bottom of the menu, you can choose individual disks themselves—if you don't have any attached disks, you just see "Macintosh HD" (or whatever you've named your iBook's hard disk).

SHORTCUT *Want to search a particular folder quickly? Open the folder (or just highlight the folder icon) in the Finder, switch to Sherlock, and choose to find items In The Finder Selection. This searches the open folder and its subfolders, instead of searching the entire hard disk.*

The Search Criteria

So now you know how to customize where Sherlock searches. But what about *what* it searches? A basic search for a filename won't always cut it. Instead, it's often clever to search by some of the other criteria—things like the size of the file, the label, or the date modified. Think of this: You could search for all files modified after a particular date—say, a week ago. Now you suddenly have a listing of documents that have recently been changed. What could you do with that? You could copy them onto a Zip, SuperDisk, or out onto the network to create a safe, backup copy!

The search criteria should be self-explanatory, although some of them get into slightly more advanced concepts. As a general rule, all these criteria are things found in the Get Info dialog box that appears when you select an icon in the Finder and choose File | Get Info. These are mostly file attributes to help you narrow your search.

You will also notice something interesting when you change from one criterion to the next—the menu after it may also change. That's because Sherlock tries to help you find relevant information, depending on the criterion you choose. If you choose to search by modified date, for instance, you probably don't want to enter an exact date—instead, you want to search by a range of dates. Sherlock helps you with that.

Some hidden criteria also exist, if you know how to find them. Hold down the OPTION key as you select the criteria menu. You'll see a couple additional Mac file attributes down at the bottom of that menu.

Add More Choices

So you've got all these ways to search for files. But what if that isn't helping much? You can narrow things down even further by mixing and matching your search criteria. Here's where the real power kicks in. Down at the bottom of the Sherlock window you see a More Choices button. Click it and your Mad Libs search sentence changes a little (see the following illustration).

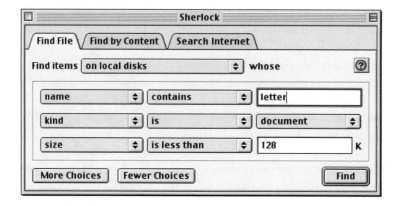

Using More Choices, you can add as many criteria lines as you need to pinpoint the file you're looking for. If you hit the More Choices button too many times, just click the Fewer Choices button to return to fewer criteria lines.

Got a completely cool search? Don't forget, you can save the criteria and use them again, if you like. Choose File | Save Search Criteria.

Custom Searches in Sherlock 2

Like the original Sherlock, Sherlock 2 enables you to customize file searches beyond simply typing the filename (or part of it) and clicking the magnifying glass. You can actually build pretty sophisticated searches with a ton of search criteria at your disposal. But, first, let's start with something a little easier.

Apple has saved some custom searches you can experiment with. Select the Custom pop-up menu in Sherlock 2 (you need to have selected the File channel by clicking the hard-disk icon at the top of the Sherlock window) and you see some interesting entries. You can select from: Applications, Larger Than 1MB, Modified Today, and Modified Yesterday. If you select one of those, you can click the magnifying glass and any file that meets the chosen criterion appears in the list menu.

Of course, you probably won't want to know every file on your hard disk that is larger than 1MB too often. More often, you want to know about files with certain filenames that meet other criteria as well. So, you can select a custom search criterion, and then enter a filename (or partial filename) in the keyword box. Now your results include files that meet both criteria—for instance, files with "letter" in their name that are over 1MB in size.

Neat-o, eh? You can do still more. Select the Edit button and you can create your own custom searches, complete with tons of different criteria. After you select the Edit button, you see the More Search Options window, shown in Figure 6-2.

If you read the previous section on adding criteria in the original Sherlock, you remember I mentioned how it can be a little like playing that game called "Mad Libs." It is in the More Search Options dialog box where you build each criterion

FIGURE 6-2   The More Search Options window is the world's most intimidating "Mad Libs" game.

for your custom search by choosing options from pop-up menus, entry boxes, and so on.

If you'd like to use a particular criterion, first click its check box. Next, select items from the pop-up menu that determine how the criterion will be limited. (They don't all have menus, but most do.) Finally, you often enter some text, date, or number, or you choose another value from a menu that will finish out the criterion statement.

It's actually pretty simple. If you want to search files that are new since 10/15/1999, click the check box next to "date created" and choose "is after" from its pop-up menu. Now, in the date entry box, enter **10/15/1999** or use the little arrows to select that date. Other criteria work similarly; you can create custom searches that check the date modified, the size of the file, the kind of file it is, the label on the file, and so on.

If you'll only be using this search once, click OK in the More Search Options window, and then return to the Sherlock 2 window, enter a filename if you want, and click the magnifying glass. Your search is conducted.

If you created a Search you really like in the More Search Options window, click the Save button. Enter a name and click Save again. Now you've got a new custom search on that custom menu back in Sherlock 2's main window. You can use it like all the other custom searches on that menu—select it, enter a filename in the keyword entry box if desired, and then click the magnifying glass to seek out files!

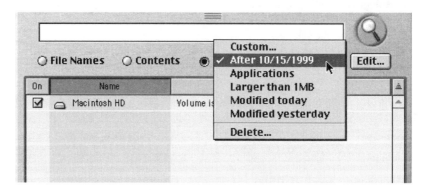

Find by Content

This is an example of how computers *should* work. For years we've been too focused on how we name our files, the little codes we use, the folders, and so on. It's too much work. What if you could just search the insides of files to find what you're looking for?

Find by Content helps you with just that. It's a fairly new technology, so it's not ready to take over for Find File completely yet. But, maybe one day. In the meantime, you can use Find by Content to help out when you just can't seem to give Find File enough information to locate a particular document.

NOTE   *Notice the use of the word "document" throughout this section. Find by Content is only useful for searching document files—files you created in applications like AppleWorks, PageMill, Microsoft Word, or SimpleText—because those are the files that contain text. (With Sherlock 2, you can also search Adobe PDF files.) If you're searching for images, applications, utilities, or other files, you need to use Find File.*

Index Documents

Find by Content requires a little work on your part. Specifically, you have to index your hard disk so Find by Content can look through your files in a speedy manner. If you don't have your hard disk indexed, then Sherlock can't search its contents. I explain how to index your hard disk in a few paragraphs.

Click the Find by Content tab in Sherlock and the first thing you see is everything to get you started—there's a box for entering the text to be sought and there's a Find button. There's also a place to choose the hard disk you want Sherlock to search. Unfortunately, all this is hidden if you don't have a drive indexed (see Figure 6-3).

To index a disk, follow these steps:

1. Click the Index Volumes button (in Sherlock) or choose Index Volumes from the Find menu (in Sherlock or Sherlock 2). That brings up the Index Volumes dialog box.

2. Here you choose the drive you want to index—probably your iBook's main hard disk. Then click the Create Index… button.

3. You see an alert box that tells you it takes a while to index the drive. If you're ready, go ahead and click Create.

Now, the index begins to be created. At this point, you might want to switch over and read your e-mail, write a letter in AppleWorks, or head out to the local theater and take in a movie. Seriously, depending on the size of your drive and the number of files on it, indexing can easily take 30 minutes, an hour, or longer—especially the first time you do it.

FIGURE 6-3 Attempting to choose an unindexed disk in Sherlock (top) and Sherlock 2 (bottom)

> TIP
>
> *Are you really going to keep working while the index is created?*
> *If so, choose Edit / Preferences. Now, use the slider bar under System*
> *Responsiveness to determine if your iBook will focus more on its indexing*
> *tasks (Faster Indexing) or whether Sherlock will be a good citizen and*
> *allow the iBook to be more responsive when you're working on other*
> *things (More Responsive).*

If you like, you can schedule the indexing. In fact, this is a good idea for keeping the index current, even if you've already created it once. As you add new documents, you have to index again to make them searchable. Getting Sherlock or Sherlock 2 to index automatically is the easiest way to accomplish that.

To schedule indexing:

1. Click the Schedule… button in the Index Volumes window.

2. Now, in the Schedule dialog box, choose what days of the week you want the index updated and at what time during the day. (It's best to schedule this for sometime when you're not using the computer—Sherlock is able to index the internal or connected disks even while your iBook is asleep.)

3. Close the Schedule dialog box once you've made your selections and Sherlock is now regularly updated for searches.

> TIP
>
> *Indexing a server drive? Make sure you have permission and then go*
> *ahead. Once a server is indexed, anyone with access to it (who also*
> *happens to have a Mac and is running Sherlock) can search that drive*
> *by content. (In Sherlock 2, you can't index a server volume unless you*
> *run Sherlock 2 from that server computer.)*

Perform the Search

Once you have the indexes created for your hard disks and other disk volumes, searching by content is easy. All you need to do is have the Find by Content tab selected in Sherlock, and then enter the text you want Sherlock to search for. (In Sherlock 2, make sure the Files channel is active—click the disk icon at the top of Sherlock 2's window—and then click the Contents button to search by contents.) Now, put a check mark next to the volumes you want Sherlock to include in its search. Click the Search button and you're off to the races. When Sherlock is done, the Items Found dialog box appears and you can manipulate the found documents, just as you would anything else found in Sherlock. (In Sherlock 2, results appear in the list area.)

Actually, you can do something special with these found documents. Because they're indexed, Sherlock has a good idea of what's in the document. As such, Sherlock can create an actual summary of the document. Want to see it? CTRL-click a document in the Items Found dialog box. You see the contextual menu appear with a Summarize to Clipboard command. Choose that command.

Now, switch to the Finder. There, in the clipboard viewer (Edit | Show Clipboard), you see a summary of the document. (If you like, you can use the Edit | Paste command in any application to paste that summary text into a document.)

 This only works with certain types of documents, including plain text and HTML documents. (Sherlock 2 can also summarize PDF documents.) Sherlock can't summarize Microsoft Word, AppleWorks, and other similar documents.

Search the Internet

Finding files and searching by content are both cool—I don't mean to take away from either of those fine features. But the real excitement over Sherlock is its capability to search the Internet from within the Mac OS—you don't have to open Internet Explorer or another Web browser. Sherlock can also search more than one Internet search site at once, meaning you don't have to jump around from search site to search site on the Web—Sherlock does all this for you.

The best part is it's easy to search the Internet using Sherlock, and it's highly customizable—many Web sites and search sites are creating their own Sherlock plug-ins, which make it possible to customize Sherlock and search for all sorts of different things using the same basic tools.

 Confused by the Internet and Web jargon? You might want to flip over to Chapter 17 quickly to read about the Web and Internet Explorer, and then come back here when you're ready to do some searching.

Start the Search

Using Sherlock to search the Internet is easy. Click the Search Internet tab and then enter words you want Sherlock to search for on the Internet. (In Sherlock 2, click the earth icon at the top of the Sherlock window.) You can simply separate the words with spaces. If you want to search for a phrase, put the phrase in quotation marks.

NOTE   *If you use your iBook's modem to connect to the Internet, you need to have established the Internet connection before searching the Internet with Sherlock. You can also set the dialer to connect automatically whenever an Internet application is launched—see Chapter 21.*

Now, put a check mark next to the Search services you want to use—they appear in the Search pane at the bottom of the Sherlock window. (In Sherlock 2, they appear in the list area.) With your search sites selected, click Search (or the magnifying glass in Sherlock 2).

Sherlock returns an Items Found list after it has searched using all the different search sites (see Figure 6-4). (In Sherlock 2, this list appears in the list area.) Each listing is a different Web page. Notice that you see three things about each page—the name, the site, and the relevance of that result. Relevance tells you how likely Sherlock believes that page is for your criteria. It's based on how many of your keywords appear in the Web page and how often they appear.

To see a summary of the Web page that's been found, click it once in the top of the Items Found window. The summary appears in the bottom pane (or the information area in Sherlock 2). You can now double-click the item to launch it in your Web browser or click the link in the summary window. If you prefer simply to save a link to that site on the desktop, you can drag the item from the top of the Items Found window to the desktop. It then becomes an Internet site document.

6

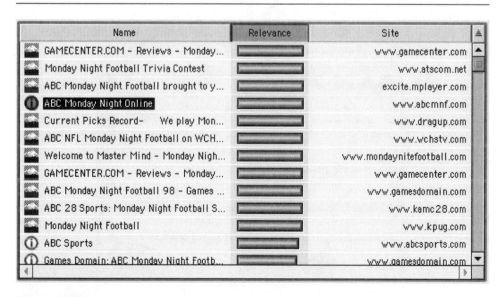

Name	Relevance	Site
GAMECENTER.COM - Reviews - Monday...		www.gamecenter.com
Monday Night Football Trivia Contest		www.atscom.net
ABC Monday Night Football brought to y...		excite.mplayer.com
ABC Monday Night Online		www.abcmnf.com
Current Picks Record- We play Mon...		www.dragup.com
ABC NFL Monday Night Football on WCH...		www.wchstv.com
Welcome to Master Mind - Monday Nigh...		www.mondaynitefootball.com
GAMECENTER.COM - Reviews - Monday...		www.gamecenter.com
ABC Monday Night Football 98 - Games ...		www.gamesdomain.com
ABC 28 Sports: Monday Night Football S...		www.kamc28.com
Monday Night Football		www.kpug.com
ABC Sports		www.abcsports.com
Games Domain: ABC Monday Night Footb...		www.gamesdomain.com

FIGURE 6-4   Results from an Internet search are ranked by relevance.

Sherlock 2's Channels

In Sherlock 2, there's a little more to searching the Internet than back in the original Sherlock. Specifically, Sherlock 2 has been updated with its new Channels technology.

Channels technology does two things. First, it places those little icons at the top of the Sherlock window, which you can click to select different groupings of Internet search sites. Click the shopping cart icon, for instance, and you see a different list than when you click the earth icon.

 You can drag the little bar between the channels icons and the keyword box. Drag it downward and you see more spaces for channels; drag it upward to cover all but the first row again.

Second, the Channels technology actually offers different *types* of channels, which enable you to search for different types of information and see results listed in different ways. Depending on the type of channel you're using for a search, the results will be formatted differently. In a regular Internet search (like the one you implement when you click the earth icon), you see the relevance-ranked results list already discussed. But, if you clicked the shopping cart icon and did a search, you'd see something different. You'd see results ranked by price and availability.

The reason for this is simple—they're different types of channels. In fact, there are four different types of channels in Sherlock 2:

- **Searching**   These channels return relevance-ranked results.

- **People**   People channels return information about the person, like e-mail address and phone number.

- **Shopping**   Shopping channels return information that includes a description, price, and availability date.

- **News**   News channels don't actually offer different results from Internet channels, which throws off my whole theory. But they're a great place to find news-oriented Internet search sites.

Try it. Select a channel and you see the different Internet search sites for each channel. Try a search in each one and you see different types of results in the different channels.

Update Your Search Sites

Sherlock notifies you when you attempt a search and one of your search sites has been updated. Click the Update button to update that particular search site. If you haven't used Sherlock in a while, you can manually have it search for updated sites by choosing Find | Update Search Sites…. If any updates are found, Sherlock lets you know.

There's no Find | Update Search Sites command in Sherlock 2.

Add New Search Sites

At some point, you may decide to add third-party search sites to your Sherlock window.

That means you can use Sherlock to search all kinds of sites, including Amazon.com (see Figure 6-5), CD-Now, Encyclopedia.com, and many others. The more you use your iBook, the more you'll see what an exciting tool Sherlock is. Apple keeps track of the plug-ins being offered by other companies. Visit **http://www.apple.com/sherlock/** on the Web for a listing and instructions for downloading those plug-ins.

FIGURE 6-5   Here's an example of searching Amazon.com, the popular bookstore, using Sherlock.

When you find a Sherlock plug-in you want, download it to your iBook using Internet Explorer or an FTP program (see Part III for much more on Internet tools).

To install the new plug-in:

1. Drag the plug-in file (called "*something*.src") to the System Folder icon on your iBook's startup disk (probably the internal hard disk).

2. Drop the plug-in on the System Folder.

3. The Finder responds by telling you the plug-in needs to be put in the Internet Search Sites folder. Click OK.

Now the new search site is available as one of the options on the Search Internet tab in Sherlock.

In Sherlock 2, new Internet search sites appear under the Custom channel (click the icon that looks like Sherlock Holmes' hat). Then, if you want to, you can drag the new Internet search site from the list area to another channel in the channel area. (More on that in the section, " How to Create a New Channel in Sherlock 2.")

6

Create a New Channel in Sherlock 2

If you have Sherlock 2 on your iBook, then you can go even a little further than simply adding Internet search sites. You can actually create a whole different channel at the top there. Then, you can drag Internet search sites from other channels to your new channel, if you want. Here's how to create a channel:

1.   Choose Channel | New Channel.

2.   In the New Channel dialog box, enter a name for the channel in the Name The Channel entry box.

3.   In the Channel Type menu, choose the type of channel you want to create. (The types are discussed back in the section, "Sherlock 2's Channels.")

4.   Now, click the up and down arrows next to the icon to choose an icon for this channel.

5.   Enter a description if you want to, then click OK.

Now you've got a new channel. You can drag Internet search sites from other channels to your channel or, if you'd dragged new Internet search sites to the System Folder to install them, you can drag those from the Custom channel (the one with Sherlock Holmes' hat) to your new channel.

Chapter 7

Get Some Help

How to...

- ■ Decide which component of Apple's Help systems to use
- ■ Use Apple Help to link to Help documents
- ■ Follow along as Apple Guide teaches you topics interactively
- ■ Use Balloon Help

O ver the years, the Mac's reputation for being easy to use has encouraged Apple's engineers to work on innovative Help systems to assist you in understanding how things work and how to get things done. In fact, they've worked so much on the Help system that they've ended up with what might be a few too many ways to get help. It can get a little confusing.

The Help Systems

These days, the main Help system is the Apple Help system. The best thing about the Apple Help system is that it's based on the same technology that World Wide Web pages on the Internet use.

This makes it easier for application developers to build the Help system for their applications, since most of them already know how to create Web pages. It also makes it a little easier for us as users; if you understand how Web pages work, you'll understand how Apple Help works. Even if you don't, it's an easy system to use.

There are other kinds of help, too, including Apple Guide, Balloon Help, application help, Read Me files, and online sites.

Every application that runs in the Mac OS has a Help menu, since Apple engineers think it's important that Mac applications all have a similar look. Select that Help menu and you'll be able to see what that particular application offers in the way of help—it might be using the Apple Help system, Apple Guide technology, or the application's own Help system, and you'll always have Balloon Help (although it won't necessarily be implemented). You can also press the ⌘-? (question mark) keys to bring up the default Help system.

> *Remember that Apple Help isn't a particular command, it's a system. So each application that uses the Apple Help system will have its own name. In the Finder, you'll find "Mac OS Help" or "Mac Help" in the Help menu—it's using the Apple Help system.*

It's rare, but if you're not finding help through the Help menu, you should also try the Apple menu. Sometimes you'll find help (or some sort of documentation) when you select About this Program (it'll actually say the program name, for instance "About Internet Explorer"). You should also look in the application's folder on your hard drive—you may find a document of some sort in the folder that offers instructions or help.

Apple Help

The Apple Help system, as mentioned, is based on the Web technology using *hyperlinks*, which allow you to move from topic to topic in the Help system by clicking the blue, underlined text. This makes it easy to learn about a topic, then click to see a related topic.

In order to see this help, open the Help menu and choose the *Application Name* Help command. An example might be "SimpleText Help." This loads the Help Viewer—the browser application that you'll use to find the help you need (see Figure 7-1).

NOTE *Actually, this won't always load the Apple Help system—sometimes it will load Apple Guide or the application's own internal Help system.*

Browse for Help

With the Help Viewer open, you have a couple of choices. You can begin by clicking on the hyperlinks on the page. The hyperlinks are the blue, underlined words. Clicking a hyperlink causes the Help Viewer to show you that topic. This method is a little like using the Table of Contents in a book. Click the topic that

FIGURE 7-1   The Help Viewer is the main online Help system for your iBook.

seems most appropriate. When the document for that topic appears in the Help Viewer, you can click the subtopic that seems most appropriate for your situation.

After you've clicked the subtopic, you'll most likely see an instructional document that walks you through that topic (see Figure 7-2). While you're reading the instructions you'll see three different types of hyperlinks. If the hyperlink doesn't have a special icon next to it, it's designed to move you to another, related topic. If the link *does* have an icon next to it, that means the link is designed to help you do something—it'll open a control panel or document, or change a setting for you.

FIGURE 7-2   Browsing for interesting topics in the Help Viewer

The third type of link points to a Web site on the Internet. If your Internet connection is running, you can click one of these links to load your Web browser and view the help that's online.

To leave a particular page, you can either click the Back button in the Help Viewer (which returns you to the list of topics) or you can click a link that takes you to another, related topic.

Search for Help

If the Table of Contents approach doesn't work for you, you can search directly for a topic using keywords. In the Search entry box at the top of the screen, enter a few words that suggest the issue you want to learn about. You don't need to enter complete sentences—something like "application menu" or "mail merge" should be good enough. (You can narrow things down by including more keywords.) Then click Search. After your iBook thinks things over, the Help Viewer will display a Search Results page, as shown in Figure 7-3.

Results from a Help search are ranked by relevance—the Help Viewer decides if a Help topic is relevant based on the number of times your keywords show up in the document. Then, it shows the Help topics in descending order, along with up to five asterisks to represent relevance. (The more asterisks, the more relevant.)

When you see a topic that looks good, click its hyperlink to see the associated Help document. If you don't see the topic you want, you can click the More Results link at the bottom of the page if the Help Viewer has identified other relevant topics. If there are no more results to examine, you can click the Broaden Search hyperlink. This forces the Help Viewer to relax the search criteria and even check other applications' Help documents.

The Help Center

In most Help menus you'll see an additional choice: the Help Center. (You can also get to the Help Center by clicking the Home button—it looks like a little house—in the Help Viewer.) The Help Center works within the Help Viewer, allowing you to search and browse across all of your applications' Help systems, including those designed for the Mac OS itself and for AppleScript. If you'd like to see help for all Help Viewer-compatible applications, fire up the Help Center.

Search Results

Page 1 of 5 about "network printing" in **Mac OS Help**

***** Printing from the desktop

***** Printing

**** Selecting a printer

**** Using infrared communication

**** Creating groups of settings (locations)

**** Security issues with Folder Actions

*** Doing other work while you're printing

*** Changing print options

** Printing on an IrDA-compatible printer

** Printing color accurately

Broaden my search   More results ▷

FIGURE 7-3   The Search Results page shows you the Help documents that might relate to your search keywords.

Apple Guide

In some ways, Apple Guide is similar to the Apple Help system—it offers both topics and a search approach to finding what you need to know. (It also offers an index of terms that is more extensive than what's found in Apple Help.) Once you find the Help topic you're looking for, the Apple Guide walks you through the process in small steps, often telling you and showing you exactly what to do on the screen. You may notice, for instance, that some Apple Guide lessons will circle menus or highlight menu commands in red to help you find them more easily. More than just Help documents, Apple Guide offers something akin to electronic lessons on different topics:

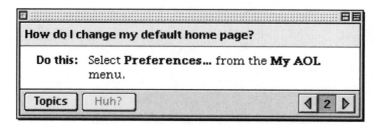

To start up Apple Guide, pull down the Help menu and look for an entry called *Application* Guide. An example might be "AOL Guide," the Help system for America Online 4.0, the version included with most iBooks. Choose that item on the Help menu, and that particular Guide system appears.

 Another way that Apple Guide is invoked is through Apple Help documents. If you see a link in an Apple Help document that starts with "Help me...," then there's a chance it will use Apple Guide technology to walk you through the steps of a lesson.

Help by Topic

With the Apple Guide open onscreen, click the Topics button to see the various topics for which Help articles have been written. On the left side of the screen you'll see general topic areas. Click one that seems appropriate, and specific Help questions appear in the Guide window. To open a Help lesson, select it and click the OK button.

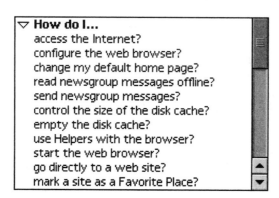

After you've chosen a topic, just sit back and be taught by the Guide. Read each screen carefully, then do what's recommended on the screen. Once you've finished everything the screen says to do (or if it only provides information and doesn't offer any specific instructions), click the right arrow.

If something on the screen doesn't make sense to you, click the Huh? button, which will help by defining the technical terms onscreen. Otherwise, continue to follow the instructions on each screen of the Guide until you've solved the problem or answered your question. When you're done, you can click the Guide's Close box to end the Help session or click the Topics button to return to the Topics window.

Index and Search

One of the best ways to get to a particular Help topic is to look it up in the index. Here's how:

1. In the main Guide window choose the Index button to look at an index of keywords that are covered in the Guide's lessons.

2. Drag the slider along the letters to change to a different letter or just click directly on one of the letters to see an alphabetical listing of keywords.

3. When you find the keyword that seems to relate to your problem, select it. A list of topic phrases appears in the right side of the window.

4. Select one of the topic phrases, then click OK. The lesson begins.

You can also search for lessons using your own keywords:

1. Click the Look For button in the main Guide window and you'll see the search box.

2. Enter keywords in the entry box, then click the Search button. (Notice that in order to type in the Guide window you'll need to click the arrow button to the left of the entry box.)

3. After you click Search, related topic phrases appear on the right side of the window.

4. Choose one of the topic phrases, and click OK to begin the lesson.

Balloon Help

Balloon Help's simple role is to tell you what something is when you point to it. Unfortunately, Balloon Help isn't universally implemented by applications. It's useful when it is, though, so it's always worth checking for Balloon Help when you have a question about an application's interface.

To turn on Balloon Help, choose Help | Show Balloons. Now, aim the mouse pointer at anything onscreen that you'd like to learn more about. If Balloon Help has been implemented for that application and that item, a small cartoon-like balloon appears, at the mouse pointer, offering information.

To turn off Balloon Help, choose Help | Hide Balloons.

You'll find that Balloon Help always works in the Finder and works in a number of commercial applications like AppleWorks, Microsoft Office 98, and America Online, to name a few. You'll also find that Balloon Help is great for identifying files in your iBook's System Folder, such as control panels, extensions, fonts, and other system file types. Just turn on Balloon Help and point at any item—in the Finder or in another application—that confuses you.

Part II

Get Things Done

Chapter 8

Create Printed Documents

How to...

- Meet AppleWorks
- Create a word processing document
- Type your document and format the text
- Format paragraphs, align elements, and create headers and footers
- Format the entire document, including margins, sections, and tabs
- Spell check and find and replace automatically
- Create Stylesheets and paragraph styles
- Use pre-built Stationery and create your own document templates

As you know, a computer makes you a better writer. My ramblings, for instance, are almost instantly translated into readable, friendly, and useful text, thanks to this iBook I use when I'm on the move. Otherwise, not only would my text be misspelled, grammatically reproachable, and improperly formatted, it would also be completely unintelligible and morally reprehensible.

OK, so that's a bit of an exaggeration. A computer isn't about writing better—it's about typing a little better, formatting documents more professionally, and being able to edit, cut, paste, and shape your document without scissors and glue.

Write with Your iBook

If you need to write documents with your iBook, you'll likely turn to a word processing application—an application designed to accept typed input and allow you to manipulate it on the page. Unless you've chosen to install a different word processing application, your best bet is to launch AppleWorks, which came with your iBook, to begin word processing.

A word processing program is designed to do a number of things. It's designed to accept text and images that you type or add through menu commands, then allow you to format the text and images in many different ways. It's worth saying that word processors are designed to help you format entire documents—from memos and letters to longer documents like reports, pamphlets, and books. Word processors allow you to do many things to long and short documents:

- Change the document size, margins, and spacing

- Insert headers and footnotes

- Change the font, style, and formatting of text

- Create documents in outline form

- Format text in tabular form

- Format text with bullets, numbers, or special tabs and indents

- Check spelling

- Change formatting for paragraphs, sections, or the entire document

In most cases, however, a word processor is not designed for creating a particular *page*. That's what layout applications like QuarkXPress and Adobe InDesign are designed for. Such applications have highly sophisticated tools that allow a page designer to drop text, images, effects, lines, and shapes onto a page and manipulate them freely to create the most stunning advertisement, pamphlet, or publication. Even within AppleWorks we'll use a different module to create newsletters and similar layouts.

So, word processing really is a little closer to the typewriter than it is to the layout table. But there is a difference between a typewriter—even most electronic, computerized typewriters—and a word processing application. Word processing applications allow you to change your mind. You can experiment with documents after the fact. That means you can create the document first, then worry about how it will be formatted.

AppleWorks vs. The Other Guys

AppleWorks is what's referred to as a "Works" application, because it's designed to perform more than one major function. While a program like Microsoft Word is designed solely for word processing, AppleWorks offers a number of different modules, allowing you to create word processing documents, spreadsheets, databases, images and drawings, and other types of documents. So why would you choose anything else?

In most cases you probably won't have to. AppleWorks is a very good program that allows you to do some rather unique things—including putting its parts together to create layouts that feature word processing, images, spreadsheet tables, and database data in the same documents. In that respect, it's a very powerful and very enjoyable program to work with.

But you may need more specialized capabilities or you may need to use a particular program—like Microsoft Word—because the rest of your office, school, organization, or clan requires it. That's okay, but you'll need to spend more money and install that application yourself.

In exchange, you'll get a program that's specifically tailored to the task at hand. Microsoft Word, for instance, offers a lot of tools for collaborating on important word processing documents—you can embed comments, track changes, and even give different human editors a different color to use within the document so it's easy to see who is making what changes. We used Microsoft Word to create this book, for instance, largely because of its collaborative capabilities.

So, you'll want to use a tool that's designed for the job. The question becomes, how do you know? Let me reiterate that AppleWorks is truly an impressive application, and you'll be able to accomplish a lot with it. If your tasks are personal, educational, or even for a small business, you'll likely find it completely adequate for your needs.

But even if it doesn't fit all of your needs, in nearly all cases, documents created in AppleWorks can be translated into documents that can be read by other applications like Word, Excel, QuarkXPress, and others when the times comes. So, feel free to try things in AppleWorks first, then move on to something else if you need more power.

Begin Your Document

To begin, launch AppleWorks or choose File | New if AppleWorks is already open. The New Document window appears, allowing you to choose the type of document you'd like to begin. In this case, you're interested in creating a word processing document, so leave that selection highlighted and click OK.

In AppleWorks, the type of document you choose helps determine what sort of tools and menu commands you see at first—you'll see the word processing commands and a blank document window now.

Start typing. There are actually a couple of rules you should follow when typing in a word processor, especially if you're used to a typewriter. Some of these rules are:

- **Don't press TAB to indent the first line of a paragraph.**   You can format paragraphs so that they are indented automatically, either before or after you type them.

- **Don't press RETURN at the end of a line.**   You only need to press RETURN at the end of a paragraph. Whenever you type to the right margin of the page, the next thing you type will automatically *wrap* to the next line.

- **Don't put two spaces after a period.**   Many typists get used to pressing the SPACEBAR twice after the end of a sentence, but that throws off the automatic spacing capabilities of a word processing program and it just looks bad with many standard Mac fonts.

- **Don't worry about double-spacing while you type.**   You'll be able to set line spacing for your document at 1.5, double-, or triple-space after you've typed it (or, as you'll see, before you begin).

- **Don't press RETURN many times to get to a new page.**   You can easily insert a page break if you're done on one page and want to begin on another one.

■ **Don't enter asterisks, dashes, or numbers for lists.** You can do all that automatically. If you need to create a list like the one you're reading right now, you can do that with commands—just enter each line and press RETURN. You'll be able to go back and format the bulleted or numbered list later.

■ **Don't do anything weird to change the margins.** You don't need to insert many spaces, add tabs, or press RETURN in order to create special margin spacing—for instance, if you want to have a block of quoted text that's squeezed onto the page. Again, you can do that with special document formatting commands, covered later in this chapter.

■ **Don't uses spaces to create columns or table layouts.** At the very least, you should use tabs and the document ruler to set up the spacing in your document. That's covered later in this chapter, too.

Most of these issues are addressed in the section "Format Your Document," which appears later in this chapter. You'll find that what you need to do while typing is pretty simple:

1. Type words.

2. When you get to the end of a sentence, type a period then press the SPACEBAR once.

3. When you get to the end of a paragraph, press RETURN.

That's pretty much it while you're typing your document. Remember, you'll be able to change just about anything once you have the words on the page. For now, that's the primary goal.

Fonts, Styles, and Sizes

Aside from the typing basics, there are two other precepts for the accomplished word processing typist. (That's you.) The first is to *save often,* which is covered in the next section. The second is to format your text as you're typing. It's not mandatory, but learning to format as you type makes creating your documents easier.

By text formatting I mean three things: the font, the style, and the size of the text. These things can be changed easily before or while you're typing a line of text, so I'll include them here while you're getting started with your word processor.

Fonts

The word "font" is used in most Macintosh applications to mean "typeface," which is defined as a general design for a set of characters. Popular typefaces are Courier, Times New Roman, Helvetica, and so forth.

If you'd like your typed text to appear in something other than the default font, you can head up to the Font menu, choose a new font, and begin typing. Your text appears in that new font.

Similarly, you can select existing text and change it to a new font. Select text by beginning to the left of the first word you want to highlight, press the trackpad button, and drag the mouse pointer to the right of the last word you want to choose, then release the trackpad button. If you want to choose all the words in your document, choose Edit | Select All. Then select the Font menu and click the font you want to use for the highlighted text. Your text should change immediately (see Figure 8-1).

You may notice one cool thing about AppleWorks' Font menu—it shows you each font name in its actual design so you can get a quick idea of how the font will appear in your document once chosen.

Styles

The text styles represent different effects you apply to the fonts for emphasis—things like italics and boldfacing. You can change the style of your text in either of the two ways that you change the font—either before you type, or by selecting text that's already been typed.

To change the style, select the Style menu in AppleWorks, then click on the style you want to use. Begin typing and your text appears in that style.

To change the style of text that already appears, select that text in the document window and then pull down the Style menu. Choose the style you want to use, and the highlighted text changes immediately to that style.

Often, though, you won't want to do it this way, especially with the four major styles: Plain, Italic, Bold, and Underlined. In these special cases, you'll probably want to learn the keyboard commands for changing text styles. Except for the Plain command, these commands are the same in many applications, including AppleWorks:

⌘-B	Boldface	⌘-U	Underline
⌘-I	Italic	⌘-T	Plain, unstyled text

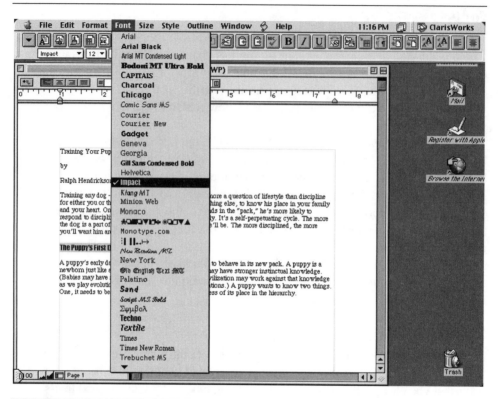

FIGURE 8-1   Choose a new font from the Font menu, and you'll see it in your document.

Knowing these keyboard commands, you can quickly switch styles while typing. Press ⌘-I, type a word in italics, then press ⌘-T to return to plain text. (You can also press ⌘-I to turn italics off again—you'll find that some applications don't support ⌘-T.) Press ⌘-U and ⌘-B and you'll be typing bold, underlined text; press ⌘-T and you're back to plain text again.

Sizes

You can change the size of text in your document by highlighting the text and pulling down the Size menu to choose the point size you want. Points are a traditional way of sizing fonts in publishing terms—72 point is about one inch, so 12 point is about one-sixth of an inch in height. Traditionally, 72-point text was reserved for newspaper headlines that declared war or the surprise winner of a presidential election—these days the biggest headline on every morning's front page is probably about 72 points.

Readable body type is typically about 12 point; 14 point looks like "big" type you find in some of those movie novelizations. Try 18 point for a subhead in your report—24 or so can look good for the title of your report (see Figure 8-2).

You can also change text sizes as you type. Pull down the Size menu and choose the new size from the menu, then type in that new size. If you want to use the keyboard commands, they might take some memorizing: ⌘-SHIFT-< makes text smaller and ⌘-SHIFT-> makes it bigger. (Note, by the way, that these are specific AppleWorks keyboard commands and don't work in all applications.)

Save Often

If you've been following so far, you might see from the figures in this chapter something terribly wrong is going on. The document I'm working on is still untitled (it says "Untitled" there in the document window's title bar), which means it hasn't been saved!

My rule: Save every three sentences. It usually doesn't take long for each save (once the initial save is complete) and it'll sure make you happy if and when your

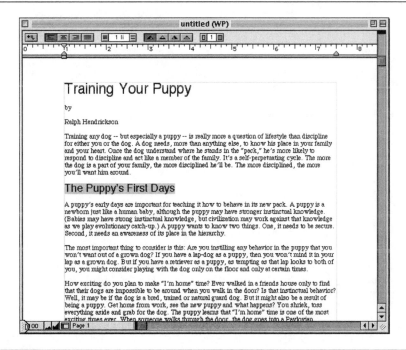

FIGURE 8-2   Different point sizes clearly define the parts of your document.

iBook or your application crashes. (It does happen.) Having saved very recently, you won't be as upset when you have to retype only a few sentences to catch up. If you have to retype an entire page or two, you won't be nearly as pleased.

To save the document the first time, choose File | Save once you've typed something. Use the Save dialog box to find the folder where you want to store the file, then give it a name and click Save.

From then on, you can just press ⌘-S to save as you're typing. Every three sentences, remember? (For more on saving, see Chapter 5.)

AppleWorks doesn't offer an AutoSave command, but it can be added with a $10 shareware program called SuperSave that autosaves in nearly every Mac application you have. See Chapter 18 for more on downloading shareware.

Format Your Document

I know I've been a little forceful about the whole "just type your document" thing—I hope I didn't scare you with that. It's just that it's so much easier to set up the document to work the way you want it to before or after you type—not during. Let me show you what I mean. This sections covers a lot of stuff in a little space, including:

- Formatting paragraphs: indenting, spacing, alignment

- Inserting elements: page breaks, headers, footers

- Formatting whole documents: margins, page numbers

- Formatting sections: book-type formatting

- Using tabs and the ruler: making changes visually

See, that's quite a bit. Whether you're writing reports, documentation, thesis papers, research, legislation, contracts, or books, you'll find you're able to get pretty deep into this stuff without filling too much of the space in your head. After all, you've got important things to store in your brain, including birthdays, phone numbers, where your aunt hid her will, and how to tie a double-Windsor knot.

Format Paragraphs

There are three basic things you'll be managing when it comes to your paragraphs, and it all happens in the Paragraph dialog box. To start formatting a paragraph, click the trackpad button to place the insertion point in that paragraph (you don't have to select the whole thing, but you can if you like). To format more than one paragraph at once, select them. (Remember that triple-clicking usually selects paragraphs.) With that out of the way, choose Format | Paragraph. That causes the Paragraph dialog box to appear:

	Paragraph	
Left Indent:	0 in	Line Spacing:	1	li ▼
First Line:	0 in	Space Before:	0	li ▼
Right Indent:	0 in	Space After:	0	li ▼
Label:	None ▼	Alignment:	Left ▼	
?		Apply	Cancel	OK

Indenting

Now, in the Paragraph dialog box you can make some choices about how that paragraph is going to look. On the left side of the dialog box, you have three choices. All three are entered in the entry boxes in inches—a standard indent is about 0.5 inches. You can indent either or both margins (usually for block quotes, programming code listings, or lists) or you can indent just the first line of the paragraph.

Click in the entry box next to the type of indent you want, then enter the number of inches you want for the indent. You can press TAB to move to the next box or press RETURN to accept the value and close the dialog box. If you'd like to see how something looks before you close the dialog box, click the Apply button. That makes your changes but leaves the dialog box open for further changes or experimentation. By the way, you can also move this dialog box around if you need to see how your paragraph looks after the change is applied.

 You don't need to type the "in" for inches when entering your own number—just the number will suffice.

Line Spacing

In the Line Spacing entry box enter a number, then choose the units for that number in the little pull-down menu next to it. If you want to double-space, you can just keep the units at "lines."

You can also fine-tune your spacing to give yourself more or less space between lines as necessary. For instance, you'll sometimes want a document to look like it's double-spaced, but you need it squeezed a bit. In that case, you should choose Points as the units for Line Spacing and select a point size that's just less than twice the point size of your text. If your text is 12 point, for instance, you could choose 20 point to get a slightly squeezed double-spacing effect.

 You'd think you could just choose 1.75 lines for the Line Spacing, but AppleWorks rounds it up to 2 lines. It will only accept whole and half values, so 1.5 is acceptable, but 1.25 gets rounded up to 1.5.

The other spacing options allow you to add additional space above and below a paragraph—this can be useful if you choose a more contemporary style for your document in which you don't indent the first line of your paragraphs. In that case, a little extra space before and after a paragraph will make it clear where it ends and the next paragraph begins.

Make a List

When you build a list in AppleWorks, you press RETURN after each list item. So, technically, you're creating a number of different paragraphs, even if they're really short. In order to turn them into a list, you can select each item and give it a label in the Paragraph dialog box. The labels vary from bullet points to numbers to Roman numerals.

There's a slightly more efficient way to make a list:

1. In the document window, type each list item and press RETURN after each.

2. Drag the mouse pointer to select every item in the list.

3. Select Format | Paragraph.

4. Choose the Label menu from the Paragraph dialog box and select Bullet.

5. Click Apply or OK.

That's it—the list is created. Every item you've highlighted becomes its own list item. If you're still in the Paragraph dialog box, you can change the item's left and right indent to taste—sometimes you'll want a list indented from the left margin to help it stand out.

If you want to change a bulleted paragraph back to a regular paragraph, select it and choose None from the Label menu in the Paragraph dialog box. That will return the paragraph to normal, non-bullet mode.

Alignment

The last little task for the Paragraph dialog box is aligning the paragraph. You can align the paragraph in four different ways:

- **Left**   Paragraph is flush with the left margin and ragged on the right margin.

- **Right**   Paragraph is ragged on the left margin and flush with the right margin.

- **Center**   Both left and right margins are ragged, but the entire paragraph is balanced toward the center.

- **Justify**   The paragraph is spaced so that the text is flush with both the left and right margins, like many newspaper columns.

To choose one of the alignments, just pull down the Alignment menu and make your choice. Click Apply and you'll see the paragraph's alignment change.

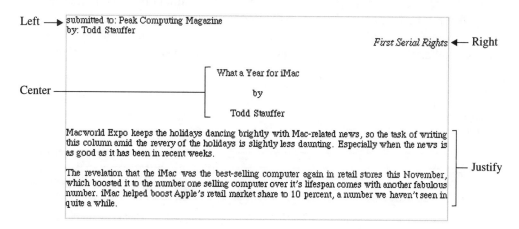

Format Multiple Paragraphs

Clearly, it could get a bit tedious to format every paragraph of a document manually like this. Fortunately, that's not mandatory. If you like, you can select as many paragraphs as you like—or even choose Edit | Select All to highlight the entire document—and perform the same Paragraph dialog box changes to them all at once.

You can also copy one paragraph's traits and apply them to another paragraph. To do that, place the insertion point in the paragraph you want to use as a model, then choose Format | Copy Ruler (⌘-SHIFT-C). This copies the paragraph settings. Now, place the cursor in the paragraph you want to change to the copied settings (or select multiple paragraphs). Choose Format | Paste Ruler (⌘-SHIFT-V). The selected paragraphs change to reflect the model paragraph's settings.

Why is this called Copy and Paste Ruler? Because the ruler in the document window reflects all of the settings you can make in the Paragraph dialog box.

Shortcut: Use the Ruler

Some of these formatting options—alignment, basic line spacing, and bullets—are offered right in the document window if you have the ruler visible. (To show the rulers, choose Window | Show Rulers. To hide rulers, choose Windows | Hide Rulers.)

Small, clickable icons on the ruler will allow you to do the same things you can do in the Paragraph dialog box.

For instance, if you'd like to align a paragraph, place the insertion point somewhere in that paragraph and click one of the alignment buttons in the ruler. You can tell by looking at the buttons how they align—left, center, right, and justify (see the following illustration). If you don't like how the paragraph looks, click another alignment button. The changes are made instantly.

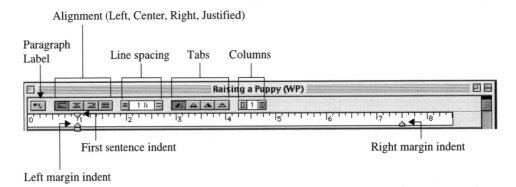

The other buttons work the same way. Select the paragraphs you want to turn into bullet items, then choose the bullet you want to use from the Label menu on the ruler. The series of paragraphs become bullet items.

For line spacing, the button on the left pushes lines together while the button on the right spreads them apart. Select the paragraph(s) you want to alter the line spacing of, then click on the line spacing button of your choice.

 Here's a cool trick—if you double-click the line-spacing number box where it says 1.5in or 2in, you'll immediately open the Paragraph dialog box.

The ruler can also be used to quickly format the indenting of paragraphs. Select the paragraph(s) you want to indent, then drag the little indent sliders. (Point at a slider with the mouse pointer, hold down the button and drag it to the right or left. Let go of the trackpad button to place the slider.)

The sliders determine how things are indented—on the left side, the top slider determines the first-line indent and the bottom slider determines the left-side indent of the rest of the paragraph. Notice what this lets you do—if you indent *only* the bottom slider, then you'll end up with a paragraph whose first line is flush with the left margin while the rest of the lines are indented, just like in academic bibliography entries.

The right margin indent slider just controls the right-side indent of the entire paragraph. Using a combination of the three you can quickly and visually accomplish anything you can do with indents in the Paragraph dialog box. Of course, you'll have to eyeball the measurements—in the control panel you can be exact to a fraction of an inch.

Insert Elements

Once you have your paragraphs nice and neat you may start to get the feeling that there are still some things missing—elements you'll usually find at the edges of your document. Here are some of the special elements you can insert into your document:

- **Headers**   Need something at the top of every page? Add a header and it'll automatically be put at the top of all your pages.

- **Footers**   Create a footer and the same thing appears at the bottom of your pages.

- **Page Numbers**   Add page numbers that automatically count up for you.

- ■ **Date and Time**   Choose a quick menu item to add these to your documents in the header, footer, or wherever you like.

- ■ **Section Breaks**   Dividing your document into sections—for new chapters, for instance—makes it easier to renumber and manage things.

- ■ **Page Breaks**   When you're ready for a new page, but not finished with the last one, you can break immediately and start a fresh page.

- ■ **Footnotes**   Writing a scientific, academic, or commercial report that needs footnotes? You've got 'em.

Headers and Footers

These small sections appear at the top and bottom of the page and allow you to add your name, the document's name, a page number, the date and time, or just about anything else required.

To create a header, select Format | Insert Header. A small section appears at the top of the current page in your document window. Now, you can type anything you need in that section—you can even adjust what you type using the paragraph formatting tools.

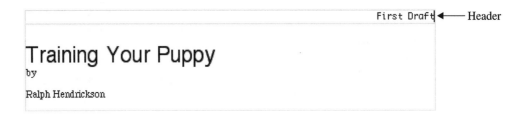

Footers work the same way—choose Format | Insert Footer and a small section appears at the bottom of the page. In either a header or footer you can press the RETURN key to add additional lines—it'll take away space from the document, not from the margins, which will always stay the same as their setting in the Document dialog box (discussed in the section "Format the Whole Document," later in this chapter).

Now all you need is something to put in the header and footer.

Page Number, Date, and Time

Over in the Edit menu, AppleWorks makes it easy to add the page number, current date, and current time into your document. You can add them anywhere, but the best plan is to put them in the header or footer of your document. And the best part is that the date, time, and page numbers will be updated automatically. The Date and Time commands are a great way to get an automatic record of when documents are modified.

To insert a date, time, or page number, place the insertion point in the header or footer where you want the date to appear. Then, choose the appropriate Insert command from the Edit menu. The element you're inserting appears, as shown here:

```
                    First Draft Modifed: 1/21/01 -- 5:19 PM   | Page Number: 1
```

Training Your Puppy
by

Ralph Hendrickson

8

TIP *Want to enter a date, time, or page number that never changes automatically? Hold down the OPTION key as you select one of the Insert commands in the Edit menu.*

When you select the Insert Page Number command, you'll get a small dialog box that allows you to choose which page-related number you want to enter. Here's the breakdown:

- **Page Number**   Inserts the current page number for that page in the document or section.

- **Section Number**   Inserts the current section's number. You can create different sections of a document—for instance, for chapters—and number them. We'll cover sections next in this chapter.

- **Section Page Count**   Enters the number of total pages in the current section.

■ **Document Page Count**   Enters the total number of pages in the document. This would be useful for something at the top of the page that said "Page 4 of 15"—you'd get the "15" to automatically update by inserting the Document Page Count command.

Beyond these, there's a Representation menu you can use to choose how the page numbers will be shown. If you want something that says "Section C, Page 4," you can have those numbers automatically updated, too.

 The point of having all of these different page-numbering options is to give you the opportunity to choose different combinations of page-numbering schemes and have them automatically updated. Plus, you can add your own text in the header to help explain your scheme.

Section Breaks

While we're on the topic of all this numbering, let's quickly look into section breaks. You can create a section break anywhere in your document—a section is simply an internal label for parts of your AppleWorks document. Sections allow you to divide a document up into chapters, lessons, segments or, well, sections. You can then number the sections separately, start over with new page numbering, and so on, as discussed earlier.

To create a section break, place the insertion point where you'd like the new section to begin, then select Format | Insert Section. Now, a line appears dividing the two sections of the document. (This line will not print in the final document.) If you've used the automatic section numbers with the Insert Page Number command, then the section numbers on subsequent pages will reflect the new section.

You can do a whole lot more with sections, too. That's discussed in "Format the Section," later in this chapter.

Page Breaks

If you're typing along in your document and you decide you want a new page, you can choose Format | Insert Page Break. That automatically moves you to the top of a new page. Plus, your text will always appear at the top of a new page after a page break, even if you add text before the page break occurs. If you just press RETURN a bunch of times to get to a new page, you'll have to go back and fix the Returns every time you reformatted, added text, or otherwise messed with the text in the document.

Footnotes

If you need footnotes in your document, they're pretty easy to add. Place the insertion point at the end of the word or sentence you want to footnote. Then, choose Format | Insert Footnote. A superscript footnote number appears next to the selected word, and you're transported to the bottom of the page (or the end of the document) where you can type the footnote text, as shown in Figure 8-3.

> **TIP** *You can choose where footnotes are added—at the bottom of the page or the end of the document—using the Document dialog box, which is covered in the next section, "Format the Whole Document." If you're currently set up to place footnotes at the end of your document, the command will be Insert Endnote instead of Insert Footnote.*

To get rid of a footnote, delete the footnote number in the body of the document. The footnote itself will automatically disappear.

Format the Whole Document

After you're done formatting individual paragraphs, you may have reason to make some more global choices—in that case, you'll want to get into the Document

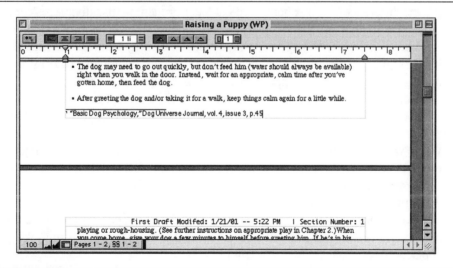

FIGURE 8-3   Adding impressive-looking footnotes is automatic and easy.

formatting preferences. Select Format I Document, and the Document dialog box appears.

```
┌─────────────────────── Document ───────────────────────┐
│                                                        │
│  ┌─ Margins ──────────┐   ┌─ Page Display ───────────┐ │
│  │ Top:      [1 in]   │   │ ◉ One Page Above The Next│ │
│  │ Bottom:   [1 in]   │   │ ○ Facing Pages Side-By-Side│ │
│  │ Left:     [1 in]   │   │ ☑ Show margins           │ │
│  │ Right:    [1 in]   │   │ ☑ Show page guides       │ │
│  │ ☐ Mirror Facing Pages│ └──────────────────────────┘ │
│  └────────────────────┘   ┌─ Footnotes ──────────────┐ │
│                           │ ◉ At Bottom of Page       │ │
│  ┌─ Page Numbering ───┐   │ ○ At End of Document      │ │
│  │ Start at Page: [1] │   │ ☑ Automatic Numbering     │ │
│  └────────────────────┘   │   Start At: [1]           │ │
│                           └──────────────────────────┘ │
│  [?]                          [ Cancel ]  [ OK ]       │
└────────────────────────────────────────────────────────┘
```

Your first Document options focus on the margins for your document. You can select the top, left, right, and bottom margins for the entire document from this dialog box. Just enter the value for each margin, in inches. The larger the margin numbers, the more white space will appear around the text in your document.

While you're in this dialog box, you'll probably want to decide whether or not you desire to work with facing pages versus pages that come one after the other. What's the difference? Think about a typical letter or memo—usually, pages come right after one another and no one really expects you to print on the backside of pages. When you finish one page you move it out of the way and read the next page.

If you're writing a book, report, pamphlet, or similar document, you'll want facing pages. That is, readers expect to turn the page in a book and read the backside of that same page, then move over to the right-side page and read that one. Those are facing pages, and you can set up AppleWorks to work with facing pages in the Document dialog box.

While working with the margin numbers you can select the Mirror Facing Pages check box in order to change the margin options slightly. The Left and Right margin options change to Outside and Inside margins. Why? Because once you have pages set up to face one another, you can adjust the inside margins together to provide a uniform look. This is important if you plan to distribute your documents in a booklet or newsletter form—you'll want facing pages to look right when placed next to one another (see Figure 8-4).

Of course, if you'll be formatting and printing your documents as facing pages, you'll probably want to view them as facing pages, so select the radio button next

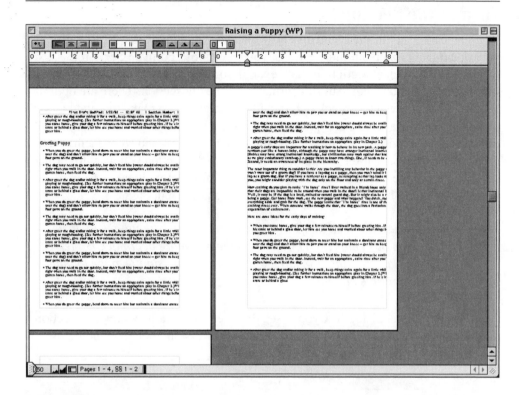

FIGURE 8-4   Facing pages need mirror-image margins to look right once they're in book or booklet form.

to Facing Pages Side-By-Side in the Page Display section of the dialog box. Now the pages are moved so that the document window looks more like Figure 8-4. (Likewise, click the button next to One Page Above The Next to return to the default behavior.) You can also make choices as to whether or not margins and page guides—the light gray lines that show you the boundaries of the page—should be displayed.

The last little section in the Document dialog box allows you to choose how footnotes will appear—if space is left for them at the bottom of every page or if they all appear at the end of the document. You can also have footnotes automatically numbered, if you desire—just check the check box and enter the number the footnotes should start with in the entry box.

Format the Section

You saw earlier in "Insert Elements" how to create section breaks. Now, with your document broken out into sections, you can choose Format | Section to format each individual section. In fact, even if you don't break your document into different sections, you can still format it as one big section. There are options in here you might want to check out, including the ability to make the first page of your document a "title page" (meaning it has no headers or footers) and the opportunity to choose different headers and footers for left- and right-facing pages.

To begin, place the insertion point somewhere in the section you want to format (or anywhere in the document if you haven't added any section breaks). Now select Format | Section. The Section dialog box appears, as shown in Figure 8-5.

 You may have noticed that I'm ignoring most things that have to do with columns in this chapter. We'll discuss them in more depth in Chapter 12, which covers creating brochures, newsletters, and similar page layouts that use multiple columns.

At the top of the dialog box you'll see that the title bar tells you which section you're working with—a handy feature. Your first decision, though, is how this

FIGURE 8-5   The Section dialog box gives you even more formatting options.

new section should manifest itself. Choose one of the following from the Start Section menu:

- **New Line**   Choose this option and the section really is pretty much invisible—it'll be for your reference, but readers won't necessarily notice it.

- **New Page**   If the section is to be a new chapter or a major section in a pamphlet, for instance, you'd choose New Page to insert a page break along with the new section.

- **Left Page or Right Page**   If you've formatted your document with facing pages (read about it in the earlier section "Format the Whole Document"), then you can choose if this new section begins with a left or right page. If the new section represents a new chapter, for instance, you'd likely choose to start it as a right page.

8

In the Page Numbers portion of the dialog box, you have some housekeeping options. If you've chosen to have your new section begin on a new page, you can now choose to have it begin a new page-counting scheme. You can have the page count start over at 1, for instance, so you can keep track of the count in the section or chapter instead of in the whole document. (You'll find that many pamphlets and booklets will number with a section number and a page number, like "C-3" or "3-3." You can do the same thing by inserting section and page numbers into the header or footer of your document.)

Finally, you can choose to have the headers and footers the same as they were in previous parts of the document, or choose to build all new headers and footers for this section. (Choose between Continue From Previous Section or Different For This Section by clicking the appropriate radio button.) If you will have new ones, you can click the Left & Right Are Different option to have different headers and footers on the left and right pages. Click the Title Page option to have the first page of the section appear without headers or footers.

Got it all set? Click the OK button and you're returned to the document, complete with its new section formatting. Now, if you chose to have new headers and footers in this section, you'll want to insert and edit them.

Tabs and the Ruler

The TAB key on your iBook keyboard can be a powerful tool in the fight against chaos in your documents. By default a standard document offers tab points every half-inch or so. But you might want more specialized tabs than that—tabs that help you align text, for instance.

There are four different types of tabs you can add to your document: left-aligned, right-aligned, centered, and aligned to a particular character, usually a decimal. What that does, in most cases, is give you an interesting freedom to align things for impromptu tables and arrangements of text in your documents.

Say, for instance, that you wanted to create a table of contents. In that case you'll need two things, a right-aligned column of chapter descriptions and a column that's aligned to the dash that separates a document's section and page number. (OK, so maybe this example is an overly regimented military report. Just bear with me.) It'd look something like Figure 8-6.

How does this work? Before you type any text, just drag the tab you want to the point on the ruler where you think it should go.

If you want a right-aligned column to end on the 2-inch mark, drag it there. If you want to align a column of currency figures, put the decimal-aligned tab on the 6-inch mark and that's where the dollars will line up.

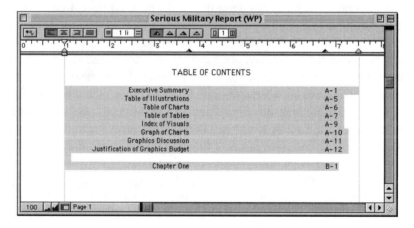

FIGURE 8-6   An orderly use of tabs

Need to switch some things around? Three rules:

■ If you need to change a tab that affects more than one row of text, select *every* row first, then change the tab in the ruler. Otherwise, you'll only change it for the row where the insertion point is. This will happen to you a lot by accident, so be wary.

■ If you need to change a tab that you've already dragged to the ruler, double-click it. The Tab dialog box appears, allowing you to make changes. For instance, you can change the alignment of the tab, add a fill (automatically fill in behind the tab with dots or dashes), or tweak the location of the tab by entering the inch mark where it should appear.

■ To get rid of a tab, select *all* rows that are affected by the tab—they need to all be highlighted—then pick up the tab and drag it back up to the top of the ruler. It'll disappear.

It's worth emphasizing that if you can't find a tab, if a tab is still there even though you moved it, or if only part of your document is lined up to tabs correctly, there's a good reason. It's because you didn't select every line in your document affected by that tab. Go back, select all the lines, and make your change once more.

Spell, Find, Change, and Count

You've finally gotten through most of your document creation. You've written the report, cleaned it up with tabs, and saved every three lines. Now that you've seen what a computer can do to help you format an important report or document, how about seeing what it can do to help you clean up and edit the words themselves? Here's where some of that computerized speed and savvy comes into play.

Check Spelling

By brute force your word processor can jump quickly through a document and check every word against an internal dictionary. If it finds one it's not familiar with, it'll suggest other words that seem to be similarly spelled. If you see the word you meant to type, you can choose it from the list. Otherwise, you can either add the word that AppleWorks doesn't recognize, you can type the correct spelling yourself, or you can just skip the suggestion.

Here's how it works:

1. When you're ready to check spelling, select Edit | Writing Tools | Check Document Spelling.

2. AppleWorks begins checking. When it finds a word it doesn't like, it pops up in a dialog box like the one here:

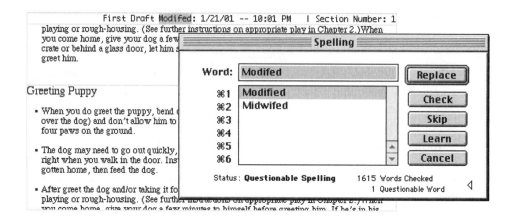

3. If AppleWorks offers the correct spelling, select it in the box and click Replace (or press the keyboard command ⌘-*number* where *number* is the number of the suggestion in the list). If you don't see the correct spelling, you can type it into the entry box. If you type something you want to check against AppleWorks' dictionary, click the Check button. If the word is spelled correctly, click Learn. If the word isn't worth worrying about (it's an odd abbreviation or something), then click Skip.

4. AppleWorks moves on to the next word it finds misspelled.

If you don't need to check the entire document, you can check just a selection of text—highlight the text you want to check, then select Edit | Writing Tools | Check Selection Spelling.

Find and Change

The Find and Change features use some of the same technology as spell checking, but instead of checking the document against an internal dictionary, it checks the file against whatever text you enter in the Find dialog box. It can then change the found text to whatever text you choose.

Need an example? As I wrote the first draft of this chapter, half the time I called this program ClarisWorks, since that's what it was called for the past ten years—and I'm a slow learner. The fact is, though, that Apple renamed it "AppleWorks," so that's what I want you to see in the final product. So, when I got to the end of the draft, I told the program to perform a selective Find and Change to help me find all instances of "ClarisWorks" so I could change most of them to "AppleWorks."

Here's how to do a Find and Change:

1. Select Edit | Find/Change. In the submenu that comes up, select the Find/Change command.

2. In the Find/Change dialog box, enter a word you'd like to search for in the Find entry box. If you plan to replace that word with something else, enter it in the Change entry box.

3. Click the Find Next button. The first instance of the word is found (if there are any instances of that word).

4. If you want to change this instance of the word, click Change. You can also click Change, Find, if you want to change the word and move instantly to the next instance of the word. If you don't want to change this instance, click Find Next.

5. Rinse and repeat. If you want to stop finding, click the close box on the Find window.

If you just want AppleWorks to find and change every instance of a word, you can click the Change All button instead of going through the entire document by hand. Think carefully before doing that, though, since you could accidentally change words you don't mean to change. Consider my example, where I found and changed nearly every instance of ClarisWorks in this chapter to AppleWorks. If I'd performed a Change All on that Find search, I would have changed the sentence right before this one you're reading. The sentence would then read: "Consider my example, where I found and changed nearly every instance of AppleWorks in this chapter to AppleWorks."

In the Find/Change window you'll find two check box options:

■ **Find Whole Word**   Check this option to find instances where the word in the Find entry box matches only a whole word in the document. If you search for the word "pup" without this option checked, it'll find the letters "pup" within the word "puppy." If you check the Find Whole Word check box, it will only find the word "pup," not parts of words that include the letters "pup."

- **Case Sensitive**   Check this option and Find will pay attention to the upper- and lowercase letters you type in the Find entry box. If you search for "Puppy" with the Case Sensitive option checked, Find will not stop on the words "puppy" or "puppY."

> **TIP**   *You can replace words with spaces or nothing at all. That's a great way to delete every instance of a particular word. You can also find just about anything you can cut and paste into the Find entry box, including spaces and line returns. Get creative—use ⌘-V to paste things into the Find entry box for more advanced searches.*

Standardize with the Stylesheet Window

If you're serious about word processing, you should get to know the Stylesheet window. What does it do? When you create a paragraph style you really like (including the font, alignment, line spacing, and other characteristics set for the paragraph), you can give it a name and save it. Then, you can invoke that style anytime by simply selecting it in the Stylesheet window. Instant high-end formatting—perfect if you do a lot of the same sort of documents and you want to stop re-inventing the wheel.

To open the Stylesheet window, select Window | Show Stylesheet Window. The window appears.

To select a style, just click it once in the Stylesheet window. The currently selected paragraph in your document will instantly change to that style. If you select more than one paragraph and then select a style in the Stylesheet window, they'll all change to that style. If you don't like the style you've changed it to, click Body or another style. You can also choose Unapply Style from the Stylesheet window's Edit menu.

To add your own style, format a paragraph just the way you want it. Make sure the insertion point is in that paragraph. Then, in the Stylesheet window, click the New button. In the New Style dialog box, give your style a name and choose the Paragraph radio button. Click the Inherit Document Selection Format option, then click OK. The style is created. You can now select it in the Stylesheet window to format other paragraphs.

> **TIP** *The Stylesheets can be used for other styles, too, including table and outline styles.*

8

Use Stationery for Automatic Documents

AppleWorks has built into it Assistants (little programs that walk you through a task) and Stationery (template documents) that can help you create a number of different types of documents. We'll focus on some of the Assistants—those that create business documents like newsletters, business cards, brochures, and such—in Chapter 12. For now, let's see some Stationery that can help you with memos and letters.

Stationery is a document template that's been pre-formatted, often by professional designers, to make you look good. When you create a new document using Stationery, you get a new document that already has some attractive elements created for you. Then, you enter your own information to finish the document. In letter Stationery, for instance, you can select the sections of the document that are currently generic looking and change them into something you can use. For example, you can change the "Company Name" section and address to your own, as shown here:

Stauffer Productions

2301 Pennings Circle
Santa Fe
New Mexico 87154
(505) 555-1541

NOTE *Actually, Stationery is a feature of Mac OS, not just AppleWorks, and you can create Stationery documents for many application. In the Finder, find a document you've created that you really like. Select the document's icon, then select File | Get Info. At the bottom of the Get Info window, there's a Stationery Pad check box. Select it and close the window. Now the document will act just like Stationery, exactly as described in the next sections.*

Create a Document from Stationery

To use Stationery, you'll begin by creating a new document by selecting File | New or pressing ⌘-N. (Or, if you are just starting up AppleWorks, the New dialog box will automatically appear.) In the New dialog box, click the radio button option for Use Assistant or Stationery. The list in the window changes to reflect the Stationery and Assistants you can use. In the menu, choose an appropriate topic—Letters and Letterhead, Memos, or something similar.

Word processing Stationery appears with a big "A" as the icon. Select a Stationery that looks interesting (under the Letters and Letterhead topic, try "Letterhead 1"), and click OK. Using the Stationery, AppleWorks creates a new, styled document.

You'll find that some Stationery is more involved than others. Some will feature special Stylesheets, for instance, that allow you to continue to format the paragraphs according to the Stationery's theme.

At some point you'll want to save the document—just save it like any other document. You can always go back to the Stationery list in the New dialog box to create another document that looks like it. An even better solution, though, is to use the document to create your own Stationery.

Save a Document as Stationery

Actually, it doesn't matter if you've created the document from AppleWorks Stationery or not—if you have a particular document design that you like a lot, you can save it as Stationery. That way you can use it to automatically create new documents that look like it.

Stationery

With the document created, choose File | Save As. Give your Stationery a name, then click the Stationery icon down in the corner. You'll be automatically transported to AppleWorks' Stationery folder. Click the Save button and your Stationery is saved. Now, the next time you want to create a document in that style, you can choose your Stationery from the New dialog box (see Figure 8-7).

8

FIGURE 8-7   Choose your new Stationery just as if it were a pre-built AppleWorks Stationery template.

TIP   *If you've created a document you need to save as an actual document, do that first. Then you may want to clear out parts of the document—like the salutation and the body—that are specific to that letter or memo so you have a more generic document to use as Stationery.*

Chapter 9

Work with Numbers and Build Charts

How to...

- See the basics of spreadsheets
- Enter and format text and numbers in your spreadsheet
- Cut, Copy, Paste, and Sort your data
- Build formulas that work with your data
- Use advanced formulas for "what-if" scenarios
- Chart your data to see it visually

The computing industry likes to think in terms of something called "killer applications" (or "killer apps" in a *Wired Magazine* hip shorthand). Basically, the killer app is a reason to use a computer that's so new and so compelling that it drives millions to buy new machines and software to join the revolution. In the mid-to-late 1980s, for instance, the Mac's early ability to offer desktop publishing capabilities—allowing you to format text, add images, and arrange pages completely onscreen, then print it all to laser or color printers—was its killer application. In some ways, the Mac is still superior for that sort of work.

Before this happened, though, there was another time in Apple's history when it saw its computer sales spike—the killer app that prompted that spike was the spreadsheet. At the time (the late 1970s), the spreadsheet was called VisiCalc, the concept was completely new, and the computer that sold like gangbusters as a result was the Apple II.

We've come a long way. With the iMac and iBook, computers have become cute, and with AppleWorks spreadsheets have become easy to use. Just you wait and see.

9

The Spreadsheet Defined

A spreadsheet application is one that allows you to create what amounts to a digital ledger book. Ebenezer Scrooge, for instance, might have tracked his accounts in one of those cool-looking, lined, leather-bound ledger books. But times have changed. These days we have electronic spreadsheets instead of ledger books. And it's the iBook that looks cool.

Why Use Spreadsheets?

So, this is a like a ledger book, but better. Why? A spreadsheet allows you to do three major things well:

- **Math**   You can concoct all sorts of formulas and impose them upon the numbers you've entered into your spreadsheet; do loan calculations, find the average or standard deviation, figure the net present value—tons of things that no human should try without computerized help. By getting your numbers into the spreadsheet—where every cell has a name—you can perform many different mathematical functions.

- **What-If**   Once you have a spreadsheet full of data and calculations, the spreadsheet allows you to change numbers quickly and see how that affects the whole. This was probably actually the *killer* part of the *app* when spreadsheets first appeared. Say you've laid out an entire budget for the next six months. What if you decide to take a job that pays less but allows you to perform that invaluable human service and boost your ego to that stratospheric level that you've had your eye on? Edit up that income number in your budget and see how things shake out.

■ **Charts**   Once you have the data entered and represented the way you like it, you can create graphics from the numbers that allow you to more clearly make your case at the next board, team, faculty, or family meeting. AppleWorks is capable of creating all sorts of charts, including exciting 3-D charts that will wow them for weeks.

So, all you have to do is enter the data, format it correctly, then get working on your calculations, what-if scenarios, and charts. Before you do that, though, you're going to have to know how to enter the data into the spreadsheet.

The Cell

The building block of any spreadsheet document is the *cell*—the conjunction of a column and a row that is given a unique name in the two dimensions of a spreadsheet. In that cell, you can put text, numbers, formulas—even images, although there's less reason to do that. As shown next, those cells, because they're uniquely named (with names like "A2" and "F18"), can be added together, subtracted from one another, even cosined and tangented, if those are words. (I never did terribly well in trigonometry.)

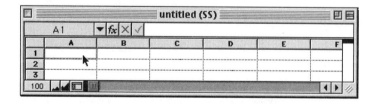

In working with spreadsheets, you need to get to know cell notation—the cell's name acts as a variable in formulas you build to work with the numbers in those cells. It's basic algebra—you create a formula that says "add C3 to C4," which tells the spreadsheet to sum the values it finds in cells C3 and C4. So how does it know which cells those are?

In the typical spreadsheet (AppleWorks included) the columns are lettered from left to right across the top of the document and the rows are numbered from top to bottom. So, the first cell at the top-left corner is A1. The cell C3, then, is the cell at the conjunction of column C and row 3.

Sound exciting yet? Let's run through how to create your own spreadsheets, doctor them up, and make them look nice. There are a couple of Stationery spreadsheets you can use to create different types of document as well; those are discussed later in the chapter.

> NOTE   *By default, a spreadsheet in AppleWorks is 40 columns wide (reaching cell "AN") and 500 rows long. You can add to them both—the limit is 256 columns and 16,384 rows.*

Get the Spreadsheet Started

Spreadsheet documents start the same way any other documents begin—with the New command. In AppleWorks, choose File | New. In the New dialog box, choose Spreadsheet and click OK. A blank spreadsheet appears.

Move in the Spreadsheet

The first thing you want to do is learn how to get around. It's pretty basic. You start out in the top-left cell, but you can click anywhere on a cell and instantly be transported there. Once you have a cell selected, you can enter something in that cell by simply typing. Notice, when you start typing, nothing actually appears in the cell.

You edit in the Entry Bar at the top of the document window. You won't see the results in the cell until you move on from the cell—you do *that* by pressing TAB or RETURN or an arrow key. The following table shows you how to move around in a spreadsheet document.

Press This	To Do This
RETURN or DOWN ARROW	Move down one cell
TAB or RIGHT ARROW	Move right one cell
SHIFT-RETURN or UP ARROW	Move up one cell
SHIFT-TAB or LEFT ARROW	Move left one cell
ENTER (RETURN with the FN key pressed)	Accept data in cell without moving to a new cell

It won't take too long before these keys become second nature to you. You just need to remember this: If you want to edit something that's already in a cell, move to that cell (with the keys or the trackpad) and edit it in the Entry Bar, not in the cell itself (the program won't let you edit in the cell).

 The arrow keys don't let you leave a cell if you're currently editing data in that cell because then you can't use those keys to move the insertion point around in the Entry Box. If you prefer arrow keys to enable you to leave a cell immediately, select Edit | Preferences. From the pull-down menu, choose Spreadsheet. Now, select Always Selects Another Cell. Notice you can also change the behavior of the RETURN key in this dialog box. Click OK to exit Preferences.

You can enter either text or numbers in a spreadsheet, although it's best to have a plan before you jump in and start entering things randomly. In general, you want series of numbers—budget numbers for every month of the year, for instance, to be in a row or a column, unbroken by other text or numbers. Figure 9-1 shows an example of a nice, neat spreadsheet that will be easy to deal with when it comes to building formulas and creating "what-if" scenarios.

Select Cells

You can select cells in the spreadsheet window in three basic ways:

- ◼ If you're selecting a single cell, click it once. Its frame becomes outlined.

- ◼ To select more than one cell, click and hold the trackpad button on the first cell you want to select, and then drag the mouse pointer across the other cells you'd like to select. When you've highlighted all the cells you need, release the trackpad button. Now those cells are selected and are ready to have some action performed on them. (Note, the first cell in your selection will not be highlighted—the frame will be outlined. It's still selected, though.)

- ◼ To select an entire row or column, click its letter or number once. In the *F* column, for instance, you can click the *F* at the top of the screen to highlight the entire column. If you want to select more than one column or row at a time, hold down the SHIFT key and click once for each column or row you want to add. Notice that multiple columns or rows must be adjacent to be selected and you can't select both rows and columns at once.

	A	B	C	D	E	F	G	H	I	J
1	Annual Household Budget									
2		January	February	March	April	May	June	July	August	
3										
4	Work Income	3000	3000	3000	3000	3000	3000	3000	3000	
5	Investment Income	200	200	200	200	200	200	200	200	
6	Savings Interest	15	15	15	15	20	20	20	20	
7	Other Income	0	0	350	0	0	350	0	0	
8	Total Income	3215	3215	3565	3215	3220	3570	3220	3220	
9										
10	Rent	750	750	750	750	750	750	750	750	
11	Car	225	225	225	225	225	225	225	225	
12	Insurance	50	50	50	50	50	50	50	50	
13	Medical Insurance	120	120	120	120	120	120	120	120	
14	Groceries	240	240	240	240	240	240	240	240	
15	Dining	200	200	200	200	200	200	200	200	
16	Entertainment	300	300	300	300	300	300	300	300	
17	Clothing	500	100	100	500	100	100	500	100	
18	Household	150	150	150	150	150	150	150	150	
19	Misc.	75	75	75	75	75	75	75	75	
20	Cash Expenses	2610	2210	2210	2610	2210	2210	2610	2210	
21										
22	Mastercard	50	50	50	50	50	50	50	50	
23	Discover	25	25	25	0	0	0	0	0	
24	American Express	75	75	75	75	75	75	75	75	
25	Credit Expenses	150	150	150	125	125	125	125	125	
26										
27	Over/Under	455	855	1205	480	885	1235	485	885	
28										
29										

FIGURE 9-1   The best spreadsheets are arranged logically in a table format.

Save the Spreadsheet

To save a spreadsheet, just select File | Save or File | Save As. The Save As dialog box appears, enabling you to name the document and find a folder to save it in. When you've made those choices, click Save. From there on, you can quickly save the spreadsheet every few minutes by selecting the Save command again or by pressing ⌘-S on your keyboard.

Enter and Format Data

In most spreadsheets, you enter text to label the rows and columns that will be filled with numbers. With both the text and the numbers, it's possible to do some rather intricate formatting, including the basics like font, size, style, and alignment. You also find some formatting options different from those in word processing—options like formatting numbers as currency, dates, or times.

Actually, it's possible to perform calculations on text, as well—you can do a number of things with text, including comparisons for word length, changing the case of text, sorting the text, adding text strings together ("concatenating" them), and so on.

Format Text and Cells

Let's begin with text because you'll likely begin with text in your spreadsheet. (You need to create labels for the columns and rows of numbers you plan to enter.) You might want to begin by typing a title into the first cell of the spreadsheet—cell A1. You can type text that's longer than the cell and all the text will actually appear just fine—as long as you haven't typed text into the adjoining cells. If you're creating the title line for your spreadsheet, that should be no problem.

 Want text to wrap within the cell instead of continuing off the edge? Highlight the cell and choose Format | Alignment | Wrap. Now text will wrap within the cell.

You can also format text using pretty much the same tools you use in a word processor—font, size, styles, and alignment. The major difference is all those commands appear in the Format menu. You can't format selected text differently within the same cell—formatting for text in the cell applies to all text in that cell.

Here's how to format.

1. Select the cell(s) that have text you want to format.

2. Select the Format menu and point the mouse at the type of formatting you'd like to change—Font, Size, Style, Font Color, or Alignment.

3. In the menu that appears, make your formatting selection.

All the text in the cell is affected, although the cell itself won't be. That can be a problem if you've changed the size of the text in the cell, for instance, and can no longer read it clearly. The solution: Resize the cell.

Actually, you can't really change the size of an *individual* cell—you either change the size of its row or its column. To change the size of a row, point the mouse all the way over at the numbers that label each row. If you place the mouse pointer on the line that appears between any two rows, the mouse pointer changes to a pair of arrows. This is your cue that holding down the trackpad button and dragging changes the size of the row, as shown in the following illustration. A column can be resized in the same way—just drag the line between the numbers.

Text is important in most spreadsheets, especially if you want other people to understand what the heck your spreadsheet is for. Text is also useful for charting data, which you learn about later in this chapter. AppleWorks likes to find text on the top and left borders of your numbers; it can use that text for labels in charts, for instance. So, think in terms of labeling your data in rows and columns—the more structured the data, the more easily it can be viewed and manipulated.

One special case is alignment—you probably want to format your columns and rows so they line up together nicely. This is best done with the Alignment commands—in fact, you can select an entire range of cells or an entire column or row and use the Alignment commands in the Format menu to align every cell in the range to the left, right, centered, or justified. In a similar way, you can choose rows of your "label" cells and format them as bold, larger text, or what-have-you.

Want to delete text? Just select the cell and press DELETE. Likewise, you can highlight more than one cell and press DELETE to clear many cells of text (or numbers and formulas, for that matter) at once.

Enter and Format Numbers

Once you have text in your cells and the rows and columns lined up the way you want them, you're ready to enter numbers in your spreadsheet. Numbers are entered the same way as text—just select a cell, type the number, and then exit the cell. The number appears in the cell.

AppleWorks automatically recognizes a number as a number (not as text) when you type a number into a cell. In fact, to type a number as text, if you need to, you must enter a sort of mini-function that looks like this: **="5467"**. Using this formula, the number is treated as if it were text. This might be useful if you needed to label a column or row with a number—for instance, if you wanted your columns to represent years. If you enter **2001**, that's seen as two thousand and one. Enter **="2001"** and it's treated as text, so you can use it as a label.

Otherwise, numbers are numbers. If you need to enter a negative number, enter a minus sign (–) before it, such as **–5467**. And, as is true with text, you can copy and paste numbers from one cell into another, if you like.

Number Formats

Numbers can be formatted in the same way as text—font, size, style, color, and alignment—by selecting the cell or cells and using the Format menu. Numbers, however, also have their own formatting schemes that can be used specifically to make them more meaningful, easier to read, or both. Those formatting options appear in the Format menu under the Number command. You can also access the Format Number, Date, and Time dialog box (shown in Figure 9-2) by double-clicking a cell.

In the dialog box you find the following option groups:

- **Number** Here you have a few different radio button options that enable you to change the appearance of your numbers—they can be regular numbers, currency, percentages, scientific notation, or fixed decimal numbers (with a certain number of decimal places shown). Using the check boxes, you can also decide the precision of the numbers and whether negative values will appear in parentheses, which is common in accounting and financial notation.

- **Date** Choose one of these radio buttons, and the numbers typed into selected cell(s) will be formatted as dates following the specific form shown.

- **Time** Choose one of these radio buttons and the selected cell(s) will accept numeric values as times, formatted as chosen.

FIGURE 9-2 Format numbers using this dialog box.

9

You probably often want to format an entire row or column with a certain type of number formatting—Currency, for instance. Go ahead and select an entire range of cells or even a complete column, row, or series of either to format. In fact, you can still have text in the same columns or rows, and the text won't be affected by what you do with the numbering (see Figure 9-3).

Cut, Paste, Fill

In spreadsheets, you can cut and paste either text or numbers easily. In the sample budget document created for this chapter's figures, a lot of numbers repeat. It's possible to select an entire range of numbers—part of a column, for instance—and then copy and paste it into the next column.

Another way to enter numbers quickly is to use the Fill Right or Fill Down commands in the Calculate menu. Enter a value for one cell, and then highlight that cell and a number of cells to the right or down from that cell. Now, choose the appropriate command—Calculate | Fill Right or Calculate | Fill Down—and all those cells are filled with the first cell's value.

FIGURE 9-3   Select an entire column, and you can format all the numbers in it at once.

Sort the Spreadsheet

Once you have a ton of data entered into your spreadsheet, you might suddenly think it'd be groovy to have that data sorted in some different way. What if, let's say, all your expenses were sorted from highest to lowest (based on the first month)? Or, if they were just listed alphabetically? Easily done.

To sort a range of data, follow these steps:

1. Select a series of rows or columns of data. You need to make sure the data is all a single data set, so you don't accidentally sort a row or column that isn't related. (When you do that, it ain't pretty.) Figure 9-4 shows an example of a good data set to sort—each column or row should have the same kind of data.

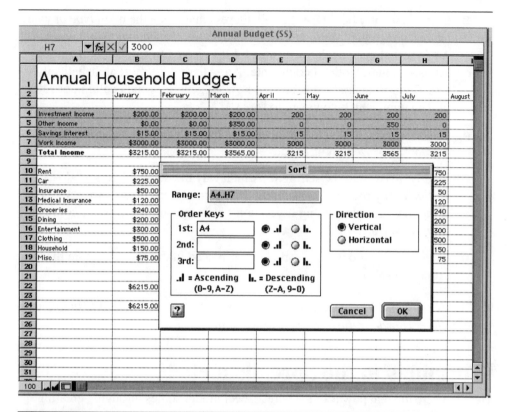

FIGURE 9-4 Select a range of "sortable" data before you perform the sort function.

By data set, *I mean data that logically belongs together. In the sample budget, each of the rows I want to sort is a similar type of data— they're all income lines. The data you choose to sort needs to be similar, so if each row (or column) gets moved around, it won't hurt the spreadsheet overall.*

2. With a series of rows or columns chosen, select Calculate I Sort. The Sort dialog box appears. At the top of the dialog box you see the range of cells to be sorted. Next, you see entries for the Order Keys. To sort, AppleWorks looks at one of the cells, which you specify, and sorts the data set based on that column (if you're sorting rows) or that row (if you're sorting columns).

3. In the first entry box, type the cell address that holds the main *type of* value against which you're going to sort the data set. (In the example, I entered **A4** to sort alphabetically; I'd enter **B4** if I wanted to sort according to the January values. Notice I could enter **A5**, **A6**, or **A7** to sort alphabetically, too. The Sort dialog just needs to know, in general, which column or row of data upon which you want to sort.)

4. Click the radio button to select whether the data set will be sorted in Ascending or Descending order.

5. Finally, make sure the setting for which way the data will be sorted—vertically (by row) or horizontally (by column)—is correct. AppleWorks sometimes gets this wrong if you don't choose complete rows or columns for your sorting.

6. Click OK. Your data gets sorted and is placed in the spreadsheet in the order you specified.

TIP

If you don't like the new sort order, immediately choose Edit | Undo and the sort order returns to its original state.

Add Formulas to the Spreadsheet

Here's where the real power of the spreadsheet model shines through—creating formulas that enable you to manipulate the data. So far, you entered text that labels data and you entered numbers that represent data. Now it's time to put some of that algebraic knowledge swimming around in your head to the task of creating formulas that work with your data. In this section, I show you the anatomy of a formula, then we move on to some of the formulas included in AppleWorks.

Anatomy of a Formula

You've already seen that by simply typing text and numbers into the cell, AppleWorks can differentiate between the two for formatting purposes. It can immediately tell the difference between a number and text.

AppleWorks can't, however, tell the difference between the cell reference "A3" and the text "A3." To differentiate a formula, AppleWorks needs a little code. That code comes in the form of an equals (=) sign. If you begin your typing in a cell with an equals sign, AppleWorks interprets what follows as a formula.

After you exit the cell, if you typed the formula correctly, you won't see it again in the cell. Instead, you see the result of that formula. (If you highlight the cell, you again see the formula up in the Entry Bar.)

Formula Types

Beyond the equals sign are two basic types of formulas you create. The first is a straight mathematical formula with addition (+), subtraction (–), multiplication (*), division (/), or exponential (^) operators. A typical mathematical formula could easily be =34+45 or =34^2, although that'd be reasonably useless in a spreadsheet (you'll see why in a moment).

The other type of formula uses a built-in function from AppleWorks. These functions range from financial to trigonometric to logical. An example might be =AVERAGE (34, 45, 56), which would return the average of those three numbers.

As you might guess, it's also possible to use these two types of formulas together in the same cell, so =34+45+(AVERAGE (34, 45, 56)) is a legal formula, too. Notice, by the way, that parentheses are used pretty liberally in these formulas to separate one operation from another. Again, it's like algebra—functions and math inside parentheses get done first, and then the result gets entered into the larger equation.

Build with Cell Addresses

What's missing, of course, is the cell address. By using cell addresses as variables, you're suddenly able to do amazing things with formulas. For instance, while =34+45 isn't terribly useful in a spreadsheet (because you could just enter **79** and be done with it), the formula =B3+B4 could be *very* useful. Why? Because if you change the value in B3 or in B4—or in both—the result changes, as well. And getting results is what spreadsheets are all about.

Now you're able to create a cell whose value is based on values in other cells. You could take this even further. How about a cell whose value is the sum of many different cells—something along the lines of =B4+B5+B6+B7? That's shown in Figure 9-5.

Notice the cell addresses are starting to get a little out of hand, even with just four—what if you were adding together 400 cell addresses? In your spreadsheet, you can use a special notation to denote a range of cells to be acted on. The range is separated by two periods, as in =SUM(B4..B7), which gives the same result as =B4+B5+B6+B7. Notice with ranges that you're forced into using functions to perform even basic math.

	A	B	C	D
	Annual Household Budget			
2		January	February	March
3				
4	Work Income	$3000.00	$3000.00	$3000.00
5	Investment Income	$200.00	$200.00	$200.00
6	Savings Interest	$15.00	$15.00	$15.00
7	Other Income	$0.00	$0.00	$350.00
8	**Total Income**	$3215.00	$3215.00	$3565.00

B8 =B4+B5+B6+B7

FIGURE 9-5   A basic formula for adding cell values together

> **TIP**
>
> *Once a formula is evaluated, you can use that formula's cell address in another formula. If you put SUM(B4..B7) in cell B10, you can type **B10** in another formula, where it will represent the result of that sum.*

Relative versus Absolute

The cell addresses being discussed here are called *relative addresses*. What does that mean? Say you wanted to use the Copy and Paste or Fill Right/Fill Down commands with a formula you created. With relative addressing, the addresses within that formula will change relative to the cell you paste it into. For example, if cell B29 had the formula =SUM(B10..B27) in it, you could copy that formula from cell B29 and paste it into cell C29. The formula in C29 is changed slightly, though, to =SUM(C10..C27). AppleWorks is just assuming that's how you want it.

But what if you don't want that automatic translation done for you? Easy. You can create an absolute address using dollar signs ($). The address $B$10 is an absolute address that always points to cell B10. If I create a formula in cell B29 that looks like =$B$10+B11, and then copy that formula to cell C29, the result will be =$B$10+C11. Because the second address was relative, it changed. But the first address is still B10.

> **NOTE**
>
> *How clever are you? If you're very clever, you may come up with a good reason to use partial absolute addressing, as in $B10. Now, the B part of the address is absolute, but the 10 part isn't—the row number will change if this reference is cut and pasted into a lower or higher row. I'm not that clever, but, then again, my finances are always a mess. Maybe there's a relationship there?*

More Operators

Want a little more confusion? First, you can use two other operators to change the way numbers are evaluated—the percent operator (%) turns a number into a decimal percentage, while the minus sign (–) can be used in front of a cell address to make it negative.

And other operators can be used in your formulas besides the numeric ones— the relational and text operators. The *relational operators* offer comparisons between two values. They are

=	Equal to
<>	Not equal to
>	Greater than
>=	Greater than or equal to
<	Less than
<=	Less than or equal to

Using a formula like =A3>A4 returns a value of either True or False, which appears in the cell. If you don't find this useful, you may want to use these operators within logical functions like the IF function. (The *IF function* does something *if* something else is true. For instance, *if* A3 is greater than A4, *then* do some sort of math or perform some function. IF is discussed later in this chapter, with examples.)

There's also one text operator, the ampersand (&), that enables you to concatenate text. The formula =B5&" "&B6 would create one long string of text with a space between the two cells' text entries.

> **TIP** *What happens when you concatenate numbers? They're turned into text. It works fine, but you won't be able to perform any math on the text-ified numbers until you turn them back into numbers with the TEXTTONUM function.*

Operator Precedence

Before you can build formulas, you need to know one last little thing about them—operator precedence. We used to call this *order of operations* back in algebra class. Say you have the formula =40+10*3. What's the answer? It depends on what you do first. If you evaluate from left to right, then 40 plus 10 is 50; 50 times 3 is 150. If you evaluate the multiplication first, then 10 times 3 is 30 and 40 plus 30 is 70. You get two different answers.

9

One way to manage this is to rely on parentheses. Because operations inside parentheses are always evaluated first, you could create the formula =(40+10)*3 to get 150 or =40+(10*3) to get 70.

Or, you could rely on the operator precedence. In this case, multiplication has higher precedence than adding. Without parentheses, the formula =40+10*3, by rule of precedence, equals 70. Multiplication is done first and then addition. The following table shows the order of precedence for all operators—the higher in the table, the sooner the operation is performed.

()	Parentheses (done first)
%	Percentages
^	Exponentials
+, −	Positive or negative numbers (sign is before a cell address)
*, /	Multiply, divide
+, −	Add, subtract
&	Concatenate text
=, <, >, <=, >=, <>	All comparisons (done last)

Whenever a precedence level is the same for two operations, the formula is evaluated from left to right. So, if a subtraction is further left than an addition, the subtraction is done first.

 When in doubt, use parentheses. That way you can decide exactly how a formula is evaluated.

Add Functions to Your Formulas

You'll soon come up with a reason to do more than just basic mathematics between a few different cells. You've already seen that the SUM function can be used with a range of cells to add them all together and to get a total. But what if you need to do something more sophisticated in your formulas?

In that case, it's time to call in a function. Here's how you add one:

1. Select the cell where you want the function to appear.

2. Next to the Entry Bar on your spreadsheet document window is the Function (Fx) button. Click it and the Paste Function dialog box appears (see Figure 9-6).

FIGURE 9-6   The Paste Function dialog box helps you enter functions into your spreadsheet.

3. Choose one of those functions and it's added to the Entry box, where you can edit it.

4. Edit the function to taste (usually, you add cell addresses and values) and exit the cell.

AppleWorks offers a number of different types of functions:

■ **Numeric**   These functions enable you to work with numbers and ranges of numbers. They include SUM (sum of numbers), RAND (generates a random number), ROUND (rounds a number), and SQRT (returns the square root of the number).

■ **Business and Financial**   These are functions like *PV* (present value), *NPV* (net present value), *RATE* (tells you the interest rate of a payment schedule), and *PMT* (figures the payment required to satisfy a particular type of loan or payment scheme).

■ **Date and Time**   These functions enable you to perform various calculations regarding time. The date, day of the week, and time can all be stored as numeric values, enabling you to do math easily using them. That's discussed in more detail later in this section.

■ **Information**   These functions are used to send information, as in alert boxes and error tones, to your user.

- **Logical**   These programming-like functions can be used to determine if a number of values are true (AND) or if any values are true (OR), or it can evaluate values and perform other calculations based on whether they're true (IF). Other functions determine whether a value is present or if there's an error.

- **Statistical**   These functions take the MEAN, find the MODE, determine standard deviation, and more.

- **Text**   Text operators enable you to find certain words programmatically, change words to uppercase or lowercase, get the length of a word, and perform similar functions.

- **Trigonometric**   Here are those crazy functions all about angles. You can figure the cosine, sine, and tangent and convert between radians and degrees, among other things.

Learn About Functions

The functions are too numerous to list here—and it'd be redundant, anyway, because you can learn about any of the AppleWorks functions through the AppleWorks Help system. Select Help | AppleWorks Help. The Help window appears. Enter the keyword **Functions**, and then look for a link that says "Alphabetical List of Functions." Click it to see every function spelled out for you, alphabetically. Click an individual function's name to get a full explanation of that particular function, as shown in Figure 9-7.

Now, when you go to add a function, you can switch between the Paste Function dialog box and AppleWorks Help to get the answer regarding your particular function.

Some Cool Functions

Okay, I'm well over my allotted pages for this chapter, but I had to show you some cool functions available for your spreadsheet. I'll try to get through these quickly, so you can get back to your regularly scheduled tutorial.

Total Selection

This is a shortcut from the AppleWorks' button bar. It enables you quickly to generate a total in a spreadsheet of numbers, like a budget or financials. I used it for the sample budget in this chapter. Here's how it works:

1. Highlight the column or row of numbers you want to total, *plus* an additional cell at the end of the list.

2. Click the Total Selection button.

FIGURE 9-7   The AppleWorks Help System explains the various functions and
their use.

That's it. The sum automatically appears in that blank cell (see Figure 9-8).
Now you can do it again for the next row or just use the Fill Right command for
all the other Total cells in that row of your budget. Because the Total Selection
creates a SUM function with relative addresses, the function will copy just fine for
the rest of the row.

Other values that work like SUM include AVERAGE, MIN, and MAX, all of
which can accept a range of cells, such as AVERAGE (B2..B10).

Total Selection button

FIGURE 9-8 Quickly create a total of an entire selection of cells.

Text to Date, Date to Text

In the spreadsheet, AppleWorks enables you to deal with dates in an interesting way—you can add and subtract them, if you like. How? It turns a typical date into a serial number. That number, by the way, represents how many days the entered date is since January 1, 1904. Pretty weird, huh?

The TEXTTODATE function accepts a text entry of the current date. (The year should be in four digits to avoid those pesky Y2K issues.) In Figure 9-9, enter the date in cell B2, in the format 00/00/0000. In cell B4, enter the formula **=TEXTTODATE (B2)**. Now, you have a serial number.

What can you do with that? You can add or subtract from it. In Figure 9-9, I'll figure out what date is seven days past the date entered by adding 7 to the serial number in cell B5 (=**B4+7**). Now, I'll use the DATETOTEXT function to turn the serial date back into one read by humans. The formula typed into cell B7 is **=DATETOTEXT (B5, 1)**. The 1 represents the date format I want to use—the numbers are explained in AppleWorks help for the DATETOTEXT function. The result? A readable date that's seven days after the one entered above (see Figure 9-9).

If you'd like to work with time, too, it works much the same way, except time's serial number is a decimal—it's the percentage of 24 hours. The time 6:00 P.M. (18:00 hours) is represented as 0.75. You could figure that out with the formula TEXTTOTIME ("18:00") or TEXTTOTIME (B2), if cell B2 contained the text 18:00.

IF Function

Here's a great one for all sorts of analysis. IF accepts a logical expression, followed by what it should do if an expression is true and what it should do if an expression is false. For instance, let's say the value of cell B22 in my budget spreadsheet represents my over/under value for the month. If I come out more than $300 ahead on my budget, then I put half of it in my retirement account. If I have less than $300, then I put 0 in my retirement account.

So, with that in mind, I can create an IF function that checks out my over/under balance and decides what to do. It'll look like this: =IF (B22>300, B22/2, 0). That

	Date Sheet (SS)		
B7	▼ *fx* ✕ ✓ =DATETOTEXT(B5,1)		
	A	**B**	**C**
1			
2	Text Date	10/06/2001	
3			
4	Serial Date	35708	
5	Add 7 Days	35715	
6			
7	Week-Later Date	Oct 13, 2001	
8			
9			
10			
11			
12			
13			

FIGURE 9-9   Use TEXTTODATE and DATETOTEXT to do math with dates.

is, if B22 is greater than 300, return B22 divided by 2 as the value. If B22 isn't greater than 300, return 0. Here it is in action:

Household	$150.00	$150.00	$150.00
Misc.	$75.00	$875.00	$75.00
Total Expenses	**$2610.00**	**$3010.00**	**$2210.00**
Over/Under	**$605.00**	**$205.00**	**$1355.00**
Retirement	$302.50	$0.00	$677.50

Chart Your Data

Once you have the data in your spreadsheet arranged, calculated, and accounted for, you may find the best way to communicate the data is to create a chart. Charts go a long way toward making numbers in rows and columns much more bearable—plus, it's possible to see the relationships between data more clearly when you're looking at a chart. Here are a few suggestions about charts:

- **Make sure your data is chart-able.** You should have data sets in your spreadsheet that have an obvious relationship that makes a comparison worthwhile. Sales figures among different regions, budget categories, and demographic numbers are all chart-able. (If your rent doesn't change monthly, it won't be effective in a graph.)

- **Charts should convey one comparison.** If I take all my expenses and chart them over six months, the graph will be unreadable. Instead, I should either chart *one* expense over six months or many expenses in one month, but not both.

- **Don't include totals.** If you graph all your expenses in one month— including the *total* of all those expenses—you'll throw your graph way off. Make sure you're not accidentally including totals when you're comparing data.

- **Totals look great on their own in graphs.** If you graph *only* totals, that's another story. In a budget, for instance, you might graph total income over six months. That'll make a great graph—especially if income has been going up.

Create the Chart

Creating a chart is easy in AppleWorks—it's more about choosing the right data than it is about using odd commands. In fact, you may need to replicate your data in another part of the spreadsheet before you can chart it. When necessary, you can always re-create a part of your chart somewhere else on the sheet. You can simply have formulas that point to another cell, like =B20, to enable you to copy the values to a part of your document that you can chart more easily. (See Figure 9-10).

Here's how it works.

1. Choose a range of data you want to chart.

2. Select Options | Make Chart. The Chart Options dialog box appears (see Figure 9-11).

	A	B	C	D	E	F	G	H	I
	Annual Household Budget								
2		January	February	March	April	May	June	July	August
3									
4	Work Income	$3000.00	$3000.00	$3000.00	$3000.00	$3000.00	$3000.00	$3000.00	$3000.00
5	Investment Income	$200.00	$200.00	$200.00	$200.00	$200.00	$200.00	$200.00	$200.00
6	Savings Interest	$15.00	$15.00	$15.00	$15.00	$15.00	$15.00	$15.00	$15.00
7	Other Income	$0.00	$0.00	$350.00	$0.00	$0.00	$350.00	$0.00	$0.00
8	**Total Income**	**$3215.00**	**$3215.00**	**$3565.00**	**$3215.00**	**$3215.00**	**$3565.00**	**$3215.00**	**$3215.00**
9									
10	Rent	$748.00	$748.00	$748.00	$748.00	$748.00	$750.00	$750.00	$750.00
11	Car	$225.00	$225.00	$225.00	$225.00	$225.00	$225.00	$225.00	$225.00
12	Insurance	$50.00	$50.00	$50.00	$50.00	$50.00	$50.00	$50.00	$50.00
13	Medical Insurance	$120.00	$120.00	$120.00	$120.00	$120.00	$120.00	$120.00	$120.00
14	Groceries	$240.00	$240.00	$240.00	$240.00	$240.00	$240.00	$240.00	$240.00
15	Dining	$200.00	$200.00	$200.00	$200.00	$200.00	$200.00	$200.00	$200.00
16	Entertainment	$300.00	$300.00	$300.00	$300.00	$300.00	$300.00	$300.00	$300.00
17	Clothing	$500.00	$100.00	$100.00	$500.00	$100.00	$100.00	$500.00	$100.00
18	Household	$150.00	$150.00	$150.00	$150.00	$150.00	$150.00	$150.00	$150.00
19	Misc.	$75.00	$875.00	$75.00	$75.00	$75.00	$75.00	$75.00	$75.00
20	**Total Expenses**	**$2610.00**	**$3010.00**	**$2210.00**	**$2610.00**	**$2210.00**	**$2210.00**	**$2610.00**	**$2210.00**
21									
22	**Over/Under**	**$605.00**	**$205.00**	**$1355.00**	**$605.00**	**$1005.00**	**$1355.00**	**$605.00**	**$1005.00**
23									
24	Retirement	$302.50	$0.00	$677.50	$302.50	$502.50	$677.50	$302.50	$502.50
25									
26	**TOTALS SECTION**								
27		January	February	March	April	May	June	July	August
28	Total Income	$3215.00	$3215.00	$3565.00	$3215.00	$3215.00	$3565.00	$3215.00	$3215.00
29	Total Expenses	$2610.00	$3010.00	$2210.00	$2610.00	$2210.00	$2210.00	$2610.00	$2210.00
30									
31									

FIGURE 9-10   Creating a section of chart-able data in your spreadsheet can make creating the chart more bearable.

FIGURE 9-11   The Chart Options dialog box is home base for creating your chart.

3. In the Gallery, choose the type of chart you want to use. Use the check boxes at the bottom of the window to add options.

4. Click the Axes button. Here's where you label each axis of the chart. Choose the X-Axis radio button, enter a label in the Axis Label entry box, and then make other choices for how you want the axis to appear in the final chart. (If you don't customize the tick marks, min/max values, and step values, they are done automatically.) Choose the Y-Axis value and make the same choices.

5. Click the Series button. Most of this you won't need to worry about. You can, however, click the Label Data check box, and then place the label, if you'd like each individual part of the chart (each column, pie piece, and so on) to include a label that gives the exact data amount it represents.

6. Click the Labels button. Here you can decide if you're going to have a title (click the Title check box) and what that title will be. You can also decide if you'll have a legend (check or uncheck the Legend check box) and how it will be arranged.

7. Click the General button. Now you get to choose the series that is listed in the legend. You can change this by clicking the Rows or Columns radio button. This is significant—the series you choose is what each colored bar or area will represent. (If your chart comes out backward from what you expected, create another one and change the series you graph.)

8. Click OK. A chart appears in the document window (see Figure 9-12).

Need to move the chart around? It's a graphical object—it's not in a cell or attached to the spreadsheet. If you like, just click somewhere in the chart and hold down the trackpad button, and then drag the mouse pointer to move the chart to another part of the spreadsheet document window.

If you need to change anything about the chart, you can double-click it to change the Chart Options, click OK, and the chart will update to reflect the new changes.

9

FIGURE 9-12   The final chart—looks pretty spiffy.

So what else can you do with your chart? Actually, you can do quite a few things, thanks to the power of AppleWorks. For one, you can copy and paste it into any other AppleWorks document. Or, you can drag the chart to your iBook desktop, where it becomes a Picture Clipping document. You can rename the chart and file it away, or you can drag it in to another document in almost any applications on your iBook.

You can even use the Show Tools command in the Window menu to view the drawing tools, which enable you to change the way the chart looks with new colors, backgrounds, text, and other elements. Using the drawing tools is discussed more in Chapter 11. And the Show Tools command is discussed in Chapter 12.

Chapter 10

File Information and Ideas with Databases

How to...

- Create the fields for your database
- Enter data in Browse mode
- Sort the database
- Create a new layout
- Build a quick report

The database module in AppleWorks is probably the most misunderstood of the components. So many people instantly associate the idea of a database with, well, computer programming or something. It seems like too much work to create a database, too much effort to get that organized.

But the fact is, the database module in AppleWorks is very easy to work with—and there are a lot of things you can track in a database. The basic rule is this: If you have something you need to store, sort, or search through, then it's probably a good idea to consider creating a database.

What's a Database?

A database is a document that stores many different *records,* each of which is composed of several *fields* in which data is stored. Databases and spreadsheets have a lot in common—in fact, you can view databases in rows and columns just like you can spreadsheets (see the following illustration). But databases are really designed to do something quite different from spreadsheets—they're designed to track data and help you create reports based on that data.

10

	Client Name	Address	City	State	Zip	Phone	Fax	Email
	Rachel	3456	Allegro	CA	91211	209-555-	209-555-	rachel@hen
	Wes	1910 El	Rapid City	CA	90123	209-555-	209-555-	wes@sprint
	Rich Mills	140 Main	Rapid City	CA	90124	209-555-	209-345-	richm@aol.c
	Harry	3987	Rapid City	CA	90123	209-555-	209-456-	n/a
	Marcia	135	Allegro	CA	91210	209-555-	209-555-	mwilliams@

Invoice Database (DB)

Records: 5 — Sorted — 100 — Page 1

The best metaphor for a computer database is probably a card catalog at the local library. Each record is a card; each field is a line item on one of those cards. The author's name is a field, the title of the book is a field, even whether or not someone currently has the book on loan is a field. As you know, electronic databases of books are popular these days in libraries. A well-made library database offers many advantages, including reports on loaned books, searches based on authors' names, searches based on titles, and so on.

When Can You Use a Database?

You probably think of databases in terms of business uses—invoice tracking, project management, contact management, phone logs, inventory, or records for a mailing list or customer tracking database. But there are other things you can do with a database for home, school, or organizations.

Sure, you can track your CDs, movies, books, and recipes. (Those are such old standards that they're built into AppleWorks' Stationery system.) But think of this: You could create a personal or professional journal in a database, creating a new record for every day, and you'd be able to search the database using keywords. That'd be great for tracking creative ideas or remembering events. Or you could create a photo database of your insured belongings. If you're planning a wedding, party, birthday, or fund-raiser, you might track people in a database (see Figure 10-1).

Same goes for your block association, church group, scout troop, or sports team—anything that needs a little tracking can be stored in a database. Membership dues, training requirements, awards and certificates, ranks and accomplishments, scoring, attendance, and grades can all be tracked in a database.

FIGURE 10-1   Databases aren't just for business.

Then, you can create reports that tell you what still needs to be followed up on—you haven't gotten an RSVP from the Williamses, you haven't gotten a medical release from your goalie, or you don't yet know what Mildred plans to bring to the bake sale. All of these items can be tracked with databases.

How Databases Work

You'll begin by creating a database file and defining the fields that will be used by the database to create each record. Once the fields are defined, you're ready to create your first record. It's shown to you using a default *layout*—the data entry screen. If desired, you can edit this layout, or you can create other layouts for your database.

Different layouts can be composed of different fields, if you desire, allowing you to look at the same record in different ways. Or, you can use alternate layouts for different methods of data entry and/or searching.

Layouts also allow you to create different reports based on the data, too. For instance, you could create a layout that shows all of the books in your classroom that haven't been returned (and who checked them out) or all of the invoices in your small business that are 30 days past due. Layouts can be very complex, if desired, since you're offered most of the same drawing and formatting tools you'll find in AppleWorks' drawing module (see Chapter 11 to learn about the drawing tools).

And a big part of using a database is generating useful reports. The fact that layouts support the drawing tools also means you can create reports that will look good (and be useful) when printed.

Create Your Database

Creating your database is really pretty simple. In AppleWorks choose File | New, then choose to create a Database document and click OK in the New dialog box. Things get complicated in a hurry, though. Immediately, you're confronted with the need to create fields for your database. And, in order to do that, you'll need to think a little about your database.

Plan Your Database

With AppleWorks you'll begin by creating a new database file in which you will eventually store records. After you've launched the new document, you're asked to create fields for that database—each record will be composed of these fields. It's important to know ahead of time what sort of data you'll be tracking, since you need to define your fields before you can begin to use the database.

10

The key to planning your database is getting a good feel for what information you'd like to store in each record. Begin with what will be unique about each entry—if you had to give each record a title, what would it be? Would it be a customer, student, or contact ID number? Would it be an invoice number? Would it be a recipe name, a CD title, the name of the photographer, or a room in your house? Once you know why each record will be unique, you may have a better idea of what you'll want to store in that record and what fields will be necessary.

For instance, I might have a database that stores information about my students in a particular class I teach. Before the semester begins, I'll want to seriously consider all of the information about each student that I'll want to record over the next four or five months. I'll want names, addresses, phone numbers, and other contact information. I also know I'll be giving five major tests and twenty graded homework assignments. I'll need to have fields available to record all of that information, too.

But what about teacher conferences? Should I include parental contact information and a check box to show that each of the three conferences have been completed? How about a special section for storing notes so I can remember what to discuss with the parents? You should ask yourself these types of questions while you're planning your database.

Field Types

AppleWorks offers a number of different types of fields you can define for your database. Some are general in purpose—text fields are designed to hold pretty much any combination of text and number characters like addresses or zip codes; number fields are designed to hold numbers you plan to use in calculations. Others do very specific, techie kinds of things like offer you a pull-down menu of options or allow you to click a radio button or check list. Table 10-1 shows you all the different types of fields.

By the way, the fact that there are a lot of fields doesn't mean that database building is hard. It can be a little intimidating, but usually only in the beginning. Once you have the correct fields set up, you'll definitely like having the database available when you need to find, search, or sort something important.

Most of the fields you create will be text fields—they're the catch-all for personal and small business databases. You're more likely to use menus, radio buttons, and check boxes—fields called *controls*—if you're designing a database for someone else to do the data entry. (Controls are a good way of limiting typos by offering multiple choices.) You'll also likely use name and date fields in most any database you create, especially for business, organizational, or social databases.

Type of Field	What It Can Contain	Examples
Text	Any combination of letters, numbers, and symbols up to 1,000 words	Salutations, personal titles, addresses, notes, phone numbers, product names, product numbers, customer ID codes, zip codes, social security numbers
Number	A negative or positive integer or decimal up to 255 characters	Dollar amounts, student grade percentages, number of children, quantity of purchased items
Date	Date, month, and year (offers different formats)	Current date, shipping date, date order received, date of birth, wedding date, party date
Time	Hours, minutes, and seconds (in 12- or 24-hour formats)	Current time, time of order, time shipped, time of birth
Name	Full, proper names	People's names, company names, organization names
Pop-up menu	A menu of values; use anytime you want a limited response from many options	Compass direction, city names, U.S. states, demographic groups
Radio buttons	Multiple choice; similar to a pop-up menu but designed for fewer choices	People's titles (Mr., Ms.), name suffixes (Jr., III), computing platform (Mac, Windows, Unix), housing payments (rent, own), marital status (single, divorced, married, widowed)
Check box	Yes or no answer	Want further information? U.S. citizen? Self-employed? Product shipped? Checked zip code?
Serial Number	AppleWorks assigns a new, ordered number for each record; good for giving each record a unique value	Customer ID, product ID, invoice ID
Value List	Choose from a list of values or enter your own	Local restaurants, election candidates, favorite computer games, magazines you subscribe to
Multimedia	An image or movie file	Photo of employee, photo of household item, movie walkthrough of property for sale
Record Info	Time, date, or name of person who created/modified data	Record creation date, date/time modified, name of entry clerk
Calculation	Result from a formula using other fields	Total of invoice, sales tax, final student grade, days since shipped
Summary	Calculation from fields in this and other records	Total receivables, total of unshipped items, class average, number of items due

TABLE 10-1   Database Fields

10

Other fields that are very interesting are serial fields (important for invoices and inventory), calculation fields, and record info fields. All of these can be used to automate your database in a way that can make it much more valuable to use. Later in the chapter, you'll see how calculations can be used to automate important database functions.

Add Your Fields

Once you know the field types, you can add them to your database. The process for that is simple. If you've already chosen File | New to create a new database document, you're presented with the Define Database Fields dialog box.

Here's the process for creating a new field:

1. In the Field Name entry box, enter a unique name for your field. You should keep it reasonably short and avoid additional non-text characters, especially if you think you might one day export this database to another database program.

2. In the Field Type menu, choose the type of field you want to create.

3. Click the Create button to create the field.

4. If desired, click the Options button to make specific choices about the field's behavior. The Options dialog box allows you to make basic choices about your field, such as setting default values, a range of accepted values, and so on.

5. Done with all your fields? When you're ready to create your first record, click OK in the Define Database Fields dialog box. (Don't worry, you can still add fields later if necessary.) The dialog box disappears, and you're presented with the entry screen for your database. Enjoy!

TIP
This is a good time to save your database by choosing File | Save and giving the database a name.

Control Fields

Certain control fields—menus, radio buttons, value lists, and record info fields—will require additional information from you before the field is accepted. If the field contains radio buttons, a value list, or a menu, you'll need to enter values for those lists. A dialog box will appear right after you click the Create or Modify button in the Define Database Fields dialog box.

Here's what you can do in this dialog box:

- To enter a value, type a name in the Item Label entry box and click the Create button (or press RETURN).

- To create another value, type a different name and click the Create button.

- To modify an existing value, highlight the value in the Items List, then type a new name for it and click the Modify button.

- To choose the default value for the control, pull down the menu in the Default section of the dialog box and choose the default value. This is the value that the control will be set to until the user changes it.

10

Click OK when you're done fixing the control. If you've chosen to create a Record Info field, you'll see a different dialog box.

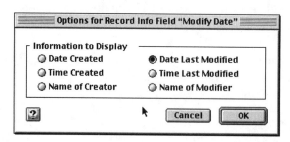

This one is more straightforward—just click the corresponding radio button to create the field you want in your database.

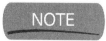 *How does AppleWorks know the name of the person creating or modifying? It looks up the iBook's Owner in the File Sharing control panel. Sneaky, huh? (See Chapter 24 for more on networking.)*

Calculation Fields

Here's another instance where you won't get away with a quick swipe of the Create or Modify button. A *calculation field* is one that requires you to enter a formula, somewhat akin to a formula in a spreadsheet.

If you're creating a calculation field, you'll be asked to create the calculation before the field is complete. To do that, you'll work with the Enter Formula dialog box, which appears when you first create a calculation field.

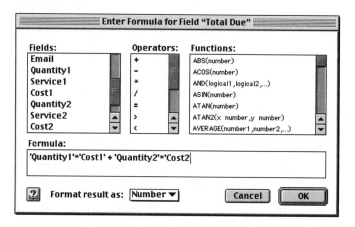

If you read Chapter 9 closely, you might notice something familiar here in the Enter Formula dialog box—the functions. In fact, most of them are exactly the same as those functions found in the spreadsheet module, although some are more limited in the database module. Still, you'll find that many of the same calculations are possible. (Refer to Chapter 9 to learn about some of the special ones.)

In database formulas, you'll find that field names are your variables—they replace the cell names in a spreadsheet when you create mathematical formulas or build functions. Most of the time you'll want to use number fields in your calculations, although you can use the built-in text functions to work with text fields, if necessary, and the date and time functions to deal with date, time, or record info fields.

There are a couple of different ways to create a formula:

- To create a basic formula, you can click a field name, click an operator, and then click another field name. (Perfect for adding together costs in an invoice, for instance.)

- If you want to use a function, you'll usually choose the function first, then choose the field name(s) it should operate on.

- Just type it—if you already know the exact field names, operators, and/or functions you want to use.

At the bottom of the Enter Formula dialog box, choose how the result should be formatted from the Format Result As menu. (Remember, when you're entering data, this field will show the *result* of the calculation in each record, not the calculation. So, you've got to decide what sort of value that's going to be, just as with other fields.)

Then click OK to save your formula. If AppleWorks thinks you've formatted things correctly, the dialog box goes away and the field appears in your field list. If not, you'll see an alert box telling you something is wrong. Fix the problem and click OK again.

TIP   *Since a calculation field only stores the result according to the field type you specify in the Format Result As menu, you can use the field name as a variable in other calculations. For instance, you can have a calculation field called Total, then a calculation field called Sales Tax, and a Final Total calculation field that calculates Total+Sales Tax. Just make sure all the results are formatted as numbers if you're going to be adding and multiplying them together.*

10

Enter and Find Records

Once you've defined your fields, you're ready to enter your first record. AppleWorks immediately drops you into Browse mode, the mode used to create records and move between them manually (see Figure 10-2). The mode is chosen from the Layout menu in the menu bar.

In Browse mode, you can click near a field name to begin entering data in that record. Press TAB to move to the next field after you've entered data; press SHIFT-TAB if you need to move back up to a previous field. Once you've entered all the data you need to enter, you can quickly choose File | Save or press ⌘-S to Save. Then, choose Edit | New Record or press ⌘-R to begin entering a new record.

List View

If you prefer, you can also do your data entry in List view, which makes it a little easier to see more than one record at a time. If you have many fields, though, the window will need to scroll quite a bit. To switch to List view, choose Layout | List.

	Client Name	Address	City	State	Zip	Phone	Fax
	Rachel	3456	Allegro	CA	91211	209-555-4635	209-555-9987
	Wes	1910 El	Rapid City	CA	90123	209-555-1212	209-555-1345
	Rich Mills	140 Main	Rapid City	CA	90124	209-555-3452	209-345-1243
	Harry	3987	Rapid City	CA	90123	209-555-4562	209-456-1342
	Marcia	135	Allegro	CA	91210	209-555-2345	209-555-6675

Invoice Database (DB)

Records: 5 Sorted 100 Page 1

TIP   *You can drag the line that separates columns to make them wider or narrower, just as in the spreadsheet module.*

Find Records

If you only have a few records in your database, it won't be that tough to click around in Browse mode and find a particular one. But if you have quite a few records, or you're interested in looking at only certain ones, then you need to instigate a Find.

FIGURE 10-2   Browse mode allows you to move through records and enter new data.

NOTE *This is easiest to manage if you select Window | Show Tools to display the spiral-bound note cards (shown in Figure 10-2) in the left margin.*

It's actually really easy to find records. Just follow these steps:

1. Choose Layout | Find.

2. You'll see a blank version of the Browse screen. Enter data in one or more of the fields that you'd like to match with your find.

3. Click the Find button in the left margin.

4. If any records are found, they'll be displayed. The found records are now a subset of the total database. You can scroll back and forth through the records and see only the found records.

Choose Organize | View All Records when you're ready to deal with the entire database again.

By the way, it might be helpful to know that number fields (and calculated fields with number results) can accept basic comparisons. For instance, if you have a field that calculates a testing average, you can enter **<65** to see every record that has an average under 65. The same goes for a number field that's holding a dollar amount—use <, >, <>, <=, >=, or = to see which records match up. And it's the same for dates and times. You can enter **<10/10/01** in a date field to find records with dates before October 10, 2001, for instance.

Save Your Search

Want to create a Find that lasts for a while? You can do it with the Search button that appears on the Tools palette in the left margin of the database window. The Search button is the magnifying glass; click the button to see its menu. Choose New Search and you can name the search before you enter criteria in the Find layout view.

Now, when you want to perform that search again, it appears right there on the Search button menu. Just click the button to see all your named searches.

Print Records

If you choose Print while viewing records in your database, the Print command automatically defaults to printing *all* visible records. (This doesn't mean the records you can see with your eye—it means records that are visible within the database after a Find command has been done. If you want to print records numbered 1-5, for instance, perform a Find to find records with record numbers less than 6.)

If you just want to print one record, you'll need to look for an option in the Print dialog box that allows you to Print Current Record. If you can't find this option, look for a pull-down menu in the Print dialog box that says General; select it and choose AppleWorks. Now you'll see the Print Current Record option.

Give It a New Layout

Whenever you create a new database, AppleWorks designs a very basic layout, called Layout 1, which offers only the rudiments of design. Fortunately, you can do something about that by editing the layout.

Layouts are used for more than just the data entry screen—they're also used for creating and printing reports. As you'll see, a report is simply a sorted, searched database that uses a particular layout to make it look good. A layout doesn't even have to include every field in your database, so you'll often create different layouts to correspond to different reports you want to build. Notice, for instance, that the report in Figure 10-3 uses only a few of the fields from the sample inventory database.

FIGURE 10-3   Here's a report layout I've created specifically to show me payments that haven't come in yet.

Since a database can have more than one layout, you might decide it's best to have different layouts for data entry and reports. It's up to you, but even if you don't create more than one layout, you can jazz up your layout so that it looks good for both a report and data entry.

Choose a Layout or Start a New One

To begin, you should figure out which layout you're currently using. Click the Layout menu to open it and look toward the bottom. Whether or not there is more than one layout in your database, the current one is the layout with a check mark next to its name. If you want to use a different layout, choose it in the Layout menu. If you want to create a new layout, choose Layout | New Layout.

If you choose to create a new layout, you'll see the New Layout dialog box. Give the layout a meaningful name, then choose whether you want the basic layout (like Layout 1), a duplicate of an existing layout, or a blank layout. You can also choose a Columnar Report, which helps you build a simple report layout that will place information about each record on its own line, as was shown in Figure 10-3.

Edit the Layout

The fun is just beginning, because you can edit as you please. To get into Layout mode, pull down the Layout menu and choose the layout to edit. Now, go back to the Layout menu and choose the Layout command. Suddenly you're in Layout mode.

What can you do? You can move your text and fields around, you can draw boxes around parts of your layout, or you can add graphics and text. For the most part, the drawing and painting tools are the same ones used in the drawing and painting modules, so I'll point you to Chapter 11 to learn things like drawing and moving shapes around. But there are a few things specific to the database layout process you should know:

- Don't forget the SHIFT key. You can click a database field, then click the field's label while holding down SHIFT. Now you can click and drag one field and the other will follow along.

- You can also use the SHIFT key to select all of the field labels at once, then you can use the Format menu to change the font, size, style, or color of the field labels.

- If you want to add something that appears at the top of every record, choose Layout | Insert Part, then choose to add a Header. You can drag the Header line around on the layout to resize it, then add the text or image above the Header line and it'll appear at the top of every page in your layout.

- If you want more than one record on a page, you'll need to edit the layout so that more than one will fit, then drag the Body line up under the abbreviated layout. If you only have a few fields and want each record to appear on one page, do the opposite and drag the Body line down to the bottom of the page.

- To change the appearance of a field, you can select it (or more than one field) and use the text formatting options in the Format menu. For both text and number fields, you can also double-click the field to quickly format it. (This includes things like formatting for currency and setting the precision of decimals.)

- Switch to Browse mode to test things (assuming you have more than a few records in your database). That'll give you a good idea how things look. You can switch back to Layout mode to keep editing.

After a while you'll have a nice, edited layout designed for data entry or for a report, depending on your needs. Figure 10-4 shows the report in Layout mode; Figure 10-5 shows that same report in Browse mode.

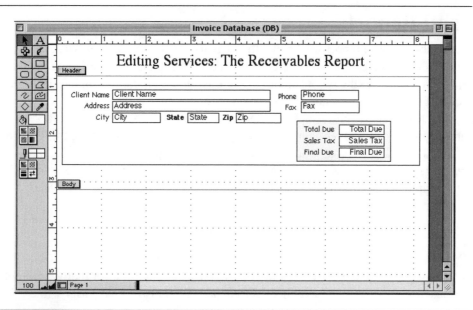

FIGURE 10-4 A new layout, still in Layout mode

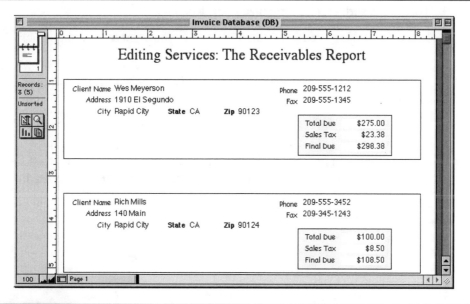

FIGURE 10-5 Here's how the new layout looks in Browse mode.

Sort and Report

The slash-and-burn report works like this: Create the layout that you want to use for the report. Perform a Find and create a subset of matching records you want to report on. Switch to the report layout in the Layout menu, then change to Browse mode. If the report looks good, print it.

You can even get more sophisticated. If you're going to be creating the same report over and over again, you can go ahead and save the whole thing—the search, the sort, and so on. You might also want to perform a quick sort before you run the report—that way you can Find whose grades in the database are below 65, for example, and you can organize the report alphabetically or based on some other criteria.

Sort

Once you get a number of records in your layout you may find, for many different reasons, that it's useful to have them sorted. This isn't always a priority while you're entering data, but it can be very important when you're ready to generate a report.

Here's how to sort:

1. To begin a sort, choose Organize | Sort Records.

2. In the Sort dialog box, select the Field name you want to sort, then click the Move button.

3. Click the Ascending or Descending button in the bottom-right corner of the dialog box.

4. Next, choose the secondary field you want to sort on. This is the "sort-within-the-sort" field. If your first-level sort is on the State field, for instance, and you have more than one record within a given state, then the records could be secondarily sorted based on, say, the Phone Number field.

5. Continue until you have enough sort fields, then click OK. Your database is now sorted.

So, things are sorted. If you add records and want to sort them again, just choose Organize I Sort Records again. The criteria should still be there in the dialog box and you can just click OK again.

Save a Sort

Want to save a sort for posterity? You might find reason to work with more than one sort. If that's the case, you'll need to head down to the Sort button on the Tools palette in the left margin of the database window. Select the Sort button (it's the one with the three bars) and choose New Sort. You'll get the same dialog box as with a regular Sort, except there's an entry box at the bottom to name the sort. Do so, then set up the sort criteria. Click OK and the sort is created.

Now you can return to the Sort button to perform the sort or edit it. Any new sorts you create show up on the Sort button's menu.

Build a Report

I'm not trying to rhyme the titles of these last two sections, I promise. It's appropriate, though, because the processes are so similar. If you're ready, it's time to head to the Report button and create a new report. The Report button is the one with an image of two sheets of paper on it.

10

Pull down the Report button menu and choose New Report. The New Report dialog box appears. Here's the crazy part—all you do is give the report a name, then choose a saved Layout, a saved Search, and a saved Sort from the menus. If you want the report automatically printed when you choose the item in the Report button menu, then check the Print The Report check box. Otherwise, you've just built and saved a report. Pretty easy, huh?

Chapter 11

Paint, Draw, and Create Presentations

How to...

- Create a painting
- Add text to your painting
- Save the painting
- Create a drawing
- Add AppleWorks elements (charts, paintings, text) to your drawing
- Create a presentation from scratch
- Get serious about presentations with the AppleWorks presentation template

People seem to love to play with the Paint and Draw modules in AppleWorks, which allow you to create some of the great graphics that Macs are known for. If you're quite the artist, especially with a mouse pointer, then you'll want to head directly for the Paint module, which puts both your free-form and shape-driven ideas on a virtual canvas.

If you're a little less abstract in your thinking, you'll prefer the drawing tools, which can be used to create diagrams, drawings, signs, labels, and even desktop layouts with precision. Drawing documents are about creating straight lines, boxes, circles, and shapes, and adding text when necessary.

With your graphics and text, then, the logical result is to create presentations. AppleWorks has the built-in ability to take over your iBook's screen and give a slide show presentation, allowing you to manually or automatically move through slides created in almost any one of the AppleWorks modules.

First you'll need to learn to draw and paint.

Painting vs. Drawing

You may be wondering why AppleWorks offers two different modules for what seem to be very related tasks. The answer is simple: *objects*. The definition of objects, however, will take a little more discussion.

The Draw module in AppleWorks allows you to create objects—shapes, lines, text—that can be moved around, grouped together, and placed relative to one another on the drawing document. This is different from the Paint module, which treats the document window more like an actual artist's canvas. Once you put a shape, line, brushstroke, or text on the canvas, that's it—it can't be moved again as an individual shape. You can select a portion of the painting and move it, but the shape itself is now part of the painting.

You *can* cut and paste portions of a Paint document, and you can erase parts, too, but you can't pick up an individual shape or text object and drag it around—you can only cut, copy, paste, or erase parts of the canvas. The difference is a little like watercolor painting versus collage art. In a collage, you can lay down elements on your canvas, then pick them up and move them around. In watercolor painting, once you paint something onto the canvas, you have to either wipe it off (if you can) or paint over it to change it. But once you've blended colors and shapes together, you can't move them again.

Of course the AppleWorks paint tools offer a little more freedom than that. After all, you can select square chunks of your Paint document and drag them around. And,

11

the Magic Wand tool can be used to grab shapes from within the painting and drag them around. But, if you want to create boxes and lines that can be moved around and organized on the page, you're better off using the Draw module.

Start Your Painting

Create a new Paint document in AppleWorks (select File | New), then choose to start a Paint document. Your untouched document "canvas" appears onscreen along with the tools you'll need to get started. If you'd like to immediately save, choose File | Save As to give this document a name and find a folder to store it in.

Document Size

Depending on your reason for creating this painting, the first thing you might want to do is create a document that's a certain size. If, for example, you're building a newsletter page or a page on the World Wide Web, you may want to create a painting that's less than the standard document size. You can then place it in the larger document, wrap text around it, and create an interesting layout.

NOTE   *Layouts are covered in more detail in Chapter 12.*

Choose Format | Document from the menu and you can determine exactly how many pixels wide and long you want your document. In the Document dialog box, use the entry boxes under Size to determine the width and height of your painting in *pixels*. (Pixels are *picture elements* or individual dots on the screen.) When you close the Document dialog box, your canvas will change to reflect your sizing.

Document

Margins		Page Display
Top:	1 in	☑ Show margins ⌘M
Bottom:	1 in	☑ Show page guides ⌘G
Left:	1 in	
Right:	1 in	Size
☐ Mirror Facing Pages		Pixels Across: 600
		Pixels Down: 400
Page Numbering		
Start at Page:	1	
[?]		Cancel ⌘. OK

NOTE *This is another distinction between Paint and Draw—the painting tools can be used for editing individual pixels if you zoom in close enough. The drawing tools can't be used on individual pixels.*

Use the Tools

With document size set, you're ready to begin work with the painting tools. There are quite a few of them, but they fall into basically four different categories: shapes, pickers, brushes, and color controls. Before you can see any of them, you'll need to make sure that Window | Show Tools has been chosen. (If you see Hide Tools when you choose the Window menu, that means that the tools are currently being shown. See 'em?) Figure 11-1 shows the different tools available for your painting pleasure.

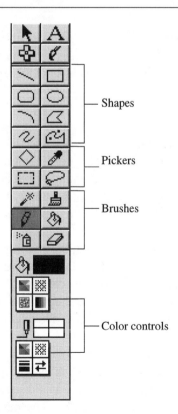

FIGURE 11-1 The different tools in the Paint module

11

Shape Tools

If you want to create a shape, simply select a shape tool by clicking it in the toolbar. Then, move the mouse pointer to the window and choose a starting place for your shape. Now, click and hold the mouse button, then drag out to create the shape. When you release the mouse button, the shape is committed to the document canvas.

 Double-click the Rounded Rectangle or Curve tool's icons to change some options that govern how the shapes look.

The first five shape tools, Line, Rectangle, Rounded Rectangle, Circle, and Curve, all work in the same way—just select and drag. The next four shape tools work a little differently. Each requires a little extra input before you can draw the shapes. Here's how to use each of them:

 ■ **Polygon Tool**   Choose this tool, then click once in the document to begin your polygon. Move the mouse pointer to the next point in the shape and click again. Continue to click for each point on the shape until the next to last one—you can double-click that point to automatically draw a line back to the original point. (The lines of your polygon can be curved, if you like—just hold down the OPTION key while you move the mouse pointer.)

 ■ **Freehand Tool**   Select this tool, then click and hold down the trackpad button in the document window. Drag around the screen to create a curvy, filled shape. When you release the trackpad button, a line is drawn straight back to the starting point and the shape is filled in. (If you're trying to create a particular shape, draw it so that you end up as close to the starting point as possible.)

 ■ **Bezigon Tool**   Choose the tool, click the trackpad button in the document window, then move to the next place you want to create a point. Click the trackpad button to create the point. To close the shape, double-click on your last point, or click very close to the original point to end the shape.

■ **Regular Polygon Tool**   This one allows you to create a polygon by dragging, just as you do with the Rectangle and Circle tools. The difference is, you get to specify the number of sides. To choose the number, double-click the tool's icon. In the dialog box, enter the number of sides for this polygon. Now, in the document window, click and hold the trackpad button and drag the mouse to create the shape. Let go of the trackpad button when you've got the shape the size you want it to be.

Selection Tools

The next set of tools are the selection tools, which allow you to select different parts of your painting in order to copy, paste, clear, or drag the part to some other section of the canvas. Here's how they work:

 ■ **Eyedropper**   This tool does one thing—pick up the color that's under it when you click the trackpad button. Choose the Eyedropper, point at a particular color, and click the trackpad button. That color then becomes the Fill color.

 ■ **Rectangular Selection Tool**   This tool is designed to select a rectangular section of the document. Choose the tool, then click and hold the trackpad button in the top-left corner of the part of the document you want to select. Now, drag down toward the bottom-right corner of the portion you want to select. Let go of the trackpad button and it's highlighted. (Double-clicking the tool icon selects the entire window.)

 ■ **Lasso**   The Lasso allows you to be a little more cavalier in your selection. Select the Lasso's icon, then click and hold the trackpad button in the document window while you draw, freehand, the shape you want to select. Release the trackpad button and your selection is highlighted.

 ■ **Magic Wand Tool**   With this tool, you won't need to drag and release—the Magic Wand is designed to "magically" select shapes in the document window. Select the tool, then head over to a shape and click it. All or part of the shape will be highlighted. If you don't get what you want, try a different part of the shape. (You can also hold down the SHIFT key while selecting in order to select more of a shape or more shapes.)

What do you do once something is selected? Hit the DELETE key and everything in the selection box will disappear. Or, pull down the Edit menu and

11

choose any of those commands—Cut, Copy, Paste, Duplicate—to perform such functions on the selection.

Brushes

With all of the brush tools, you hold down the trackpad button and move around on the document window when you want to draw; release the button when you don't want to draw. Brushes do a couple of specific things:

- **Paint Brush**   Use this tool to paint brushstrokes of color onto your document. You can change the shape and size of the brush by double-clicking the tool's icon. Select a new size and/or shape and click OK. Also, notice the Effects menu, which allows you to change the way the Paint Brush works, offering more sophisticated special effects like blending and tinting.

- **Pencil**   Use this tool to draw thin lines or to fill in a drawing at the pixel level. The pencil can be used at high magnification to fill in individual pixels with color. Double-click the pencil to switch instantly to 800% magnification.

- **Paint Can**   This is the fill tool—choose the Paint Can and click in your document and any shape or form is filled in with color. You can draw a closed shape, then fill it with this tool, or click outside of a closed shape to fill the entire screen with color.

- **Spray Can**   The Spray Can creates a spray-painting effect, making it look as if some paint is scattered. The more you spray on one particular area, the better the coverage of paint in that area. Double-click the Spray Can to change the size of the dots and the amount of coverage the Spray Can shows.

■ **Eraser**   The last brush tool is actually an "anti-brush" of sorts—the Eraser. It erases all layers of shapes and color on your document, taking it back to the original white background.

Options for most of these brushes can be found in the Options menu, where you'll also find options to change the Paint Mode from the standard Opaque to Transparent Pattern, and Tint, which mixes your paint color with any colors you paint over.

Color Tools

The last tools in the toolbar are the color tools, which offer two different ways to color—Fill and Line. The Fill color is used for the bulk of all shapes you create; it's used whenever you use one of the brushes, and it's used when you select the Fill Paint Can. The Line color is used for drawing lines and for outlining shapes.

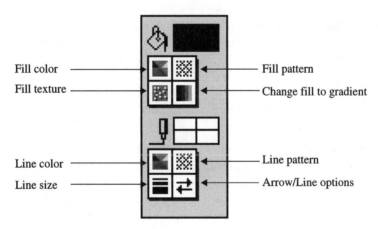

Fill color — Fill pattern
Fill texture — Change fill to gradient

Line color — Line pattern
Line size — Arrow/Line options

11

Let's start with the Fill color tools:

■ **Fill Color**   To change the Fill color, click on the Fill Color button. A palette of colors appears. Select one of the colors; the palette disappears, and the Fill color indicator changes to show the new color.

- **Fill Pattern**   Next to the Fill Color button is the Fill Pattern button. Click it once to see the various patterns you can fill with. Select one and the palette goes away. (Note the first two patterns in the palette. The first one causes no fill to appear; the second is the solid Fill color with no pattern.)

- **Fill Texture**   Open this palette and choose a texture to fill with instead of a color.

- **Gradient Fill**   If you'd like to fill shapes and paint with a gradient instead of a Fill color, choose one from this palette. A *gradient* is a pattern that moves from one color to another gradually across the shape or background you fill. You can edit the gradients by choosing Options | Gradients.

Want one of these palettes on the screen all the time? All you have to do is click and hold the particular button that interests you, then drag the mouse pointer along and off the end of the palette. That *tears* the palette off the menu. When you release the trackpad button, the menu *floats* above the document, so you can change colors or patterns on a whim.

NOTE   *You can edit the color palettes if you want to. Choose Edit | Preferences. In the Preferences dialog box, choose Palettes from the pull-down menu. Click the option for Editable 256 Color Palette. Now, back in the document window you can tear off the color palette. Then, you can double-click an individual color on that palette to edit the color.*

Below the Fill tools you'll find the Line tools. These tools determine the color and pattern used for lines and the outlines of shapes. Each one of these works just like the other palettes—click the icon, then click to select the color or pattern. Here's what each does:

- **Line Color**   Choose the color for the line from the color palette.

- **Line Pattern**   Same as Fill Pattern, but it pertains only to line and outline patterns.

- **Line Size**   Choose the size of the line in points. If you want something larger than 8 point, choose Other, then enter the point size desired.

- **Line Arrows**   Choose whether or not you want arrows on the end(s) of your lines.

> TIP
>
> *Want my limited artistic tips? When painting an object or landscape, remember your light source. Figure out where the light is coming from, then use darker versions of your colors on the farther side and use lighter versions of your colors on the side closer to the light. Also, a nicely placed shadow goes a long way to making a painting look more realistic, if that's your goal. You can use the tint and transparency options to create distance and perspective effects, too.*

Add Text

Here's the last thing I'll show you in the Paint module—you're going to have to figure out the artistic part yourself. Hopefully you've already got a start. If you need to add text to your masterpiece, it can be done. Here's how:

1. At the top of the toolbar, choose the Text tool (the letter "A").

2. Click in the document where you want the text to be. An insertion point appears.

3. Head up to the menus and format the text just as you would in the word processing module.

4. Type the text you want. If you need to change formatting, quickly type ⌘-A to invoke the Select All command, then format the text.

5. When you're done entering and editing the text, click somewhere else on the document outside of the text box. You can click the Pointer tool in the top-left corner of the toolbar to switch back from the Text tool and use the painting tools.

Once you've placed the text, it's there for good. It can't be moved (unless you also move the background behind the text) or edited. It has become part of the painting, just like a brush stroke or a shape. (Sometimes, but not always, you can manage to select text with the Magic Wand, especially if you zoom in close, as discussed in Chapter 12.)

Save Your Image

You know that File | Save allows you to save your Paint image in AppleWorks document format. But if you'd like to use the Paint image in other programs—to edit the image in PaintShop or add it to a professional layout or World Wide Web page, for instance—you'll need to save it as a more common file format. To do so, you can choose File | Save As. In the dialog box, give the file a name, then choose the file type from the Save As menu.

If you plan to use the document in an earlier version of AppleWorks or in ClarisWorks for Kids, select one of those options. If you want to use the image in an application other than AppleWorks, save it as one of the remaining four image file types. Click OK to save the file.

 Need to know more about image file types? They're described in Chapter 13.

Draw Objects and Text

The drawing tools can be used in much the same way as the painting tools—for fun, for artistic creation, or for logos and images you'll use elsewhere. More so than the Paint module, the Draw module can be used for a variety of business-like reasons. As I've said, the drawing tools are a good way to present information graphically. Using these tools, you'll be able to create signs, posters, certificates, and more. In Chapter 12 we'll take a close look at some of the Stationery that's provided for the Draw module and all of the publications you can create with its tools.

Draw in Databases and Spreadsheets

By the way, the drawing tools are also found elsewhere in the AppleWorks suite, including the Database module and the Spreadsheet module when you're dealing with charts. You'll notice that a lot of the object manipulation commands (as well as some of the drawing tools) are found in those parts. If you're trying to create a database layout or improve the appearance of a chart, what you'll learn in this section on the drawing tools will help.

Create Objects

To begin, open a drawing document by choosing File | New, then select Drawing and click OK. A new drawing document appears.

You can place text, graphics, shapes, other multimedia objects, and even spreadsheet objects in your drawing document. When you're in the Draw module, everything is an object, meaning that everything you add to your drawing document remains its own entity. You can pick them up, move them around, and even stack objects on top of one another (see Figure 11-2).

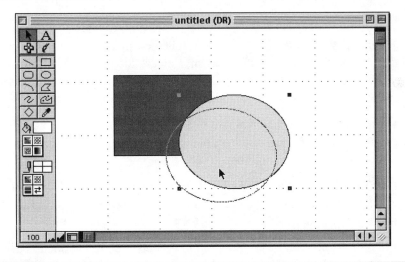

FIGURE 11-2   In the Draw module, you create objects that can be moved around.

There are three basic types of objects you'll create in the Draw module: shapes, text, and objects from other modules. That includes spreadsheet objects, charts, painted images, scanned photos, QuickTime movies, and other multimedia objects you can bring in from other applications.

Shapes

The shapes you find in the Draw module are a subset of those found in the Paint module, and they work pretty much the same. One important thing to remember is that most objects in the Draw module can easily be reshaped or resized after they've been created, so your dimensions don't have to be as perfect as they do in the Paint module.

Here are the tools you can use to draw different shapes:

- ■ **Line Tool**   Click the Line tool, then click once in the document window. Move the mouse pointer and click again to create a line between the original point and the final location.

- ■ **Rectangle Tool**   Choose the Rectangle tool, then click and hold the mouse button in the document window. Drag the mouse to create your rectangle, then release the trackpad button when the rectangle is the size and shape you want it.

- ■ **Rounded Rectangle Tool**   Choose this tool, then click and drag in the document window to create the oval. Release the trackpad button when you've got it the right size. To shape the corners of the rounded rectangle, make sure the tool is selected, then choose Edit | Shape Corners.

- ■ **Oval Tool**   Select the Oval tool in the toolbar, then click and drag to create the oval. Release the trackpad button when it's the correct dimensions and circumference.

- ■ **Arc Tool**   Select the Arc tool, then click and drag in the document window until the arc is the correct size. To change the arc's characteristics, make sure the Arc tool is selected, then choose Edit | Arc Info.

- ■ **Polygon Tool**   Select the Polygon tool, then click in the document window to place the first point. Move the mouse pointer and click to place a second point; repeat until all the points for the shape have been laid out, then double-click to draw a line between the last point and the first point, closing the polygon.

- ■ **Freeform Tool**   Select the tool, then click and drag in the document window. Drag out the shape you want to create, ending as close to the starting point as possible. In the Draw module, this shape isn't forced closed—it can just be a squiggly line, if you prefer.

- ■ **Bezigon Tool**   Select this tool, then click in the document to create the first point. Now, move the mouse pointer and click to create additional points for the shape. End as near the first point as possible, then double-click to complete the shape.

- ■ **Regular Polygon Tool**   Select this tool, then click and drag in the document window to create a polygon. To change the number of sides, make sure the tool is selected, then choose Edit | Polygon Sides.

> **TIP** *The SHIFT key can be used to constrain many of these tools. Hold down the SHIFT key while you draw a line (or draw the side of a shape) and the line will be perfectly straight. Hold it while using the Rectangle tool to draw a square. Hold it down while using the Oval tool to draw a circle. Hold it down while drawing an arc to keep the arc symmetrical.*

The Draw module also includes an Eyedropper tool and the same color tools described in the Paint section. The color tools work slightly differently, though. You can select a shape that's already been created, then choose a color, texture, or pattern if you like. Same with lines—even if they've already been created, just select them in the document window and choose a new color, pattern, or size, or add arrows. You can always change them back later, if desired.

> **TIP** *To change the Polygon tool's behavior, choose Edit | Preferences and make sure the Topic menu shows Graphics. Now, click to change the shape-closing behavior in the Polygon Closing section. With the Manual option, you need to click to place the last point pretty much right on top of the first point in a shape.*

Text

To create a text object, click the Text tool in the top of the toolbar. It's the tool that looks like a capital "A"; it allows you to click and drag in the document window to create a text box.

Notice that this is a little different from painting. You've actually created a word processing object within the drawing document here—it's almost like you opened up a little window into the Word Processing module. Watch carefully and you'll notice that the button bar and menus change when you're editing inside the text box. The insertion point appears and you're ready to type.

Type your text, then format it using the menus. When you're pleased with your text, click the Pointer tool in the toolbar or click outside the text box to switch back to the drawing tools.

If you want to edit the text again, just double-click it if the Pointer tool is selected, or select the Text tool and single-click the text. The text box appears (it may be a little smaller), the menus change, and you're ready to edit the text.

Other Objects

We'll get into this topic in much more detail in Chapter 12, but I want to touch on it here. You can create spreadsheet and painting objects right here within the Draw module. Just as you can create a text object that switches around your menus and button bars, you can create spreadsheet and paint objects.

For a spreadsheet object, select the Spreadsheet tool (the small cross) at the top of the toolbar, then click and drag in the document window to create the spreadsheet object. A table of cells appears and the insertion point is ready to edit. Start your spreadsheet. You can enter anything you might enter in a typical AppleWorks spreadsheet.

You can even create a chart. Try it. Enter data that works for a chart, then choose Options | Make Chart. (If you don't see that option, double-click the spreadsheet to make sure it's selected for editing.) Now, create a chart as discussed in Chapter 9. When you click OK, the chart appears in your document. Best of all—it's an object, just like everything else (see Figure 11-3).

It's a similar process to create a paint object within your Draw document. Select the Paint Brush, then drag out a paint object in the document window. You'll notice that the tools and menu commands change to those of the Paint module. Paint all you want inside the paint object, then click outside it when you're done.

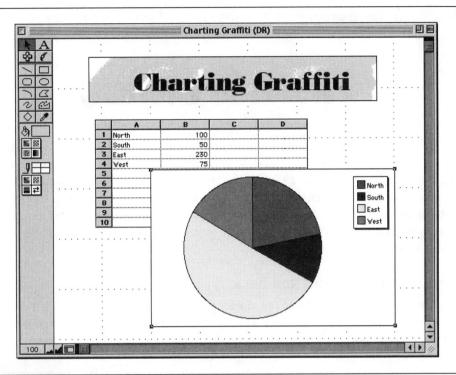

FIGURE 11-3   A chart from spreadsheet data can easily be added to your Draw document.

Manipulate Objects

Once you've got your objects created, you're ready to work with them. The key is to figure out how to select and drag them around—that part's pretty easy. With the Pointer tool selected, point to an object, then click and hold down the trackpad button while you drag the object around the screen. Drop the object when you're done moving it by releasing the button.

Don't forget Undo! Most of these manipulations can be immediately undone by choosing Edit | Undo right after you perform the change.

Select Objects

If you want to change an object's size, just click once on it to select it. You'll see the resizing handles appear. You can click and drag one of the handles to make the object larger. This includes text boxes, spreadsheet objects, and paint objects, all of which can be stretched to offer you more space to work in.

Charting Graffiti

But that's not all you can do. With an object selected, you can hit the DELETE key to delete it from the document, or choose any of the Edit menu commands like Cut, Copy, or Paste. You can paste an object from any AppleWorks module into any other module. (The major exception is the Paint module, which will accept the Paste command, but won't store the object as an object—it just turns it into part of the painting document. That's even true of spreadsheet objects, which can be painted right over in the Paint module.)

Arrange Objects Front and Back

Sometimes you'll find you have one object that's "on top of" another object—it's obscuring part of the second object. This often happens, for instance, if you decide to create the background for a text object after you've created the text object. Drag the background to the text and it'll obscure the text.

If you really want that background in the, well, background, then make sure it's selected and choose Arrange | Move Backward or go for the gold and choose Arrange | Move to Back. In either case the selected object is moved behind other objects. The Arrange | Move Backward command is designed to move objects back one layer at a time (just in case you have three or four objects stacked on one another). Move to Back immediately moves the selected object to the back of all objects on the screen.

As you might guess, you can bring objects to the foreground just as easily. Select an object, then choose Arrange | Move Forward or Arrange | Move to Front.

Align Objects

There are two different ways to align objects. You can select a particular object and choose Arrange | Align to Grid. This only does something if you've previously selected the Options | Turn Autogrid Off command. Autogrid is what forces objects to "snap" to a particular position on the page whenever you drop them. It keeps you from making precise little movements, but helps you by aligning everything to the grid. If you've turned it off, but you now want an object aligned to the grid again, choose the Align to Grid command.

The Align Objects command is even cooler. Select two or more objects that you want to align relative to one another. Now, choose the Arrange | Align Objects command. You'll see the Align Objects dialog box.

See the options? Decide how you want objects aligned, asking yourself some questions like:

- If your objects are in a vertical column, do you want them aligned on the right or left edge? Should the vertical distance between the objects be distributed evenly?

- If it's a horizontal row of objects, should the bottom or top be aligned? Should the horizontal distance between the objects be distributed evenly?

- In either case, should the centers of the objects be aligned?

Make your choices and click OK.

Reshape Objects

As mentioned, objects in drawing are unique because they can be changed and reworked after they've been created. One way to do that is to change the way the shape is made with the Reshape command. This works with objects created using the Arc, Polygon, Freehand, Bezigon, and Regular Polygon tools. Choose Arrange | Reshape and you'll see resize handles that let you change the shape of the object.

After you've changed the shape, you'll still be in Reshape mode until you select Arrange | Reshape again. So, click another object and reshape again. Or choose the menu command to return to normalcy.

Free Rotate

The Free Rotate command works much the same way that the Reshape command does:

1. Choose Arrange | Free Rotate from the menu and you're in Free Rotate mode.

2. In the document window, select an object to rotate.

3. Now, click and grab one of the image's handles, then move the mouse pointer. You'll see the object rotate along with your mouse pointer movement.

4. Release the trackpad button when you have the object where you want it.

Don't forget to choose Arrange | Free Rotate again when you're done rotating to leave Free Rotate mode.

Flip and Rotate

These are more precise controls that allow you to do exactly as much rotation and flipping of an object as you'd like. For these, you'll select the object in the document window first, then choose the command from the Arrange menu. Here are the commands:

- **Flip Horizontally**   Quickly flips an object from left to right.

- **Flip Vertically**   Flips the top and bottom of an object.

- **Rotate**   Brings up a dialog box that allows you to enter how many degrees the object should rotate. Rotation works counterclockwise (entering **90** causes the object to rotate counterclockwise 90 degrees), but you can enter a negative number to rotate clockwise. (Note that **–90** and **270** give the same results, since rotation covers the total—360—degrees in a circle.)

- **Scale by Percent**   Brings up a dialog box that allows you to reduce or enlarge your object vertically or horizontally. Enter a percentage for each to stretch or enlarge the object.

Group and Lock

With the Lock command, you make it so an object can't be moved, reshaped, or rotated. Locking is simple—just select the object and select Arrange | Lock (⌘-H) from the menu. The object becomes locked—it can't be moved or shaped. (You can edit text and make changes in spreadsheets and similar objects, though.) To unlock the object, select it and choose Arrange | Unlock (SHIFT-⌘-H).

The Group command allows you to take two or more objects and cause them to function as a group—move one and you'll move them all. They become, in essence, one object. To group objects, select them all (hold down the SHIFT key as you click additional objects in order to select more than one). Choose Arrange | Group (or ⌘-G) and the different objects become one object. You'll notice that the object handles change so that the entire group can be selected, moved, resized, shaped, or rotated as one object.

To ungroup, select the object and choose Arrange | Ungroup (SHIFT-⌘-G). Once you've created a grouping, you can also group that grouping with other objects (and so on, and so on) although that can get a touch complicated.

Obviously, it's best to group related elements, especially things that always need to be together as one object or together but a certain distance apart. (It can be annoying to get everything set up correctly and then accidentally move one of the related objects. Just group them and that can't happen.) It's also easy and recommended that you group objects temporarily when you want to move them, together, across the screen. Select, group, move, ungroup—you can do it very quickly and it keeps all those objects the same relative distance from one another.

11

Create a Slide Show

I've mentioned that the Draw module is a great way to communicate information graphically, and it doesn't end with creating flyers or posters. In fact, many of AppleWorks' parts also have the ability to display documents on the screen in the form of a slide show—the type you might use for a presentation or for a kiosk of some sort.

So, you can create a series of Word Processing, Spreadsheet, Draw, Paint, or Database screens (usually pages within a document or a series of documents) and create a slide show that advances automatically or can be advanced by pressing a key or clicking the trackpad button.

 Need more than one page in a drawing or painting document? Choose Format | Document, then enter the number of pages across and down for your document.

Start the Show

You'll start by creating multiple screens or pages within a document that can be used for the slide show. You'll want the pages or documents to be pretty much the same size, have a similar appearance, and generally work well as a group. Here's how to display them as a slide show:

1. Load the document you want to display as a slide show. Make sure it's frontmost in AppleWorks.

2. Choose Window | Slide Show.

3. Now you'll make some choices. Begin by deciding whether your pages are going to be opaque or transparent. Click on the transparency icon next to each page to change its condition (see Figure 11-4). A transparent page simply builds on the page before it, allowing you to see the content from both pages. This is a clever way to build slides if you want it to appear that text or images are appearing on a slide that already exists (for example, a new bullet point appears on the same slide when you click the mouse button).

It's okay to create every third or forth slide as an opaque slide, while the ones in between are transparent. That way you make each bullet point (or other element) appear when you're ready to talk about it. Each opaque slide covers up the previous transparent ones so you can move on to a new slide and add bullet points again.

4. In the top-right corner of the dialog box, you can change how the page will appear onscreen, although the defaults are usually good choices. You can also determine whether you'll see the cursor on the screen. The cursor can be used for pointing and emphasis, but probably isn't necessary for an automated kiosk or display.

FIGURE 11-4 The Slide Show setup window

5. Still in the top-right corner of the dialog box, you can also choose to Fade between slides (which provides an attractive transition effect) and to Loop so that when the last document is shown, the first one is repeated and the show goes on. Finally, click the Advance Every option and enter the number of seconds between each slide in the entry box.

6. If you want, you can choose a Background color or pattern for your slides. The background of your document pages (the pages that are being turned into slides) will show up, but if your document doesn't completely fill the screen, the background surrounding your document will be this color or pattern. The Border palettes can simply be used to create a border around the slide window, which you may or may not find attractive.

7. The final option, QuickTime Settings, is only relevant if you have QuickTime sounds or movies stored in your slide show document. If you do, you can choose to have the QuickTime sound or movie auto-play when the slide appears. If you have more than one QuickTime element, you can choose to have them play simultaneously. If you have the slide show set to auto-advance, you can choose the final option, Complete Play Before Advancing, to force it to complete the QuickTime sound or movie before moving to the next slide. (If this option isn't on, you'll need to click or OPTION-click the movie to get it to start.)

TIP *Consider the possibilities! You could actually record your own voice or some music and have it play when a new slide appears. It's an instant, self-running, narrated slide show.*

8. You're ready to begin. Click the Start button to start the slide show. You can stop the show by pressing Q.

While the show is running, you'll have some choices for controlling it:

To go to the next slide	Press SPACEBAR, RIGHT ARROW, DOWN ARROW, or RETURN
To go to the previous slide	Press SHIFT-SPACEBAR, LEFT ARROW, UP ARROW, or SHIFT-RETURN
To go to the beginning of the show	Press HOME
To stop the show	Press Q or ESC

As you might imagine, the size of the pages can affect the way the presentation looks and you might need to play with document sizes—or make sure you're only typing in certain parts of your document. If you can set the pixel size of your documents (like in Paint documents), you should choose 640 × 480, 800 × 600, or a similar multiple that matches typical screen resolutions.

NOTE *If you plan to show the images on another Mac, you need to take that Mac's screen resolution into consideration when you set up your Paint documents.*

The Presentation Template

Having trouble getting things to line up and look good? Or are you creating a class, lecture, or business presentation from scratch? You might consider using Stationery to create a well laid-out presentation (see Figure 11-5). The best one is provided within AppleWorks, although the module where you'll find it might surprise you. It's a Database document.

NOTE *Actually, there are two different approaches to presentations; there's also a Presentation Assistant that will walk you through creating a presentation in the Draw module. You can find it under the Slide Backgrounds Stationery.*

To create a presentation using Stationery:

1. Choose File | New.

2. Select the Use Assistant or Stationery option.

3. Choose the School Curriculum menu item, then choose the Making a Presentation database Stationery.

4. Click OK and your presentation database is built.

Why does using a database to create a presentation make sense? Because all you have to do is enter a new record to create a new slide. It's really pretty brilliant. Each slide (record) has four major fields that you can use to enter your points. Then, you can present it as a slide show, moving from record to record (or slide to slide) very easily.

FIGURE 11-5   The Presentation stationery helps you build a presentation using the database module.

The first thing you'll want to do is edit the slide layout—it's not the most gorgeous layout I've seen. Choose Layout | Layout to change how each of your slides will work. In Layout mode, you can use the Layout tools discussed in Chapter 10 to change the way the layout looks. Also, select Window | Show Tools and you'll have some drawing tools you can use to make your slides look that much better.

When you're done designing the slide, switch back to Browse mode and start entering the data for each slide. (To begin with, you'll probably want to change the first four slides, which contain instructions for the Stationery.) Each field is a new line in your discussion. To create a new slide, just create a new record. You can format each individual field for font size, emphasis, or whatever else you'd like.

When you're done creating slides, choose Window | Slide Show, then go through the options and begin the show. It's that easy, and the template makes things look really good. Experiment and have fun— it's a great way to build a quick presentation.

Chapter 12

Use AppleWorks for Layout

How to…

- Work with page layouts
- Use Assistants for common documents
- Create a layout using drawing tools and text frames
- Add images and wrap text around them
- Draw shapes and create floating text for your layout
- Create layouts quickly using the word processing tools
- Merge data from your databases with your layout documents

Y ou've learned about text layout and management in Chapter 8, numbers and calculations in Chapter 9, data management in Chapter 10, and artistic creation and communication in Chapter 11.

Now, what if you could put all this stuff together?

AppleWorks is a special sort of program. Although we've taken a reasonably thorough look at the individual parts and what they can do for you, in this chapter we'll look at AppleWorks as a whole. If you're interested in creating dynamic, professional-looking, and creative documents, you're going to enjoy this chapter.

How Layouts Work

These days, the desktop publishing revolution has made it so that most of the *page layout* process—the steps used to create a newsletter, newspaper, or magazine page—happens on a computer screen. You type and edit your story in a word processor, then you simply cut and paste it (or some close equivalent) into *frames* that are laid down in a special desktop publishing program. With the text laid down in columns, you can change fonts, sizes, spacing, and alignment. Then you can drop digital images right into the document itself and move them around on the page.

Popular programs for this sort of layout include Adobe PageMaker and QuarkXPress. They usually cost hundreds of dollars apiece and can take a little training to master.

Or, you can use AppleWorks and get somewhat similar results. The tools aren't all as advanced as those in the layout programs, but AppleWorks does offer you the ability to format documents in columns, create text frames, add images, and even create graphic elements in the Paint and Draw modules. The best part is how all the modules work together.

The AppleWorks Frame

You already know that you can create different types of documents—word processing, spreadsheet, Paint documents, and so on—in the different AppleWorks modules. What you may not have realized is that you can use almost any of the tools and commands to create one single document.

You do that by creating frames in a particular document. While you'll have a basic document in the background—say, a Draw document—you can create a word processing frame or a spreadsheet frame and place it on the Draw document,

12

the same way you might lay out a strip of typeset text on a paste-up board to create a newspaper. Figure 12-1 shows an AppleWorks document with multiple frames.

A frame is sort of a window into another part of AppleWorks—when you double-click in the frame, the AppleWorks menus and tools change to the tools that are available in that module. Double-click a spreadsheet frame and you'll see the spreadsheet tools and commands; double-click a text frame and you'll see all

FIGURE 12-1 Using multiple frames in an AppleWorks document makes sophisticated layouts possible.

the word processing tools. With frames, you can create a sophisticated document that communicates very effectively.

What Can You Lay Out?

So, you'll be able to use AppleWorks to lay out many different sorts of documents using all the different frames and tools at your disposal. What sort of things can you create? You can use just a few frames in a document to spice it up, or you can create entire documents out of nothing but frames that work together to create a whole. Here are some ideas:

- Add charts and graphs to your word processing reports.

- Create text frames in spreadsheet documents that explain the spreadsheet or help the novice user enter data in the spreadsheet form. You can similarly use a text frame in a database layout to offer instructions.

- Add Paint or Draw images to your spreadsheet, database, or word processing document.

- Create text frames within text documents in order to create headlines, pull quotes, or other special elements (like the Tips and Notes you see in this book) on the page.

- Create spreadsheet charts within other types of documents, like Draw or word processing documents.

- Create text and image frames within a database to create a presentation, slide show, or flash cards that can be used for teaching or lecturing.

- Create a merge, in which data from a database can be merged into a word processing document or a text frame. This is great for mail merges (personalizing form letters and addressing envelopes) and it works for other things, too.

And there's much more—you can use layouts to create brochures, holiday letters, reports, and newsletters; you'll likely use all the different permutations. Want to create a newsletter that features text, graphics, painted objects, drawn objects, charts, and spreadsheet data? How about a newsletter that does all that,

12

then allows you to print multiple copies and automatically address them from a database of names and addresses?

Don't ever let anyone tell you AppleWorks isn't a powerful program.

Assistants

In fact, AppleWorks is so powerful that you don't even have to create your own layouts—you can start with help from the Assistants. There are five Assistants to help you create different layouts:

- **Business Cards**   This Assistant walks you through adding the company name, address, title, and phone number to create a business card, which it then generates as a database document. Using the database tools, you can modify the card in Layout mode, then switch to Browse mode, which automatically fills a page with eight instances of the card. The cards can then be printed to plain paper and taken to your print shop, or printed on card stock and cut at home. You can also get perforated card stock at most office supply stores, which can be used to create business cards.

- **Calendar**   Using the spreadsheet tools, this Assistant quickly creates a monthly calendar, automatically placing the dates correctly, based on the month(s) you choose. There's really only once choice—a single month per sheet of paper.

- **Certificate**   This Assistant quickly tosses together a certificate, award, diploma, or something similar. The result is a Draw document that can easily be edited.

- **Envelope**   This Assistant walks you through the process of setting the alignment and printing path for the envelope. Envelopes can be tough to print—you'll need to read your printer's manual carefully to figure out how to orient and feed the envelope to your printer. Then you can make an informed decision on how to set up this Assistant, which generates a word processing document that's easily edited.

- **Newsletter**   This Assistant automates the process of creating a newsletter in the Draw module, providing between 2 and 16 pages worth of columns, headlines, boxes, and so on. I think the final layout can be somewhat lacking (some of the Stationery options for newsletters are better), but it's a decent start for using the techniques you'll learn later in this chapter.

To use an Assistant, choose File | New from the AppleWorks menu bar. Click the Use Assistant or Stationery option in the Open dialog box, then choose Show All Assistants from the Category pull-down menu. Choose an Assistant and click OK.

Assistants work by asking you a series of questions about your document. You enter information in the Assistant dialog box, then click the Next button to move on to the next series of questions.

When you get to the end of the Assistant, you'll see a Create button, which causes the Assistant to take all the information you've input and create the document based on that information. You can also click the Cancel button to leave the Assistant, click the Back button to go back to the previous questions, or click the Begin button to return to the beginning of the Assistant.

Now, you're ready to learn how to jazz up that Assistant-created document by moving things around on your layout.

Layout Basics: Text Frames

Let's begin by creating a newsletter that incorporates all the different sorts of frames. We'll create text frames in columns, drop in images, add headlines—it'll be fun. Plus, what you learn in creating a newsletter can be applied to any sort of layout, from creating business cards and brochures to report letterhead and mail merge documents. We'll get to those other things later in this chapter, but right now let's cover the general instructions for dealing with frames on a page.

With a newsletter, there's actually a more fundamental problem to broach before you can start typing and framing things. You need to choose which type of AppleWorks document—word processing or Draw—to use as the foundation for your newsletter. Here's the basic rule—if you're more interested in the text than you are in the layout, then choose the word processing module for creating the basic document. Your newsletter may come out looking a little more like a pamphlet, but you'll have a more structured document with headers, columns, and other tools for automating the layout.

If your primary focus is the appearance of the newsletter—you want it to be visually pleasing, creative, and incorporate a lot of different framed elements— then you'll want to create a Draw document. Draw documents give you the most flexibility, since they're specifically designed for creating and moving objects around in the document window.

Getting Started

Create your Draw document by choosing File | New, selecting Drawing, and clicking OK. The first thing you need to do is make sure you're seeing all the drawing tools— they'll be important throughout this process (Window | Show Tools). You'll also probably want to view the rulers in the document window (Window | Show Rulers), since you'll be lining things up and spacing them evenly.

Next up is a little tool we've ignored until now: magnification. You'll find that changing the magnification is a handy thing to do when you're trying see the whole page at once and get a feel for its overall design. The magnification level allows you to see more of your document (decrease magnification) or to see a smaller portion of your document up close (increase magnification). It's helpful to drop back to 75 or 67 percent sometimes, because then you'll be able to see the whole page. Then, return to 100 percent so you can actually see the text and detail in the images. While you're at it, you can also zoom in up to 800 percent to get a very close look at part of an image, text layout, or other feature of the page.

To change the magnification, select the percentage in the bottom-left corner of any AppleWorks document. It's actually a menu—you can simply choose the percentage to change the size of the document.

TIP *You can use multiple "views" to open different windows showing the same document at different magnifications. To create a new view, choose Window / New View. Notice that the title bar of the new view has ":2" in it. It's still the same document—this is just a convenient way to look at the same document in two different magnifications so you can switch quickly between the two.*

Next, you'll probably need to set up the document's margins and pages. This works the same as with any other Draw document. Choose Format | Document, then enter numbers for the margins on the page and the number of pages down or across you'd like the document to have. (I prefer to place all my pages horizontally, since that just looks more like a newsletter to me. Your approach is up to you, though.)

NOTE *Most inkjet printers and many laser printers can't print all the way to the edges of a page, so you'll probably want a minimal margin even if you plan to use most of the page for your layout. If you're using a typical letter-sized page, a margin of .25 inch on each side gives you 8 inches for your document's width and 10.5 inches for the height; .5 inch for each margin leaves you 7.5 by 10 to work with. Later in the chapter you'll be measuring things pretty closely, so keep these numbers in mind.*

Now you're ready to create the frames that will hold the different parts of your newsletter. If you're serious about creating a newsletter *right now*, remember that you can pre-type your stories in the word processing module to get them nicely spell-checked and formatted, and you might want to have some graphics or images on hand to drop into the layout. (Chapter 13 discusses manipulating digital images, while Chapter 23 discusses scanners and digital cameras.)

You can also type directly into the layout, as you'll see, but sometimes it's easier to have written the story beforehand so it can be checked and edited.

Create Text Frames

Much of your layout will likely be composed of text, so you'll be working with text frames a lot. Fortunately, they're pretty flexible. After all, a text frame is sort of a window into the word processing module of AppleWorks. Draw your text frame on the page, and you'll have all the text tools at your disposal.

In drawing projects you'll create a text frame, type text, and then the text will become an object. Unfortunately for our newsletter, AppleWorks, by default, collapses the text frame around the typed text so that only that text becomes the text frame, regardless of the size of the frame you draw.

12

That won't quite work for us in the newsletter, since we want the column to stay a fixed size. That way we can move text around within the columns and the column won't change sizes just because we don't have enough text to fill it. It can be convenient to have the frame grow around your text in certain cases. But in order to build a newsletter-type document, you'll want to create frames that are a fixed size.

To do that, you must create a *linked* frame (this might be a good time to drop back to 67 percent magnification, by the way).

1. With the Pointer tool selected, choose Options | Frame Links.

2. Now, select the Text tool and drag out a frame on the page.

3. Release the mouse button and the insertion point appears—you can type in the frame if you want.

4. To see the entire linked frame, click once outside of the frame. Its handles appear to show you the entire frame object.

The text frame is an object in the same way that a drawn rectangle or line is an object—it can be rotated, resized, moved, or even sent to back or sent to front (see Figure 12-2).

So why is it called a "linked" frame? Well, it'll take some explaining, which I'll do later in this chapter in the section called "Link Text Frames." For now, suffice it to say that linked frames allow text to flow from one frame to another, like text flows from column to column on a newspaper page.

> TIP *The frame borders keep disappearing after you select other objects! To see your frames at all times, select them and choose to surround them with a line (choose Hairline from the Line Width button menu on the Tool Panel at left). Just don't forget to remove the lines before you print the document.*

Add Text

There are four basic ways you can add text to a linked frame. The first three start with clicking in the frame to make sure it's selected for input—the insertion point appears and you can type, if desired. In fact, that's the first way to add text:

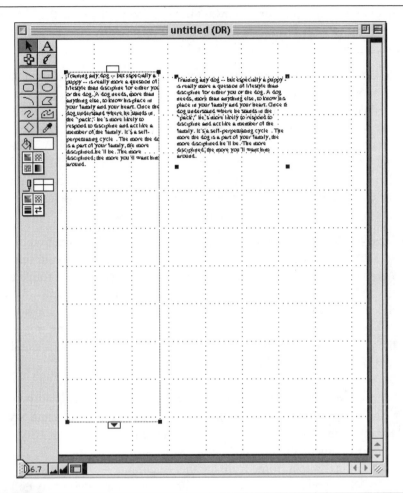

FIGURE 12-2   On the left, a linked text frame; on the right, a typical text frame—it collapses around the text instead of maintaining its shape.

- **Type**   You'll notice that, when you're in the insertion mode in the text frame, your tools (menus and the button bar) are all the same as they are in the word processing module. That should make it easy to type, format, and even clean up your newsletter story.

- **Cut and Paste**   If you have parts of an existing word processing document that you'd like to drop into this frame, you can open the document, select the text you want in your frame, then use the Edit | Copy and Edit | Paste commands to copy the text from the word processing document into your frame.

- **Insert Command**   A real pro does it this way. (That's a challenge, not an admonition.) You've already created your story in the word processing module, you've edited it, and you're ready to simply drop it into your layout. Select the text frame, then choose File | Insert. Find the word processing document you want to insert, then click OK. If you subsequently want to change the inserted document, you can select all the text by choosing ⌘-A, then insert a different document. (Or you can clear the text first and then insert the document.) Note that changing the text once it's been inserted doesn't affect the original word processing document's text at all.

- **Drag-and-Drop**   If you have good hand-eye coordination, you can select text in a word processing document and drag it into your text frame. Arrange the document windows so that you can see the text frame even if you have the word processing document in front of the Draw document. Select the text in the word processing document, then click and hold the trackpad button on the selected text and drag the text to the frame. When the frame becomes outlined in blue, release the trackpad button and the text should appear in the frame.

Again, once you have text in the frames you can format it just as if you're working in the word processing module—pull down the Font, Size, and Style menus, for instance, or use the Stylesheet button bar (select Window | Stylesheet) to change the alignment, create lists, and so on.

If you insert text into a frame from another document—or if you simply have a lot to type—then you may run into a little problem, because you may end up with a frame that's too big after it has been resized to fit your text. You can use the frame's handles to move the frame around and try to make things fit, but that probably won't work if you're creating a newsletter, report, or similar document. Instead, you'll probably want to move the additional text to a new frame and have it flow nicely so the story continues onto the next column. Almost as if, say, those frames were *linked*. Hey now!

Link Text Frames

If you've created one text frame that's overflowing with text, you can create another one to link to it so that it takes up the slack. Here's how:

1. Select the first frame to see its frame handles.

2. At the bottom of the frame, locate the continue indicator. Click it once.

3. Now you're ready to draw the linked frame. Drag to draw the frame onto your page. (Don't worry—you can resize it later.)

4. When you release the trackpad button, text flows into the frame from the original frame. They're linked. When selected, the new frame will show a linked indicator (a little chain link icon) at the top and, if the story is long enough to overflow the frame, it'll show a continue indicator at the bottom, as shown in Figure 12-3.

What's important to realize about linked frames is that they flow just like different pages in a word processing document flow. So, if you go back to the original frame and add or delete text, the linked frame will change to reflect the added or subtracted text. If you simply had two frames into which you'd cut and pasted text, you'd be in for quite an experience if you added text to or subtracted text from either of them, because you'd need to do some crazy cutting and pasting to make the columns look right again.

12

NOTE   *If you're used to expensive desktop publishing programs, you'll find these linked frames useful but limited. You can't re-order the links or link to an existing frame. You can only create linked frames by clicking the continue indicator and drawing the frame. Also, cutting or copying the frame breaks the link—a pasted frame can create its own linked frames, but it's no longer linked to the original.*

Frames don't have to be the same sizes or shapes to be linked, so you can link a narrow column of text to a large rectangle of text and it will still flow fine. In fact, you can create a linked frame on a new page, if you like.

Link indicators

Continue indicator

FIGURE 12-3   Linked frames allow text to flow from one frame to the next.

Resize Frames

Once you've got a couple of text frames on your page you'll probably realize that it's nearly impossible to get them to look like perfect columns on the page—after all, you're drawing and arranging them by hand. This can be frustrating, to say the least.

Fortunately, there are some tools to help you. The first is the Size window, which allows you to make some very precise decisions about how each frame will appear. Choose Options | Object Size and the Size window appears.

⊞▣ **Size** ▣⊞	
⊢	7.47 in
⊤	0.13 in
→⊣	9.83 in
⊥	7.39 in
⊢→⊣	2.37 in
⊤⊥	7.26 in
↺	0°

This is a great little window, because it gives you amazing precision in placing and aligning your frames as columns. From top to bottom, the measurements are listed here:

- **Left Location**   The point, in inches, where the left side of the frame appears.

- **Top Location**   The point, in inches, where the top of the frame appears.

- **Right Location**   The point, in inches, where the right side of the frame appears.

- **Bottom Location**   The point, in inches, where the bottom of the frame appears.

- **Object Width**   The width, in inches, of the frame.

- **Object Height**   The height, in inches, of the frame.

- **Rotation**   Amount of rotation, in degrees, of the frame.

While you're creating your layout, you should keep in mind how useful these measurements are. For instance, if you want all of your frames to be aligned at their tops, you can choose a measurement and enter it for each. Similarly, you can check all your columns to make sure their bottoms align exactly. This will also help to keep the text aligned across columns so the column layout doesn't look jagged. An example of what you *don't* want is shown in the following:

12

> The dog may need to go out quickly, but don't feed him (water should always be available) right when you walk in the door. Instead, wait for an appropriate, calm time after you've gotten home

> let him see you home and worried about other things before you greet him.
> When you do greet the puppy, bend down to meet him but maintain a dominant stance (lean over the dog) and don't allow him to paw you or

Probably the best tools here are column width and height—two measurements that are almost impossible to eyeball. Select one of your columns and check its width—if you've got three columns, it's probably about 2.5 inches or so wide, right? Go ahead and make it a nice, round number. Now, select another column and make it 2.5 inches wide. Do it for the last one, and your columns will all be a uniform width.

Align the bottoms of your frames, then give them all the same height measurement if you want them to align at the tops, too. Columns of different heights simply can't align at both the top and bottom. It goes against the laws of physics.

While you're doing these measurements, you'll probably want to keep in mind a little mathematics. By default, a Draw document shows all 8.5 inches of a standard letter-sized sheet of paper. If you have margins for your document, you probably have 8 or 7.5 inches for your document's width. If you have an 8-inch wide document with three 2.5 inch columns, that will leave you 0.25 inches for the *gutters*—white space—between the columns. (There are two gutters for three frames, remember.) That's a good size. If you only have 7.5 inches to work with, though, you'll need to pare back those column widths a bit to get a decent gutter—say, about 2.333 inches for each column, which would give you back 0.25 inches per gutter.

You can select more than one column (or another frame) at the same time by holding down the SHIFT key as you select them. Then you can apply uniform sizing to them all at once.

Align Frames

Keep repeating to yourself that frames are objects and objects can be manipulated, as we saw in Chapter 11. You're using the Draw tools, so all of the same tools for shapes can be used to manipulate frames. That includes the alignment tools.

Here's a neat trick to align frames as columns and get that gutter just perfect:

1. On your layout, place your left- and right-most columns where you want them on the page relative to the edges.

2. Now, select all three frames by holding down the SHIFT key while you click them.

3. Choose Arrange | Align Objects.

4. In the Align Objects dialog box, choose Distribute Space in the Left To Right section.

5. Click Apply.

See what happened? Your columns snapped into place, distributing the remaining space equally between the two gutters. Perfect. If you like what you see, click OK to get out of the Align dialog box. Or, you can use the other settings—like Align Bottom Edges under the Top To Bottom options—to change other alignment issues regarding your columns.

Lock Frames

When you've finally got your frames in place the way they need to be, go ahead and lock them down. That'll keep you from accidentally moving the columns around once they've been carefully arranged. Select the frames to lock (hold down the SHIFT key as you select more than one frame), then choose Arrange | Lock. You can still select the frames and edit text within them, but you can't move them on the page until you unlock them.

Graphics, Floating Text, and Shapes

Once you have your main column frames created and locked down, you're ready to start adding text and images around the columns in order to create a more vibrant layout. The basic concept is simple—you create frames that can be placed near or even over the existing frames that you've created. Then, using a special command, you can force text to wrap around the floating frames, creating the effect that an image or block of text is diverting the columns around it, drawing attention to the visual element. Fortunately, it's very easy to do.

Add Graphic Frames

Let's begin by adding images to your layout. The graphics can be from a variety of sources, including graphics you create or one of the many images that come with AppleWorks, which you can find by selecting File | Library. And you can just as easily scan graphics or digital camera images into your computer and store them as image files. Any of these are easily added to your layout.

There are four basic ways to add graphic images to your layout:

- **Build the Graphic** Using either the tools in the Draw module, a Paint frame, or a spreadsheet frame, you can add images (or spreadsheet cells) you've created in AppleWorks.

- **Insert from File** If you don't have a frame selected and you choose File | Insert, you can search your hard disk (or connected network disks) for image files that can be added to your document as their own frames.

- **Insert from a Library** AppleWorks offers libraries of *clip art*—small images, royalty-free, that you can add to your documents—which can be used to augment your layout.

- **Cut and Paste** In most cases, you can select images or parts of other documents, then copy and paste them into your Draw document using the Edit | Copy and Edit | Paste commands. They'll show up in their own frames that can then be moved, stretched, rotated, and so on.

You already know from Chapter 11 how to create and manipulate AppleWorks graphics, and you know how to cut and paste. Let's look at adding a graphic from a file or library.

To add a graphic from a file, make sure no frames are selected in the document (so that AppleWorks doesn't try to add the graphic into that frame), then choose File | Insert. The Insert dialog box appears. Find the file you want to add and click OK. The graphic appears in your document in its own frame. Note that the file *format* of your graphic is important—you'll need to have it in PICT, TIFF, JPG, GIF, BMP, or a similar format. (You can see them all by pulling down the Show menu in the Insert dialog box.) Graphic file formats are discussed in detail in Chapter 14.

If you're adding from a library, choose File | Library, then select the type of clip art you'd like to look at. (The topics appear in a submenu that pops up when you select the Library menu.) That opens the Library window.

Find the graphic you want to use by selecting the name in the bottom half of the window—the top half will change to show the graphic. Once you find the graphic you like, simply drag it from the Library window to your document (see Figure 12-4). It becomes an object in your layout. If you're done with the Library window, click its Close box.

Notice your floating graphic and your text co-mingling in an uncomfortable way? We'll cover that in the section "Wrap Text," coming up shortly.

How to ... **Add Inline Graphics**

12

You can also add graphics in another way—as inline graphics (or other objects) that become embedded in the text. Instead of floating freely in their own frames, embedded images are placed at a specific point in the text. You accomplish this by inserting, pasting, or choosing an image from a library while you have the Text tool selected and the insertion point placed somewhere in the selected text frame. The image appears as part of the text instead of in its own frame. You can learn more about this in "The Word Processing Layout," later in this chapter.

Graphic created using Draw tools

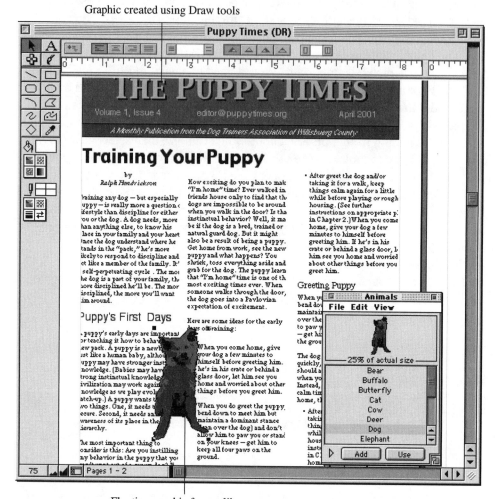

Floating graphic from a library

FIGURE 12-4
Drag the image from the library to your document, where it becomes an object.

Create Floating Text

You've already seen quite a bit on adding text in frames—this really isn't much different. You may find that creating a linked frame is the best approach here, if only because a linked frame doesn't collapse around the text. You likely won't actually be linking it to anything—you just want the additional control it gives you. Here's how to create floating text:

1. Make sure Frame Links is selected (with a check mark next to it) in the Options menu.

2. Click the Text tool and drag to create a text frame on the page.

3. Enter the text (a pull-quote, headline, and so on) for this floating text frame. Format the text.

4. Click outside the text frame. The text frame should be selected, with handles showing. (If it's not, click it once to select it.)

5. Click and drag the text frame to its final destination. It's OK if the frame obscures the text beneath it—you'll fix that momentarily. (See Figure 12-5.)

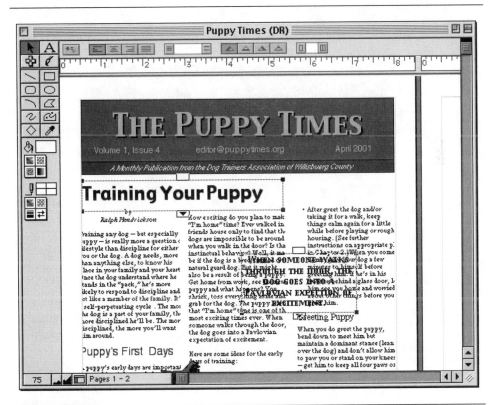

FIGURE 12-5   Floating text can be used to create effective pull quotes and headlines.

Wrap Text

Whether it's a text frame or a graphic, if you've created a frame that you want to float among the columns of your layout, then you'll want to wrap text around it. This is a great way to add visual appeal and a hint of professionalism to your document. It's also simple to do:

1. Select a graphic or text frame that's currently overlapping text. (It may be a little tough to select—try to make sure the underlying columns aren't also selected. If they are, SHIFT-clicking one of the selected frames will de-select it while leaving others highlighted.)

2. Choose Options | Text Wrap.

3. In the Text Wrap dialog box, choose the type of wrap you want. Regular wraps text around the frame, while Irregular will wrap the text around the actual image or shape within the frame. No Wrap, of course, eliminates the text wrap if it was there.

4. Enter a number for the gutter, if desired. This determines the number of points to keep between the frame (Regular) or graphic (Irregular) and the wrapped text. The typical text size of typed output is 12 points, so something like 6 points might be good for each side (6 points is 1/12 of an inch).

5. Click OK.

That's it, the text is wrapped either regularly or irregularly, as shown in Figure 12-6. This gives your layout a great look, although you'll still need to look at it carefully to make sure everything is lined up nicely. If things aren't working out, you may need to resize the graphics frame or choose Regular instead of Irregular wrap. Notice, for instance, in Figure 12-6 that the irregular wrap around the dog clip art has resulted in some odd text placement. Regular wrap might be preferable for this particular graphic.

FIGURE 12-6   Text wrapped around frames and graphics

Note that not all of your floating text will necessarily have other text wrapped around it. You can use this same approach to create two-column headlines over three-column stories.

Shape and Lines

In Chapter 11, you saw how to create various shapes and add them to a drawing. Your layout is also a drawing, meaning it can just as easily accept lines, shapes, and curves if you'd like to use them. Just draw them right on the document, then arrange them—back to front, text-wrapped, and so on—as you like.

A couple of ideas stand out. First, you can take an odd shape—a curve, oval, jagged shape or something similar—and group it with an image or text frame, putting the shape behind the text or image.

Now, if you choose to make the border of the shape invisible and wrap text around it, you can create some very interesting text wrap shapes that will give your layout even more artistic flair. Similarly, you can create a shaded or patterned background for your floating images or text, if you like.

You can also use shapes around individual stories in your layouts—surround shorter stories with boxes (or boxes with light-colored backgrounds in them) to separate them from the surrounding text. And, of course, you can use shapes combined with text and use other Draw tools to create special elements like a table of contents for your newsletter.

This Issue...

Wagging the Owner.................1
On Leashes........................2
Visit the Vet....................2
Life at Ten......................3
Smell and Seek...................4
Adoptables.......................5
Editor Letter....................6

Lines are also a great addition to layouts, especially since they no longer require the special "border tape" that was required in the days of yore. (That same tape still decorates the drafting table I have my iBook situated on at this very moment. It was certainly a big part of the journalist's life at one time.)

You know how to draw the lines. My only suggestions are

- **Remember the different sizes and shapes available.**   If you like, you can pattern lines so that they're dashed, broken, or otherwise more interesting.

- **Arrange your lines To Back.**   Traditionally, gutter lines go behind other elements, including images and shaded backgrounds. You can get this effect by selecting the lines, then choosing Arrange | Move to Back.

- **Lock your lines!**   Put the lines in the gutters of your document, then select Arrange | Lock to keep them there. Nothing gets more annoying than replacing your lines every few mouse movements because you've accidentally selected and moved them.

■ **Copy and paste.** Want lines that are the same size, width, and orientation? Copy an existing line, then immediately paste it into the layout. It shows up as an object, ready to be added to the layout.

Figure 12-7 shows some of these line suggestions in action.

Build Layouts Quickly

The Draw tools, as we've seen, are exceptional for creating dramatic layouts. You can use many different elements to design a few pages and create complex newsletters and other documents. But you can also see why people have full-time jobs as graphic designers and layout artists. It can take quite a while to get each page right.

What if, instead, you're trying to create a good-looking layout that takes a little less time to create? There are a number of templates and assistants in AppleWorks to help you do just that—you can create business cards, brochures, flyers, invitations, signs, birthday cards, posters, and many other publications. If you're creating a more serious report or similar document, you can also get it done more quickly by sticking

FIGURE 12-7   Lines help break up the text, offering a professional flair.

12

with the word processing module. You'll get a less graphical, more formal
publication, but it can be accomplished much more quickly.

The Word Processing Layout

Say you've already typed a long document as a word processing document and
you'd prefer not to format it using drawing tools. And yet, you're interested in
adding some graphical elements to the text—in fact, you might even want to
format the document as a newsletter. It can be done.

Columns

To begin, you can place the document in columns. This is much easier than creating
columns in the Draw module, although it gives you less flexibility. You can create the
columns in two ways:

- **Click the More Columns button.**   In the ruler bar of the word processing
  document, click the More (or Less) Columns button to add (or remove)
  columns for the document. The columns are added immediately.

- **Add columns to the section.**   Choose Format | Section. In the Section
  dialog box, enter the number of columns for that section in the Number of
  Columns entry box.

The Section dialog box also allows you to choose the width of the columns
and/or the width of the gutters (choosing one affects the other, by necessity). Note
that if you have more than one section defined in your document, you'll need to
define columns for each section.

Graphic and Spreadsheet Frames

You can use any of the four previously discussed methods to add graphics or spreadsheet frames to your word processing document: draw them, use the File | Insert command, copy them from a library, or paste them in. (See the section "Add Graphic Frames," earlier in this chapter.) You can also move them around, wrap text, and generally have the same sort of rollicking good time you can have in the Draw module.

If you're inserting or pasting an object into your word processing document, you must have the Pointer tool selected in the word processing document. That allows you to add an item as a frame. If you have the Text tool selected, the pasted, inserted, or library graphic (or other object) will appear *inline*. In this case, the image appears as part of the text, not as a floating object. An inline image is useful for those little graphics people like to put in newspapers and newsletters that show you when a story has ended.

> • If he's in his crate or
> behind a glass door, let
> him see you home and
> worried about other things
> before you greet him. End

NOTE   *This book is using the same inline vs. floating concept. The graphic just above is inline—it flows with the text so I can talk about the image and ensure that it's in the same place as the text that discusses it. This book also features "floating" images—they're the ones with Figure numbers.*

12

Draw and Text Frames

You can't create a text frame in the word processing module, supposedly because a word processing document is sort of one big text frame. This can be a little annoying, though, since it's tough to create pull quotes and multicolumn headlines without using text frames. (You can create Paint frames with text in them, but it's not the same since Paint frames can't be edited as objects.)

The trick is to create your text frames in a Draw document, then copy and paste them into your word processing document. It's convoluted, but it works:

1. Create (or switch to) a Draw document and create your text frame.

2. Select it and choose Edit | Copy.

3. Switch to the word processing document.

4. Make sure the Pointer tool is selected in the word processing document (you may need to choose Window | Show Tools first) to verify that you're placing the frame as an object and not as inline text.

5. Choose Edit | Paste. The text should show up in a text frame.

Now you can move the text frame around, use Text Wrap, and generally do the same things that are possible in the Draw module. It's just a little more of a pain. You'll probably want to keep a Draw document open just as a sort of "scratch" document to allow you to create these objects and paste (or drag-and-drop) them into your word processing layout.

This is actually the process used to get any complex drawn object into the document. You can draw basic shapes—rectangles and circles—directly on the word processing document. But if you have a more complex drawn object, then you'll want to create it in a Draw document and transfer it to the word processing document as an object. Then you can manipulate it just like any other frame, making things look good.

At least you saved a lot of time by not having to worry about creating columns!

Stationery

The Stationery options that help you create layouts are too numerous to mention— you'll just have to take a look at them. They range in capabilities from fax cover sheets to memos to letterhead to full-fledged newsletter layouts. And, of course, there is other Stationery available for other types of documents, like spreadsheets, databases, and drawings.

You saw how to use Stationery in Chapter 8—just select Use Assistant or Stationery in the New dialog box, then select the Stationery to use and click OK. The document pops up in AppleWorks, ready for you to save it under its own name and then edit it.

One way to get a sense of what Stationery is available is to choose About Stationery from the Category menu in the New dialog box. (It appears when you've selected Use Assistant or Stationery.) A number of Stationery indexes appear; each index is a document that shows two or more related types of stationery. It's a quick way to get a sense of what's available and how many options you have for quickly creating a new layout or document (see Figure 12-8).

Mail Merge

The ultimate meeting point for automating documents and generating layouts is the concept of mail merge. Mail merge allows you to take data elements that are stored in a database document and automatically create new layouts that fold the information into the document automatically.

FIGURE 12-8 Here's the Home Tools index, which shows you the Stationery options for a variety of uses around the house.

It's called a "mail merge" because the most obvious use for this scheme is to take names and addresses out of a database file and drop them into a letter or newsletter so that they can be mailed. You're creating a form letter. While it's possible to create a form letter as a layout in the database module, a mail merge allows you to use all of the sophistication of the word processing part—spell checking, sections, footnotes, and headers—to create more advanced form letters. In fact, any form letter more than a page long is best created in the word processing module.

A mail merge is created in three different steps: setting up the database, altering the document, then generating the merge.

Set Up the Database

First, you need to make sure your data is well arranged for a merge. AppleWorks' Help offers this example: If you want to use a salutation in your merged letter that includes a first name, then you're going to need a field in your database that stores that first name. You're also going to need logical address fields—address lines, city, state, zip—if you want to add addresses.

Remember that you can create any sort of merge you want using database fields. If you need to add fields that correspond to invoice numbers, products ordered, hair color, registration number, or whatever you have stored, you can put those fields in your database.

Now, before you create the merge document, find and sort the database as if you were creating a new report. If you only want certain documents in the merge, you should find them now. Similarly, you should sort to put the database in the order in which you want the merged documents generated. After doing this, leave the database open in the background.

Add Field Variables to Your Document

Now you're ready to edit the document. What you're going to do is add *field variables* to your document. The field variables tell the mail merge which field's data should be inserted into the document and where.

Here's how to add field variables to a document:

1. Open the document you're going to merge with your database.

2. Choose File | Mail Merge.

3. In the Open dialog box, find the database you want to use for the merge. Select it and click OK. (You need to perform this step even if the database document is already opened in AppleWorks.)

4. The Mail Merge window appears. Choose the field you want to add as a field variable, then click the Insert Field button.

5. Meanwhile, you can still edit the document, adding text around the fields being merged, punctuating them, and so on (see Figure 12-9). You can add the same field variable more than once, if desired. And, you can put the variables anywhere within the document. If you're building a form letter, for instance, you can even have field variables within paragraphs of text.

If you'd like to see the data in the document (instead of the field variable names) put a check mark in the Show Field Data box. You can then scroll through each document of data and see what they'll look like, just by clicking the up and down arrows next to the Record Number box.

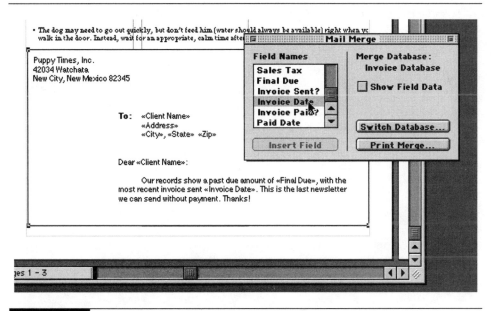

FIGURE 12-9   The field variables fit right in with any sort of text, formatting, or punctuation.

> **TIP**
>
> *Creating a mailing label for your newsletter or brochure? You can make a text frame that includes your field variables and use the Arrange / Rotate command to rotate the text 180 degrees, so you can fold the newsletter over and have the address printed correctly. The merge still works, even upside-down!*

Print the Merge

When you're done adding field variables, you're ready to print the merged documents. This part is simple. Click the Print Merge button in the Merge window. Your printer's Print dialog box appears. Click Print and the merge begins. If all goes well, you'll have an entire database of merged documents coming out of your printer.

> **TIP**
>
> *Scared? If your large mail merge has typos, you could waste a lot of paper. Click the Print Preview button in the Print dialog box to make sure everything looks OK before you go ahead with the entire printing. You could also consider finding only a few documents in your database to test the merge the first time around, then, if it looks good, give it a go for the whole database.*

Chapter 13

Movies, Sounds, and Images

How to...

- View a movie
- Work with images
- View and edit images
- Edit a QuickTime movie
- Create and record sounds
- Play an audio CD

Macs are known for their *multimedia* capabilities—their ability to integrate sound, video, and images. The technology behind a lot of the multimedia capabilities of any Mac, including the iBook, is something called QuickTime.

So what can you do with QuickTime? With both QuickTime and other technologies, you can play digital movies and movie clips, create and edit digital sounds, and work with images to incorporate them more easily into your documents.

QuickTime Movies

Just as your iBook requires underlying technologies to allow it to print—you may have noticed that nearly every application offers almost identical Print dialog boxes—it also benefits from underlying technology to play digital movies and digital sound. That technology, developed by Apple, is QuickTime.

What QuickTime Is to You

QuickTime is a rather advanced digital technology that, in a way, mimics an animation flipbook. It stores images in the form of ones and zeros, then displays them in rapid order, usually between 10 and 30 frames per second. (For comparison, a film is generally shown at 24 frames per second, while television is displayed at about 30 frames per second. Any more than about 10 frames per second gives a reasonable sensation of movement to the viewer.)

QuickTime is also capable of recording audio and layering it in with the video so that it can be synchronized with the video or complementary to it. Audio can also stand alone within a QuickTime "movie" file, then be played back at any time using the QuickTime Player application or many others that support QuickTime technology.

QuickTime is also a translation technology—built into it is the ability to translate between different audio, video, and image file formats. Different applications and computer platforms (like those from Microsoft, Sun Microsystems, Silicon Graphics, and other computing companies) save files in different formats. QuickTime, and applications that take advantage of QuickTime, offer the capability to translate to and from Macintosh file formats. In that way, it's easy to play or display nearly any movie, sound, or image file you find on the Internet or elsewhere (see Figure 13-1).

13

NOTE   *It can be a bit confusing, but documents saved in QuickTime are all called "movies" even if they contain only audio and no video component.*

FIGURE 13-1   QuickTime can play many different movie formats, including this movie that was originally designed for Microsoft Window–based computers.

Want QuickTime to do more? It can. QuickTime VR is a special technology that allows certain special QuickTime movies to behave more like the "virtual reality" scenes you may have seen in movies. QuickTime VR isn't quite that sophisticated, but it does allow you to explore 3-D panoramas by dragging the mouse around to change perspectives and clicking on objects or "hot spots" that take you elsewhere in the virtual tour.

QuickTime Streaming is a technology that makes it possible to view QuickTime movies as they are transferred over a network connection—generally, this is done over the Internet. In most cases, you'll open a movie document that is stored on your iBook's hard disk. With streaming, it's possible to view a movie as it arrives, instantaneously, over long distances. This has many applications, not the least of which is the possibility that you can watch live events via *Webcasts* or "narrowcasts." This can be a very interesting technology, especially if the event wouldn't otherwise be broadcast for television.

Finally, QuickTime is multimedia. You've probably heard that catchphrase before and wondered why it's significant. *Multimedia* is defined as the bringing together of many different media—audio, video, still imagery, text, virtual reality—to communicate ideas, educate, or entertain. Obviously, QuickTime fits the bill quite nicely.

The QuickTime Software

The manifestation of QuickTime on your iBook comes in the form of Mac OS Extension files that are stored in the System Folder on your iBook's hard drive. These files include QuickTime, QuickTime MPEG Extension, QuickTime Musical Instruments, QuickTime Powerplug, and QuickTime VR.

There's also a QuickTime Settings control panel stored in the Control Panels folder in the System Folder. If these extensions aren't in the Extensions folder in the System Folder, then some or all of your QuickTime movies won't play correctly. They're most likely there, but you can have trouble with QuickTime if you start your iBook with Extensions Disabled (by holding down the SHIFT key while the iBook starts up), or if you move the extensions for some reason.

> **NOTE** *Dealing with extensions and control panels is covered in Chapter 27.*

Although they're not integral parts of the QuickTime technology, a big part of the QuickTime experience for us humans is the QuickTime Player and PictureViewer applications. Both of these can be found in the Applications folder on your main hard disk. You also probably have an alias to the QuickTime Player on your iBook's desktop if you haven't deleted it (it's installed there automatically). You can just double-click that alias anytime you want to launch the QuickTime Player.

> **TIP** *There's often another alias on the desktop, too, called Get QuickTime Pro. It's just an annoying advertisement from Apple trying to convince you to upgrade! You can safely toss it in the Trash. (More on upgrading to QuickTime Pro in the next section.)*

13

Getting QuickTime Pro

Most of this book talks about how useful the software bundled with your iBook is and how to get things done exclusively with that software. Although I definitely recommend that you buy some shareware and consider some computer peripherals, it won't be often that I recommend spending money to get something like QuickTime Pro. (After all, your iBook already has a lot of free capabilities.) But the upgrade is worth it.

To get QuickTime Pro, you must register with Apple and pay a small fee
(about $30 at the time of this writing). In exchange, you'll get a registration code
that does a number of things to QuickTime and its associated tools:

■ It opens up the capabilities of the QuickTime Player, upgrading it to
QuickTime Player "Pro" (you won't see the name change in the Finder, but
I'll call it "QuickTime Pro" to differentiate between the two).

■ QuickTime Pro adds the ability to create a number of different types of
multimedia and gives you more options for creating and saving movies in
different formats.

■ The upgrade gives you a more robust PictureViewer ("PictureViewer Pro")
that allows you to edit, save, and translate graphic file formats.

■ You get an advanced QuickTime plug-in for Web browsers that makes it
possible to save certain QuickTime movies from the Web, and to perform
a few other tricks.

■ Upgrading does away with the annoying splash screen that Apple pops up
to convince you to upgrade every time you open the QuickTime Player. As
much as I'd like to discourage this behavior by Apple, I should point out
that paying the fee will get them off your back about upgrading!

Even if you don't get QuickTime Pro, you'll still be able to use a lot of
the information in this chapter. (I'll specifically point out when I'm using the
advanced features.) If you're into this multimedia thing at all, I think you'll
enjoy the reasonably priced upgrade. To register, visit Apple's QuickTime Web
site—**http://www.apple.com/ quicktime/**—and select the button or hyperlink to
upgrade to QuickTime Pro.

The QuickTime Player Application

If you have a QuickTime movie that you've downloaded over the Internet or copied
from a CD-ROM, you can double-click it to launch the movie file. When you do, most
likely the QuickTime Player application will launch (see Figure 13-2).

The QuickTime Player offers controls that look a lot like a cassette recorder's or
a VCR's controls. When you have a digital movie file loaded, you'll find Play, Stop,

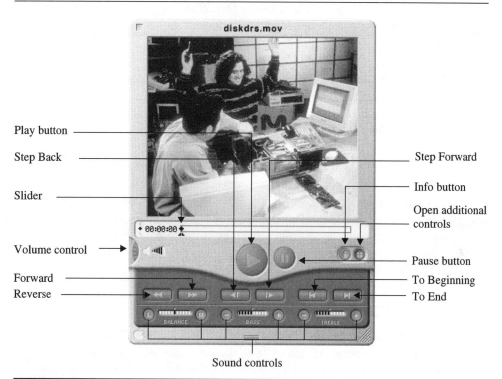

Play button

Step Back

Slider

Volume control

Forward

Reverse

Step Forward

Info button

Open additional controls

Pause button

To Beginning

To End

Sound controls

FIGURE 13-2   The QuickTime Player interface is a little like a VCR, but with a bunch of other little features.

and Fast Forward buttons. You'll also find a slider bar that shows the progress of the movie as it's playing. Grab the slider and drag it back, and you can play part or all of your movie again. You'll also find you have control over the volume by dragging the little volume wheel up and down with the mouse.

Select the Movie menu (from the menu bar) and you can choose the size at which your movie will display. Movies generally open at their optimum size for quality viewing. If you'd like to see the movie a little larger, you can choose Movie I Double Size. The quality of the video won't be as good (it'll most likely appear more "pixelated" or jagged) but it'll be larger. The further back you sit from your monitor, the better it will look.

You can also get some information about the movie—click the Info button to see the Info window. Here, you can find out about the different audio and video tracks in the movie and view other relevant information.

13

NOTE *There are three kinds of tracks that a QuickTime movie can have: video, audio, and text. Each track is a separate line of data in the movie document that is synchronized with the others. The digital data stored in the video and audio tracks is compressed because video and audio, without compression, require huge amounts of storage. These compression schemes are called codecs, which stands for "compressor/decompressor." The better the codecs, the better the quality of a QuickTime movie file and the smaller and more transportable the movie will be.*

By default, you may not be seeing all of the controls in the QuickTime Player window. That's because some of them—that panel of reverse and forward, step (frame-by-frame) controls, and sound controls—are hidden when you open the QuickTime window. Toward the bottom right of the display window is a small button with four little dots on it—that's the button you use to reveal the additional controls. Click it to get access to more options. (See Figure 13-2 to figure out those buttons.)

QuickTime Player Favorites

Down at the bottom of the QuickTime Player is a little "drawer" of sorts—you can click on the four little lines in the middle of the drawer, then drag down to open it up. There you'll find your QuickTime Player Favorites—movies or Internet locations you can access to view QuickTime over the Web. With the push toward QuickTime "streaming" technology, Apple has made it possible to view things like newscasts, music videos, and live events over the Internet, just using the QuickTime Player.

With the Favorites drawer open, you can single-click one of the favorites to load it into the QuickTime Player. If it's an Internet site (as most of the pre-saved favorites are) then you'll probably need to have your Internet connection active (or set to automatically connect) before the movie can be played in the viewer. Eventually, depending on the speed of your connection, you'll see a new movie appear in the window. It may be a streaming video, or it may be a special screen that incorporates Macromedia Flash technology. In this case, you can actually click in the movie window to view different types of content.

You can save your own movies as favorites, if you like. Usually, you open movies using the File | Open command or by double-clicking a movie in the Finder. If you'd like to open a movie from the Favorites drawer, you'll need to add it first. With the movie open in QuickTime Player, choose Favorites | Add Favorite. Now, a small icon appears in the Favorites drawer that represents your newly added movie file. When you return to QuickTime Player, you can open the drawer and click that movie again to add it.

You can do this with streaming movies over the Internet, too. If you find one you like, just add it to the Favorites. Now you can single-click it in the Favorites drawer anytime you get the urge. You'll be connected to that Internet site and the movie will play—if it's still out there.

To edit your favorites, choose Favorites | Organize Favorites from the menu. Now you'll see a dialog box that lets you scroll through and select the favorites you've saved (along with those that were pre-saved by Apple). Select a favorite, then click Delete to remove it from the drawer or click Rename to give it a new name. Click Done when you're finished with your editing.

13

You can also drag favorites from the Favorites drawer to the Finder's Trash icon to delete them. Likewise, you can drag movie icons from the Finder to an open slot in the Favorites drawer to add them as favorites.

View a Streaming Movie

You've actually already seen one way to view a streaming movie—by selecting one of the brand-name favorites in the Favorites drawer, you'll often be connected over your Internet connection to a streaming movie site, then the movie will appear in your QuickTime Player window.

 Again, don't forget that a streaming movie doesn't necessarily have video. You can listen to National Public Radio (NPR), for instance, using one of the QuickTime Player's favorites. The live broadcast is sent as a streaming "movie" (since that's what all QuickTime media is called) but it only has an audio component. You'll just hear it—you won't see any video in the Player.

There are other ways to viewing streaming movies, though. The most common way is to locate a streaming QuickTime *feed* somewhere on the Web using your Web browser application. You'll click a link or a button on a Web page that begins the streaming movie. When you do that, QuickTime Player is often automatically launched (or switched to if it's already running) and the streaming movie appears. You might see indications of the streaming process before the movie actually starts—QuickTime Player gives you messages to show what's happening, like "Connecting," "Negotiating," and "Buffering." Those are all indications that your streaming movie is being loaded over the Internet and preparing to play.

Your streaming movie experience may be a little different than playing a movie. First, you'll probably notice that your streaming movie is lower quality than a typical QuickTime movie you play from your hard disk or a CD-ROM. Why is that? Because the data has to be sent in *real-time* over the Internet. Real time means it's played almost as it arrives, to give you a seamless viewing experience. Good quality QuickTime movies need a lot of data to flash up a pretty picture 15-30 times per second, and many Internet connections can't handle that sort of demand. So, picture size and quality are compromised in order to allow you to see *something* in your QuickTime Player. The slower your Internet connection (and the slower the Internet server computer that's sending the movie data) the worse the picture quality. That's one good reason to get a cable modem or special DSL access from the phone company! (See Chapter 20 for more on high-speed access.)

The second thing that's a little weird about streaming video is the way fast forward and rewind work. Usually, a regular hard disk or CD-ROM movie allows you to flip through each frame or use the fast forward/rewind buttons to shuttle through the movie just like a VCR does. With a streaming movie, though, things don't work that way. You can often go to a different section of the movie, but you generally do this by moving the slider bar in the QuickTime Player. Then, the connection has to be renegotiated (you'll see those messages again) before the movie can begin playing in its new spot.

If the streaming movie you're watching is a *live event* or *live broadcast,* then you obviously can't fast forward or move to a later part of the movie, since it hasn't happened yet! With live broadcasts you also generally can't pause the movie and return to the same spot—when you click Play again, you'll see the connection negotiated and you'll start at the current spot in the live broadcast. In other streaming movies, you can pause and play again at the same spot.

View a QuickTime VR Movie

QuickTime VR movies—often called *panoramas*—have slightly different controls since you're supposed to "look around" and "move through" a QuickTime VR movie (see Figure 13-3).

You don't "play" a QuickTime VR movie—you manipulate it. Point the mouse at the video image. The cursor you see will tell you what to do next. If you see a little circle that looks sort of like a dartboard, hold down the trackpad button, then move in any direction to explore the 360 degrees of the panorama. (In most QuickTime VR movies you can spin all the way around, but can only tilt up or down about 10–20 degrees.) While you're holding down the trackpad button, the cursor changes to an arrow that points in the direction you're scrolling the panorama. The closer to the edge of the image you get, the faster you scroll.

If you move the mouse pointer around (without holding down the trackpad button) and your cursor changes to a hand pointing at a globe, that's a *hot spot.* Click there once and release the trackpad button and another node of the VR

13

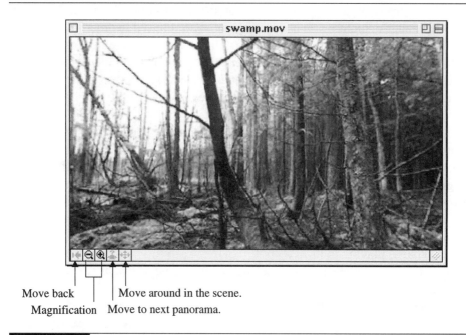

Move back
Magnification   Move to next panorama.
Move around in the scene.

FIGURE 13-3   QuickTime VR works a little like a video game, allowing you to "move around" within the movie.

movie loads—you move to another part of the image where you'll have another 360-degree panorama to enjoy.

The controls at the bottom of a VR movie screen really just allow you to magnify or widen your view of the panorama. You can also accomplish this with the keyboard. Hold down the SHIFT key to magnify; hold down CTRL to pull back and see more of the panorama.

QuickTime Web Browser Plug-in

Along with the QuickTime Player comes the QuickTime plug-in, an addition to Web browsers that allows them to display QuickTime movies directly within the Web browser's document window. You'll notice that the controls are pretty much the same whether you're viewing a movie with QuickTime Player (playing from your hard disk) or with a Web browser (playing across the Internet).

QuickTime movies must be embedded in the Web page for them to appear in the browser—otherwise they're downloaded to your iBook first, and you view them in the QuickTime Player. If they're embedded in the page with special HTML codes, the movie, QuickTime VR, or QuickTime audio movie plays from within the browser screen itself. This works great for streaming QuickTime, which allows you to watch a movie *while* it is being transmitted over the Internet.

NOTE   *If QuickTime movies aren't displaying correctly, the QuickTime plug-in may not be in the right place. It should be stored in the Plug-ins subfolder found in your Web browser's folder. If it's not there, do a quick Sherlock search for QuickTime Plugin, then copy a version of the file to the Plug-ins folder.*

If you've upgraded to QuickTime Pro, you'll be given a few other options with the plug-in, including the ability to save movies directly from Web pages. Click and hold the trackpad button on an embedded QuickTime movie (or CTRL-click the movie) and a pop-up menu appears. Choose Save As to save the movie to your iBook's hard disk. Then you're free to view it in the QuickTime Player.

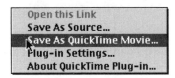

PictureViewer and Images

The PictureViewer is a small utility program that uses QuickTime's ability to work with various digital image file formats. Like movies, sounds, and other document types, there are many different types of digital images floating around in the computing world. They've been created in different programs, on different types of computers, and following differing standards. So how can you possibly work with all of them?

Well, there's a lot of translation that needs to happen. At its most basic, the PictureViewer simply displays images onscreen and allows you to view them. You can do some very basic manipulation, but you can't save the images unless you have QuickTime Pro, so there isn't much point. In its basic form, PictureViewer is a convenient tool for examining images.

View Images

To load an image into the PictureViewer, you can usually either double-click the image file, drag-and-drop the image document on the PictureViewer icon, or choose File | Open from within PictureViewer.

13

If the image isn't immediately opened in PictureViewer or in another application or utility, the Mac OS may not know which application to use. You can pick PictureViewer from the list and it will most often load the image.

Once you have the image open in PictureViewer, you can change the size at which the image is displayed by selecting one of these commands: Image | Half Size, Image | Normal Size, Image | Double Size, or Image | Fill Screen. You can also rotate the image by choosing Image | Rotate Left or Image | Rotate Right, or you can flip the image by choosing Image | Flip Horizontal or Image | Flip Vertical. These commands help you when viewing an image—if you happen to get your hands on an image that's been scanned, downloaded, or saved "sideways," then you can flip it accordingly to see the full image.

You can also make some changes using the trackpad and modifier keys:

- Drag the bottom-right corner to resize the image.

- Click SHIFT and drag to resize the image with different proportions.

- Click SHIFT-OPTION and drag to resize the image in increments of 12.5%, 25%, 50%, and 75%. You can also hold down SHIFT-OPTION and drag all the way out to return the image to its original size.

Image Format

If you're working with an image from a digital camera, one that's been scanned into a computer, or one that's been created in a high-end graphics application, the big question is: What format is it saved in? There is no single standard for digital images, although there are a handful of common ones.

In order for different types of applications and different types of computers to be able to read and display these image files, we need some standard formats. QuickTime's PictureViewer, for instance, can read many popular formats, as shown in the following table:

Format	Extension	Description
BMP	.bmp	The Microsoft Windows "bitmap" graphics format, the native format for Windows-based computers.
GIF	.gif	Graphics Interchange Format, originally developed by CompuServe. This format is popular for non-photographic images (like buttons, arrows, and stylized text) that are created for the World Wide Web.

Format	Extension	Description
JPEG	.jpg	Joint Photographic Experts Group format, developed by the group of the same name. This one is used on the World Wide Web for photographic images because it offers high-quality images with lots of color information, and it compresses into small files that don't take up a lot of storage space on hard drives.
PICT	.pic, .pict	Macintosh Picture file, the native format for Mac OS. When you take a screenshot (⌘-SHIFT-3), or copy and paste images, this is the format that results. Many graphics programs can save files to PICT format and exchange them.
PNG	.png	Portable Network Graphic, a file format designed to replace the GIF format for Web development because GIF relies on patented technology. PNG is gaining some popularity, but GIF remains very popular.
QuickTime Image	.qif	QuickTime image format, best used for editing frames within QuickTime movies.
TIFF	.tiff, .tif	Tagged Interchange File Format, used extensively in publishing. This high-quality format creates very large files that take quite a bit of storage space but maintain clean scanned and edited images.

One way to identify the different sorts of images is to look at the filename's extension, especially if you've downloaded the images from the Internet or otherwise transferred them from non-Macintosh computers. Unix and Windows both deal heavily in these filename conventions that help each program figure out what format a particular file is using.

Save Images

If you've upgraded to QuickTime Pro, then the PictureViewer Pro is capable of saving files to a number of different formats, effectively working as a file format translator. Once you have an image loaded in PictureViewer in any of the listed formats, you can save it as a BMP, PICT, PCX, QuickTime image, or Photoshop image file. Here's how:

1. Choose File | Export.

2. In the Save As dialog box, choose the file format from the Type menu.

3. Click OK and your image is saved.

13

Notice that PictureViewer will automatically append a filename extension to the file's name, making it easier to transfer this file between computing types (from Macs to Unix or Windows, for instance).

QuickTime Player Pro: Edit Movies and Sound

If you've upgraded to QuickTime Pro, you also have QuickTime Player Pro capabilities at your disposal. QuickTime Player Pro is a mini-recording studio of sorts, allowing you to edit movies, make changes to the compression schemes, layer in new audio tracks, and much more.

Like the PictureViewer, the QuickTime Player can read and play a number of different file types. Likewise, QuickTime Player Pro can save movies in a number of different formats, effectively serving as a translator between different movie file formats. The QuickTime Player allows you to cut and paste movies, record audio, and more.

Movie Types

The first thing you might want to do is translate to and from the QuickTime movie format. Again, there are a number of popular formats used by different types of computers and different applications that deal with digital movies. Here are a few that QuickTime can translate and that QuickTime Player can read directly:

Format	Extension	Description
MPEG	.mpg, .mpeg	Motion Picture Experts Group, a standard in digital video editing that rivals QuickTime for popularity. It's used in a variety of situations including multimedia CD-ROMs and on the Web.

Format	Extension	Description
AVI	.avi	Audio/Video Interleave, the Microsoft Windows standard. Popular on the Internet and some CDs, especially those designed more exclusively for Windows users.
DV	.dv	A standard for storing and transmitting digital video between DV camcorders and computers. QuickTime can work directly with these files, both inputting and outputting in DV so that QuickTime Player and other QuickTime applications are able to edit DV video easily.

Sound File Formats

QuickTime Player can also import and work with sound files as well, whether it's to store the sound as its own audio-only QuickTime movie or to integrate the sound into an existing QuickTime movie as an audio track. To open a sound, just choose File | Open, then look for the sound file. Select it in the Open dialog box and the Open button changes to Convert if it's a sound format that QuickTime recognizes. Click Convert and the sound file appears in the QuickTime Player.

How to ... Build Your Own Video

Are you an artist or cartoonist? You can create a QuickTime movie from a series of images you've created in another program:

1. If you have a series of images, give them the same name with a number appended to the end, like image1, image2, image3.

2. In QuickTime Player, choose File | Open Image Sequence.

3. In the Open dialog box, choose one of the numbered images.

4. The Image Sequence Settings dialog box appears. Choose the number of seconds per frame from the menu to determine how long each image should stay onscreen. Then click OK.

The images appear in the form of a QuickTime movie.

13

Since sound files don't have a video component, nothing shows up but the controls and slider bar.

Which sound files does QuickTime deal with? There are a number of sound files out there on the Internet and elsewhere, including some that can be translated using special utilities available for the Mac. QuickTime handles the following sound file formats:

Format	Extension	Description
AIFF	.aiff	Apple's Audio Interchange File Format is an older standard that offers decent sound, but isn't as compressible or as high-quality as more recent standards.
AU	.au	Also know as the μlaw format. This popular format was originally used by Sun and Next Computer systems. It's a common, low-quality format used on the Web often.
WAV	.wav	This format is native to Microsoft Windows and very popular among PCs and on the Internet. It offers decent quality and can be compressed with many of QuickTime's codecs.
MPEG	.mpeg	Both the MPEG audio and video formats set the standards in multimedia, especially in consumer applications like DVD-video and high-quality audio. MPEG Level II is a popular standard for recording sounds to your own hard drive; MPEG Level III offers FM radio–to-CD quality audio that can be downloaded over the Internet.

If you plan to save audio that you're creating yourself, you'll probably want to choose either AIFF or MPEG, although you can also save audio tracks as QuickTime movies if you like. If you plan to send your sounds to a Windows user, then WAV is the best way to go.

Edit Video

Although QuickTime Player doesn't really offer the highest forms of editing, programs exist—like Apple's Final Cut, Adobe Premiere, or Macromedia's Director—that give you amazing control over the fades, wipes, effects, sound synchronization, and similar components of a good movie.

With QuickTime Player, it's more like cut and paste. You can still create some interesting effects, though, and have fun doing it.

Say you've got two movies and you want to add part of one movie into the middle of another movie. That's easily done:

1. In QuickTime Player, select portions of a movie by moving the small selection triangles at the bottom of the movie window (right below the slider bar). If you want to select the entire movie, choose Edit | Select All.

2. For minor corrections to your selection, click one of the selection triangles, then tap the left or right arrow keys.

3. Now, select Edit | Cut or Edit | Copy (if you don't want to cut the selection from the original movie).

4. To paste the selection into the other movie, choose the point on the slider bar (by moving the diamond selector or clicking the slider bar once) where you want the selection to enter the first movie. Then, choose Edit | Paste. The selected part of the first movie is now part of the second movie. You might notice that this works best, by the way, when the movies have the same-sized video image.

If you'd like to trim a movie down a bit, you can do that, too. Use the slider and the SHIFT key (or just drag the little selection triangles) to select the section of the movie that you want to *keep*—it should be the part that's highlighted. Now, hold down the OPTION key as you select the Edit menu. You'll see a new command, called Trim. Select that and the highlighted segment becomes the whole movie.

Work with Tracks

13

A QuickTime movie can be composed of different tracks—one or more video tracks, one or more audio tracks, and a text track. Each track needs to be added to the movie separately, and it's pretty easy to do.

Sound Track

Let's say you want to add an audio track to an existing QuickTime movie. Here's what you should do:

1. Load the audio file so that it becomes a QuickTime movie of its own.

2. It's not absolutely necessary, but your audio track should probably be about the same length as the video track that you're adding it to. You can check by making sure the audio movie is selected, then choose Movie | Get Info. In the Info box, choose the track from the left-side menu, and General from the right-side menu. You'll see the duration of the track. Check this against the entry for the Video track in the other movie file.

3. Select the portion of the audio track you want to add to the movie by holding down the SHIFT key while you drag the slider. If you want to select the entire track, choose Edit | Select All.

4. Choose Edit | Copy to copy the track.

5. Click the window of the movie that has your video track to bring it to the front, then hold down the OPTION key as you choose the Edit menu.

6. A new command, Add, appears. Select it.

That's it—the sound selection is added as a new sound track for this particular movie. You can check to make sure in the Get Info window for the movie—you should see both tracks in the left-side menu.

Text Track

QuickTime Movies can handle a little text track—formatted text can be cut and pasted as a new track that appears at the bottom of the screen. It can be used for credits, closed captioning, or whatever you think is useful. Here's how:

1. In any program that allows you to type and format text, create the text you want to add as a text track.

2. Select the text and choose Edit | Copy.

3. In QuickTime Player, select the movie to which you want to add the text track.

4. Hold down the OPTION key and select the Edit menu.

5. Select the Add command.

Now the text will appear at the bottom of the movie screen. If you'd like to place the text at a certain place in the movie, move the slider bar to that portion of the movie first, then select the Edit | Add command while holding down the OPTION key.

Add Scaled

What if you need the track you're adding to fill a certain amount of time? There's a slightly different Add command for that. Here's how you do it:

1. Select the audio, text, or other data you plan to add to the movie.

2. Now, in the target movie's window, use the slider or the selection triangles to select the amount of time you want the new track to fill.

3. Hold down the OPTION and SHIFT keys as you access the Edit menu.

4. You'll see a new command, Add Scaled. Select that command.

Now your new track fills the allotted time. If it's text, then it'll just stay at the bottom of the window for the time allotted. If you add audio at a scaled rate,

13

realize that the audio will be sped up or slowed down to fit the scale that you've chosen. If you take a sound clip that's half as long as you scale it, the audio is going to sound very odd since it'll be slowed way down.

Extract, Delete, Enable

Once you have a track in your movie, you can do a few more things with it—you can extract, delete, or enable/disable the track. Use these commands in the Edit menu:

- **Extract** Allows you to pull an individual track out of a movie file and save it as its own movie file or export it as a different kind of multimedia file.

- **Delete** Allows you to do away with the track.

- **Enable** Allows you to enable or disable the track, but leave it in the movie file.

When you choose a command, you'll see a dialog box that allows you to select the track you want to affect. Click OK in the dialog box and the command is performed.

Saving the Movie

When you're ready to save the movie, you may have to make some choices first. If you want to simply update the movie you've made changes to, choose File | Save. If you want to change the name and create a new movie with your changes (a good idea so that you don't overwrite the original), choose File | Save As. In the Save As dialog box, you'll need to find a folder to store the movie in and give it a new name. You'll also choose from one of two options:

- **Save Normally** Creates a dependency on the original movie, which means the original movie needs to be on the same hard disk as this version of the movie in order for it to work correctly.

- **Make Movie Self-Contained** Saves the movie as a completely new movie file, allowing you to move it to another computer and use it. This makes for a much larger file (since it includes all of the movie data needed to play the movie), but this way you don't have to remember to copy the other files that this movie is dependent upon.

When you've made your choice, click Save to save the file.

Export Video or Sound

Once you have a movie open in the QuickTime Player, you can export the video, audio, or both to other file formats. This is actually one of the more common uses for QuickTime Player at the hobbyist level of audio and video production. QuickTime Player allows you to deal with many different types of audio and video, as do other applications based on QuickTime. Then you can feed these exported files into other applications that deal with them on a more sophisticated level.

To do this, choose File | Export. The Export dialog box appears. Here you'll name the file, find a place to store it, then choose how you'd like it saved. You have three basic categories of choices:

- **Export to Image File**   This allows you to export the frame of the movie currently being shown in QuickTime Player as an image. Your choices are Movie To BMP, Movie to Image Sequence, or Movie To Picture (PICT).

- **Export to Movie File**   This exports the entire movie to another movie format, including Movie to AVI (Microsoft Windows' primary format), Movie To DV Stream (for sending to digital cameras), Movie to FLC (to save as a FLI/FLC animation), Movie to Hinted Movie (to create a movie suitable for QuickTime streaming), or Movie To QuickTime Movie.

- **Export to a Sound File**   This takes the audio track of the movie and stores it in the sound format of your choice. The sound choices include Sound To AIFF, Sound To System 7 Sound, Sound To Wave, and Sound to μLaw.

After you've chosen the type of export you plan to perform, you can choose some options from the Use menu. These options generally determine how the file is going to be compressed, making it smaller (for one) and suitable for a variety of different purposes.

The Use menu changes according to the type of file you're exporting to. Here are some of the options you'll find, based on the type of export you're trying to accomplish:

- **Movie to AVI**   Choose the type of compressor to use depending on where the AVI movie is going to be run from by your user. In most cases, 2x CD-ROM should be fine.

13

- **Movie to BMP**   The compressor is BMP, but you can choose the number of colors and the quality of image. The fewer colors and lower the quality, the smaller the resulting file will be.

- **Movie to DV Stream**   In this one, you just pick your local TV format, PAL or NTSC, and the MHz level. NTSC is standard in the U.S. and Japan; PAL is used for cameras in Europe.

- **Movie to FLC**   For animations, you select the type of colors and the frames per second of the animation.

- **Movie to Image Sequence**   Choose the type of movie images you want to create and the frames per second that should be exported.

- **Movie to Picture**   Photo JPEG is appropriate if you want the image compressed, or choose Uncompressed for the best quality. Choose PNG to use the Portable Network Graphic format for Web graphics.

All of the sound exporting options also allow you to choose 8-bit or 16-bit sound (8-bit is lower quality but takes up less storage space), and mono or stereo (mono takes up less storage space). An 8-bit mono sound is somewhere around the quality of AM radio, while a 16-bit stereo sound file can approach CD quality, depending on the file format and compressor used.

You can also use the Options button to set more advanced options for each of your Export file types. Choose the type from the Export menu, then click the Options button to choose a particular compressor and set other options. This gets a bit complicated, but you can learn more about the various options by selecting Help | On-line QuickTime Player Help. This loads Apple's latest QuickTime Help files in your Web browser (you'll need an active Internet connection.)

Play Audio CDs

Your iBook comes with a special AppleCD Audio Player application that allows you to play Audio CDs using the CD-ROM drive that's built-in. The AppleCD Audio Player works a lot like a home CD player, allowing you to access individual tracks of an audio CD, name the tracks, program it to play songs out of order and so on. If you're into CD music at all, you'll enjoy this program.

Launch AppleCD Audio Player

To launch the AppleCD Audio Player, choose it from the Apple menu. If you don't find it there, it's in the Applications folder on your hard disk. You'll see the player's interface appear on your iBook's screen. Now, pop an audio CD in the CD-ROM drive if you don't already have one in there. Figure 13-4 shows the AppleCD Audio Player.

> **TIP** *You'll probably want to hook up headphones to your iBook for best sound—the built-in speaker doesn't offer the best listening experience. You can also connect powered speakers to the iBook's headphone jack (get computer-style speakers for magnetic shielding). See Chapter 23 for more on upgrading your iBook.*

You'll note that many of the controls are already familiar to a CD hound like yourself—you have all the usual suspects like Play/Pause (the same button), Stop, Eject, Forward, Backward, and so on. (The volume slider on the edge just changes the volume on the CD, not the system volume, which you can change from the Sound control panel or the control strip's Sound module.)

The player also has some familiar program buttons, like Shuffle, which randomly switches between tracks on the CD. Prog can be used to program the playlist—you'll see that in a minute.

FIGURE 13-4   The AppleCD Audio Player lets you control audio CDs in your iBook's CD-ROM drive.

Customize Tracks and the Playlist

To see details on each track, click the little triangle to reveal more information about the disk. Here you can do some interesting things. For one, you can actually double-click on the name of the CD (currently "Audio CD") and give it a name. Click outside the name to save your editing. You can do the same thing for each individual track—double-click its name, then start editing (see Figure 13-5).

You may have already guessed that you can't actually save data to a CD, since it's not designed to store computer data (and it's read-only, anyway, like all CDs in your iBook's CD drive). Good call. But what you may not know is that it doesn't matter, since these changes are actually stored in your iBook's System Folder, in the

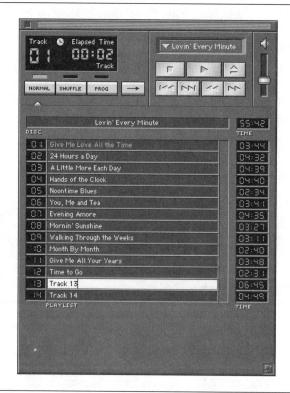

FIGURE 13-5 You can edit the name of your CD and each audio track.

Preference folder. The iBook can tell which CD you pop in, and will automatically load the name and tracks correctly the next time you go to listen to it.

But wait, there's more! If you'd like to customize the way your CD is played, you can do that, too. Select the Prog button and a new panel—the Playlist—appears. You can drag tracks from the left side (the correct order of the CD) to the Playlist side to customize how the CD is played. Want to play the same track three times in a row? Just drag it to three of the slots. Drag others around on the Playlist, too—there's a little arrow that appears next to the Playlist to show you where a song will be placed. Release the trackpad button and it's put there in order.

Now, click the Play button and listen to your newly customized CD!

NOTE

There's an option in the Options menu called AutoPlay that allows your audio CDs to play automatically when you pop them in the drawer. If you like that idea, make sure there's a check mark next to AutoPlay. The next time you insert an audio CD, it will begin playing, even if the AppleCD Audio Player isn't active.

Chapter 14

Track Your Schedule and Contacts

How to...

- Schedule appointments on your calendar
- Deal with your To Do's
- Jot down quick reminders
- Track your contacts
- Sync your iBook with a Palm OS handheld computer
- Install Palm applications

The iBook ships with the Palm Desktop, an application from 3Com that allows a Palm Pilot or Palm OS handheld computer to synchronize data with a Macintosh computer. Of course, the iBook doesn't come with a Palm Pilot (don't I wish), but the Palm Desktop is perfectly functional with or without a Palm Pilot. On its own, the Palm Desktop is a complete calendar and contract manager, allowing you to track appointments, To Do lists, notes, and information about people you know in your work or personal life.

NOTE   *A Palm Pilot is a popular handheld computer made by 3Com, Inc.'s Palm Computing division. 3Com, Inc. is a not particularly popular company in San Francisco because it bought the rights to rename the venerable and already interestingly-named Candlestick Park. (Other companies also make handheld computers that run the Palm OS, including IBM's Workpad and the Mindspring Visor. The Palm Desktop software works with those handheld computers, too.)*

In fact, Palm Desktop is a good program precisely because Apple wrote it—at least, initially. When it was clear that the Palm handheld computer was going to be popular with Mac users, 3Com bought Claris Organizer, a datebook and contact manager program, from Apple. (Claris was a subsidiary company of Apple before it was folded back into Apple in early 1998. The Claris people are the same folks who wrote AppleWorks, which was once called ClarisWorks.) Using Claris Organizer as a basis, the Palm Computing/3Com folks wrote the new Palm Desktop software that not only tracks appointments and contacts, but also syncs up nicely with a Palm handheld computer. Then, even cooler, they released the software for free and allowed Apple to bundle it on the iBook.

Get Started with Palm Desktop

14

Palm Desktop isn't installed initially on your iBook, although the software is already there on your hard disk. In the Applications folder, open the Palm Desktop folder and double-click the Palm Desktop Installer. This will step you through the installation process. At the end of the installation, you'll enter a name to associate with Palm Desktop's original data file when it first launches. Enter a name and click Continue.

After you enter a name, you can choose whether or not to set up HotSync. If you click Setup Now, you'll be asked to choose the type of connection for your Palm OS handheld's connection—with the iBook, you're likely to use a USB connection for your Palm OS handheld. (You'll need a special USB connection kit, which is a separate purchase for your Palm device.) To set up HotSync later, click Setup Later.

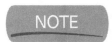 *Setting up HotSync is discussed in more detail later in the section "Synchronize with a Palm Device."*

The Palm Desktop adds some extensions and control panels, so you'll need to restart your iBook after it's installed.

Instant Palm Desktop Menu

Once Palm Desktop is installed (and your iBook has been restarted after the installation), you'll see something different about your iBook's desktop. It will likely have a small icon up in the corner of the menu bar, next to the clock. This is the Instant Palm Desktop menu, a special menu that allows you to quickly access the Palm Desktop software and the HotSync capabilities for getting your iBook to talk to a Palm Pilot.

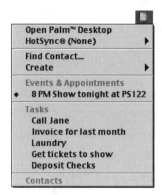

The menu also has a Create menu, which allows you to select individual items you'd like to create within Palm Desktop. And, if you have anything that's currently scheduled or due, you can see those things quickly by looking at the menu instead of opening up or switching to the Palm Desktop software.

If you need to launch Palm Desktop, switch to it if it's already open, or just quickly check your current tasks and appointments, pull down this menu. It's a lot easier than finding the Palm Desktop icon and launching the program.

If you'd like more information about a particular task or appointment that's listed, select it in the menu. A dialog box will appear for that particular item, with the complete text of the item, the date, times, and whether or not an alarm is set. You can change things in the dialog box or just click OK to dismiss it.

The Palm Desktop Interface

Once you've gotten the Palm Desktop launched or switched to, you'll see a more complete application ready for just about any data you'd like to organize. The nerve center of the Palm Desktop software is its toolbar, which gives you quick access to just about every major command available in the software.

NOTE   *You can use the trackpad to point at a button in the toolbar if you don't know what it does. Its name will appear just below the button. If you don't see the name, click the disclosure triangle at the far-left end of the toolbar so that it's pointing down. Now you'll be able to see the names of buttons.*

As you can see, the toolbar allows you to accomplish quite a lot without ever touching a menu. Just aim your mouse pointer at a button and click it to execute that command.

By default, you'll also see the calendar window, and you'll likely keep it up most of the time, since it can be tucked behind other windows (like the Task List, Note List, and Contact List), always hanging out there in the background.

To quit the Palm Desktop, choose File | Quit. Even though the Palm Desktop quits, the Instant Palm Desktop menu will always stay on the menu bar—it's actually a Mac OS system extension.

14

Manage Appointments, Events, and Tasks

Since the Calendar is what you'll see first in the Palm Desktop interface, let's go ahead and talk about it first. The Calendar allows you to manage three different things—appointments, event banners, and tasks. You can also manage these things from three different views—Daily, Weekly and Monthly. Each gives you a different overview of the items you've scheduled. Figure 14-1 shows the daily calendar; Figure 14-2 show the weekly calendar; Figure 14-3 shows the monthly calendar.

To change the view, click the tab on the far-right side of the Calendar window. This immediately switches you between different views. If you're currently viewing a weekly or monthly view, you can switch to a daily view by double-clicking a date (the actual number) in the calendar.

As you can see, the different views are useful for different reasons. Daily lets you jump into today (or some day in the future) and get an exact idea of all the appointments you have and the tasks that need to happen. The Weekly view gives you a sense of what's going on over a five-day period, especially when it comes to appointments. The Monthly view is simply useful for knowing roughly what's going on at some point in the month and just generally what a busy person you are.

FIGURE 14-1   The Daily calendar gives you a look at the day's appointments and tasks.

FIGURE 14-2   The Weekly calendar is good for getting a handle on your immediate tasks.

FIGURE 14-3   The Monthly calendar shows you an entire month at a glance.

14

The toolbar has buttons for Go To Date and Go To Today, if you'd like to quickly get to a particular date on the calendar.

The Calendar views can be handy not just for getting a sense of what you need to do, but also for creating events and moving things around. For instance, most items on your calendar will respond to drag-and-drop—just point at an item and hold down the trackpad button. The mouse pointer should turn into a fist. Now, drag the item to the time or date where you'd prefer to see it and release the trackpad button. It's moved.

 If you'd like to see just the appointments or just the tasks in a particular view, open the View menu and select Calendar, then choose either Show Appointments or Show Tasks. The Show command that you select will have its check mark (in the menu) removed and those items will no longer be shown. To see them again, return to the command and select it to replace its check mark. The items reappear in the calendar.

Before you can move events around, though, you'll probably need to create some.

Create an Appointment

To create an appointment you can do a number of different things, depending on where you are in the Calendar view (or even if you're not looking at the calendar):

- From anywhere, pull down the Instant Palm Desktop menu and choose Appointment from the Create menu.

- From within the Palm Desktop software, click the Create Appointment button in the toolbar.

- On a Monthly view, double-click the box that represents the day on which you'd like to set the appointment. In the dialog box, select Appointment and click OK.

- On a Weekly or Daily view, point at the start time within the day's schedule area and hold down the trackpad button while dragging to create the new appointment. If you aim well, you can create the appointment for the correct start and end time. You can then begin typing the text for your appointment. When you're done, click elsewhere on the calendar.

In all but the last case, you'll see the Appointment dialog box, where you can enter the text for your appointment, set the date and time, set an alarm, and choose categories for the appointment.

Choose the date from the pop-up calendar.

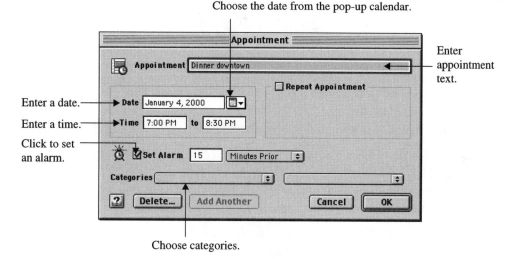

Enter a date.

Enter a time.

Click to set an alarm.

Enter appointment text.

Choose categories.

> NOTE
>
> *In Weekly or Daily view you can double-click an appointment to see its dialog box, which you'll need to do if you want to set an alarm or the categories for the appointment. Likewise, you can double-click any existing appointment to view its dialog box.*

To move between each element in the Appointment dialog box, press the TAB key. Here's how each part of the dialog box works:

■ **Appointment**   In the Appointment entry box, enter the text that describes the appointment. It can be reasonably long, if you like, but if you have extensive notes that relate to the appointment, those are best stored as a separate note, which I'll describe a little later in this chapter.

■ **Date**   Either enter a date in the Date entry box, or you can choose one from the Calendar pop-up menu. Select the menu and you'll see a small calendar. You can use the arrows to move between the months, then click the particular date on which you'd like to set this appointment.

14

- **Time**   Enter the beginning time and the ending time in the entry boxes. Note that when you enter a beginning time and press TAB, the ending time is switched to one hour after the beginning time automatically. This may not be what you want, but it's helpful when it's right.

- **Set Alarm**   Check this box if you want to be reminded (by a tone and an alert box) of this appointment. Once checked, you can enter a number and then choose from the pop-up menu whether the number represents the number of minutes or hours before the appointment that the alarm should appear.

- **Categories**   You can choose a category for this appointment from the pop-up menu. If you like, in fact, you can choose two categories.

When you're done creating the appointment, you can click the OK button to dismiss the dialog box or click the Add Another button to add another appointment without getting rid of the dialog box. This clears it out and let's you create a new appointment without going to the hassle of invoking another command.

Create a Banner Event

Do you have an event that isn't quite an appointment and doesn't exactly fit the bill of a task? Then it's probably a banner event. Banner events can span one day, many days, or many weeks, if desired, and they aren't tied to a particular time. As a result, you can set an alarm for a banner event, and they don't show up in lists like tasks do.

I use banner events in two ways. The more obvious way is for vacations, trade shows, or anything that will take me a couple of days, or for events that take one day but are special. With a banner event, you'll see immediately when you have a trip scheduled or a birthday or anniversary coming up, especially in Weekly and Monthly views.

The other way I use them is to track project deadlines. Since I'm a writer (by trade if not by calling), a lot of what I deal with are chapters. I'll create banner

Set a Repeating Appointment

If you have an appointment that needs to repeat on a regular basis, you can set that in the Appointment dialog box. (If you're not currently viewing the particular appointment's dialog box, double-click the appointment in the calendar.) To set a repeating appointment, place a check mark next to Repeat Appointment in the Appointment dialog box. (So far, it ain't brain surgery.)

Next, you'll see a pop-up menu appear. Select from that pop-up menu how often you'd like the appointment to repeat. If you don't see the right time frame in the menu, you can select More Choices to set the frequency yourself. In the More Choices dialog box, use the radio buttons, pop-up windows, and check boxes to determine exactly how often this appointment should occur. When you're done, click OK.

Back in the Appointment dialog box, you'll see an entry box labeled Until. Enter the date when this repeating appointment should stop repeating or choose it from the Calendar pop-up menu. Now, your repeating appointment is scheduled and added to your calendar.

14

events for each chapter and place them on the dates when they're due or when I plan to get them done. Then, when I need to reschedule (as my editors well know, this happens more often than not) I can simply drag the banner event to a new day. If things are getting tight, I can drag two or more banners to a particular day and virtually see the work starting to pile up.

In any case, creating a banner event is easy. Here are the different ways to do it:

■ From the Instant Palm Desktop menu, choose Create | Banner Event.

■ With the Palm Desktop software active, select the Create Banner Event button in the toolbar.

■ From the Palm Desktop software, choose the Create menu, then choose Banner Event.

■ From a Monthly view, double-click a day's box in Monthly view and choose Event Banner from the dialog box, then click OK.

■ In a Weekly or Daily view, double-click just above the appointment area, just below the date and day of the week.

After choosing one of these fabulous options, you'll see the Event Banner dialog box. Don't worry—this one is easy.

Enter the text for the banner.

Choose a start date.

Enter the duration of the event.

Click if this event repeats every year.

Choose categories.

In the Event Banner entry box, type the text for your banner. Then, enter a start date in the Date entry box (or choose it from the Calendar pop-up menu) for the banner. Next, enter the duration of the event if you want it to last more than one day. Choose categories for the event banner from the Categories menus, if desired.

TIP *If this is an event that repeats annually, click the Repeat Annually check box. Once it's selected, you can choose to be reminded of the event a number of days before it happens—perfect for birthdays and anniversaries.*

When you're done, click the OK button to dismiss the dialog box, or click Add Another if you'd like to create another Event Banner. When you're done, you'll see your event banner back in the Calendar window. The banner will span the relevant dates in the Monthly view, or you'll see it at the top of the window in the Weekly view or the Daily view.

Add Your Tasks

Aside from appointments and banner events, you can use the Palm Desktop to manage your tasks or To Do's. By default, your tasks appear in the calendar on the day for which the task is scheduled. Plus, tasks will be held over and shown on subsequent days if you haven't checked off the task once it's completed. If you often use Daily or Weekly views in the calendar, then you'll be able to conveniently view both your appointments and tasks from those views.

You can also manage your tasks in a special list. The list makes it easy to see all pending tasks, including those scheduled for the future. And it's a simple matter to add and delete tasks from the task list. I'll cover both ways in the following sections.

Create a Task

First, you need to create a task. You can do that in a number of ways:

- From the Instant Palm Desktop menu, choose Create | Task.

- With the Palm Desktop software active, select the Create Task button in the toolbar.

- From the Palm Desktop software, choose the Create menu, then choose Task.

- From a Monthly view, double-click a day's box in Monthly view and choose Task from the dialog box, then click OK.

- In a Weekly or Daily view, double-click in the Tasks area of the window. (In the Weekly view, this is at the bottom of the window. In the Daily view, Tasks are on the right-hand side.)

Once you've chosen to create a task, you'll see the Task dialog box. Here you'll enter the information for this particular task.

14

Here are the different items you can enter or set for your task:

■ **Task** Enter the text that describes the task.

■ **Priority** Choose a priority level. In the various task areas and the Task List, you can sort by priority so that the most important tasks appear at the top of the list.

■ **Schedule Task** If selected, the task will have a due date. If you check the box to deselect it, then the task will simply appear in your task list on the current day.

■ **Date** Enter the due date or choose it from the pop-up calendar.

■ **Carry Over After Due** If you'd like this task to continue to appear in your task areas or the Task List after its due date, select this box. Now it won't ever leave until you purposefully mark the task as done.

■ **Remind** If selected, this option will allow you to enter the number of days before the due date that the software will remind you of the task (via an alert box).

■ **Categories** If you'd like to associate particular categories with this task, select the categories from the pop-up menus.

When you're done entering the information for your task, you can click the OK button to store the task, or click the Add Another button if you'd like to continue adding tasks without dismissing the Tasks dialog box.

Manage Tasks in the Calendar

Once you've entered some tasks, you'll see them in your Calendar window. They're easier to see in the Weekly and Daily views, since those calendars have special areas for tasks. In the Monthly view, tasks appear in the same listing as appointments, below the appointments in a date box. (They have a bullet point before the task description instead of a time.)

In the Weekly and Monthly views, you can select a task and drag it to another day. This changes the start date of the task, not the due date. If you drag a task past its original due date, the due date will disappear.

 Tasks without due dates will have the date the task was created in parentheses after the task description. Task with due dates will have "due:" plus a date in those parentheses.

In the Daily view, you can't drag a task to a different day, because there aren't other days to choose from. Instead, you can drag a task to a different location in the task area if you'd like to see your tasks in a different order.

To edit a task, double-click it in any view. This brings up the Task dialog box.

In the Daily and Weekly views, you can do one other thing to a task—you can mark it as complete. When you've completed a particular task, click the small check box that precedes it in the task area. You'll see a check mark, marking that task as complete. Now it won't show up in the task area in future days' listings. (To do this in the Monthly view, double-click the task and place a check in the Completed box.)

SHORTCUT *Don't forget that your current tasks also show up in the Instant Palm Desktop menu, so you don't even have to open the Palm Desktop software in order to see what you need to accomplish for the day.*

14

Manage Tasks in the Task List

Want to see all your tasks in one place? Just click the View Task List button in the Palm Desktop toolbar or choose View | Task List from the menu. Now you'll see the Task List (see Figure 14-4).

The Task List can make it easier to view and manage your tasks all at once. It allows you to view quite a bit of information about the tasks, including the description,

	Task	Priority	Date	Categories	Completed
☐	Call Jane	Highest	January 12, 2000	None	
☐	Invoice for last month	High	January 10, 2000	None	
☐	Get tickets to show	Medium	January 10, 2000	None	
☐	Deposit Checks	Medium	January 12, 2000	None	
☐	Laundry	Medium	January 12, 2000	None	
☑	Dennis's Birthday	High	August 6, 1999	Employees	October 25, 1999
☑	Sonia's Birthday	High	November 16, 1999	Suppliers	October 25, 1999
☑	Denise's Birthday	High	November 18, 1999	Suppliers	October 25, 1999
☐	Jennifer's Birthday	High	October 13, 2001	Customers	
☑	Make another resolution list	Lowest	January 1, 2002	Personal	January 12, 2002
☐	Take car for new tires	High	January 20, 2002	Personal	
☐	Clean desk!	Medium	January 20, 2002	Personal	
☐	Prepare For Sales review meet…	Medium	January 20, 2002	Business	
☐	Call Lei	Medium	January 21, 2002	Business	
☐	Call Kathy, confirm lunch	Medium	January 23, 2002	None	
☐	Prepare For Staff meeting	Medium	January 24, 2002	Business	
☐	Jennifer's Birthday	High	October 13, 2002	Customers	
☐	Prepare For New products mee…	Medium	January 22, 2003	Business	

FIGURE 14-4 The Task List lets you manage tasks without flipping through the calendar.

priority, date, and any categories. Here are some management tasks you can accomplish in the Task List:

- To check off a completed task, click the check box at the far left of the item's row. If you check an item you haven't completed, you can click the check box again to remove your check mark.

- To edit a task, double-click it in the Task List. You'll see the Task dialog box, where you can change the description, priority, schedule, or categories for the task.

- From the View menu in the top-left corner of the Task List, you can choose to view All Tasks, this week's uncompleted tasks, or today's uncompleted tasks. You can also create your own views by selecting View | Memorize View. You'll then see a dialog box that lets you give the view a name and decide what, exactly, is memorized. Once you've created a memorized view, you can select it at any time from the View menu. (You'll want to change things around elsewhere in the Task List, as described in the next bullet points.)

■ You can sort the list by any of the columns listed. For instance, if you want to sort by date, click the heading Date in the Task List. Your list is sorted by date.

TIP *Want to move the columns around? Click-and-drag the column name to a new location in the Task List and it'll appear when you release the trackpad button.*

■ You can also use filters to help you see exactly what you need to see in the Task List. To do this, select the small triangle next to one of the column headings. In the pop-up menu, you can choose one of the filters in the menu. For instance, if you choose the Priority column's pop-up menu, you can see only tasks with the Highest priority by selecting that filter. With the Date column's pop-up menu, you can view tasks dated for the next week or for today and tomorrow, for instance. To return to the unfiltered view, choose the pop-up menu again and select No Filter.

SHORTCUT *If you've filtered like mad and you want to quickly get back to the entire list of tasks, choose the Show All button up in the top-right corner of the Task List. This will immediately do away with all filters and show you the complete list.*

■ You can create your own filters if you don't see one that meets your needs. From a column heading's pop-up menu, choose Custom Filter. You'll then see a dialog box that allows you to create a filter that will work for that column head—each dialog box is different since each column offers a different type of information.

14

NOTE *The checked column has its own Filter menu, too. You can choose that pop-up menu and select Unchecked if you'd like to see only the tasks that haven't yet been checked as completed.*

To close the Task List, just click its Close box. You can get back to it at any time through its toolbar button or the View | Task List command.

Manage Your Contacts

Aside from serving duty as your task master and datebook, the Palm Desktop can also replace that dog-eared address book you have floating around your desk...somewhere. You can create and manage individual contact records for everyone you know, then view them all at once and edit at will. If you've got a Palm OS handheld computer, you can then synchronize your contact list with the handheld so you can carry your address book with you.

Plus, contacts can be attached to Calendar items in the Palm Desktop software. If you've got an appointment with John Doe or Jill Buck, you can attach that contact to the appointment and access that person's information quickly from within the Calendar.

Create a New Contact

Before you can manage your contacts, you'll need to create some. These can be colleagues, family members, or friends.

TIP   *If you need to create colleagues or friends, you might consider getting a job, developing a profession, or joining a sports team, hobby group, or a fraternity or sorority. Creating family members is something I'll leave up to you.*

Once you have these sorts of people at your disposal, you can create a contact record within the Palm Desktop software to track them. There are, of course, a number of ways to create a contact record:

- From the Instant Palm Desktop menu, choose Create | Contact.

- From within the Palm Desktop software, click the New Contact button in the toolbar.

- In the Palm Desktop software, choose the menu command Create | Contact.

Now you're ready to enter information about your contact in the Contact dialog box.

To enter information, just begin typing. The first entry box by default is the First Name—type this person's first name, then press the TAB key. Keep entering information in each entry box. If you get to an entry box that you don't have information for or you otherwise want to skip, just press the TAB key again.

SHORTCUT   *Many items have a small triangle pop-up menu next to it. After you've entered a few contacts, you'll notice that these arrows will include the entries you've made previously. And, you'll notice a little "auto-fill" going on: As you type the first few letters of items in many fields, they will be automatically filled in with previous entries. If those entries aren't correct, just keep typing. If the auto-fill entry is correct, you just press TAB to move to the next field. This is a great way to quickly enter data that you've typed before.*

14

The Contact dialog box is divided into different sections, each of which includes different entry elements that help you enter information about this person. When you reach the end of one section (like the Name section) pressing the TAB key takes you to the first entry box in the next section. If you'd like to go directly to another section, select it with the mouse pointer and click once.

You'll also find that some of the entry options include pop-up menus. For instance, in the Phones section you can choose the type of phone number you're entering from the pop-up menu next to each entry. Options include Fax, Home, Main, Mobile, Work, and others.

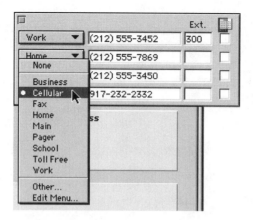

> **TIP** *You can create your own entries for these menus. Choose Other... to enter a one-time name for this menu, like "Upstate" or "Vacation home." When you choose the Other command, you'll see a dialog box that lets you enter this one-time name. If you'd like to permanently add an item to the menu, choose Edit Menu from the pop-up menu. Now you'll see the Edit Menu dialog box that lets you delete, edit, or add items to the menu.*

Now, just move through each section and add information that you have about this person. You'll find that in some of the boxes you can choose the type of information you're entering from a pop-up menu—for instance, you can choose the type of address you want to enter from a pop-up menu in one of the address sections. You don't have to enter a Work Address and Home Address (the defaults). You can choose School or Business or your can customize the menu to reflect a different type of address (like billing, shipping, vacation, or whatever you'd like to enter).

In the Other Information section, you'll see a number of Custom entry boxes. To change the name of a Custom entry box, double-click the existing name. In the dialog box, you can customize a number of features, including the name, whether or not items in the entry box are capitalized automatically, whether or not the entries typed are saved to the triangle pull-down menu, and whether or not the entry will include a button icon that runs an AppleScript when clicked. You'll notice that in the Script File menu there are a few AppleScripts that have already been set up for you.

TIP

Know something about AppleScript? If you do, you can create more scripts to associate with buttons in the Contact dialog box. Place those scripts in the Scripts folder inside the Palm folder on your hard disk and the scripts will appear in the Script File menu.

Done with all that data entry? Click the Contact dialog box's close box and the entry is saved.

View the Contact List

Once you've gotten a few contacts entered, you're ready to manage them from the Contact List. To open the Contact List, choose the View Contact List button in the toolbar or choose View | Contact List from the menu. You'll see the contact list in all its shimmering glory, as shown in Figure 14-5.

14

FIGURE 14-5 The Contact List shows you contacts and selected information about them.

Once you've got the Contact List open, there are plenty of management tasks you can perform:

- To edit a contact, double-click it in the Contact List. You'll see the Contact dialog box, where you can change the information for this contact.

- If you have a contact who has information that's similar to another contact you'd like to create, select that contact and choose Edit | Duplicate Contact. Now you can change what's different about your new contact, but leave the other information intact.

- You can sort the list by any of the columns listed. For instance, if you want to sort by company, click the heading Company in the Contact List. Your list is sorted by company.

TIP *Want to move the columns around? Click and drag the column name to a new location in the Contact List and it'll appear when you release the trackpad button.*

- You can also use filters to help you see exactly what you need to see in the Contact List. To do this, select the small triangle next to one of the column headings. In the pop-up menu, you can choose one of the filters in the menu. For instance, if you choose the Categories column's pop-up menu, you can see only contacts within your Personal category by selecting that filter. With the Company column's pop-up menu, you can view contacts who work for a particular company by selecting the company name. To return to the unfiltered view, choose the pop-up menu again and select No Filter.

SHORTCUT *If you've been filtering a bit and you want to quickly get back to the entire list of contacts, choose the Show All button up in the top-right corner of the Contact List. This will immediately do away with all filters and show you the complete list.*

- You can create your own filters if you don't see one that meets your needs. From a column heading's pop-up menu, choose Custom Filter. You'll then see a dialog box that allows you to create a filter that will work for that column head—each dialog box is different since each column offers a different type of information.

■ From the View menu you can choose All Contacts if you've been filtering and sorting. If you've created a series of filters and sorts that really tickle your fancy, you can store that view of the Contact List by selecting View | Memorize View. You'll then see a dialog box that lets you give the view a name and decide what, exactly, is memorized. Once you've created a memorized view, you can select it at any time from the View menu.

TIP *You can view different columns of information, if you'd like to. To select the columns to view, choose View | Columns. In the Columns dialog box, click an item to place or remove the check mark that denotes whether or not the item will appear in the Contact List. You can then drag items to new locations to change the order in which the columns will appear. A small number next to the check mark indicates its order (from left to right) in the Contact List.*

Attach Contacts to Items

One of the really powerful features in Palm Desktop is the ability to attach a contact to appointments, events, or tasks on your calendar. This makes it easy to associate data between the different parts of your calendar in many different ways. For instance, you can associate a contact with a particular task that involves that person, like a task you create that reminds you to call Pamela. If you attach Pamela's contact info to the task, you won't have to go digging for her number.

Attach from the Contact List

One way to attach a contact to a particular item is from within the Contact List. With the Contact List open, select the Attach menu for the contact in question (it's the file folder icon with a paperclip on it). In the menu, choose the item you'd like to attach this contact to from the Attach To menu. If you choose Existing Item from the Attach To menu, a small window opens up at the bottom of the screen.

14

```
╔═══════════ Attach Existing Item ═══════════╗
║                                          ▣  ║
║  To attach this contact to another item:    ║
║     1) Locate the other item.               ║
║     2) Drag this contact onto that item.    ║
║                                             ║
║     ┌─────────────────────────────────┐     ║
║     │▐  Nancy Eison (International Bak...│     ║
║     └─────────────────────────────────┘     ║
║                                             ║
║  [?]              [    Cancel    ]          ║
╚═════════════════════════════════════════════╝
```

You'll notice that this window is holding a little draggable version of the contact you've chosen. Now, switch to the Calendar or Task List and find the item to which you'd like to attach this contact. Once you've found it, drag the contact from its Attach Existing Item window to the event. When you drop the contact on the event, they become attached.

 ◄─── Attachment icon

Now, when you encounter that event, you can select the attachment icon to bring up a menu that allows you to view the attached contact, detach the contact, or attach it to another item.

 If you have both the Contact List and the Task List or Calendar open, you can drag a contact straight from the Contact List to the item to which you'd like to attach the contact. This attaches the contact instantly.

Auto-Attach

If you don't feel like opening the Contact List, you can attach contacts from within the Calendar or while you're creating an item. If you create an item that has part of a contact's (or more than one contact's) name in the entry, you'll see the Auto-Attachments dialog box after you've created the item. For instance, creating an appointment called "Lunch with Bob" will bring up the Auto-Attachments dialog box, complete with listings of contacts that may fit the description.

If one of the contacts matches, you can click that contact to place a check mark, then click the Attach button in the dialog box. That attaches the contact to the item you've created.

If you want to attach a contact to an existing item that includes part of the contact's name, click the item, then choose Create | Attach To | Instant Attach. That will cause Palm Desktop to analyze the event and see if any contacts might match.

Create and Manage Notes

If you synchronize the Palm Desktop software with your Palm OS handheld computer, you'll probably see the immediate value of creating notes in the Palm Desktop program. After all, it can be nice to have extensive notes and reminders on your handheld computer, but it can put a cramp in your style to have to write all of those notes on the handheld's little screen. Well, what if you could type them up (or copy and paste from your iBook's applications) first, then get them on the handheld computer with a quick menu command?

Even if you don't have a handheld, the notes feature in Palm Desktop is worth using. It's a great place to put thoughts, ideas, lists, or anything else you'd like to keep track of. Plus, you can attach notes to events, appointments, and tasks in your calendar, making it easy to add extra text to a calendar event. If you've got directions to a meeting, for instance, you can store them in a note, then attach them to an appointment (or to a task or a contact). That way the note is safely stored away, and it can be attached to a future item if necessary.

Create the Note

If you've been reading along in this chapter so far, you know there are multiple ways to create items with Palm Desktop. Creating a note is no exception. Here's how:

- From the Instant Palm Desktop menu, choose Create | Note.

- From within the Palm Desktop software, click the New Note button in the toolbar.

- In the Palm Desktop software, choose the menu command Create | Note.

All of these result in a new Note window appearing in Palm Desktop, as shown in Figure 14-6.

To create your note, just enter a title in the Title entry box, then press TAB to move on to the Date. Today's date and time are entered automatically, but you can edit them if desired. (Usually, the date is used to reflect when the note was created.

14

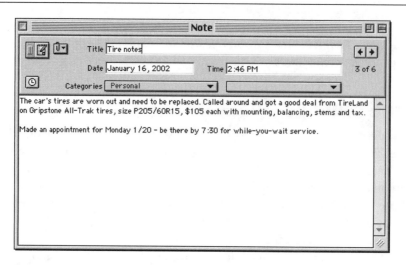

FIGURE 14-6 The Note window allows you to title, categorize, and edit your note.

Next, you can select a category or categories for the note. Then you're ready to edit. Type your note in the text area of the note.

TIP *Want to insert the current date and time without typing them? Click the small clock icon on the left side of the window, just about the text area. That automatically inserts the current date and time at the insertion point. You can do this at different times if you like to keep a running journal or add to an existing note.*

Notes are pretty much plain text—you can't format with fonts, boldface, italics, and other styles. One of the reasons for this is simple—most Palm OS handheld computers can't handle too much styled text, so anything you do in the Note window wouldn't translate well anyway.

Once you're done creating the note, you can click the close box in the Note window. Your note is done.

NOTE *The Note window is also used for reading notes that you've written previously. In the top-right corner you'll find two arrow keys that can be used to move back and forth between the notes that you've saved. This makes it easier to read notes quickly.*

View the Note List

As with contacts and tasks, you can view all of your notes using the Note List. To open the Note List, click the View Note List button in the toolbar or choose View | Note List.

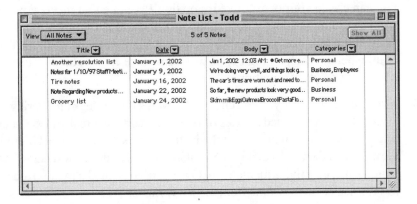

And, as with the Contact List and the Task List, there are a number of management tasks that you can accomplish in the Note List:

- To edit a note, double-click it in the Note List. You'll see the Note window, where you can re-title, edit, or add to your note.

- You can sort the Note List by any of the columns listed. For instance, if you want to sort by title, click the heading Title in the Note List. Your list is sorted alphabetically by title.

Want to move the columns around? Click and drag the column name to a new location in the Note List and it'll appear when you release the trackpad button.

14

- You can also use filters to help you see exactly what you need to see in the Note List. To do this, select the small triangle next to one of the column headings. In the pop-up menu, you can choose one of the filters in the menu. For instance, if you choose the Categories column's pop-up menu, you can see only notes in your Personal category by selecting that filter. To return to the unfiltered view, choose the pop-up menu again and select No Filter.

If you've been filtering a bit and you want to quickly get back to the entire list of notes, choose the Show All button up in the top-right corner of the Note List. This will immediately do away with all filters and show you the complete list.

- You can create your own filters if you don't see one that meets your needs. From a column heading's pop-up menu, choose Custom Filter. You'll then see a dialog box that allows you to create a filter that will work for that column head—each dialog box is different since each column offers a different type of information.

- From the View menu you can choose All Notes if you've been filtering and sorting. If you've created a series of filters and sorts that really tickle your fancy, you can store that view of the Note List by selecting View | Memorize View. You'll then see a dialog box that lets you give the view a name and decide what, exactly, is memorized. Once you've created a memorized view, you can select it at any time from the View menu.

Attach Notes

As with contacts (and most other events, for that matter), you can attach notes to other events in Palm Desktop. This is great for situations where you'd like to store extensive notes about something—say, a log of phone conversations or written directions to a meeting site—and then associate them with a contact, appointment, or other event. Plus, you can associate one note to any number of events, making it easy to cross-reference an important document while you're viewing an event or contact.

Attaching a note works pretty much the same as attaching any other event. There are two basic ways to accomplish it:

- From the Note window, open the Attach menu (the small menu that looks like a folder and paperclip). Select Attach To..., then choose the type of item. If you choose Existing Item, an icon for the note appears in a floating window. Locate the existing item and drag the note icon from the floating window to that item.

- From the Note List, drag a note to an item in the Calendar, Contact List, or Task List.

Synchronize with a Palm Device

Although Palm Desktop is a powerful organizer program in its own right, ultimately its goal is to synchronize calendar and note-taking data with a Palm OS handheld computer. If you have one of those, and you have a USB-based PalmConnect kit (which allows a Palm cradle to connect to an iBook, iMac, or similar computer via USB), then you can synchronize your calendar, contacts, and notes with the handheld computer easily.

 You don't have to have a PalmConnect USB connection kit, although that's certainly the easiest way. Some USB adapter manufacturers make USB-to-serial connection kits that allow you to connect a serial PalmConnect cable to a USB port on your iBook. See Chapter 23 for details on adapters.

Set Up HotSync

Once you have your Palm's cradle connected to your iBook, you'll want to make sure you've got HotSync configured correctly. From within Palm Desktop, choose HotSync | Setup. Now, in the HotSync Software Setup window, check to make sure that HotSync is enabled. You may also wish to make sure that the option Enable HotSync Software At System Startup is checked, so that you can synchronize data by pushing the cradle's HotSync button instead of using a menu command.

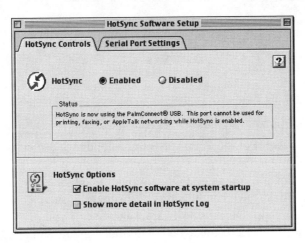

Click the Serial Port Settings tab to set up the connection for your Palm's cradle. With these settings, you can choose whether you'll be synchronizing over a local connection (most likely the USB cable), a modem connection (if your Palm OS handheld has a modem), or both if you'd like the option of switching between the two. Then, set up the speed and port for each relevant setup. (For the local setup, you'll likely choose As Fast As Possible and PalmConnect USB from the pop-up menus.)

Set Conduit Settings

Your next step is to determine what, exactly, you'd like to have synchronized when you perform a HotSync between the Palm OS handheld and your iBook. To do that, choose HotSync | Conduit Settings.

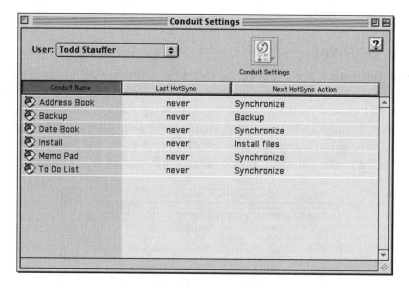

The Conduit Settings window shows you the currently installed applications that include a *conduit*. For the Palm software, a conduit is a mechanism by which a Mac OS application and a Palm OS application can share data. For instance, all of the standard applications on a Palm OS computer (To Do, Memo Pad, Address Book, and Date Book) have conduits that allow them to share data with their counterparts in the Palm Desktop software. Likewise, if you install other applications that can share data via a conduit, that conduit will appear in the Conduit Settings window.

To alter a particular conduit, double-click it in the window. Now you'll see a Settings dialog box that gives you the options for that particular conduit. (While the bundled conduits are similar, you'll find that third-party conduits vary more greatly.) Change whatever settings you think are necessary, or leave things as they are and click the OK button when you're done.

Note that for the bundled applications, the conduit settings allow you to change the way a HotSync works. By default, a HotSync causes all data to be synchronized between the two devices—that is, any event or item that appears on one computer but not the other will now appear on both computers. That's useful, but it may not be how you always want things handled. If you'd prefer to have one of the two computers be the dominant partner—for instance, so that all data on the handheld is overwritten with the data that's in the Palm Desktop software, you can choose that from the Settings menu for certain conduits.

Synchronize Data

Once you've got your settings in place, synchronizing between the Palm OS handheld and the Palm Desktop software is simple. Simply place the handheld in its cradle and press the HotSync button. You'll see the HotSync alert box appear and a status bar will indicate that your Palm OS handheld is being located, then that data will be synchronized.

If you don't see the HotSync alert dialog, check the connection between the Palm's cradle and your iBook. You should also ensure that HotSync is enabled on the HotSync Enabled dialog box and that your local connection settings are correct on the Serial Port Settings tab.

Install Palm Applications

You can also use the Palm Desktop software to install applications on your Palm OS handheld. To do that, choose HotSync | Install Applications from the menu. In the Install Handheld Files dialog box, drag Palm OS applications to the Applications list. (Palm applications have the three-letter extension ".prc" as part of their filenames.) Figure 14-7 shows files being dragged to the Install Handheld Files window.

Now, the next time you perform a HotSync, these files will be installed on the Palm OS device. To perform the HotSync immediately, place the Palm OS handheld in its cradle and press the HotSync button.

FIGURE 14-7   Installing files on your Palm OS handheld

Chapter 15

Play Games and Learn Things with iBook

How to...

- Play Nanosaur
- Play Bugdom
- Check out your iBook's 3-D capabilities
- Adjust the Input Sprocket for game controllers

Since Apple's strong showing in the consumer market with the iMac computer, Apple has been pushing for more and more gaming titles on the Mac platform. That push has paid off with new and exciting titles being released for Mac OS computers. The iBook is another part of this equation, offering pluses for gamers including a fast processor and video circuitry designed to display three-dimensional game graphics more quickly and with more colors. Notebook computers aren't often considered ideal for gaming, but the crispness of the iBook's screen and its support for USB peripherals are both nice nods to the gamer in you. You'll find it more than adequate for most Mac games out there.

In this chapter we'll take a specific look at some of the games that come with the iBook, and you'll learn how to install, optimize, and use other games. Plus, we'll take a quick look at the World Book Encyclopedia that's included with your iBook.

Play Nanosaur

Nanosaur, shown in Figure 15-1, has gotten something of a cult following since the release of the iMac. After being included on every iMac made, and now every iBook (at the time of this writing), more than two million copies of Nanosaur have been distributed with the machines, leading to quite a bit of Nanosaur fever. It's pretty well deserved, since the game's theme makes it appropriate for reasonably young kids, even if it is what's called a "first-person shooter" (meaning that you follow just behind your character and shoot at the enemies).

NOTE   *Nanosaur is not installed by default on some iBooks. Instead, you'll find its installer on the iBook Software Install CD. You'll find it in the Nanosaur folder inside the Applications folder.*

In this game, you're a Nanosaur—a type of genetically altered dinosaur brought back to life by humans in the future. Unfortunately, the humans die out, but the Nanosaurs thrive and create a technological civilization. You've been elected to head back in time, to recover the eggs of different species of dinosaurs from the pre-extinction days. That'll give the Nanosaurs more genetic material to work with to ensure their survival.

The point is to run around the screen and find the colorful eggs. You then go back to a certain place where you toss the eggs into a time portal and they are sent back to the future. You only have a limited amount of time before a meteor crashes into the Earth and drives the dinosaurs to extinction. (Too bad you didn't set that time machine further back a few months.)

15

FIGURE 15-1   Nanosaur is a first-person "shooter" where you play the dinosaur.

The eggs of different species are different colors—the first egg is worth 20,000 points, and subsequent eggs of that same color are worth 5,000 points. The ultimate goal is to find the eggs of all five species and send them back through the time portal so that life can be wonderful back in the future. (You also get a bonus of 150,000 for accomplishing such a feat.)

Get Started

Once Nanosaur is installed on your iBook, open the Applications menu and look for the Nanosaur folder. Open it up and you'll see the game; double-click the Nanosaur icon to start the game. You'll see the Nanosaur opening screen—press the SPACEBAR. You'll see the opening animation; when you see the dinosaur running, you're ready to access the game's controls—press the SPACEBAR again.

You move between the game's control commands by pressing the LEFT and RIGHT ARROW keys—you'll see that the ring rotates and a new picture will be in your view. To select that particular option, press the SPACEBAR.

Here's what each command means:

■   **The Dinosaur**   This allows you to start playing the game.

- **The Check Box** Press the SPACEBAR to see some options you can change. The fewer options selected, the faster the game can be played.

- **The Question Mark** This is the Help screen—it shows you the keys used for commands during the game.

- **The Exit Sign** This allows you to quit the game.

- **The Medal** This shows you the high scores and scorers.

When you're ready to play the game, put the dinosaur to the front, and press the SPACEBAR. The game begins.

Play the Game

As the game starts, your Nanosaur is dropped to the ground, ready to start running around the screen. You move with the ARROW keys, which allow you to run in all four directions. Immediately, you'll see a *power-up*—gamers' lingo for something that you're supposed to run directly into and which gives you extra powers or some other goodies. In this case, the power-ups you initially see are to give you more ammunition for your laser gun, which is the weapon you have at the start of the game.

Move and Jump

There are a number of different controls you'll want to master right away. These commands enable you to move the dinosaur and play the game:

Press This	To Do This
ARROW keys	Move the dinosaur
SPACEBAR	Fire weapon
⌘	Jump
OPTION	Pick up (egg)
SHIFT	Change to next weapon
A/Z	Move up and down with the jetpack

You'll move using the ARROW keys, then press the SPACEBAR to fire at any hostile dinosaurs. Your typical T-Rex takes about two shots before he disappears—other dinosaurs can take more or fewer.

15

Jumping can be very useful—in fact, you should get used to both jumping and double-jumping. If you press the ⌘ key once, you'll jump; press it twice in succession (or anytime while the Nanosaur is still in the air) and you'll jump again, doing a flip in the process.

Win at Nanosaur

Here are some hints for playing the game:

- **Move quickly.**   If you want to win the game, you've got to get eggs back through time, fast.

- **Don't gather all eggs.**   You get 5,000 points for each egg gathered, but each species of egg (that is, each different color) is located on a different "section" of the map. For instance, the first egg color is found in the marshes where you begin the game; the next egg color is found in the lava flow portion of the world. Keep moving along. There are five different-colored eggs you need to gather.

- **Learn to use the jetpack.**   You can fill the jetpack by standing over a gas vent that's shooting up out of the ground. Then, use the jetpack, but spend as little time in the air as possible—it uses up fuel fast.

- **Pick your weapons.**   The SHIFT key lets you toggle between weapons. Some weapons—like the "nuke"—are only appropriate when you need to hit many enemies at far range. Make sure you've selected the best weapon for the job.

- **Try new things.**   There are a few different "tricks" that will help you get more points or additional bonuses. For instance, you can jump on the backs of pterosaurs (the flying ones) if you do a double-jump at the right moment. That'll result in some interesting bonuses.

Gather Eggs

When you find an egg, move up close to it and stand still, then press the OPTION key. The Nanosaur bends down and attempts to pick up the egg in its mouth. If you've got it, it's time to return to a time portal, since you can only carry one egg at a time. Check the temporal compass and head off in that direction.

Once you arrive at the time portal, you need to toss the egg into its time stream. Press the OPTION key again. You'll see the egg leave the Nanosaur's mouth and fly straight forward—hopefully it encounters the time stream before it hits anything else or lands on the ground. Try not to hit OPTION accidentally while you're running with an egg, since you could accidentally toss the egg into water, lava, a crevice, or under a dinosaur you don't feel like getting close to. (Fortunately, those sturdy dinosaur eggs don't break.)

Change the Camera and Options

Aside from the commands for controlling your Nanosaur, there are some other keyboard commands that allow you to change the gaming environment listed in the following table.

Press This	To Do This
< > (brackets)	Spin the camera around
1/2	Zoom the camera in and out
CTRL-M	Toggle music on and off
CTRL-B	Toggle sounds on and off
+/-	Raise or lower volume
F8	Show the current frame rate (performance of the game)
ESC	Pause the game
TAB	Change the camera mode (look from behind the Nanosaur or look through the Nanosaur's eyes)
G	Toggle the GPS map on and off (which gives you an overview of your current position and the surroundings)

15

The Quit command is the same in Nanosaur as in other applications—press ⌘-Q to quit the game. There are no Save and Load commands—you simply have to play a new game straight through or quit.

Get More Help and Update Nanosaur

You've learned enough here to start playing quickly, but you'll want to consult the Nanosaur manual, an Adobe PDF document (discussed in Chapter 6), to learn more about weapons, power-ups, and the creatures you'll encounter. You'll find the manual in the Nanosaur folder in a file called Nanosaur Instructions.

You should also check **http://www.pangeasoft.net/** for updates and information about Nanosaur.

> NOTE   *Free updates can take Nanosaur to version 1.1.6 or beyond for bug fixes and better performance. You can download the Nanosaur update, then unstuff it to see the new application, which you can simply drag into your Nanosaur folder—no need to download the entire thing.*

Play Bugdom

Bugdom, by the same Pangea folks who brought you Nanosaur, is a painfully cute game. Ideal for kids but addicting for adults (at least, this one), this is a nice game to have included on your iBook.

The story is simple: After years of benevolent rule by the Rollie Pollies and the Lady Bugs, Bugdom has been swarmed by hostile forces—the Fire Ants and the bugs they've recruited to perform their evil. The kingdom is now ruled by King Thorax, who holes up at the anthill. You, Rollie McFly, have to get to the anthill, defeat Thorax, and crown yourself king, hopefully returning the kingdom to the peaceful paradise it once was.

As Rollie, your basic job is to walk through Bugdom kicking things. (This seems to be Rollie's forte. I guess when you have that many legs, you develop certain skills.) A number of things can be kicked, including the power nuts (walnuts scattered around that include power-ups), enemies, and the cages that hold Lady Bugs hostage (see Figure 15-2).

The point of the game is to kick walnuts to get power-ups, keys, and other special powers, like buddy bugs. (You can use buddy bugs, who follow you around, to dive-bomb your enemies.) You also seek out Lady Bugs who are trapped in cages and kick their cages to free them. As you proceed through gates and tunnel between levels, your ultimate goal is to come up against King Thorax and defeat him.

FIGURE 15-2   Rollie kicks up a little walnut dust.

Get Started

When you first launch Bugdom you'll see the main menu (shown in Figure 15-3), which allows you to view the high scores, change settings, load saved games, read the credits, or begin the game.

Here are some things you can do from the main menu:

1. To load a saved game, double-click the Saved Games icon. You'll see an Open dialog box that allows you to locate a saved game.

2. Double-click the High Scores icon to see who has done the best at the game.

3. Double-click the "?" walnut to see the credits for the game.

4. Double-click the Start icon to begin the game.

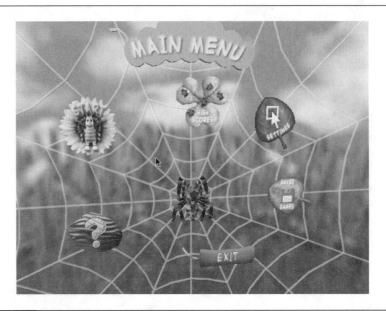

FIGURE 15-3   The main menu in Bugdom

To change settings, double-click the Settings icon. This brings up a dialog box where you can choose a few different settings for the game:

1. **Easy Mode**   Select this option if you'd like Rollie to sustain less damage when attacked.

2. **Configure Input Sprocket**   Click this button to bring up the Input Sprocket dialog box, where you can alter settings for your input device (joystick, gamepad) if you have one that supports the Input Sprocket. (See "Configure Input Sprocket" later in this chapter.)

3. **Keyboard Controls Are Player-Relative**   Select this option if you'd like controls to be player-relative instead of camera-relative. (This is discussed in the "Control Rollie" section.)

4. **Rage II Mode**   This option allows you to downgrade the quality of graphics for the original iMac or other early Power Macintosh G3 computers. It's not necessary on the iBook.

5. **Clear High Scores**   Clear out the names and scores when you're sick of seeing your sibling's or children's embarrassingly superior scores.

Once you're done setting options, click OK to return to the main menu.

Play the Game

As the game starts, Rollie appears on the ground, ready to start running around the screen. You move with the ARROW keys, which allow you to run in all four directions. Immediately, you'll see a walnut that likely contains a power-up. Go and kick it by pressing the OPTION key. In this case, the early power-ups you kick to reveal are likely clovers, which add bonus points to your score.

Control Rollie

Rollie has two basic modes—bug mode and ball mode. (Remember, he's a Rollie Pollie.) Press the SPACEBAR to switch between modes. While he's a bug, Rollie can jump, kick, and walk. While he's a ball, he can either roll or he can roll *faster*. As a ball, he can also roll into enemies, walnuts, and Lady Bug cages instead of kicking them.

There are a couple of different ways you can control Rollie:

- **Trackpad**   You can use the trackpad to move Rollie in any direction, and click its button to kick. If he's in ball mode, clicking the button gives him a turbo boost while rolling.

- **Mouse and Keyboard**   Using either the trackpad or a USB mouse while holding down the SHIFT key, you can control Rollie's direction while he walks forward. This is the recommended mode of play, although I'd only recommend it if you have an external mouse hooked up. Otherwise, your trackpad finger will get mighty tired.

- **Keyboard**   Using only the keyboard, you can use arrow keys to get Rollie to move just as you would with the trackpad. In this case, the OPTION key is used to kick or boost speed, depending on Rollie's mode.

> *You can switch to what Pangea calls player-relative controls, which allow you to use the UP ARROW to move him forward, the DOWN ARROW to move him backward, and the LEFT and RIGHT ARROWS to turn him without moving him. Used in concert, this gives you more control with the arrow keys, but it can also be tough to get used to.*

TIP

You can also use the keyboard to accomplish a few other things including jumping, changing modes, or launching a buddy bug. This table shows the controls.

15

Key	What It Does
OPTION	Kick in bug mode, turbo boost in ball mode
SPACE	Switch between bug and ball mode
⌘	Jump (in bug mode only)
TAB	Launch your buddy bug at an enemy
+/-	Raise or lower the volume
⌘-Q	Quit the game
ESC	Pause the game
M	Toggle music on and off
1/2	Zoom in/Zoom out
</>	Swivel camera

You can also freeze the screen (and the game) in a special pause mode that allows you to take a screenshot. Press F12, then press ⌘-SHIFT-3 to take a picture of the entire screen.

Scoring Points and Tracking Health

You score points in two ways, by gathering clovers (within walnuts that you kick open) or rescuing Lady Bugs. Each is registered in the status bar at the top of the screen.

At the far left of the status bar you'll see the number of lives Rollie has left. Next to it, you'll see the two types of clover you'll encounter—each new clover you discover in a walnut and walk over to pick up is added to its respective four-leaf clover in the status bar. In the middle, you'll see Rollie holding up any special items he's found, like keys or money. Next, you'll see the Lady Bug gauge. If the image of the Lady Bug has wings, then you've freed all Lady Bugs on this level. If not, you still have work to do. On the far right you'll see a tally of how many Lady Bugs you've freed.

There are two indicators near the picture of Rollie in the middle of the status bar. The green curved indicator tells you how much more "ball time" you have—Rollie can only stay in ball mode for so long. If you've depleted your ball time, you'll have to find a power-up that gives you more. The red straight line is a health indicator. Run out of health and you'll lose a life.

A third indicator appears whenever you're fighting a level "boss" (a meaner bug that you have to defeat to end some levels). That indicator, which appears on the bottom of the screen, tells you how much health the boss has left.

> **TIP**   *Whenever you see a large candy cane–colored pipe with a bubble of water coming out of it, you've reached a checkpoint. Jump up to pop the bubble and register at the checkpoint. Now, if you lose a life while playing, you'll return to this checkpoint instead of the beginning of the level.*

Fight Bad Bugs

One of Rollie's strengths seems to be running away, and since you don't score additional points for beating up an enemy, you can run away with impunity. That said, sometimes you've got to stop, clinch your feet into fists, and take on the bad bugs.

Some bugs can't be beat, like the snails. Instead, avoid those. Others have to be kicked (or rolled into) more than once before they're knocked out. It's easier to roll into bad bugs than kick them, especially if they have weapons. Remember that you only have a certain amount of ball time before you have to stand up and take it like a, uh, bug.

You've got another trick up your sleeve—the buddy bug. If you've got a small bug following you around that you can't get rid of (after kicking a walnut where he was hiding) it might be because he's your buddy. While you're in a fight, press the TAB key to launch the buddy bug at an enemy. He can knock most of them silly with one punch.

Get More Help and Update Bugdom

As with Nanosaur, Bugdom has a manual that can help you learn more about it. The Bugdom manual is an Adobe PDF document (discussed in Chapter 6), to help you learn more about the power-ups, levels, and creatures you'll encounter. You'll find the manual in the Bugdom folder in a file called Bugdom Instructions.

You should also check **http://www.pangeasoft.net/** for updates and information about Bugdom.

Check Your 3-D Specifications

Your iBook features an ATI graphics chip that's designed to accelerate the drawing of 3-D images. With the correct ATI drivers installed, your iBook should take advantage of the 3-D acceleration code built into popular games, especially those that support QuickDraw RAVE or ATI Rage acceleration. You should look for this sort of support when you're buying a game—check the side of the box.

 The graphics chip in the iBook is an ATI Rage Mobility graphics accelerator with 4MB of RAM. If you come across a game that requires ATI Rage II or Rage Pro graphics, then you're compatible.

Similarly, games may require a minimum processor speed. Your iBook has at least a 300MHz processor and at least 32MB of system RAM, just in case the game asks. The original iBook also has a 3GB hard disk. Your iBook's video mode can be set to display millions of colors at resolutions of 800 × 600 or lower.

 These are just specifications for gaming reference. To learn more about screen resolutions, see Chapter 21. To learn more about upgrading RAM, see Chapter 23.

Add Game Controllers

One other variable when you're playing games on your iBook is the controller. In many cases, you'll play the game using the keyboard—a lot of games are designed to allow you to do that. Others will specifically encourage the use of a joystick or gamepad. (Joysticks work like flight sticks in fighter planes; a gamepad is usually similar to the controllers that come with Nintendo or Sony Playstation game boxes.)

On the iBook, joysticks require driver software to allow them to operate correctly. That driver software can come in three forms:

■ It can be a generic driver that allows the controller to be a substitute for the mouse with a particular game.

■ It can be a specific driver that works with certain games.

■ It can use the Input Sprocket driver software created and installed by Apple for easy gaming.

The easiest way for this to work is with the Input Sprocket driver software, but then the game must specifically support GameSprockets, a special technology that Apple has created to make gaming easier. Unfortunately, not all games use this, so sometimes you have to get creative.

Configure Input Sprocket

If your game and controller are both compatible with the Input Sprocket, then
configuration is simple. The controller should say on the box that it's compatible
with Input Sprocket or Game Sprockets, and the controller should include a CD
that allows you to install such drivers. You'll install a driver for your particular
controller (in some cases), then you'll install a compatible game. Once support
for both has been established, you're ready to set things up.

   In the game itself, look for an option to change controller preferences.
That will cause a special dialog box to appear—the Input Sprocket configuration
dialog box (see Figure 15-4). In this dialog box, you'll be able to choose what each
button on your controller will do. Click a particular button to see a list of different
options available for your particular controller. Each game has its own control
mappings, so look carefully at each. For instance, in Future Cop (the Ariston
Hermes example shown in Figure 15-4) there are three different weapons at your
disposal—each needs to be mapped to a particular button on the gamepad.

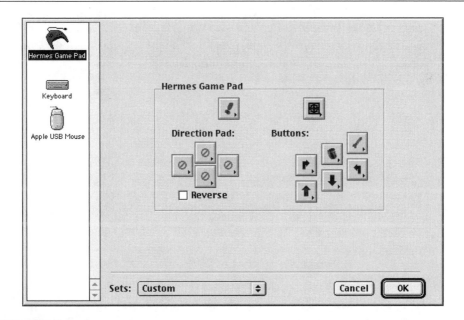

15

FIGURE 15-4   Configuring a joystick using Input Sprocket

Since this dialog box is designed as part of Apple's Input Sprocket software, you'll find it's similar for nearly every device you use and every game you play that supports Input Sprocket.

Other Drivers

If your input device supports other sorts of drivers, you'll be able to do one of two things. First, you may simply be able to use your input device as a substitute for an external mouse. If that's the case, use the preferences in the game to select a mouse as one (or the only) input device. You can use the joystick instead, although the game will believe you're using a mouse.

Second, you may be able to use your joystick specifically with a particular game. Some games offer built-in support for certain joystick brands with specific features—for instance, many controllers from Thrustmaster and Microsoft are specifically supported by particular games. Likewise, your controller may offer a special driver that makes it act like popular controllers that are supported by individual games.

NOTE *At the time of this writing, a shareware driver for some USB devices was making it possible to use USB gaming controllers with non-Input Sprocket games. Basically, the driver, called USB Overdrive, maps USB buttons to keys on the keyboard. You'll need to figure it out on your own, but if you're an advanced iBook gamer and you'd like to experiment with the driver, check out **http://www.montalcini.com/**.*

Part III

Get Online

Chapter 16

Manage Your E-mail

How to...

- Set up your e-mail account
- Check your mail
- Read messages and respond
- Create new e-mail messages
- Send and receive e-mail attachments
- Create mail rules to automate your mail
- Add more than one account or more than one user

You may have bought your iBook for the express purpose of getting e-mail—a lot of people do. Even if it wasn't your primary goal, you probably think e-mail is a big part of the computing experience. Electronic mail (e-mail) gives you the opportunity to communicate inexpensively and rather quickly in a written format. What were once letters between family, friends, and business associates have become electronic messages. What used to take days now arrives in seconds.

In this chapter I'll focus on Outlook Express, Microsoft's full-featured e-mail program that's included with the iBook. If you want to experiment, though, you'll find a number of demos and shareware versions of e-mail client applications online—check out the sites mentioned in Chapter 18 that allow you to download and install shareware applications. Popular e-mail programs include Eudora Pro and Eudora Lite (**http://www.eudora.com/**), Mailsmith (**http:// www.barebones.com/**), and the Messenger components of Netscape Communicator, which is also included with your iBook (**http://www.netscape.com/**).

NOTE
*The latest version of Outlook Express, version 5.0, became available during this writing and is covered in this chapter. Many iBooks, however, shipped with Outlook Express 4.5. I'll try to point out the differences between the versions in this chapter, but if you have an earlier version, you can upgrade by visiting **http://www.microsoft.com/oe/** on the Web.*

Is Your Account Set Up?

The first thing you'll need before you can send and receive e-mail is an e-mail account. Most likely you already have one—after all, an e-mail account is created for you when you sign up for Internet access. And the best part is, with most ISPs you'll have an e-mail account that corresponds to your Internet account name. If you were given the user name toddstauffer when you created the account, for instance, then your e-mail address is probably toddstauffer@earthlink.net (assuming, of course, that you're using the Earthlink service).

Plus, if you've walked through the Internet Setup Assistant in Chapter 1 and taken a quick look at getting your e-mail in Chapter 2, then you've already tested to see if your e-mail account is properly set up. If everything works and you can receive e-mail, move on to the section "Get, Read, and Reply to E-mail," later in this chapter. If you're having trouble, though, you may need to set up the account manually, which is covered in this section.

How E-mail Addresses Work

In order to receive e-mail, you have to tell others your e-mail address. You may
also need to enter the e-mail address when you set up your e-mail program. (Or if
you ever change e-mail programs, you may need to enter it again.)

The e-mail address can be broken up into three or more different parts:

- **Account Name**   The name that identifies you or your e-mail account
  (if more than one person is using it) is unique among the accounts on
  your ISP's mail server computer. That's the "toddstauffer" part of
  toddstauffer@earthlink.net.

- **Server Computer**   Some, but not all, mail servers will include the
  actual name of the mail server computer in the address. An example
  might be todd@mail.mac-upgrade.com where "mail" is the actual mail
  server computer.

- **Domain Name**   The domain name is a name given to a group of
  computers at a particular organization. If you work for Apple, for instance,
  your address might be todd@apple.com. The "apple" part suggests the
  domain for that company.

- **Domain Name Extension**   Sometimes considered part of the domain
  name, the domain name extension suggests the type of organization you're
  dealing with. A commercial entity (like Apple) gets a .com, while an ISP
  (like Earthlink) generally gets a .net extension, as in earthlink.net. Other
  extensions include .edu (educational), .mil (military), .org (organization),
  and country codes for organizations and companies outside the United
  States like .uk (United Kingdom), .fr (France), and .au (Australia).

It's not terribly important to remember what each part of an e-mail address is
intended to signify. What's more important is remembering that whenever you
enter an e-mail address, you need to enter the entire address as you've been given
it, so that it can reach its destination account. Otherwise, you may not be entering
enough information to deliver the e-mail. I still have that problem with people who
don't put the suite number in my office address. I can't get the package if it's not
properly coded, just as with e-mail.

The Internet Control Panel

Using the Internet control panel, you can quickly and easily customize your e-mail account setup. You've likely already used the Internet Setup Assistant, so the basics are already entered regarding your e-mail account. If you dig into the Internet Control panel, though, you can change some options, too.

The Internet control panel serves as a repository of information about your Internet account(s) and preferences. This is good because it means you can change e-mail or Web applications and still have all of your arcane Internet addresses stored within the Mac OS itself. That way, you don't have to repeat the setup process if you decide to use a different application (see Figure 16-1).

FIGURE 16-1   The Internet control panel is a convenient repository of Internet addresses for e-mail, Web browsing, discussion group preferences, and more.

16

The Personal tab is where you enter information that recipients of your e-mail messages will see. This is an important distinction; technically, you can enter anything you want and it won't affect the way that your e-mail program logs into your ISP's mail server computer—that stuff is on the E-mail tab. These entries are still important, though, because they tell your recipients who you are and how to respond to you. Here are some things you can customize on the Personal tab:

- **Name** This is your full name as you'd like it to appear in e-mail messages. The "From" section of messages would include a portion with your full name, like "toddstauffer@earthlink.com (Todd Stauffer)" if you enter your name here.

- **E-mail Address** You can create a special "reply to" address. This may or may not be different from your e-mail account. For instance, I have a domain name set up for my Mac-Upgrade Web site—mac-upgrade.com. I like people to send e-mail to todd@mac-upgrade.com. It's easy to remember and I can change it easily if I change ISPs. The actual e-mail *account*, though, is "todds@isp.net" because I have an ISP that manages that mac-upgrade.com account. Since the ISP manages it, I actually log into the todds@isp.net account on that ISP's mail server, not on a todd@mac-upgrade.com account. The *e-mail account* is entered on the E-mail tab. The one you're entering here is the e-mail address where people can reach you.

NOTE *There isn't always a difference between an e-mail address and e-mail account. For instance, if you have a regular Earthlink account, you probably don't have a separate e-mail address and e-mail account. They're probably both you@earthlink.net. There can also be subtle differences, like an e-mail address of tstauffer@tamu.edu and an e-mail account of tstauffer@science.tamu.edu.*

- **Organization** Enter the name of your organization, if it's relevant. It'll show up in the *headers,* the information at the top of your e-mail message.

- **Signature** This is a block of text sent at the bottom of your messages to identify you, offer related Web sites, and so forth. People usually put three or four lines of text saying who they are, give a phone number, list accomplishments, a favorite quote, or a joke. Etiquette dictates that this be kept to six lines or less and not be overwhelmed with dashes, asterisks, and so on—just tasteful and interesting.

```
----------------
Todd A. Stauffer
<TStauffer@aol.com> <http://shutup101.com/todd/> for Book Updates

It's Here!! Mac Upgrade and Repair Bible <http://www.mac-upgrade.com/>
Disk Doctors -- Knowledge TV, 8:30 PM (EST) Thursdays
   <http://www.jec.edu/ktv/index3.html> for local channel info
```

Now, click the E-mail tab and you're ready to enter the information your e-mail program will need to access the ISP's mail server computer and get your mail. Most of these entries have already been completed for you by the Internet Setup Assistant. You can change them if desired or necessary—sometimes you'll get a new password or a mail server address from your system administrator. You'll enter those here on the E-mail tab. (You can also re-run the Internet Setup Assistant, which is located in the Internet folder on your main hard disk.)

There are two elements I want to point out for customizing purposes:

- **E-mail Notification**   In e-mail programs that fully recognize the Internet control panel, you can determine how they'll tell you about new messages by placing a check mark next to every option you want active.

- **Default E-Mail Application**   Choose the application that gets loaded whenever you double-click the Mail icon or otherwise click an e-mail link in an Internet-savvy application.

Get, Read, and Reply to E-mail

The checking part is easy—in fact, we've already gone over it in Chapter 2. If you have modem access to the Internet, fire up your Internet connection (either via the Remote Access control panel or the Control Strip's Remote Access button). If you have an Ethernet or wireless connection to the Internet, you don't need to do anything special.

You can set your Remote Access connection to dial your ISP automatically whenever you use an Internet application. See Chapter 20 for details.

16

Once the Internet connection is active, click the Send and Receive button on Outlook Express' window. (If you don't see it, select Window | Outlook Express.) You can also use the keyboard shortcut ⌘-M to send and receive all mail.

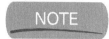 *If you have Outlook Express 5.0 or higher, you can use the Send & Receive button in the toolbar as a menu, where you can choose to download e-mail from individual e-mail accounts if you have more than one.*

If you have mail, you'll see the Progress window appear, complete with an indicator that shows you how many messages you have and how many are left to come in. The progress bar indicates that Outlook Express is communicating with the mail server. If you don't see the Progress window, you can view it by selecting Window | Progress.

Once all of your mail has been downloaded, it'll appear in the Inbox window pane of Outlook Express. If you don't see it, you may not have the Inbox selected. Click the Inbox icon on the left side of the Outlook window, and the Inbox will appear. (You may also need to scroll up or down in the Inbox to see your mail if you already have lots of messages.)

Read Your Mail

Unread mail appears in the Inbox's message list in bold type, so that it's clear you haven't read it yet. To read it, just click once on the topic of the message—the message text appears in the bottom window (the *preview pane*, as Microsoft calls it), where you can scroll to read the message. If you prefer, you can also double-click a message subject, which causes a new window to appear, containing that message.

Once a message has been read, it stays in the Inbox message list, but its subject and other information switch to plain text, so that any other unread messages stand out with bold type.

Change the View

Want to switch the view around a bit? Each message in the Inbox message list takes up a full row—the columns represent the subject, sender, date, and other information. You might notice that these columns work a little like the columns in Finder windows. You can click the column heading in each case to change the organization of the Inbox (see Figure 16-2).

Once you have the message list arranged according to one of the column headings, you'll notice that it's in a particular order, either ascending or descending. You can change that order by clicking the heading again. You'll notice that the little triangle flips sides to indicate that you've switched from ascending to descending order or vice-versa.

Click the heading to organize by that column.

Click again to change the order.

Click a subject to
read the message (the
message list).

The Folder List

Message appears here (the preview pane).

FIGURE 16-2 The Inbox interface

You can choose the columns that are shown in the Inbox. Choose View / Columns, then choose the column you want to display or hide. A displayed column has a check mark next to it. Also, you can organize the Inbox by read/unread status. Just click the column at the far left. Click it again to change the sort order.

16

Filter the Mail

If you have a whole lot of messages in your message list, you can filter the view—that is, you can show only messages that match a certain string of characters or a particular word.

In Outlook Express 5.0 you have two menus—the first menu allows you to choose what portion of the message to filter (from, to, subject) and the second menu allows you to choose how to filter (starts with, contains). Then you enter the letters or keyword you want to use for the filter. The result will be many fewer e-mail messages listed, since only those that meet your criterion will appear.

 In Outlook Express 4.5 there is only one menu. Choose what to display from the small menu just above the subject headings, then enter a few letters or a keyword that indicates what you're trying to find.

Reply to a Message

If a message deserves a reply, then click the Reply button while you're viewing that message and a new window appears, ready for your reply.

You should see that the original message has already been "quoted" for you—that just means that the original message has been included in your reply so that the person you're replying to can have his or her memory jogged about what, exactly, you're replying to. Now you can just begin typing, creating a message that probably looks something like:

```
Mike:
I'm glad to come. You know me...I'll bring my queso dip!
- Todd
----------
>From: Mike L. Lawrence <mike@earthlink.net>
>To: <toddstauffer@earthlink.net>
>Subject: Party
>Date: Feb 14, 2001, 9:50 AM

>I was hoping you could come to the party.
>So far, people are just signing up to say what they'll bring.
>
>ml
```

Notice that the quoted part appears at the bottom of the message with the new reply (the part I wrote) at the top of the message. This is Outlook Express' default treatment of quotes. You can tell the quoted text, by the way, from the greater than sign (>) that comes in front of every line.

Another common method is to go through the message itself and reply after a particular quoted spot. That makes it looks something like this:

```
>>I was hoping you could come to the party.
I'm glad to come!
>>So far, people are just signing up to say what they'll bring.
You know me...I'll bring my queso dip!

- Todd
```

This is the more common Internet tradition for quoting. First, it gives a solid sense of a back-and-forth conversation. It also takes up less space, since Internet etiquette dictates that you edit the message so that only the relevant parts are quoted. Third, in many e-mail programs (including Outlook Express) the quoted text is a different color than the reply text when you receive a message with quotes in it. That makes it really easy to quickly read the new message.

Of course, the Outlook Express default method doesn't force your readers to page through the message to see the new parts—everything new is right up top. If the readers need their memories jogged, they can scroll down. So, the final decision about quoting is really up to you, as long as you remember to keep your quoted sections as short as possible.

16

You can change the way OE handles quoting by default. In Outlook Express 5.0, choose Edit | Preferences, then click the Compose tab and select "Place Insertion Point After Default Text." In Outlook Express 4.5, choose Edit | Preferences, then click Message Composition. Put a check mark next to the Use Internet Style Replies option. Your cursor appears at the bottom of the quoted text (ready for you to edit the message) instead of at the top.

When you're done with the reply, you're ready to click buttons in the Reply window:

- **Send (or Send Now)**　This one sends the message immediately if you're still online. If you're not connected, and you don't have your connection set up to connect automatically, Outlook Express will store the message in the Outbox and wait until you're online next.

- **Send Later**　In Outlook Express 4.5 and above you have the option of clicking the Send Later button. This places the message in the Outbox even if you're currently online. The message is sent the next time you select the Send and Receive All command.

- **Save (or Save as Draft)**　This saves the message in the Drafts folder. It won't be sent until you open it and click the Send button. Drafts are just that—rough versions of e-mail messages you don't yet want to send.

Don't forget your drafts. The Drafts folder label becomes boldface when it contains mail that hasn't been sent. When you see that boldface label, don't forget to check every once in a while so you don't forget about a message you still need to edit and send. (I do it all the time.)

- **Add Attachments**　Click this button to send an attachment. I'll discuss sending and receiving attachments later in this chapter.

- **Signature**   Click this button to add your signature to the bottom of the message. This will only work if you've actually added a signature in the Internet control panel or in the Outlook Express preferences.

- **Contact**   This allows you to open the Contact Manager so you can find and add other recipients if you need to do so. (This menu does not appear in Outlook Express 5.0.)

- **Options**   In Outlook Express 5.0, you can use the Options button menu to choose from a few different options, including whether or not the message is formatted in HTML, what priority is assigned to the message, what character set to use, and whether or not the sent message should be stored in a folder after it's sent successfully.

- **Rewrap**   In Outlook Express 5.0, you can click the Rewrap button to clean up the display of the text if it's not wrapping correctly in the text window.

 Reply to All Senders

This is a special case—if you're reading a message that was sent to more people than just you, you can send your reply to all recipients. If Mindy sends a message to you, Jack, and Tina, the question is whether or not you want to send a reply just to Mindy, or if you want everyone to see the reply. If you want to send it just to the original sender, click Reply; if you want to send it to all recipients to keep the group conversation alive, click Reply All.

Otherwise, things work the same. Edit the message, then click Send to send it or Save as Draft to save the message for editing later.

16

Create a New Message

If you're interested in sending a new message, it's even a little easier to do than replying. The only difference is that you need to know the e-mail address of the person you want to send the message to and write a subject for the message.
    Here's how to send it:

1. Click the New button in the toolbar or select File | New | Mail Message.

 If you have more than one account set up in Outlook Express, you should choose the account from which you want to send the message in the Account menu.

2. In the window, enter an e-mail address for the To box. In Outlook Express 5.0, press TAB to enter another To recipient.

 In Outlook Express 4.5, you can type a comma (,) between each e-mail address if you're entering more than one. You can also press TAB to move between entry boxes in Outlook Express 4.5.

3. Now, select the CC tab to type an e-mail address if you'd like to send a "courtesy copy" to anyone.

4. Next, you can select the BCC tab and type an e-mail address in the BCC box (blind courtesy copy). If you do so, this person's e-mail address won't appear to any other recipients. Only you and the BCC recipient will know that you sent a copy to that person. You can have more than one recipient on this line, too—type a comma between e-mail addresses.

5. Now you'll enter a subject for your message. With any e-mail message your subject should be informative without being terribly long. Press TAB.

6. Type the message in the body of the message window, then press the Signature button if you're set up to add a signature to your messages.

From here it's pretty much like a reply—press Send or Save, or add attachments as I'll discuss later in this chapter.

You can set up Outlook Express to check the spelling of all outgoing messages by choosing Edit / Preferences, then clicking the Spelling button. Put a check mark next to the options you want active. Choose Always Check Spelling Before Sending, for instance, to have the spell checker look over a message after you've pressed the Send button. This only works if you have Microsoft Office installed, since Outlook Express uses the dictionary capabilities of Microsoft Office to provide spell checking.

Delete a Message

You can highlight a message in the message window and click the Delete button to delete it from the message list. It's not gone forever, though; it's simply moved to the Deleted Items folder, where it stays until a prescribed time, usually the next time you quit Outlook Express. Open the Deleted Items folder to get a message back, if you like. You can also drag messages from the message list to the Deleted Items folder to delete them without going through the process of clicking the Delete button.

Empty the Deleted Items folder by selecting it in the folder list and choosing Tools | Run Schedules | Empty Deleted Items Folder.

You can set Outlook Express 5.0 to empty the Deleted Items folder when you quit the program. To make this setting, choose Tools | Schedules and double-click the Empty Deleted Items Folder entry. In the When section of the Define Schedule window, pull down the menu marked Manually and choose On Quit. Now click OK in the window.

NOTE *In Outlook Express 4.5, you switch to the Deleted Messages folder and choose Edit / Empty Deleted Messages. You can also set Outlook Explorer to automatically empty the Deleted Messages folder by selecting Edit / Preferences and choosing Startup & Quit. Under the Quit Settings, place a check mark next to Empty Deleted Messages Folder.*

Format Your Message

You may have been wondering why I haven't mentioned those text tools—font size, bold, italics, and so on—there in the message editing window. (If you don't see the tools, open a new message and choose Format | HTML from the menu. In

16

Outlook Express 4.5, the command is Format | Rich Text.) These tools use the HyperText Markup Language—the same language used to create Web pages—in order to format the document. That makes it look pretty and add practical value, like giving you the freedom to create bullet lists and align your text.

There's a reason I haven't mentioned those tools: HTML e-mail can be annoying. Not everyone has the capability to read HTML e-mail, so, instead of seeing a formatted document, they see something that looks more like Figure 16-3.

If you plan to use HTML controls, you'll want to do so only when you're reasonably sure that your recipients are also using an HTML-aware mail program. If they are, though, go ahead and format. You'll find that most of the

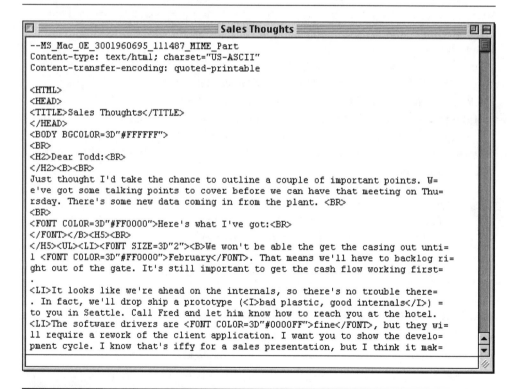

```
--MS_Mac_OE_3001960695_111487_MIME_Part
Content-type: text/html; charset="US-ASCII"
Content-transfer-encoding: quoted-printable

<HTML>
<HEAD>
<TITLE>Sales Thoughts</TITLE>
</HEAD>
<BODY BGCOLOR=3D"#FFFFFF">
<BR>
<H2>Dear Todd:<BR>
</H2><B><BR>
Just thought I'd take the chance to outline a couple of important points. W=
e've got some talking points to cover before we can have that meeting on Thu=
rsday. There's some new data coming in from the plant. <BR>
<BR>
<FONT COLOR=3D"#FF0000">Here's what I've got:<BR>
</FONT></B><H5><BR>
</H5><UL><LI><FONT SIZE=3D"2"><B>We won't be able the get the casing out unti=
l <FONT COLOR=3D"#FF0000">February</FONT>. That means we'll have to backlog ri=
ght out of the gate. It's still important to get the cash flow working first=
.
<LI>It looks like we're ahead on the internals, so there's no trouble there=
. In fact, we'll drop ship a prototype (<I>bad plastic, good internals</I>) =
to you in Seattle. Call Fred and let him know how to reach you at the hotel.
<LI>The software drivers are <FONT COLOR=3D"#0000FF">fine</FONT>, but they wi=
ll require a rework of the client application. I want you to show the develo=
pment cycle. I know that's iffy for a sales presentation, but I think it mak=
```

FIGURE 16-3 An HTML formatted e-mail in a non-HTML mail program tools work the same way that they do in a word processor or similar program. Here are the basics:

- **Text** You can either select a text size or style before typing, or highlight the selection and format its size or appearance (bold, italic, underlined) after typing it in. You can also press ⌘-B for bold text, ⌘-I for italics, and ⌘-U for underlining while typing.

- **Lists** You should type each list item, pressing RETURN between each. Then, highlight the entire list and choose either the Bullet List button or the Numbered List button.

- **Indent** Again, you're probably best off typing the paragraph first, then choosing to indent it. This is actually called a "blockquote" in HTML parlance—the entire paragraph is indented as if it were a long quote in an academic paper or book.

- **Alignment** Choose alignment before or after typing. There is no justified setting—just left, center, and right.

- **Color** Specify the text color before or after typing (highlight the text, then choose the color). Click on the triangle next to the Text color button (the letter "A" with a color under it) to choose the text color. You can also click on the triangle next to the background color button (the paint can) in the formatting toolbar to choose a background color from the list.

Send and Get Attachments

Outlook Express can help you send a file—a document, application, or compressed archive of different sorts of files—to recipients through Internet e-mail. In fact, you can even send attachments to recipients using Intel-compatible PCs. The only major limitation is that it can take a while to upload and download attachments. While most e-mail messages are about 5-10 kilobytes in size, the typical graphical image document—a photo, for instance—begins at 50,000 kilobytes and spirals upward from there.

There are two rules about sending attachments to someone. First, etiquette dictates that the person should be expecting the attachment or otherwise not likely to balk at receiving it (for instance, they're employees or colleagues and they need the file). It's important to remember that a lot of people pay for their time online and their e-mail service—a very large download could cost them time or money.

16

Second, make sure that the attachment arrives in the correct format for them to use. For that to be the case, know what sort of computer and e-mail program they're using. That way you'll know how to *compress* and *encode* your attachment.

Encode the Attachment

By definition, Internet e-mail programs are designed to send text, not computer files like documents, programs, or system code. Because of this limitation, it's historically been up to other Internet protocols, like the File Transfer Protocol, to focus on sending files from one place to another.

There is a way to get around this limitation, though, and it's exactly what Outlook Express and many other mail programs do to send an attached file—it's called *encoding*. Through the process of encoding, a file made up of binary data (ones and zeros) is literally translated into a transmittable format following a particular encoding method. Once the file arrives on the other side of the Internet transmission, it's decoded back to its original form. In the meantime, even after you've sent or received the file, it's useless until it's translated back to a usable format.

There are four basic methods for encoding supported by Outlook Express:

- **uuencode**   Also called "Unix-to-Unix encode," this one is most popular when sending to Unix machines. These days, despite the name, most versions of Netscape and many Windows-based e-mail programs recognize the format.

- **BinHex**   This is probably the most popular Mac format, especially useful when sending from a Mac to a Mac and if you're transmitting Mac-specific documents and/or applications. Some, but not all, Unix- and PC-based e-mail programs recognize BinHex.

- **Base64/MIME**   This is arguably the most popular encoding/decoding format for Microsoft Windows. This one is a safe bet if you know you're sending to a Windows PC.

- **AppleDouble**   This is probably the best to choose if you regularly send files to both Windows and Mac users. It maintains the special elements of a Mac file (if you're sending to another Mac) while being compatible with most Windows e-mail programs, too.

In Outlook Express, you can't individually encode an attachment. In Outlook Express 5.0, open the Preferences (Edit | Preferences) and choose the Compose tab, then click the button marked "Click here for attachment options." (In Outlook Express 4.5, set the encoding preference by selecting Edit | Preferences and clicking Message Composition. You'll see a pull-down menu for the encoding process.)

It's probably best to choose AppleDouble (which is safest for most circumstances), then come back and change to uuencode if you plan to send specifically to a Unix user or to Base64 if you're having trouble with AppleDouble when sending to Windows users.

Compress the Attachment

Files can be compressed (as described in Chapter 18) so that they're easier to transmit over the Internet. You can perform the compression two different ways. The first method allows you to compress from within Outlook Express. Choose Edit | Preferences and click the Compose tab. Now, click the button "Click here for attachment options." Now, turn on the option Macintosh (StuffIt) under the Compression heading. Attachments are compressed using the StuffIt format. The problem with this, though, is that the StuffIt standard is not as prevalent on the Windows platform as it is on the Mac platform. (Aladdin Expander for Windows is available, but it's not as universally available as it is on Macs, iMacs, and iBooks, where StuffIt Expander and DropStuff are actually installed with many applications.)

In Outlook Express 4.5 you can turn StuffIt compression on and off by choosing Message | Compress Attachments. This activates the option so that any subsequent attachments are compressed.

So, the second method is to compress the file beforehand using another program such as PKZip, discussed in more detail in Chapter 18. That way, simply attach the file after it's been compressed and send it on its way.

Most of these compression utilities do it automatically, but if you're sending compressed files, especially to Windows users, you'll want to make sure the filename has its three-letter extension like .zip (PKZip or WinZip) or .sit (StuffIt).

Add the Attachment

In Outlook Express, add an attachment to an outgoing message by dragging it from the Finder into the message window or selecting Message | Add

16

Attachments. To remove attachments that you decide not to send, select Message | Remove Attachments. Now, send your e-mail as usual and the attachment goes right along for the ride. Remember, it may take a while to transmit over the Internet, especially if the attachment is an image, application, or large document.

Get an Attachment

E-mail messages that include attachments appear in your Inbox list with a small paperclip icon. There are a number of different ways you can receive an attachment from an e-mail message if one has been sent to you:

- Highlight a message with an attachment in the Inbox list (or another folder's list) and choose Message | Save All Attachments. This displays a dialog box that allows you to choose a folder on your iBook where the attachments will be saved.

- In Outlook Express 5.0, click the disclosure triangle labeled Attachments in the preview pane or message window. You'll see icons for the attachments. You can highlight attachment(s) and click Open to open them in their associated application or Save to save them to your iBook's hard disk.

- In Outlook Express 4.5, you'll see attachments in the paperclip menu that appears in the preview pane when you view a message that has attachments. From that paperclip menu, choose All to save the files to your iBook's disk or choose the attachment's name to open it in its associated application.

- In Outlook Express 4.5, you can view the full message window and drag the icons for attachments from the bottom of the window to the desktop.

CAUTION   *Opening attachments to e-mail messages is one known way to contract a computer virus. You should only open or use attachments from known senders and only when the attachment is expected from that user. It's possible for some viruses to automatically send virus-infected attachments automatically from a user's e-mail program, making it look like the user sent the message to you. If you're not expecting an attachment, don't open it until you've talked to the sender and confirmed that he or she meant to send you the attachment.*

Use More Than One Account

Do you have more than one e-mail account? You'll be happy to know that Outlook Express can handle mail from more than one e-mail account, allowing you to download it all at one time, manage it all in one Inbox, and, as we've already seen, send your e-mail from the account of your choice.

> **TIP** *One way to get additional accounts is to sign onto a Web-based e-mail service like HotMail (**http://www.hotmail.com/**) or USA.Net (**http://www.usa.net/**). Look for one that offers "POP" (Post Office Protocol, the standard e-mail server protocol) access so you can download your mail to Outlook Express. Or, if you have Outlook Express 5.0, it specifically supports downloading e-mail from your HotMail account.*

Creating a new account is pretty much the same as creating the original account except that you don't get to use the Internet Setup Assistant or the Internet control panel. You'll have to dig into Outlook Express' preferences.

Here's how to add an account to Outlook Express:

1. In Outlook Express 5.0, choose Tools | Accounts. In Outlook Express 4.5, choose Edit | Preferences (or click the Preferences button on the Outlook Express window) and click the E-mail button.

2. In Outlook Express 5.0, choose Mail from the New button menu. (In Outlook Express 4.5, click the New Account button near the top of the dialog box.)

3. In Outlook Express 5.0, the Account Setup Assistant takes over from here. You can use the assistant to set up an existing or new e-mail account. You can also create a free HotMail account from within the assistant. If you're using Outlook Express 4.5, enter a name for the account and choose POP. Click OK.

4. Now, in Outlook Express 4.5, enter all of the information for this account. Notice that Account ID just requires your e-mail account name, not the full e-mail account address. The e-mail address up top, though, should be your full reply-to address.

16

5. If you want this to be your default account (the one that you've
automatically set up to send e-mail from, unless you change it), then
choose Make Default. When you're done entering information, click OK.

The account is created. Now, whenever you create a new message, you have
the choice of using the new account instead of your original one. Similarly, when
you select Send & Receive, both (or all) of your e-mail accounts will be accessed
and the new e-mail will show up in the Inbox. (Notice that each message has a
column entry that tells you what account it was sent to.)

You can also check this account individually. In Outlook Express 5.0, choose
the account name from the Send and Receive button menu. Or, in all versions,
choose Tools | Send and Receive, then select the name of the account that you
want to check.

> TIP   *Want this account to not get checked for new messages when you check
> others? In Outlook Express 5.0, open the Accounts window (Tools |
> Accounts) and double-click the account name. Now, you can use the
> option "Include this account in my 'Send and Receive All' schedule" to
> determine whether or not it is checked when you check others. In earlier
> Outlook Express versions, head back to Edit | Preferences, click E-mail,
> and choose the account from the menu at the top of the dialog box. Now,
> click Advanced. Among other options you'll find Do Not Include This
> Server With Send & Receive All. Select that and you'll only be able to
> check the e-mail individually.*

Note that this is how you manage multiple accounts that the *same* person uses.
If you have more than one person using Outlook Express, check out the section
"Add Another User," later in this chapter.

Organize Your E-mail

Once you start to get some messages you'll probably become interested in
managing those messages, putting them into folders, and storing them away.
Outlook Express makes that easy enough to do, allowing you to create folders and
subfolders for filing your e-mail. But Outlook Express does more than that to help
you organize your e-mail.

Create and Delete Folders

The most basic organizational step is adding folders to the folder pane that runs down the side of the Outlook Express interface. You may have already experimented with these folders—if you click them once, the contents appear in the right-side pane. You can also double-click a folder to open it in its own window.

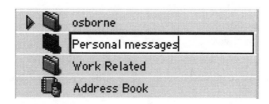

Creating a new folder is simple—just choose File | New | Folder. The folder appears in the Folder List, with the name highlighted and ready to edit. Type the name for your folder and press RETURN when you're done. If you need to re-edit the folder name, click once on the name and wait a few seconds, just as though you're editing a folder name in the Finder.

To move messages to the folder, select them in the message list, then drag-and-drop items from there to the folder. You can also CTRL-click on a particular message, choose Move To from the pop-up menu, then choose the folder to which you want to move the message.

To delete a folder, select it in the Folder List, then choose Edit | Delete Folder.

Create a Subfolder

You may find it useful to place subfolders within main folders in the Folder List. That makes it easier to stay organized and see the entire list at once without forcing too much scrolling. To create a subfolder, select the folder that will be its parent in the Folder List, then choose File | New | Subfolder. The subfolder appears, ready to have its name edited.

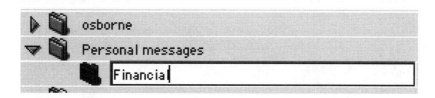

16

You can also take an existing folder and drag-and-drop it on another folder to cause the dragged folder to become a subfolder. The parent folder now has a triangle. When it's pointed down you see the subfolder; when it's pointed to the right, you don't.

With the subfolder created, you may think it's harder to drag-and-drop messages from the message list to a subfolder, but that's not true. There are two ways to do it. The obvious one is to click on the triangle to reveal the subfolders, then select your messages in the message list and drag them to one of the revealed subfolders.

There's also another way. Select and drag your message(s) from the message list to the "closed" triangle. Point directly at the triangle, and it should pop "open." Now the subfolders are revealed and you can drag the message(s) to the subfolder of your choice.

TIP   *Folders in the Folder List are alphabetized, so the rules for organizing the Apple menu apply to the Folder List—a space in front of the name moves folders to the top of the list and a bullet (OPTION-8) can move items toward the bottom of the list.*

How to ... Compact Folders in Outlook Express 4.5

After working with folders for a while in Outlook Express 4.5, you'll find that it's a good idea to *compact* your folders, a process that cleans up the database entries and recovers the storage space that had been used for deleted files. You can either compact your folders manually or automatically. To do it manually, select Tools | Compact and then select the folder you want to compact or All Local Folders. You can see the potential savings by pulling down this menu. Entries like "Inbox (+25k)" tell you that you can save 25 kilobytes of space by compacting that folder.

The option to automatically compact folders is in the Preferences dialog box under the Startup & Quit settings. There you can check the Automatically Compact Folders option and type in the entry box how much space will be saved before the automatic compacting takes place. (You can wait until 50 or 100 kilobytes will be saved, for instance, before the compacting process is begun automatically.)

Automate Using Rules

Need to automate your e-mail? Outlook Express allows you to build filters (called *rules*) that look at incoming mail and compare the messages against certain criteria. You create a rule for what happens to a particular e-mail message. If the mail matches a rule, then a certain action is taken—the message is deleted, moved to a particular folder, or automatically replied to, for instance.

Rules in Outlook Express 4.5

Here's how to create a rule in Outlook Express 4.5:

1. Select Tools | Mail Rules.

2. The Mail Rules window appears. Click New Rule to create a new filter.

3. The Define Mail Rule window appears (see Figure 16-4). This one looks a little intimidating, but it makes sense. Begin by giving the rule a number in the Rule Name entry box. You can leave the Apply To Incoming option checked if that's the sort of rule you're planning. (You can also apply rules to outgoing messages, but you'll probably find less reason to do that.)

4. In the Criteria section, build your "rule" using the menus and entry boxes. Pull down each menu to build a statement against which each piece of mail will be compared. This can require a little thought, since you need to consider why you're filtering and what it is the messages will have in common.

5. If you want more than one criteria statement, place a check mark next to the second entry and build another rule.

6. In the Execute Actions If menu, choose whether one or all of the criteria need to be met.

7. Now, select an action. You'll usually only have one, but you may have more than one. Notice that most of the actions will need a little more information in order to be complete, so they'll create another menu or entry box depending on which action it is.

8. The last thing to decide is whether to leave the Stop Applying Rules To This Message check box active. If it's active, then a message caught in this rule won't be compared to any other rules. That's probably what you want (once this rule finds a valid message, you'll perform the actions and be done with it), but you may occasionally want such a message to go through the rest of the rules, too.

9. Click OK.

16

Choose whether one or all criteria must be met.

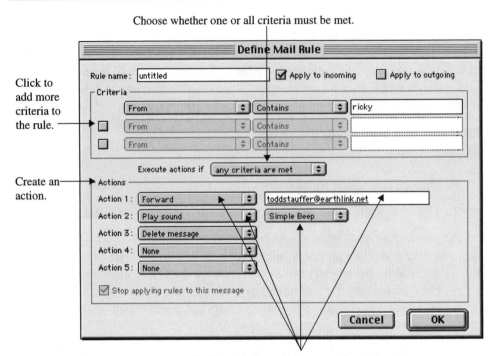

Click to
add more
criteria to
the rule.

Create an
action.

FIGURE 16-4   Creating mail rules to automatically filter incoming mail

Build a rule from the menus and entry boxes.

Rules in Outlook Express 5.0

If you have Outlook Express 5.0, the tools for creating mail rules are a little
different—you have more options while, at the same time, the dialog box has been
simplified a bit. Here's how to create your rule:

1. Choose Tools | Rules.

2. In the Mail Rules dialog box, select the tab for the type of mail or news
   account for which you'd like to create a rule. If the rule is for a standard
   POP e-mail account, choose Mail (POP).

3. Click the New button, or choose the type of rule you'd like to create from
   the New button's menu.

4. In the Define Mail Rule window, give the rule a name in the Rule name
   box (see Figure 16-5).

FIGURE 16-5 The Outlook Express 5.0 Define Mail Rule window

5. In the If section, build your rule using the menus and entry boxes. Pull down the menu that says "All Messages" and choose the beginning of a statement against which each piece of mail will be compared. (You might choose From, for instance, to create a statement that will compare the From portion of every incoming e-mail message against your criterion statement.) This can require a little thought, since you need to consider why you're filtering and what it is the messages will have in common.

6. If you want more than one criterion statement, click the Add Criterion button.

7. In the Execute Actions menu, choose whether one or all of the criteria need to be met. You can also choose "unless any criteria are met" or "unless all criteria are met" if you're filtering in that way.

8. Now, in the Then section, select an action. You'll usually only have one, but you may have more than one. Notice that most of the actions will need a little more information in order to be complete, so they'll create another menu or entry box depending on which action it is.

16

9. The last thing to decide is whether to leave the Stop Applying Rules To This Message check box active. If it's active, then a message caught in this rule won't be compared to any other rules. That's probably what you want (once this rule finds a valid message, you'll perform the actions and be done with it), but you may occasionally want such a message to go through the rest of the rules, too.

The Logic of Rules

Building rules can be tough—in a sense, it approaches the logic you need to create an AppleScript or a similar computer program. It's a basic "IF…THEN" statement—in order to use mail rules, you'll have to think that way.

Once you get your mind set to the problem, you'll find solutions. Let me tell you about a couple of rules I use. I have an e-mail newsletter I send out once a week to subscribers. People subscribe by sending an e-mail to a particular e-mail address (subscribe@mac-upgrade.com). The e-mail is automatically forwarded to my main mac-upgrade account. So, the first rule is: Was the message sent to subscribe@mac-upgrade.com?

```
To Is subscribe@mac-upgrade.com
```

Next, the user can either enter **subscribe** or **unsubscribe**, depending on what they want to do. So, the second rule is this: Does the subject say "subscribe"? (If it says something else, it'll need to be caught by another mail rule, for instance, that's designed to notice that the message is sent to subscribe@mac-upgrade.com but with the subject "unsubscribe.")

```
Subject is subscribe
```

Now, if those two criteria are met (I'll choose All Criteria Are Met from the Execute Actions If menu), the rule will go through a series of actions. The rule adds the sender's name to a mailing list I've created in the Contacts window of Outlook Express. Then the rule automatically replies to the sender to say that he or she was successfully added. Finally, it'll file the sender's message in a special folder I've created that allows me to quickly check the number of subscribers and access the subscription e-mail messages if there's a problem. So, the actions are:

```
Action 1: Add Sender to mailing list
Action 2: Reply
Action 3: Move message
```

NOTE *In Outlook Express 5.0, the first action would be "Add Sender to group."*

Because all criteria have to be met in order to invoke this rule, it's OK to keep the Stop Applying Rules To This Message check box checked, since only messages that met all the criteria have been affected. Other messages have already met a "try again" command in Outlook Express and have moved on to the next rule.

Add a New User

We've already seen that you can add a second or third e-mail account and integrate it into Outlook Express. But what if you want to share Outlook Express between two users? Having two people's mail come into the same Inbox can be confusing at best, unworkable at worst. Fortunately, there's a solution—creating a new user. Here's how:

1. In Outlook Express 5.0, choose File | Switch Identity. (In Outlook Express 4.5, choose File | Change Current User.) You'll go through a short process of closing down Outlook as if you were quitting the program. Then the Select a User window appears.

2. Click the New or New User button.

3. In the New User dialog box, enter a name for this user profile and select the existing user or default upon which Outlook should base this new user's initial settings. Click OK to create the new user. (In Outlook Express 4.5, click Save.)

4. In Outlook Express 5.0, you'll now see the Outlook Express Setup Assistant, which walks you through the process of creating a user. In Outlook Express 4.5, the program comes up as if it were the first time anyone had used the program. You add an e-mail account, create folders, organize mail, and build rules all without affecting any other user's setup.

Whenever you need to switch back and forth between users, just choose File | Switch Identity or File | Change Current User. After shutting down the current user, Outlook Express will offer up the Select New User window and allow you to choose who's using Outlook Express now. Highlight the user name and click OK.

16

Chapter 17

Surf with Internet Explorer and Netscape

How to...

- Figure out how Internet addresses work
- Get on the Web and surf the hyperlinks
- Choose a home page and set it up
- Manage your browser history, your favorite sites, and your bookmarks
- Fill in forms and check for secure connections
- Add plug-ins and work with Java applets

Throughout this book I've mentioned Web sites that you might enjoy visiting, so hopefully you've already had some experience with your Web browser. In this chapter we'll take a look at how you can get online with your Web browser and use the basic tools, then we'll move on to the more advanced features so you can become a power surfer.

Web Browser Basics

The World Wide Web is really a *protocol*—a set of computer-coded rules for transmitting information—more than it is a place or program. While it may seem that you're connecting to a central computer or some mechanism that broadcasts information like a TV network, the fact is that Web server computers are distributed all over the Internet and, therefore, all over the world. Since each individual server has its own address and each one speaks the same HyperText Transport Protocol (http), it's possible for you to connect to and read documents from computers all over the globe.

Consequently you don't really "log onto" the Web. Instead, you connect to the Internet through your ISP (Internet Service Provider), then you use your Web browser to visit particular server computers and view their documents.

The Web Browser

You may be surprised to learn that the Web browser is a fairly simple program. It's designed to read Web documents and format them to fit on your screen. The documents have instructions—things like "make this text bold" and "place an image document here on the page" that the Web browser interprets. Those instructions are in the HyperText Markup Language (HTML), which is actually fairly simple to learn.

These Web pages can include instructions to the browser to load all sorts of different documents and files, which is why the Web seems more complicated than it really is. For instance, a Web page can include a special instruction that says "load a Java program" or "display a QuickTime video." When this happens, part of your Web browser screen is given over to the video or Web program. But the Web page itself really isn't terribly complicated.

Instead, your Web browser's features are more about helping you organize, search, and approach the Web in a structured way. The browser includes Bookmarks or Favorites to help you save pages you like, a History file that helps

17

you track the pages you've seen, and other features that make it easy to send e-mail, download files to your iBook, and view or save images. The Internet Explorer (IE) and Netscape Communicator versions included with your iBook also feature advanced security and encryption to help you make online payments and transactions safer.

The Internet Address

The basis of surfing the Web is the Uniform Resource Locator (URL), which serves as the primary mechanism for addresses on the Web. The idea of the URL is simple—every Web document has its own address on the Internet. That way, if you want to view a particular document on a particular computer in a particular country, you simply enter the address.

Some URLs are simple, such as:

```
http://www.apple.com/
```

This URL points to the *index* page of Apple's Web site. In fact, the full address above is **http://www.apple.com/index.html**, although you don't have to type that entire address since it's assumed that if you don't enter a particular page name, you want to view the index page.

Another address might be:

```
http://www.mac-upgrade.com/ibook/index.html
```

This URL allows you to load the index page of the site that's dedicated to this book. In fact, it's pointed directly at that page—this is a unique address for a particular document on the Internet.

URLs are made up of three basic components—the protocol, the Web server address, and the path to the document. In the above example, *http://* is the protocol, *www.mac-upgrade.com* is the Web server computer's address, and */ibook/ index.html* is the path on the Web server computer to that file.

Here's what each component does and how they work:

- **Protocol** The protocol tells the browser what sort of Internet server you're trying to access. Enter **http://** for Web servers, **https://** for Web servers that have security enabled, and **ftp://** if you're accessing a File Transfer Protocol (FTP) server (FTP allows you to download files).

> **NOTE** *Actually, there are protocols for any kind of Internet service, although they vary a bit. For instance, mailto: is a protocol of e-mail from a Web browser—mailto: tstauffer@aol.com results in a new e-mail message addressed to me opening in your e-mail application. Other protocols include gopher://, news:, and telnet:.*

- **Server Computer Address**   Often this starts with *www*. It's simply the address to a particular computer (or group of computers) that is running a Web server application. That can even be an individual Mac, since modern Macs (and all iBooks) include Web server software. In that case, the server computer address will be a numbered address like *206.100.129.49* instead of a named address like *www.csindy.com*. In fact, as far as the Internet is concerned, all computer addresses are numbers, not names. The names are just for human convenience.

- **Path Statement**   A path statement tells the server computer what folder a particular document is stored in. Something like */ibook/index.html* tells the server computer to "look in the *ibook* folder and get me the *index.html* file." The server computer complies and sends a copy of that document, which is then displayed in your Web browser.

In order to load a page (or access some other Internet service) in your browser, enter a URL. There are a few different ways you can do that, as described in the next section.

> **TIP** *The browsers included with your iBook (Internet Explorer and Netscape Communicator) both allow you to enter Web addresses without the full URL. If you prefer, type **www.apple.com** or **206.100.129.49** without the protocol. It's a little quicker.*

Start Up and Open an Address

Once you understand the concept behind a URL, you're ready to load that URL in your Web browser. It's actually quite simple.

Before you can enter a URL, start up your browser. You can do that a number of different ways. To begin, open your Internet connection using the Control Strip

17

or the Remote Access control panel, if necessary. When you're connected to the Internet, do one of the following:

- Double-click the Browse the Internet icon on your desktop.

- Choose Internet Access | Browse the Internet from the Apple menu.

- In the Finder, double-click the icon for Netscape or Internet Explorer.

Now you'll see the browser start up and the default page—called your *home page*—will appear in the browser window. (I'm assuming you're connected to the Internet.) Now you can enter a URL in the Address entry box in the browser window.

Actually, there's another way to open your Web browser and enter a URL all at once. From the Apple menu, choose Internet Access | Connect To. (If you have Mac OS 9 on your iBook, you may not have this option.) This doesn't immediately open your browser—it opens a dialog box that asks you to enter a URL. Enter it, click Connect or press RETURN. Your Web browser starts up and the page associated with that URL will be loaded.

If you don't like your default browser, you can change it. (Internet Explorer is the "factory" default.) Open the Internet control panel, click the Web tab, and change the default browser. (Chapter 20 discusses the Internet control panel in more detail.)

Surf the Web

It's called "surfing" because, just like riding waves in the ocean, you never know exactly how you're going to get somewhere or how far down the beach you'll end up. In a Web browser, though, you surf by clicking a hyperlink.

Once you've loaded your first page (or when you're looking at the home page) you'll probably see hyperlinked text. A *hyperlink* is text or an image that can be clicked in the Web browser window. When you click the hyperlink, a new URL is automatically entered into the Address entry box and you're taken to a new page. That's the point of a hyperlink—it loads a new page.

Text link

A graphical link

'ork's Silicon Alley seems to have played a part in the decision,
; by Apple iCEO Steve Jobs' comment that, "Many of our
ers and developers live in or near New York City."

MacWorld Expo

net Slashes Prices

: Technologies this week announced a steep price cut on its Encore
5MHz/1M processor upgrade card for the Power Mac G3 line.

ed for high end systems running power-hungry applications, the

It's shipping! I hope this

Sometimes people have to adjust to single-clicking hyperlinks—they only need to be clicked *once*, not twice. This can be counterintuitive for many users, since we're used to double-clicking. But that's not true in a Web browser; you'd tire quickly by continually double-clicking links.

> **NOTE**   *Don't forget about those Back and Forward buttons we discussed in Chapter 2. They're a convenient way to maneuver while surfing.*

When you pass over a hyperlink using Internet Explorer or Netscape Communicator, your pointer icon will turn into a hand with an index finger sticking up—that means the pointer is over a hyperlink that can be clicked. To select it, just click the mouse once.

> **NOTE**   *Don't be surprised if some links open a new Web document in your window. There's a special code Web authors use to make a link open a new window. It's harmless enough, but if you don't like it, click the Close box in the new window.*

Click a Multimedia Link

Actually, a hyperlink can be used to load other things, such as images or multimedia, or you might even click a link that allows you to download a file.

17

Other than loading a new Web page, there are three different things that can happen when you click a link:

- ■ **A helper program is invoked.**   Your Web browser recognizes many types of files and passes them on to the appropriate application. For instance, if you click a link to a RealAudio file—a document that streams audio over the Internet—it will be passed on to the RealPlayer application, assuming it's installed. Similarly, clicking a hyperlink that leads to a mailto: URL activates your e-mail application.

- ■ **A plug-in is activated.**   The most common plug-in is QuickTime, which allows you to watch movies in your Web browser. There are also others, including plug-ins for Macromedia Flash documents, virtual reality documents, audio and video formats, and others.

NOTE *Plug-ins and helper applications are discussed in more depth later in this chapter.*

- ■ **A file is downloaded.**   If a link points to a file using an FTP protocol URL, the file will be downloaded to your iBook's hard disk. You can view it with another application, decompress it with StuffIt Expander (which is often done automatically), or perform a similar task.

Sometimes you'll click a hyperlink to a particular file and the Web browser won't recognize it. In that case, you can usually choose to download the file, ignore it, or search for the correct application to view it, as instructed by the dialog box.

Work with Frames

With some Web sites you'll encounter an *HTML frames* interface. This is a special sort of page that actually breaks a single Web browser window into different window panes (hence "frames") that are used to display different pages. In most cases, the idea is to click a link in one of the frames, then have the page change in another frame. Frames allow you to view many pages, worth of information without refreshing the entire window every time (see Figure 17-1).

If necessary, you can choose commands to allow you to go Back, Forward, and so on within that particular frame. Click and hold the mouse button within a frame to see a pop-up menu. You can then choose Back, Forward (if applicable), and other commands that will affect only that frame.

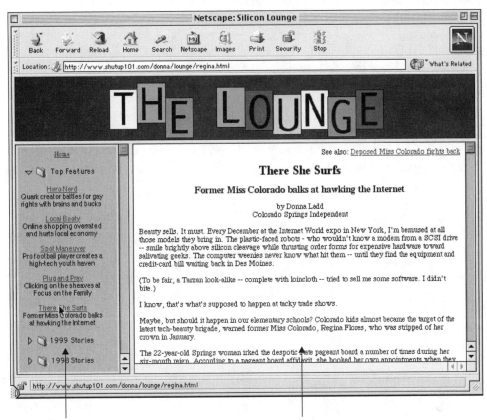

Click items in this frame…   …and the page in this frame changes.

FIGURE 17-1   A Web page that uses an HTML frames interface

Choose a Home Page

If you plan to spend a lot of time online, you'll want to get organized. The best starting place I know for getting organized is a good home page. In Internet Explorer or Netscape Communicator, it's easy to decide on a particular home page where you'd like to start your Internet adventure every time you sign on. (In fact, the home page is usually loaded every time you open a new browser window.) You can link to your company page, a page you particularly enjoy reading, a

17

professional *portal* page (a home page with news, sports, and other topical headlines) from one of the big Internet companies, or even to a page you create yourself.

Change Your Home Page

When you use Internet Explorer or Netscape Communicator for your Web surfing, your home page is already set for you—it's the Excite Live home page (see Figure 17-2). If you don't need or want to change from these defaults, skip down to the section "Edit the Home Page." You can change the home page, though, if you find one you like more or if you just want to experiment.

FIGURE 17-2 One of the popular "portal" home page sites

Popular sites that allow you to customize your own home page include:

My Excite	http://www.excite.com/
Apple Excite (offers Apple news)	http://apple.excite.com/
My Netscape	http://www.netscape.com/
Microsoft Network	http://www.msn.com/
My Snap	http://my.snap.com/
Go Network	http://www.go.com/
My Yahoo	http://my.yahoo.com/
Earthlink Personal Start Page	http://start.earthlink.net/

You don't have to go with one of the big names. Equally useful may be a smaller site that you enjoy visiting—one associated with a hobby or interest of yours. Of course, it should also be the sort of page that changes often—making a home page out of a page that's never updated is a little dull, unless it's filled with interesting hyperlinks.

Making any page into your home page is pretty simple, although you have a decision to make. Do you want to set this as your home page for all Web browsers you might open, or just for the current browser?

All Browsers

If you want to set your home page for all your browsers, do the following:

1. Open your potential home page in your browser.

2. Highlight the URL and choose Edit | Copy or press ⌘-C.

3. Select the Apple menu and choose Control Panels | Internet.

4. Select the Web tab in the Internet control panel.

5. In the entry box for the home page, highlight the contents of the box and delete the address that's currently there.

6. Select Edit | Paste or press ⌘-V to paste your home page URL into the Home Page entry box.

7. Press TAB or click the Close box in the control panel. When you do, you'll be asked if you want to save the new settings. Choose Save.

17

Now, the Home Page button in your Web browser should lead you to the new home page whenever you click it. Similarly, you'll see the home page every time you open a new browser window while you're connected to the Internet.

Specific Browser

If you want to set the page just for one particular browser, you'll follow different directions depending on whether you're using Internet Explorer or Netscape:

- **Internet Explorer**   Open the page you want to use as a home page, highlight the URL, and choose Edit | Copy. Now, choose Edit | Preferences and click the Home/Search button. Paste the URL into the Address entry box under Home Page.

- **Netscape Communicator**   Open the page you want to use as a home page. Choose Edit | Preferences and click the Navigator entry. Under Home Page, click the Use Current button.

Edit the Home Page

If you're using one of the major services for your home page, you should realize that you'll probably be able to edit it, if desired. Look for a link that says "Personalize This Page" or something similar. Click that link and you'll likely find yourself with tools that allow you to change what you view on the home page and the order in which you view it.

In the case of the Apple Excite page you'll actually register the first time you click Personalize, then you'll choose a few topics. The next time you choose Personalize is when you specify the order of things and how they look.

In most cases, you'll place a check mark next to items you want on the page. You'll then enter a number next to each item to choose how you want it prioritized—whether you want it to appear at the top or bottom of the page, for instance. You should be able to choose from a variety of topics, financials, types of news, entertainment, and so on.

You'll also likely be asked for some demographic information, as well as your ZIP code and perhaps your birthday (especially for horoscopes). If you're worried about the information getting out, look for a link to the company's privacy statement; also, look for an option you can check telling them they can't sell or use your information for advertising purposes.

Manage Bookmarks, Favorites, and History

Eventually you'll come across a site that's worth remembering, and at that point you'll want to create a Bookmark (Netscape) or a Favorite (Internet Explorer). These browser features each do the same thing—save a URL for future reference. It's pretty easy to do.

To set a Bookmark or Favorite, open the page in the browser window. Now, in Netscape, choose the Bookmark menu (it's actually a little Bookmark icon) and select Add Bookmark. In Internet Explorer, choose Favorites | Add Page to Favorites. When you do this, the browser stores the URL to the open page and places the title of that page on the Bookmarks/Favorites menu.

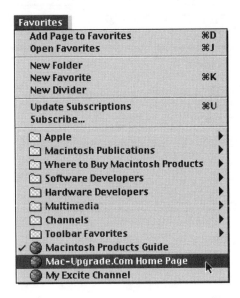

Now, whenever you want to return to that page, simply choose the Favorites or Bookmarks menu in your Web browser, then select the site. Your Web browser will find that page again and display it.

Each Web browser also provides tools for editing the Favorites/Bookmarks once you've created them.

Edit Favorites

In Internet Explorer you can edit your Favorites list by choosing Favorites | Open Favorites. In the Favorites window, you can drag-and-drop Favorites to move

17

them into folders or to change their order. When you're dragging a Favorite around, notice that a thin black line moves along the window with you to show you where it will appear when you drop it. You can rename a Favorite the same way you rename a file or folder in the Finder—click once on the name and wait a few seconds. When the name becomes highlighted, type the new name.

You can also create folders and dividing lines by choosing Favorites | New Folder or Favorites | New Divider. If you want to create a Favorite from scratch, choose Favorites | New Favorite. You'll then need to manually enter a name and URL for this Favorite.

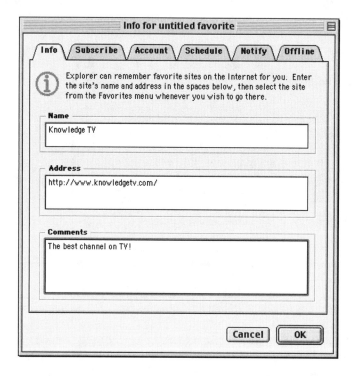

To delete a Favorite, select it in the Favorites window and choose Edit | Clear, or drag the Favorite from the Favorites window to the Trash can in the Finder. (You can also press ⌘-DELETE.)

In Internet Explorer you can edit the Toolbar Favorites to change the favorite items that appear on the toolbar just below the Address entry box.

Edit Bookmarks

To edit your Netscape Bookmarks, choose Edit Bookmarks from the Bookmarks menu. In the Bookmarks window, you can move folders and individual Bookmarks around by dragging and dropping. A black line moves with you to show you where the Bookmark (or folder) will appear in the list when you drop the item.

To edit the name or URL of a Bookmark, select the Bookmark and choose Edit | Get Info. The Info window appears where you edit the name or URL and/or enter a description. Click OK.

To add folders or separator lines, choose File | New Folder or File | New Separator. You can also manually create a Bookmark by choosing File | New Bookmark. This allows you to enter a new title and URL for the Bookmark using the same Get Info window.

Close the Bookmarks window; the Bookmarks menu has been changed with your edits.

Follow Your History

Both Netscape Communicator and Internet Explorer maintain a *history* of the sites you visit using two completely different methods. The history is simply a list of recently visited URLs that you can revisit from the Go menu in both browsers. Netscape Communicator maintains a history of each window individually and only for the life of that window.

17

In both browsers you can open a new window by selecting File | New Window. In fact, you can browse simultaneously in two, three, or more windows. In Navigator each window has its own history tracking that is deleted once you close the window. Explorer tracks them all and remembers visited sites despite closing windows.

In IE's history, visited sites are tracked and saved regardless of the windows you use. What's more, IE also tracks history for many days, limited only by a Preference setting on the Advanced button in the IE preferences.

You can also edit the history in IE if you'd like to delete items or if, perhaps, you'd like to drag-and-drop between the History window and the Favorites window. Choose Go | Open History to open your history, where you can drag the links from the History window to the Favorites window, the browser window (to view that Favorite), or the Trash (to delete that link from the History).

In Internet Explorer you can access both your History and your Favorites by clicking the tabs located at the left side of the browser window. This opens up the tabs to reveal a panel where links (either History Links or Favorites) are listed. Click a link and the main window will show that page.

Fill In a Form and Buy Things Online

Web browsers are capable of displaying Web pages that include form elements. Interface items that you might find in a dialog box within the Mac OS can be added to a Web page so that you can send information back to the Web server computer. These elements include familiar items like entry boxes, menus, check boxes, radio buttons, and regular buttons. All of these form elements are used pretty much like they are within the Mac OS.

The difference is, you're usually filling in personal information that you plan to send to the Web server computer so that it can be processed in some way. Perhaps you're buying computer software or subscribing to an online newsletter—or maybe you're setting up a home page, as discussed earlier in this chapter.

Fill In the Form

Web pages can allow you to fill in information and send it across the Internet. Usually filling in a form is pretty easy—you just enter the information necessary by typing in entry boxes and choosing items in lists or menus (see Figure 17-3).

FIGURE 17-3 Filling in a Web-based form

Other elements are also familiar. Press TAB to move between most of the parts of the form (you'll probably have to use the mouse to choose items from pull-down menus).

Once you have the form filled in, you'll need to look for a way to *submit* that form. Your data needs to be sent to the Web server computer, but it can't go until you say it can. In most cases you'll see a Send or Submit button that you click with the mouse. You may also see a Clear button that will clear the form of everything you've just entered. Don't click that button unless you're sure you want to clear the form.

Click Submit (or Send, or Search, and so on) and your data is sent over the Internet to the Web server computer where it's processed. In most cases clicking

17

the Submit button also loads a new page into your Web browser that either includes results from your data or a page telling you that your submission has been received.

Did I say your data is sent over the Internet? But what if it's private data like credit card numbers, salary figures, or e-mail addresses? Are you sure you want them floating around?

Check for a Secure Connection

In most cases where a Web site wants you to send financial or private information, they'll do so over what's called a *secure* server. What this means is simple—the Web site and your browser establish a connection over which data is encrypted. It's coded like a military transmission. The code can only be broken once your data gets to the server computer.

Each browser reports a secure connection in a similar way. In both Internet Explorer and Netscape, you'll see a small padlock icon in the bottom-left corner—it's locked and glowing when connected to a secure page.

Browse Offline and Automatically

Internet Explorer has a few different features that help you automate the use of Internet Explorer and, when used together, enable you to even browse the Web without actually being connected to the Internet.

Subscribe to Sites

Subscribe to a Web site and have Internet Explorer automatically update the site on a regular basis. This does two things for you. Periodically, while you're connected to the Internet, a site that you've subscribed to can be checked automatically. When the site is found to have changed, the Favorite will appear with a check mark next to it in the Favorites folder. If the Favorite happens to be a Toolbar Favorite, you'll see the icon next to it change to a sort of starburst, suggesting the site has new changes since the last subscription check.

You don't need permission and the site itself doesn't need to be specially set up in order for you to subscribe to it—IE is simply automatically checking the site for you to see if there have been changes.

Here's how to turn a Favorite into a subscribed Favorite:

1. Open the Favorites list for editing by selecting Favorites | Open Favorites.

2. Select the Favorite which you'd like to subscribe to and choose File | Get Info.

3. In the Info window, choose the Subscribe tab.

4. Place a check next to Check This Site For Changes. This causes the site to be subscribed; it will be checked according to the Subscription preferences.

5. If you'd like the subscription checked at some different interval, select the Schedule tab in the Info window for that particular Favorite. Place a check next to Use A Custom Schedule For This Site. Then, change the options in the window to reflect how you'd like the site updated.

Java and Plug-ins

You've already seen that your Web browser is capable of displaying and arranging images and text in the browser window. But Web browsers are also capable of giving over part of the browser window to other mini-applications that allow you to interact with an online program of some sort. These are called *embedded programs*—in the case of Java, they're often called *applets*. That just means that they're small programs that allow you to perform a simple task. Let's take a look at each.

Embedded Plug-in Files

Using plug-in technology, the Web browser can actually give control of part of the browser window to another little program which can be responsible for dealing with user input and displaying things on the screen. In most cases, these plug-ins add more multimedia, perhaps offering animated graphics, a unique interface to the Web site, and so on. One very popular plug-in technology is Macromedia's Shockwave technology, which allows you to view animated graphics within the browser window (see Figure 17-4).

NOTE *Your iBook comes pre-installed with the Shockwave, Flash, and QuickTime plug-ins. For best results, though, don't forget to check those software publishers' sites for updates.*

17

FIGURE 17-4   Plug-in technology adds interactivity (and visual effects) to Web pages.

Shockwave (**http://www.shockwave.com/**), a very popular plug-in, can be used for audio and video—most often for presentations, although you'll find comic books, advertisements, games, and other multimedia experiences authored in Shockwave.

Other plug-ins let you view a variety of embedded multimedia documents, like the Real Networks RealPlayer (**http://www.realnetworks.com/**). With RealPlayer you can view streaming audio and video (audio and video that are played as they arrive across the Internet in a data stream so you don't have to wait a long time for the data to download). Other popular plug-ins offer 3-D vistas, Virtual Reality Modeling Language (VRML) controllers, and so on. A great place to find many of the plug-ins available today for Web browsers is at Netscape's Browser Plug-in Web pages (**http://home.netscape.com/plugins/index.html**).

Of course, one of the most important plug-ins is the QuickTime plug-in, which is installed automatically. See Chapter 13 for more on using the QuickTime plug-in.

Add Plug-ins

Plug-in programs need to be placed in a particular folder—the Plug-ins folder—that's located within your Internet Explorer or Netscape Communicator folder. Most of the time you'll simply download the plug-in installer application, which will automatically place the plug-ins in the correct subfolder within your Web browser's folder.

But if you need to install a plug-in manually, begin by quitting the browser. Then, drag the plug-in program to the Plug-ins folder located within your Internet Explorer or Netscape Communicator folder. Drop the plug-in program in that folder.

Now, when you restart your Web browser, it will automatically search for and detect new plug-ins. Their functionality will be noted and the next time you encounter an embedded multimedia document, the correct plug-in will be loaded and used.

Work with Java

Aside from being an incredibly popular buzzword in the computing world, Java is two things. First, it's a programming language invented in the past few years, offering advanced programming language constructs that many programmers really like. It's a lot like the C++ language, which is popular among computer scientists.

Second, Java is a virtual platform or virtual machine. What that means is simply this: The Java virtual machine allows a Java language program to run, unaltered, on just about any sort of computer made. It does this by emulating a less sophisticated virtual "Java" computer.

With most applications, you have to specifically buy a Mac OS application or a Microsoft Windows application. And, as you know, one type of application won't run on another type of computer. Java changes that by allowing a Java program to run on the virtual machine without forcing it to notice which computer it's actually being run on. The Java virtual machine is written specifically for the particular OS—Apple writes the MRJ (Macintosh Runtime for Java), for instance, that makes it possible for you to run Java applications on your iBook.

Read about MRJ and download updates at **http://www.apple.com/ java/**. This is a good idea because Apple often updates MRJ (even between Mac OS updates) to make it much faster and cooler. To figure out what version you currently have, open the Apple Extras folder, open the Mac OS Runtime for Java folder, and see what ReadMe file is in there (About MRJ 2.1, for instance). If the Web site offers a newer version, download and install it.

In most cases, Java works seamlessly on your iBook—there's nothing in particular you need to do. In fact, if you download and install a Java applet on your iBook, it'll work just like any other iBook program.

Often, though, Java applets are loaded over the Internet and displayed in your Web browser. To use Java applets, if it requires any user interaction, simply point and click the mouse like you would with any Mac application (see Figure 17-5).

17

FIGURE 17-5 Java allows small applications to appear within the Web browser window.

Troubleshoot Java Applets

If you're encountering trouble with Java, change the virtual machine and alter some other options in Internet Explorer. (As of this writing, Netscape Communicator 4.7 and lower uses its own Java virtual machine which can't be changed.) In IE, here's how to choose the Java virtual machine:

1. Choose Edit | Preferences in IE.

2. Click the Java button.

3. At the top of the preferences window, make sure Enable Java is checked.

4. In the Java Virtual Machine menu, choose MRJ. (Or choose Microsoft Virtual Machine, if desired. The Microsoft Virtual Machine, if installed, may give you different capabilities and performance characteristics. For most situations, however, MRJ is a good choice.)

5. Click OK.

If you've changed the Java machine you're using, you'll need to restart Internet Explorer. If you continue to have trouble, you may need to increase the amount of memory that's allocated to Internet Explorer (or run IE with fewer applications in the background). See Chapter 21 for more on allocating memory to your applications.

Chapter 18

Download, Back Up, and Transfer Online

How to...

- Back up files from your iBook to the Web
- Use the File Transfer Protocol to upload and download
- Compress and decompress files
- Create and use floppy disk images
- Find and use shareware and freeware applications

The iBook is designed to live on the Internet, more so than most computers. It's built to transfer files online, back up files online, and get most of its updates, new installations, and new tools online.

In this chapter, let's take a look at how you upload to and download from the Internet. (*Upload* means to send files from your iBook to a distant computer, while *download* means to bring files from a distant computer across the Internet to your iBook.) You'll also see how to back up your iBook files using the Internet and learn some ways to get new applications and application updates into your iBook over the Internet.

Transfer Files over the Internet

There are several different ways you can transfer files over the Internet. We've already discussed one of them in Chapter 16: You can attach files to e-mail messages in order to transport them from one computer to another. This is one way that some iBook users move documents from work to home, for instance—if you have different e-mail accounts for each location, then you can just mail an attachment to yourself.

You can also send files via the File Transfer Protocol (FTP) using special applications for the task. You'll need to download the applications, but it's really very convenient after that. We'll discuss that method in a moment.

First, though, let's use the familiar Web browser to access an online storage method that has gained in popularity since the iBook was first introduced.

The Virtual Floppy

One great way to transfer files is to take advantage of a number of Web sites that offer a service called the *virtual floppy*. In essence, a virtual floppy is a few megabytes of storage space available via Web browsers, allowing you to upload a file to the Web site using one computer, then download it again using another computer. These services are usually provided free of charge because they sell advertising.

All of these sites can have slightly different interfaces, so you'll need to read the instructions posted at the site. Let's look at one example—a site called imacfloppy.com.

18

You need a membership in order to create your virtual floppy the first time. Head to the site and choose the New User button (or Sign Up Here!) to create a membership. There's some optional demographic information when you sign up, but all that's required is a name and e-mail address.

Here's how to transfer files using the imacfloppy.com service:

1. Connect to the Internet and use your Web browser to go to **http://www. imacfloppy.com**.

2. Now, log in with your member name and password. Your download space is password-protected so nobody else can access it.

3. When you get to the main screen, you'll see two boxes—one represents your online space, while another represents your iBook (or the computer that you're currently on). Now you can copy a file from your computer to the virtual floppy. To do that, click the Browse button on the "my computer" side.

4. Now, in the Open dialog box, find the file you want to upload to the virtual floppy. Select the file and click Open.

5. The filename appears in the window next to the Browse button. Click the arrow (>>) button to send the file on its way.

6. After the upload takes place, you'll see a dialog box letting you know the transfer was successful. Click OK and you'll see the new file appear in the file list on the right.

Filenames	Date	Size
⦿ Chapter One.cw4	1-12-99	10.5k
○ Invoice	2-28-99	6.4k
○ Law Abiding ...	1-4-99	9.8k
○ SBM05SC.DOC	2-1-99	96.6k
○ The Spot - T...	1-4-99	12.7k
○ The Spot Script	1-4-99	46.2k
○ linux.rtf	1-1-99	11.2k

7. If you're done transferring, log out. Down at the bottom of the Web page you'll find a link that allows you to log out from the site. Click this link to leave the site.

The file has now been uploaded and is being stored on your iMacFloppy. Now you can go to another computer where you want the file to ultimately arrive (at work, at the beach house, at grandma's house) and download it. Here's how you download files:

1. Log into imacfloppy.com again as you did before.

2. When you see the main transfer screen, find the file on the iMacFloppy side that you'd like to download. Click that file's radio button.

3. Now, click the left arrow (<<) button to send the file from the iMacFloppy down to your computer. (I'd say "your iBook" instead of "your computer" but remember, you can do this from any computer, as long as the file that you're uploading and downloading is compatible with both computers.) You'll see the Download Manager (in Internet Explorer) or a download window (in Netscape Navigator). The file will be downloaded to your computer.

File	Status	Time	Transferred
√ DJ800USB.SIT	Complete	11 Minutes	5.9 MB
√ Nanosaur 1.1.2 Instal...	Complete	28 Minutes	10.0 MB
√ ATIMac33.sit	Complete	15 Minutes	1.9 MB
√ nano11inst.sit	Complete	5 Minutes	718 KB
√ Nanosaur™ (iMac 2...	Complete	5 Minutes	636 KB
● Invoice(*)	Transferring	unknown	0 bytes

4. Finally, you should see the file on the desktop or wherever the default folder is for downloaded files on your computer. (The default folder is set in the Internet control panel, under the Web tab.)

Now you'll want to manage your files at iMacFloppy. First, you can view files within your iMacFloppy, assuming they happen to be files that can be easily viewed by a Web browser (that includes text files, HTML documents, GIF and JPEG documents). Click the radio button next to the file you want to view and click the View button in that window. The document will appear in a new window, assuming the browser can display it. You can close the Viewer window by clicking its Close button.

You can also delete files from the iMacFloppy. Click the radio button next to the file you want to delete, then click the Trash icon. This will immediately delete the file (there's no "Are you sure?" dialog box).

File Transfer Protocol

You should get to know how FTP works, especially if you have large files, many files, or if you'd simply prefer knowing that your files are privately stored and not located on a commercial server. (Even though it's unlikely anyone will bother with your files, you might sometimes feel like being extra careful.)

The process is simple—you download a particular type of application designed to allow you to transfer files over the Internet. These programs make file transfer simple—in most cases, it's a drag-and-drop procedure.

 You can also use a Web browser to download files from FTP sites, but using an FTP program offers you more options and control, especially for uploading files.

Once you have the application, you'll also need some FTP storage space, most likely through your ISP. If your ISP offers Web storage space, then you can use that—otherwise, you might ask them if they make storage space available to users. It's rare, but they may do it for an extra charge. In most cases, standard Internet accounts have at least some storage space available.

The FTP Address

FTP servers have an address, just as Web servers do. The difference is, some FTP servers will require you to log in as a registered user of that server, then you'll get access to certain or all files on that server. You'll be able to use the FTP program to upload and download files that are stored in your Internet space. So, the burning question you need to ask your ISP is, "What is the address I use to access my Internet space?" In most cases it'll be an address like ftp.*mac-upgrade.com* or, perhaps, www.*companyname.net*, depending on the type of server computer.

Please Login to a Server

Address:	ftp-www.earthlink.net
Username:	toddstauffer
Password:	••••••••••••••••
Directory:	

Connect

NOTE *Some FTP servers, called "anonymous" servers, allow you to log in and download files without specifically having an account on the system. Anonymous FTP access is discussed later in this chapter. For servers where you'll be uploading files, you'll generally need to be a registered user.*

You may also need an account on that computer—presumably, you have one if you're using the free space provided by your ISP. If that's so, then you'll just need to know your username and password in order to access the FTP server computer. (That's where you'll be storing your files.) Most likely they're the same as your username and password for the dial-up connection, but they may be different. Ask your ISP.

The FTP Application

So what should you use for an FTP application? It's up to you, although any of them need to be downloaded from the Internet before you can use them. My personal favorite is a relatively new FTP application called Transmit, shown in Figure 18-1. I like the way it looks, for one, and I like the way it makes it easy to see what's on your computer vs. what's on the Internet computer. In a sense, it's a little like the iMacFloppy.

Transmit is written by Panic Software and can be downloaded from **http://www.panic.com**. It costs $24.95 to license the software if you like it. (It's shareware, which is discussed later in this chapter.)

Other popular FTP programs include Fetch (**http://www.dartmouth.edu/pages/softdev/fetch.html**) and Anarchie (**http://www.stairways.co.au/**), both

18

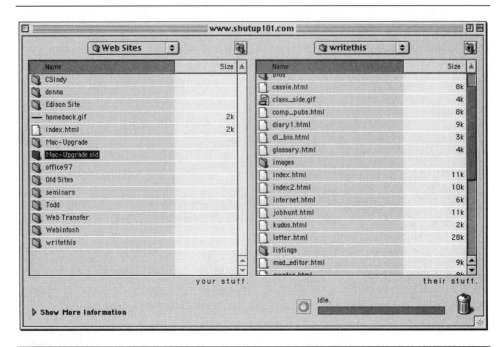

FIGURE 18-1   Transmit makes it easy to transfer files via FTP—just drag-and-drop.

of which are great programs with a long history on the Mac platform. They work slightly differently from Transmit, but the concepts are the same.

Upload and Download

Once you have your FTP program installed and you've made sure that your Internet connection is active, you're ready to transfer files to the distant site. In FTP parlance, uploading a file uses the Put command and downloading a file requires the Get command. If you're using Transmit, you won't see these commands by default, but Anarchie and Fetch both use them.

1. Start up the FTP application and enter an FTP server computer address. You should also enter username and password information, if relevant. Click the button that allows you to log on.

2. Once you've successfully logged on, you'll see a file list. Create a folder that you can use for uploading and downloading files. (In Transmit, use

File | New Folder). I like to call my folder "Transfer" since that's what I tend to use it for.

If the free FTP space offered by your ISP is for a Web site, then you may be shown, by default, a folder that is available to everyone on the Web. Instead, you need to create a private folder. Ask your ISP how to do that. If your FTP space has a folder called Webpage, then it's possible that the parent of that folder is where you can create a private subfolder.

3. Double-click that subfolder.

4. Now, if you're using Transmit, you can select the files you want to upload in the My Stuff window, then click and drag the files to the Their Stuff window. If you're using Fetch or Anarchie, you can drag files from the Finder to the open folder in that application. (You can also use the Put command in Fetch or Anarchie.)

That's it—you should see the files now available in that folder. To retrieve or download a file, the process is reversed—you can drag-and-drop a file from the Web server folder to the desktop or a folder in the Finder. Or you can select the file and drag it to the My Stuff window (in Transmit), click the Get button (in Fetch), or choose the Get command (in Anarchie). The file is downloaded and saved on your hard disk.

Encode as MacBinary

Before you get too busy uploading and downloading, there is one basic issue we need to touch on—encoding. As you may recall from Chapter 16, it's often necessary to encode files before you can send them as attachments through e-mail. That's not quite the case with FTP, which has built into it the ability to save and store files in a binary state.

That said, uploaded files are often not stored in a Mac-native state. That is, the unique elements of a file that make it a Mac file—things like the icon, the document association that allows a document to launch its parent application, and so on—can be lost when you upload to another computer, especially a Windows or Unix server. So, you have a choice to make.

If the file is cross-platform anyway—a Microsoft Word document, a GIF or JPEG graphic, or a text file like an HTML document—then it's fine to store it as a regular FTP binary file. But if the file or document is Mac-specific—or if you'd

18

simply prefer to maintain all the Mac-like qualities of your uploaded files—then you should save them as MacBinary as you upload them. You can usually accomplish this by choosing to save them as MacBinary either from the preferences of your FTP program or as you're uploading them.

In Transmit you can encode a file as MacBinary before you upload it—select the file in the My Stuff window and choose File | Encode as MacBinary. Notice that the letters ".bin" are appended to the document's name. Now you can upload the file without worrying about its saved state. When you download the file back to another computer, you can decode the MacBinary encoding and use the file.

NOTE *If you plan to download a file for use on a Windows or Unix computer, then store it as a typical FTP upload instead of encoding it first. If you need to transfer a file from your iBook to a Windows/Unix computer and then, finally, to another Mac, encode it in the MacBinary format. The Windows/Unix computer can transmit such files, it just can't use MacBinary files as documents.*

Compress Files and Decompress Files

Since large files take a long time to transmit over the Internet, it's sometimes preferable to *compress* them. This is another encoding process—using sophisticated algorithms, the compression software is able to reduce redundant information in a document or program and make the file more compact. The catch is that the file is completely useless until it's expanded using the reverse of the compression scheme.

The other thing you can often do with most compression schemes is create a compressed archive of more than one file, so that a number of files or an entire folder can be stored and sent within a single archive file, almost as if it were a shipping envelope. Once the file arrives at its destination, the decompression program is used to separate the files and bring them back to full size.

To do all this, you need to pick a compression scheme. There are three major schemes used for compressing files on the Internet. They are:

- **StuffIt Expander** This format (with the filename extension ".sit") is used almost exclusively by Macs, although there is a Windows version of StuffIt Expander available. Windows users who have Aladdin Expander for Windows can expand "stuffed" archives created on a Mac.

- **PKZip**   This format is used almost exclusively in the Windows world. A number of utilities are available on the Mac to create PKZip (or just ".zip") files, and StuffIt Expander can expand .zip files if the Expander Enhancer is installed.

- **Gzip and Unix Compress**   These formats are generally used by Unix machines (the files have .gz and .Z extensions). StuffIt Expander can decompress these files if the Expander Enhancer is installed.

StuffIt and DropStuff

For decompressing files that you download, StuffIt Expander will work with any files created on a Mac, even older formats like Compact Pro. If you need to decompress archives created on Windows or Unix machines, you must make sure you have DropStuff with Expander Enhancer installed.

DropStuff is shareware; you'll pay $25 if you find it useful. In the meantime, install it to add the ability for StuffIt Expander to decompress .zip, .gz, and .Z archives along with its built-in ability to decompress .sit archives. Just drag the files to StuffIt Expander once DropStuff has been installed.

*There may be a more recent version of StuffIt and DropStuff available since you purchased your iBook. Check **http://www.aladdinsys.com** to find a new version.*

The procedure for *decompressing* most archives is to simply drag-and-drop the archive onto the StuffIt Expander icon. (It's a good idea to create an alias to StuffIt Expander and place it on the desktop if you download files often.) When you drop an archive on StuffIt Expander, it will expand the archive if it possibly can. And StuffIt knows quite a bit about expanding archives.

You can usually decompress .sit files easily by double-clicking them. Also, many Web browser and e-mail applications, including those bundled with your iBook, will automatically decompress .sit files when you access them.

How about *compressing* files? If you're sending a file to a Macintosh, compress it as a StuffIt file. To do that, simply drag-and-drop the file, folder, or group of files (and folders) to the DropStuff icon. When you release the mouse button, DropStuff goes into action, stuffing the files into an archive.

18

You don't always have to compress a file yourself before sending it. Outlook Express, for instance, can be set to automatically compress a file before you send it as an attachment. See Chapter 16 for details.

If you're only stuffing one document, then the archive file is named for that document with a .sit filename extension. If you're stuffing more than one document, you'll get a file named archive.sit. You can rename the file just as you can rename any other file. One suggestion, however: Keep the .sit part so that your receiving party (assuming you're sending this to someone else) knows to drag it to StuffIt Expander.

 If you encounter a file with the extension .sea, it's a self-extracting archive. It doesn't require StuffIt Expander in order to decompress—just double-click it and it will decompress itself. It has a tiny version of Expander built into it.

Compress Using PC/Unix Formats

If you're sending a file to a Microsoft Windows machine, use PKZip. And if you're sending to a Unix machine, you should probably skip compressing the file. (After all, it's unlikely that you're sending a binary document or application to a Unix machine.) If you really need to compress the file, there are utilities available. Here are the main ones:

Utility	Description	URL
ZipIt	Creates and decompresses Windows PKZip archives	http://www.awa.com/softlock/zipit/
AsiZip PKZIP for Mac	Creates and decompresses Windows PKZip archives	http://www.asizip.com/products/pkzipmac.htm
MacGzip	Creates and decompresses Unix Gzip archives	http://persephone.cps.unizar.es/~spd/gzip/

Back Up Online

Since an iBook has no floppy drive (or other built-in removable disk for storage), one important option to consider is backing up online, especially if you haven't bought an add-on external disk drive or if your iBook doesn't connect to a local network where you can back up your files. It's vital that you back up your files—even your personal documents—so that if something happens to your iBook, you still have your data. If you use your iBook for business or for school, or even if you just use it for your personal financial tracking in AppleWorks, you should definitely back up regularly.

One way to back up your files is to use an application to transmit your backup data to a storage area on the Internet. Such storage space can be a little pricey—starting at $15–30 a month—and the backup can take a long time to transmit if you have a lot of documents. Still, if you're considering backing up a limited amount of data and you'd like it done without purchasing a removable drive or over a local network, then Internet backup is the way to go.

NOTE *Using a removable drive for backup is discussed in Chapter 23.*

By far the best software for backup is Retrospect Express, a lower-cost version of the most popular Mac backup utility, Retrospect. Retrospect Express can be purchased at local computer stores and popular online software stores. You can also find information about it and purchase it directly from Dantz at **http://www.dantz.com/**.

You'll also need an online backup service. You can use FTP space that you lease from your ISP or other company, and it may be inexpensive. (The data files generated by Retrospect Express can be compressed and encrypted, so your ISP won't really have access to your files.) The only issue then becomes, how much do you trust your ISP to guarantee the *integrity* of your data? You might ask them if they're backing up and if they recommend you use their FTP servers for online backup.

Some services exist specifically to help you with online backup. They generally guarantee a certain level of security, privacy, and redundancy—some go so far as to have redundant servers in secure buildings in different parts of the world. Here are some backup services recommended by Dantz:

Recover-iT!	http://www.recover-it.com/
MacBackup	http://www.macbackup.com/
Portland Communications (UK)	http://www.portland.co.uk/retrospect.html

18

Work with Floppy Images

Now we're going to deal with floppy disks—even though the iBook has no disk drive. Instead, we'll talk about floppy *disk images*.

Floppy disk images are files that act just like floppy disks (or similar removables). Once you double-click a floppy disk image, the floppy disk is mounted.

Once the floppy disk is mounted, it acts just like any other disk. You can drag files to its icon, for instance, to copy files onto the disk. Similarly, you can double-click the floppy disk to open its window and copy files from (and sometimes to) that window. But it's not a disk at all—it's just a special kind of file.

Types of Floppy Images

There are two different kinds of floppy-disk images—self-mounting images (.smi) and regular-disk images (.img). A self-mounting image can be used on any Macintosh, since it mounts itself. This is how most update and other software is distributed by Apple these days, making it easy to download the images and double-click to mount them. Then you can install from them as if they were regular disks.

To use regular image files, you'll need the Disk Copy software, which can be downloaded from the Apple Software Updates site (**http://asu.info.apple.com/**). (It should also be installed in the Utilities folder on your hard disk.) Once you have the Disk Copy software downloaded or copied from the Mac OS CD-ROM and installed, you can mount regular image files just as if they, too, were regular disks. Just double-click them.

Create an Image File

You can create your own image files as well. This can be useful in two ways. First, you can take any folder or group of documents and mount it onto a disk image. You can then transfer that image to other Macs so that they can use the folder of files. Plus, the disk images are compressed, just like StuffIt files. So, the files are compressed, convenient, and very cool—and these disk images are easy to understand and use.

Second, you can use a Mac *other than* an iBook to create a floppy image of a particular floppy disk that you need to use. Once the disk image is created, the disk image file can be transmitted to your iBook and used as if it were a diskette. That makes it that much easier to move old documents or backups you may have stored on floppies to your iBook.

> **TIP**   *A good use of floppy images is to store them on CDs. Check with your local Macintosh retailer, Apple Specialist, or Mac User Group to see if they offer a floppy-to-CD service. It's a valuable service to have your floppy disks copied onto a CD that you can use with your iBook. With over 600MB of capacity on a CD, that's over 425 floppy disks!*

Here's how you create an image file:

1. Start up Disk Copy (discussed in the previous section).

2. When the Disk Copy window appears, drag-and-drop the folder or the floppy-disk icon you want to create an image of into the window. (Remember, if you're using a different Macintosh that has a floppy drive, you can create the image from an actual floppy disk icon that has been mounted on your desktop.)

3. The Save Disk Image As dialog box appears. Give the disk image a name and choose a folder in which it should be stored. (You may want it saved on the desktop.) You can also choose various options, including whether the image will be Read Only or Read and Write (if it's Read and Write then you'll be able to save files to it when it's mounted) and whether the image should be mounted once it's created. You can also choose the size of the image, from a fixed size like 1.4MB or 500MB, or you can choose the Data Size option, where the size varies with the data you're creating an image of. Once you've made your choices, click Save.

4. Disk Copy goes to work and creates an image of the disk or folder and places it on the desktop.

> **NOTE**   *Remember, even if your disk image is in a folder, the mounted disk icon will always appear on the desktop, just like any other disk.*

18

Find and Use Shareware and Freeware Programs

One of the main reasons to learn the nuances of uploading and downloading programs is so that you can start to work with shareware and freeware programs. These are computer programs available on the Internet (or online services) for downloading and using immediately on your iBook.

If the software is shareware, you'll find yourself with a grace period during which you can use the program—often 30 days. If you go past the 30 days, a number of things might happen. You may not be able to save documents anymore. You may not have access to all the features. Or, you may be able to use the program as before, but you'll see "nag" screens—screens that pop up reminding you to pay for the program—more frequently.

 "Demo" versions of commercial software often work like shareware, at least in some respects. Usually you'll have a demonstration period where you can use all or most of the software's features. After the demo period expires, you generally have to pay for the software to continue using all of its features.

With freeware, the program is simply free, although there may be other licensing restrictions. (It may be free in certain settings, like education and non-profit, but not free for corporate use, for instance.) As you can tell, much of freeware and shareware is sold on the "honor system," and this is done for two reasons. First, it's easier for smaller companies and individuals to distribute software this way on the Internet because they don't have to pay for boxes, books, and shipping to major retail stores. Second, these applications and utilities are often meant for a more focused audience—people who need a specific solution to a problem, not a general application or utility.

Don't for a moment think that shareware and freeware aren't good programs just because they aren't sold at electronics stores. (By way of comparison, shrink-wrapped, packaged programs are called *commercial* software.) There is a lot of great shareware and freeware available for downloading—programs that do amazing things and have wonderful interfaces. In fact, you've already learned about Transmit, Fetch, and Aladdin's StuffIt products, all of which are distributed as shareware. (And StuffIt Expander is freeware!)

If there's an application or utility (or even a game) that you currently desire, it's a great idea to pop online and search for such a solution in an online library of shareware solutions. You might find exactly what you're looking for, and shareware is often cheaper than a trip to the computer store.

Find Good Shareware

Fortunately, you're not on your own when it comes to finding decent shareware. There are a number of ways to use your browser for shareware, including great services that help you search for exactly what you're seeking. You can usually search by keywords, or you can take a look at the most popular downloads, most recent additions, and so on.

These days, some of the Macintosh magazines—MacAddict (***http://www.macaddict.com***)*, Mac Home* (***http://www.machome.com/***)*, Inside Mac Games* (***http://www.imgmagazine.com/***)*—and many of the large Macintosh user groups, like Arizona Mac Users Group (AMUG,* ***http://www.amug.org/***)*, offer CD subscriptions. Subscribe and you'll regularly receive a CD-ROM in the mail, allowing you to sample the latest shareware and freeware as sampled by the editors of that magazine or CD service.*

Web Download Sites

You can begin by heading out to a Web download site using your browser. There, you'll be able to search using keywords and locate shareware and freeware that can solve the problem or fill the gap that you want filled. Many of them even feature weekly updates, stories that suggest new programs, and ways to figure out what would be best for you (see Figure 18-2).

Here are a few of my favorite places to find shareware on the Web:

CNet's Download.com	Repository of all sorts of downloadables, including shareware, demos, patches, and updates	http://www.download.com
CNet's Shareware.com	Great search engine for shareware and freeware	http://www.shareware.com
ZD's Macdownload.com	Mac focus with ratings from the Ziff-Davis Mac magazine staffs (*Macworld, MacWeek*)	http://www.macdownload.com
Version Tracker	Tracks new programs and new versions, both commercial and shareware, available on the Internet	http://www.versiontracker.com
SoftWatcher	Tracks new programs and updates; offers a Mac-specific section	http://www.softwatcher.com/mac/

18

FIGURE 18-2   The Macdownload.com site is a popular destination for finding Mac shareware and freeware.

Each of these sites has its strengths, including cataloging, reviewing, and rating popularity. In most cases you'll search or browse for a particular title, then you'll follow the links in order to download the file. It'll show up in your default folder for downloads (which is set using the Internet control panel) or on the desktop.

Often, these sites will point you to the original Web site offered by the program's author or some FTP repository of Mac downloadables. But what if you could access such an FTP site directly?

Anonymous FTP Sites

One of the main repositories of Mac software is the Info-Mac archive, which is maintained by the Info-Mac organization. It's distributed to many, many different *mirror* sites, however, so you won't ever really access the Info-Mac servers themselves; instead, you'll access a site that serves as a mirror image of the original archive at Info-Mac.

Log In to Anonymous FTP

In many cases, public servers are available for accessing downloadable software. With FTP, you get less information and a less friendly interface than with a Web site. You'll probably need to know the exact name of the file you want to download. Armed with that knowledge, however, you can easily log into and access these files using your FTP program. You can also often use a Web browser to access an FTP site—just remember to enter the URL to the site as ftp://ftp.*mysite.com*/ instead of http://ftp.*mysite.com*/ in the browser's entry box. That tells the browser you want to initiate an FTP session.

The trick is to log in anonymously—enter **anonymous** as your username in your FTP program when accessing one of the public servers. (You skip this step if you're using a Web browser.) You'll probably be able to get by without a password, but etiquette dictates that you enter your e-mail address as your password—that way the public server administrators can get a hold of you if there happens to a be a problem or a concern. It's very, very unlikely that anyone would ever contact you using the e-mail address, but it can't hurt to add it. (Some sites, like Apple and Microsoft, don't require you to enter a username or password.)

```
┌─────────────── New Connection... ───────────────┐
│ Enter host name, userid, and password (or        │
│ choose from the shortcut menu):                   │
│                                                   │
│ Host:       │ uiarchive.uiuc.edu            │     │
│                                                   │
│ User ID:    │ anonymous                     │     │
│                                                   │
│ Password:   │ ●●●●●●●●●●●●●●●●               │     │
│                                                   │
│ Directory:  │ /pub/systems/mac/info-mac     │     │
│                                                   │
│ Shortcuts:  ▼    [ Cancel ]   [  OK  ]            │
└───────────────────────────────────────────────────┘
```

There are a number of such FTP mirror sites that you can log into anonymously. Two FTP mirror sites are Apple's (**ftp://mirror.apple.com/mirrors/Info-Mac. Archive/**) and America Online's (**ftp://mirrors.aol.com/pub/info-mac/**).

18

For a complete listing of mirror sites, you can access any of the Info-Mac archives, look for the help directory, and access the document mirror-list-html.txt. The best way to work with the file is probably to download it to your iBook, then open it using your Web browser.

Once downloaded, you're ready to decompress, install, and use the shareware, freeware, or demo on your iBook. You've seen how to do all this stuff already, earlier in this chapter. Now you're ready to make it happen!

 Downloading files causes many computers to catch viruses since infected files are usually transmitted via the Internet. Many public archives check their files with virus checkers, but not always. If you'd prefer to be on the safe side, read about virus checking in Chapter 27.

Recommended Shareware Titles

You've already seen how to download and decompress the programs, so now let's look at different titles. This is by no means an exhaustive list as there are thousands of shareware titles available for your iBook. Instead, I'll offer a few titles that have proven themselves among Mac users and are popular with many, many people.

All of these files can be found on the public servers—**http://www.download. com/, http://www.macdownload.com/,** and so on.

- **GraphicConverter (Shareware)**   Designed as an inexpensive ($35) Photoshop-killer, GraphicConverter is important to have on hand if you work with a lot of digital images, perhaps for Web sites or for publishing. The program allows you to convert between popular image formats, edit those images, and apply different effects to an image. There are even drawing, text, and shape tools allowing you to draw on and transform a digital image.

- **SoundApp (Freeware)**   This program allows you to play and save sound files in various formats, many of which are discussed in Chapter 13. You can also create a Play List and play your digital sound files in the background while you work on other tasks.

- **SndSampler (Shareware)**   Using either an add-on USB microphone or an audio CD in the CD-ROM drive, or by plugging a line-level microphone or other line-level device in the iBook's sound-in port, you can record sounds using this application. (You'll see more about adding sound equipment in Chapter 23.) SndSampler offers a very straightforward, tape-player–like interface that makes it clear what you're attempting to do—record audio.

- ■ **BBEdit Lite (Freeware)**   BBEdit is the premiere text-editing application for Macintosh, designed for programming, creating HTML documents, or even working with AppleScript. BBEdit Lite is the freeware counterpart to BBEdit—it does many of the same things and it's available at no charge. It's perfect for when SimpleText can't open a document because it's too large, or when you want to take a look at how a particular HTML document works.

Chapter 19

Get on America Online

How to...

- Distinguish between AOL and the Internet
- Sign on to AOL
- Customize your screen name, including Parental Controls for kids' accounts
- Get your e-mail and send some of your own
- Visit the different channels on the service
- Check out the chat rooms
- Post in message areas
- Get on the Internet with AOL's tools

There's often confusion over what, exactly, the America Online service is. AOL is an online service that uses its own special application software for accessing the information, e-mail, chat groups, and message areas that are run by AOL staff. Ultimately, your iBook uses the AOL application to dial into server computers in AOL's headquarters in Virginia, which send requested information (news, stocks, e-mail) back to your iBook.

AOL is not the Internet, although you can use AOL as your Internet Service Provider and you can access Internet services through AOL. Instead, the AOL service is its own distinct place, complete with news, sports, magazines, interest groups, chats, and more. With more than 17 million users, it's a very popular place to be.

But AOL *can* be your only connection to the Internet if you so desire. In fact, the AOL software can work just like the Remote Access software in the Mac OS. All you do is sign onto the service, then start up Internet Explorer, Netscape Navigator, or an FTP program and start surfing.

AOL is easy to use, it's accessible from most anyplace in the United States (and most places around the world), and it offers a lot of unique content. If you don't want to mess with other ISPs, then sign onto AOL and enjoy yourself.

Sign Up and Dial In

For the America Online service, you'll need an account name and password—if you don't have those things, you can sign up directly via the service. If you already have an AOL account, then you can skip a few steps. For any connection, though, you'll need to start up AOL by double-clicking its icon in the AOL subfolder of the Internet folder, or you can choose America Online from the Apple menu.

Before starting this process, check the sound volume on your iBook and turn it down a bit. When AOL goes to dial the modem the first time, it can be very loud and obnoxious, and you can't change the volume until it's done dialing.

Dial In the First Time

Here's what happens the first time you start up AOL:

1. You'll see the AOL Setup screen. Choose Begin Automatic Setup. AOL will try to find your iBook's modem, which it should do with no problem. Wait until this process is complete.

2. Next you'll see the Confirm Your Connection screen, where you're asked to confirm that you want to use the iBook's internal modem. If you want to do this, just click Next. You may also want to use a TCP/IP or LAN connection. (This would be true if you prefer to connect to AOL over the Internet using either the Remote Access control panel or an Ethernet connection.) Select that option and click Next. AOL will attempt to sign on over your TCP/IP connection. If it does, move ahead to the next section, "Create an Account."

3. Now you'll need to make some dialing choices (assuming you're still on the modem path). If you have a touch-tone phone, you're fine. If you have special dialing needs, select the appropriate check boxes and make whatever changes are necessary for your particular phone system. (A comma, entered in any situation where numbers will be dialed, tells the AOL software to pause for a few seconds.) Click Next.

4. Now, choose the country you're dialing from and, if appropriate, the area code where you are currently located. Click Next.

5. AOL is about to dial its special toll-free number. Make sure the phone line is clear and click Next.

6. The dialing takes place. Hopefully, everything is successful and you'll move on to the Search for AOL Access Numbers screen.

7. Now choose a local phone number for AOL to access (assuming one is listed). Highlight that number on the left and click the Add button. Your iBook is most compatible with V.90/Flex connections, but it should work fine with any of the other V.90 connections, as well as 33.6, 14.4, and so on. The smaller the number, the slower the connection, with V.90 being the fastest. Each time you click Add, you'll see a screen that asks you to set up the number exactly as it should be dialed.

8. After you've selected all the phone numbers you want to use, click Next.

9. Now AOL will hang up and dial in to the first local access number you've selected. It will attempt to connect to the service (you'll hear the modem screeching). If successful, you'll see the Create an Account screen. At this point, things diverge slightly.

Create an Account

If you plan to create a new account, follow these instructions. If you already have an account, head to this chapter's next section, called "Use Your Existing Account."

Here's how to create a new account:

1. Select You Want To Create A New Account in the Create Your America Online dialog box. Click Next.

2. Now, enter a bunch of information about yourself, pressing TAB to move to each entry box. Click Next when you're done.

3. Now, read all about the exciting new membership that awaits you, then click Next.

4. Choose the credit card you want to use for your billing, or explore other options by clicking the Other Billing Options button. If you click that button, other credit cards and a checking account option are shown. Select one and click Next.

5. You'll then pass through various screens that ask you to enter credit card information, verify it, and so on.

6. After entering your credit card or banking information, you'll read and accept the member agreement. To read it, click the Read Now radio button, then click Next. If you've read it and you agree, click the I Do button and click Next.

7. Once all that is out of the way, you can choose your screen name. Enter the name you'd like to use for your main AOL account. Enter something that sounds good and click Next.

8. AOL may report that it's able to set up your screen name, but probably not. Instead, AOL will offer a contraction of what you entered, probably with some randomly generated numbers. If you like that one, click Next. Otherwise, choose the radio button next to I'd Like This Screen Name

19

Instead. When you select the button, another text box appears and you can enter a different name. Click Next when you've typed it. You may have to go through this a few times, but, eventually, you'll either break down and accept that awful name, or you'll hit on something that works.

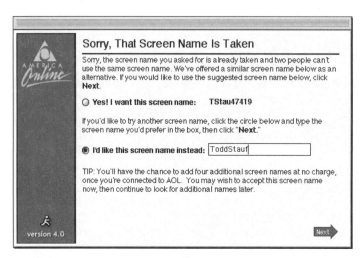

9. Next, you confirm your screen name and click Next.

10. Now you'll enter a password. Your password should be at least six characters long and can include both letters and numbers. The best passwords have nothing to do with your life—but those can be tough to remember. So, a combination of remembrances—something like your childhood house number plus that funny name your college roommate used to have for his one green sock—can mix into something no hacker could ever guess. After you've entered the password twice (to verify that you're trying the same thing both times), click Next.

11. Now you may be asked dumb demographic question(s). Click to answer them.

That's it. You're online. You'll be "welcomed" and told that "you've got mail." Don't get too excited, though—it's just a canned message from Steve Case, president of AOL. If you like, you can click Yes, Let's Get Started in the QuickStart dialog box and take a tour of AOL. (Notice you can click Don't Show Me This Again if you don't want and don't need a tour of AOL, thanks very much!)

OK, now skip a section in this chapter (lucky you!) to go see how you'll generally go about signing on and off AOL.

Use Your Existing Account

If you already have an AOL account and you just want to set up your iBook to use that account, you can do that, too. Here's how:

1. On the Create Your America Online page, choose You Already Have An AOL Account You'd Like To Use.

2. Two entry boxes appear where you can enter your name and password. Do so, then click Next.

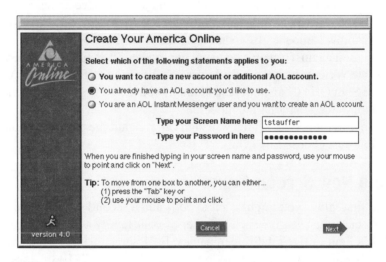

Easy enough, right? As long as you've entered a valid user name and password, you're set. Now you can learn about signing on and off in the next section.

Sign On and Off

Generally, you'll start your AOL session at the Welcome screen, where you'll see your screen name (and any others you've created) along with space for your password. Here's how to sign on:

1. Make sure your modem and phone line aren't currently in use. (You can't sign on while someone is talking on the phone or while your iBook is busy accepting a fax.)

2. Choose a screen name you'd like to use to sign on from the Select Screen Name menu.

19

3. Enter the password for the chosen screen name.

4. Choose the location you're dialing from, if appropriate, in the Select Location box.

5. Click Sign On.

Now the modem will dial (if your connection uses the modem) and the familiar connection screen appears. Watch the messages to see how things are going. Once you've gotten through the log-on process, you'll see the regular screen and you'll be welcomed, then told "you've got mail" if, in fact, you have some.

Once you're signed on, there are really three ways to sign off. First, you can sign off and allow someone else to access AOL or otherwise leave AOL active so it can be used again. (It won't be using the modem; it'll simply be open and waiting at the Welcome screen.) To do this, choose Sign Off | Sign Off. You can also choose Sign Off | Change Screen Name if you'd like to change to a new user without being forced to redial the modem.

You can also quit AOL, which will sign off and quit the program all in one swift motion. Just choose File | Quit.

Create a New Screen Name

One of the first things you might want to do is add a second screen name to your account. In fact, you can give each member of your family a unique screen name up to AOL's limit of five total screen names. Each screen name gets its own individual e-mail, its own storage folders, and even its own 2MB of storage space for Web pages. You can also change the Parental Controls for a particular screen name, limiting what can be done on AOL while that screen name is signed on. And the best part is, only the original screen name is the administrative account, so as long as you keep that screen name's password to yourself, you have total control over the other screen names.

To create a new screen name:

1. Sign on to the service under your original screen name (that's the administrative account) and wait until you've been fully connected. Once you've seen the main screens, you can select My AOL | Screen Names. (Pop-up menus appear when you select many of the buttons in AOL.)

2. In the dialog box that appears, double-click the Create A Screen Name entry.

3. Now you'll see another dialog box that allows you to enter a screen name that you'd like to add to this account. This is the same process you went through when you were trying to create your main screen name—you may or may not get your first choice.

4. If you don't get your choice, then AOL will respond with an alternate name. If you like it, choose Create A Screen Name. If you don't, enter another name and then click Create A Screen Name. You'll go through the process until you get a name you like.

5. Once you've hit on an acceptable name, you're ready to enter a password for this account. Enter that same password in each box, then click OK.

6. Now you're able to set up the age group for this account. Basically, this screen allows you to invoke the Parental Controls that are built into AOL. Choose the age group you feel is appropriate for this user—the younger the group, the less access the user will have to parts of the service that may offer more adult content. Click OK when you've chosen.

NOTE   *You can read more about Parental Controls by selecting Help | Parental Controls.*

7. Now you'll see the New Screen Name confirmation, which will include information about the particular Parental Control you've chosen (if you've chosen one). Click OK to head back to the service, or click Custom Controls to move on to customizing the Parental Controls for each screen name in your account.

Parental Controls

AOL really gives you a lot of control over how your account and screen names can be set up. Parental Controls allow you to choose what parts of the service a particular screen name can use, which allows you to decide, for instance, that a particular screen name can't accept e-mail with attachments or can't chat in chat rooms.

Beyond that, you can move on to the Custom Controls, which allow you to fine-tune the Parental Controls to the levels that you feel are appropriate for a given screen name. So if you don't like the AOL defaults, you can change them.

To set Parental Controls:

1. Choose My AOL | Parental Controls.

19

2. In the dialog box that appears, choose the Set Parental Controls Now button.

3. In the dialog box, you'll see a menu at the top of the screen that allows you to choose each screen name you've created. Choose one from the menu, then click the button next to the type of Custom Control you want to change (E-mail control, Chat control, IM control, Web control, and so on).

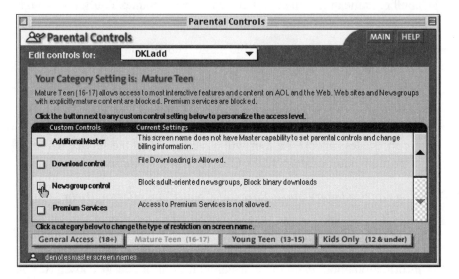

You can also click the category at the bottom on the screen to choose a general restriction setting from the options: General Access, Mature Teen, Young Teen, and Kids Only.

Once you've chosen a Custom Control, you'll see a dialog box that gives you various options to set regarding that particular control. In the Newsgroup control, for instance, you can choose to have all newsgroups blocked, you can block newsgroup downloads, or you can block a list of newsgroups or newsgroups that have certain keywords in them like "binary" (which usually means pictures, often adult-related) or "games" if you feel games are a waste of time for this particular user. Click Save in the Custom Control settings dialog box and you're returned to the Parental Controls where you can do more management.

Delete a Screen Name

To delete a screen name, you need to be signed on with the original account name (or a Master Screen Name). Here's how you do it:

1. Select My AOL | Screen Names.

2. In the dialog box that appears, click Delete A Screen Name.

3. Click Continue in the Are You Sure dialog box.

4. Now, choose the screen name to delete from the menu, then click Delete. The screen name is deleted.

Restore a Screen Name

Just because it's gone doesn't mean a screen name is gone forever—at least, not if it's been less than six months since you deleted it. To recover a screen name:

1. Select My AOL | Screen Names.

2. In the dialog box that appears, click Restore A Screen Name.

3. Now you'll see a dialog box that includes recoverable screen names. Select one, then click Recover.

Click OK in the dialog box that confirms recovery, and you're ready to roll with the screen name, now back from the dead!

Get Your E-mail

If you're like most AOL users, you're itching for that e-mail. Well, reading your e-mail is easy, assuming you have some. You'll usually know—if the volume control is allowing any sound to get through your iBook's speakers, you'll hear "you've got mail" when you sign onto the service if you've been sent some. (This e-mail can be from another AOL user or any Internet user with an e-mail account.)

To read that mail, just click the You Have Mail icon that appears in the corner of the Welcome screen.

You'll see the Mailbox with a list of messages you've received.

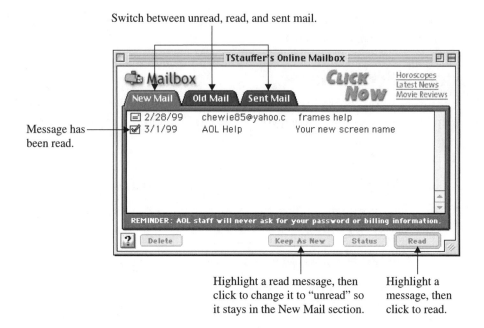

Switch between unread, read, and sent mail.

Message has been read.

Highlight a read message, then click to change it to "unread" so it stays in the New Mail section.

Highlight a message, then click to read.

If a particular message looks interesting, double-click it (or select it and click Read) to open it up in its own window (see Figure 19-1). This window allows you to read the message using the scroll bars down the right side of the message window. But it also allows you to do a lot more than that. You can reply, forward the message, delete it, or just move on to another message.

Here's what each of the controls does:

■ **Arrows**   If you choose the right arrow, you can move to the next message without returning to the Mailbox. The left arrow gives you the previous message in the list.

■ **# of # Box**   This is actually a button, which shows the current message you're reading of a certain total number of messages. Clicking the button returns you immediately to the Mailbox.

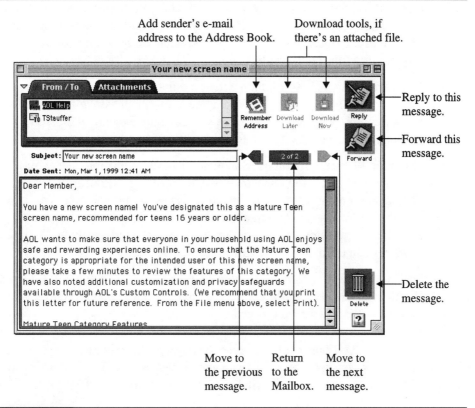

Add sender's e-mail
address to the Address Book.

Download tools, if
there's an attached file.

Reply to this
message.

Forward this
message.

Delete the
message.

Move to
the previous
message.

Return
to the
Mailbox.

Move to
the next
message.

FIGURE 19-1   The Read E-Mail window gives you a number of choices for dealing
with your incoming messages.

■ **Delete**   Choosing the Delete button causes the message to immediately
leave the Mailbox. A deleted message is not kept in the Old Mail folder
(part of the Mailbox); messages that are read but not deleted are left in
the Old Mail folder for a few days or weeks (depending on your volume
of mail) before they're deleted.

■ **Remember Address**   This adds the sender's e-mail address to the Address
Book, which can be accessed from the Mail Center button menu in the AOL
toolbar.

■ **Reply**   Highlight the text you'd like to *quote*—text that you'd like to
appear in your message reply that reminds the recipient what he or she

19

originally said in the e-mail to you. Then, click the Reply button to create a new message that includes the sender's e-mail address as the recipient of the reply. Now type your message and click the Send Now or Send Later button to send the reply.

- **Forward**   Click Forward, then enter an e-mail address in the Address section of the new message to whom you want this message forwarded. Click Send Now or Send Later once you have the forward addressed properly. (You can also type a few lines, if you like.)

- **Download Later**   If you have an attachment with this message, you can choose to add it to your Download Manager—a part of AOL where different download files can be specified. Then, at a given time, you can choose to download them all at once, instead of waiting for each to download. This allows you to get up and move around, since the Download Manager can even sign off automatically.

- **Download Now**   Select this button to download any attached files to your iBook immediately. You'll get a Save dialog box so you can choose where you'd like the attached file saved.

And, as always, you can simply close the message you're reading by clicking its close box. A check now appears next to its name in the Mailbox. The next time you open the Mailbox, the read message will have been moved to the Old Mail tab.

 Just FYI—AOL staff members will never ask you for your account password, nor will they direct you to a Web site that asks you to enter such information. Any e-mail you get that suggests that you need to enter your password (usually in exchange for something free) is a hoax. That's just bad users trying to get your password so they can create some mischief.

Create a New Message

If you'd like to create a new message from scratch, the beginning part is simple— just click the Write button in the AOL toolbar. That causes a new message window to appear (see Figure 19-2).

By the way—you don't have to be connected to start a message. You can write messages without being signed on to AOL, then choose Send Later (after writing the message) to send it once you've signed on. You'll see how to do that at the end of this section.

Choose the type of recipient from the menu.

Enter a recipient.

Get an address from the Address Book.

Attach files.

Choose when to send.

Type your message.

Enter a subject line.

FIGURE 19-2   The New Message window offers many options for formatting your e-mail.

NOTE   *Many of the issues discussed in Chapter 16 are relevant to e-mail in this chapter too—things like the memo-style headers, formatting your e-mail, and so forth. If you haven't already, check out Chapter 16 to learn more about how e-mail works and some of the etiquette involved.*

Once you've got the new message window open, you're ready to address the message. Remember that if you're sending e-mail to another AOL user, you can simply enter his or her screen name. If you're sending to a user elsewhere on the Internet, enter his or her full e-mail address.

To address your message, either type an e-mail address that you happen to know for your recipient, or select the Address Book button, then choose a name from the Address Book window. Highlight a name, then click the appropriate button—Send To, Copy To, or Blind Copy—depending on how you want to send the message. When you're done with the Address Book, click its close box. (To get rid of a recipient, select the name in the To window and press the DELETE key.)

19

If you need to add an attachment, click the Attach Files button. An Open dialog box appears, where you can find an attachment. Select it, then click the attach button. If you choose to compress the attachment, click the Compress Attachments check box. (The attachments are compressed with the StuffIt format, which is not recommended for sending to Microsoft Windows or Unix users.) The files are now attached—you can see them by clicking the Attachments tab. You can remove them by highlighting the filename and clicking the Detach Files button.

Now you can click in the body of the message and type your message. Remember that you only need to press RETURN at the end of a paragraph, just as when you're typing in a word processor. At this point you might want to make formatting decisions about your e-mail—again the tools for bold, italic, or underlining are like those in a word processor.

AOL also offers some other formatting tools for your messages, which allow you to do more e-mail–specific things.

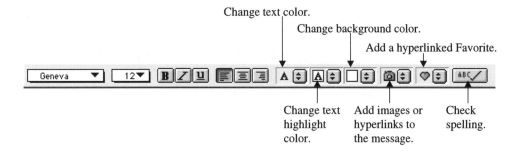

AOL offers many options that you can learn more about from the Mail Extras button down in the bottom-right corner of the message. Most of them allow you to add Web page–like tools—such as hyperlinks and graphics—to your e-mail documents.

NOTE

As discussed in Chapter 16, it's not always advisable to send messages as HTML documents instead of as plain-text e-mail. To avoid problems, simply refrain from formatting your messages with bold, hyperlinks, and so on. If you know your e-mail recipients can handle HTML documents (if, for instance, they use Outlook Express or Netscape Communicator), then go nuts.

When you've completed the message, you might want to click the Check Spelling button, then you can click Send Now to send the message immediately. If you're not currently connected to AOL you can click Send Later and it'll be sent when you sign on.

Send Waiting Mail

If you've elected to Send Later, you can send your mail all at once. You do that by opening the Mail Waiting to Be Sent window from the Mail Center button menu. You'll see the window, which allows you to click Send All or select individual messages and click Send to send them over the Internet.

This is great if you want to compose your messages offline, then sign onto AOL and send them quickly. It keeps you from tying up the phone lines, spending money on long distance, or eating into your connect time if you have a limited-time plan for your AOL access.

Move Around the Service

There's a lot to do on AOL besides get your e-mail. In fact, figuring out where to go can be tough, so there are many different ways to search and be guided around AOL to get a full sense of how it works.

In most cases, moving around AOL is simple. You click buttons to move to another section—sometimes there will be hyperlinks, too, which take you to a new topic. If you want to get rid of a window, click its close box.

Welcome

Aside from access to your Mailbox, the Welcome screen usually offers the latest and most exciting news on the service. You can click any link to jump into a news or entertainment story. You can also click the AOL logo to find a special section, What's New on AOL. Once you become a seasoned AOL surfer, you'll probably spend some time with this service, since it tells you what's changed most recently on the service.

Channels

The place to start is probably the Channels, which you can access through the Channels window (which appears when you sign onto the service) or through the Channels button on the AOL toolbar. The Channels allow you to quickly explore different topic areas on AOL like Travel, Finance, Education, Sports, and Kids Only. Choose a channel and you'll see its main page. From there click the latest links to see what's going on in that particular topic area.

People Connection

I'll discuss this section in more depth in the section "Chat and Read Message Boards." The People Connection is an area where you'll learn about AOL chatting,

19

find out what's available online that day (what celebrities and notable folks are chatting today), and discover how to go about all this chat business. Plus, there's plenty of advice on meeting people and getting to know one another better, virtually. You can get to the People Connection from the Channels screen or by choosing People | People Connection.

Find by Keyword

Keywords are quite a commodity on AOL—if you happen to know the keyword for a particular area, you can get there immediately by typing the keyword into the entry bar at the top of the screen and clicking Go or pressing ENTER. Keywords often make sense. The keyword **writer** opens the Writers Club, the keyword **dog** opens the Pets Interest page, the keyword **finance** takes you to the Personal Finance area, and the keyword **movies** takes you to the reviews pages.

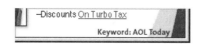

Keywords and searches can work on the World Wide Web, too—enter the keyword **Time**, for instance, and AOL takes you to *Time Magazine*'s Web site.

Use AOL Favorites

If you find a place you like on AOL, you can turn it into a Favorite. That way it's easily accessible from within the Favorites button menu. This works a lot like a Favorite in Internet Explorer or a bookmark in Netscape Communicator. (In fact, you can use the Favorites feature from within AOL's Web browsing tool.)

To use a Favorite, click the Favorites button in the toolbar, then select the Favorite from the menu that appears.

To create a Favorite, all you need to do is locate the small heart in the top-right corner of the window—it should show up in any window that can be designated a Favorite. Click that heart. Now you'll see a dialog box that allows you to choose what to do with this particular page. In this case, you want to add it to your Favorite places, so click the appropriate button, then click OK.

You can figure out a site's keyword pretty easily once you've visited it. Just check the lower-right corner, where you'll see the keyword.

Chat and Read Message Boards

Another major reason to fire up America Online and spend some time connected is to get to know people through special-interest groups, informal chats, or online forums. First, of course, you've got to find that stuff.

Chat: the People Connection

The place to find informal chats on pretty much any subject is the People Connection. Using the People Connection, you can find chats on all sorts of topics, ranging from romance to fan chats to particular, and serious, topics regarding current events, the news, or regional discussions. Here's how:

1. Open the People Connection by selecting People | People Connection.

2. In the People Connection window, click Find a Chat.

3. Now, highlight a category, then click View Chats. You'll see the Chat Groups change on the right side of the window.

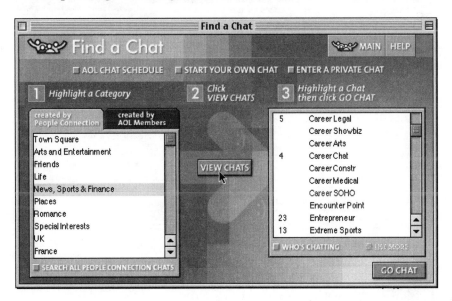

4. When you see a chat that interests you, highlight it and click the Go Chat button. Now you'll enter the chat room.

You'll also find chat rooms elsewhere on the AOL service, including in special interest and hobbyist areas. Instead of searching for those, just double-click an icon to enter the chat room.

NOTE   *Sometimes a chat room is full. If that's the case, AOL will ask you if you'd like to be automatically routed to a similar chat topic.*

Once you're in a chat room, the interface is pretty much the same (see Figure 19-3). You'll see the people who are chatting on the right side of the window, while the actual chat lines scroll down the left side. (These are lines that have been typed by other folks who are participating in the chat.)

Chatting is actually pretty easy. You just type a line of text in the entry box, then click the Send button or press RETURN. You can also format your entry, if you

Chat window   Double-click a person to see options.

Format the message, if desired.   Click to send.

Type your message here.

FIGURE 19-3   The AOL chat room interface

like, just to add some color and style. Once you click Send, your message (sometimes after a brief delay) will appear in the Chat window.

The real options come when you're dealing with individual users. In the User window, you can double-click a particular user name to bring up a dialog box about that user. Here's what you can do:

■ Click Ignore Member if this person is annoying, obnoxious, or bothersome. You now will no longer see their comments in the Chat window.

> Information about TStauffer
>
> ☐ **Ignore Member**
>
> ○ **Send Message**
>
> ○ **Get Profile**

You can also use Ignore Member in a more positive way—if you're chatting in a large room with many people in it, you might choose to ignore members that aren't currently participating in your conversation. That will make your discussion easier to follow.

■ Click Send Message to send an Instant Message to this user. Instant Messages are special one-on-one chats between AOL users (or Internet users with the special AOL Instant Message software installed).

■ Click Get Profile to see if this person has a Member Profile on file.

TIP *You can create your own Member Profile by choosing My AOL | My Member Profile.*

Read and Write in Message Boards

You'll find message boards more in the interest areas on AOL. While you're wandering around AOL, anything that says "read what others have to say" or "exchange messages with like-minded folks" is probably a message board. Message boards are areas that work almost exactly like Usenet newsgroups— you read the messages, post your replies, mark things as read, and so forth.

If you're looking at a typical AOL list, the message boards stand out because of their card and thumb-tack icon. (This suggests a "bulletin board" where you can post your bulletin for others to see and reply to.)

Double-click such an entry and you'll see the message board interface—it's remarkably similar to the Usenet newsgroups interface. Double-click a topic to see its listing window, then double-click a subject to read the posts. Posts are simply a series of replies to a particular topic of discussion. Once you get down to the post level, you're seeing each individual message.

To read the next post in this same subject, click the Next Post button; to read the next subject, click the Next Subject button. To reply to the subject (that is, to add your own post to the ongoing discussion), click Reply. You'll see the Reply window, which offers some features of its own (see Figure 19-4).

Notice that your reply can be sent two different ways—you can post it to the message board, or you can send it as an e-mail directly to the person who is shown in the message when you click Reply. You can also do both, or you can enter a different screen name if you'd like to send this message to someone else (perhaps to alert them to an interesting topic).

It's important to note that if you decide to post the message, it doesn't actually have to be a reply to the original poster. You don't even have to quote their

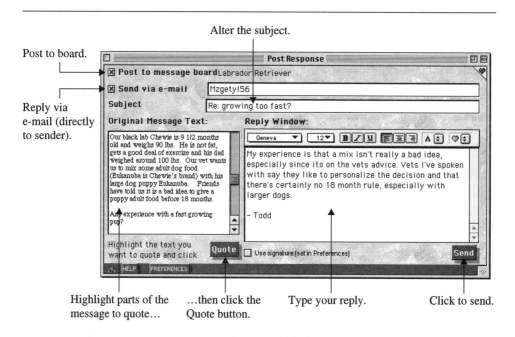

FIGURE 19-4   The Post Response message window

message—you can simply go off on some other topic and post the message at the end of the particular subject. Or, you can highlight text, click Quote, then reply specifically to a particular person's comments. It's up to you.

When you're done entering your post, click Send.

> NOTE
>
> *Your post is available for all to see, including AOL. Make sure your post doesn't violate AOL's terms of service and that you're really saying what you want to say to people—not just something angry in the heat of the moment. You should also double-check the entries to make sure you're doing what you want with the reply. If you're trying to send an e-mail, for instance, you'll want to make sure that you've checked only the Send Via E-mail option.*

Use AOL Link and Get on the Internet

You may already have noticed that AOL is tightly integrated with the Internet. As you move from topic area to topic area, you'll find that Internet links are mixed in with the regular links—after all, AOL 4.0 has an integrated Web browser that is actually a version of Internet Explorer. (With America Online's acquisition of Netscape Corporation, this may change in future versions.) The browser tool is certainly capable, and assuming you have a reasonably fast connection, it's pretty painless to surf the Internet from within America Online.

But you can also, as mentioned, use AOL as your Internet Service Provider and run other Internet applications, using AOL as your connection to the Internet. All you have to do, in most cases, is fire up the Internet application and start working. AOL takes care of the rest. We'll see more on how that works in the section "AOL Link and Internet Applications."

AOL's Internet Tools

You've already seen that you can load AOL's internal Web browser tool simply by clicking on a Web link of some sort. You can also choose a Favorite that happens to point to a Web site. If you do, then the browser tool opens and you'll view that site.

If you'd like to enter a URL directly, you can do that, too. In the Find entry box in the toolbar, enter the URL directly. Press RETURN and AOL will attempt to load that page. You'll notice in this illustration that the AOL toolbar actually turns into a sort of browser toolbar, complete with Back, Forward, Refresh, and Home buttons as well as the location entry box.

Back Stop Home History menu

Forward Refresh Find menu Location entry box

You can access the History menu (the arrow just to the left of the location box) to revisit pages you've been to recently. You can also pull down the Find menu (in the toolbar) and choose Find on the Internet to open up a search page and begin searching the Internet.

 Want to set your own home page? Choose My AOL | Preferences. In the Preferences dialog box, click WWW. Now you can enter a new home page, and many other preferences regarding Web browsing. Click OK when you're done.

Other Tools

AOL offers support for FTP as well. (FTP, short for File Transfer Protocol, is a common way to transfer files to and from other computers over the Internet.) You can use keyword: **FTP** to get to the special FTP tools, or enter an FTP URL in the location box and use the browser tools to download files.

And AOL has tools built in for accessing Usenet newsgroups. You can get there by entering the keyword: **Newsgroups**. The controls are similar to AOL's Message Board interface discussed in this chapter.

 Basic Usenet usage and terminology is discussed in Chapter 16. FTP is discussed in Chapter 18.

AOL Link and Internet Applications

AOL uses the AOL Link technology to allow America Online to serve as an ISP connection for some of your other Internet software. If you're connected through a dial-up connection to AOL, you could go to Control Panels in the Apple menu and choose TCP/IP. You'll see that the current profile is an AOL profile. That means that instead of using just the AOL software, you can use other TCP/IP applications, too—Web browsers and FTP programs like Transmit or Fetch. Just launch the application and start using it. This is a cool feature, since AOL's Web browser and FTP tools aren't the most advanced available. Instead of being limited to those tools, you're free to make your own choices and use Internet applications that you like more.

> NOTE
>
> *Occasionally, you'll notice AOL asking you to switch to AOL Link as you're starting up. AOL does this if the TCP/IP control panel is set to use some other connection (like Ethernet or Remote Access) and if you're trying to use AOL to dial your modem, instead of using AOL over an existing Internet connection. If that's the case, AOL will switch to AOL Link in the TCP/IP control panel to run its Web tool and other Internet programs.*

So, with AOL up and running over a modem connection, just choose Browse the Internet or launch your FTP tool to get started. Note that e-mail programs will work, too, but only for accessing e-mail in ISP-based accounts. You'll still have to use AOL to retrieve your AOL e-mail. (Claris Emailer, an e-mail application that's sold by Apple, can also access AOL e-mail.)

AOL's Web Storage Space

Every AOL screen name gets access to 2MB of storage space that can be used for Web pages. The pages can be accessed by anyone with a Web browser and an Internet connection by entering the URL **http://members.aol.com/*username*/** where *username* is one of your screen names. Upload pages through the My Place interface, which works almost exactly like the FTP controls discussed in the earlier section, "AOL's Internet Tools." In order to upload your Web files, you'll access keyword: **My Place**, then upload your documents to the My Place directory. Those files will then be available to anyone who has Web access.

Chapter 20

Customize the Internet and Go Faster

How to...

- Customize your Internet connection
- Connect to the Internet wirelessly
- Get higher-speed Internet access for your iBook

The iBook is usually simple to get up and running with an Internet Service Provider (ISP) and a modem—that's part of the reason I've left all the gritty details to this chapter, instead of explaining all the Internet-related settings and control panels earlier in the book. After all, there's the Internet Setup Assistant and the setup procedures in the Internet applications that make them all pretty easy to use.

So, if you're happily signing on and off with your Internet connection and you're not particularly intrigued by how it works, then there probably isn't much reason to read this chapter.

But if you're having trouble with your connection, if you're interested in customizing your setup, or if you'd like to explore new, faster Internet connection technologies, you've come to the right chapter.

Configure TCP/IP, Modem, and Remote Access

In order to have an Internet connection you need two things. First, you need a method for connecting to the Internet—this can be an Ethernet cable, a telephone line (connected to your iBook's modem), or a wireless connection if your iBook has an AirPort add-on card installed. Then, you need to configure the software for your connection. For a modem, that means configuring the Remote Access and TCP/IP control panels. For Ethernet, you'll just configure TCP/IP. For a wireless connection, you'll configure the AirPort application, the AirPort Base Station, and TCP/IP.

So how does this configuration take place? Through control panels: the TCP/IP control panel, the Remote Access control panel, the AirPort application, and the Modem control panel. You may also find reason to use a fourth control panel, the DialAssist control panel, if you have a particularly complicated dial-out process for your modem.

 The Internet Assistant, encountered when you first turn on your iBook, manages most of these options for you. If you've already used it and had great success, there's no reason for you to bother with this chapter.

The TCP/IP Control Panel

This control panel is used to set up the basics of your Internet connection, whether or not you're using a modem. In the control panel you can choose the type of connection that will be used and enter a bunch of different Internet addresses that tell the computer where it's located and how to access the Internet (see Figure 20-1).

20

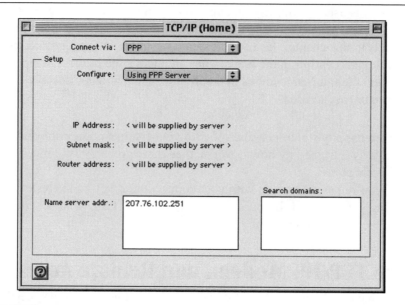

FIGURE 20-1 The TCP/IP control panel

The best way to get these numbers (the IP address, subnet mask, router address, and name server addresses) is to ask your ISP or system administrator what they should be. If you're connecting via PPP, you won't need to know the exact IP address, subnet mask, or router address, since those will be assigned to your iBook when you dial into your ISP. You will need to know your name server addresses and what sort of configuration scheme you'll use for PPP.

NOTE *A fixed IP address simply means that your Internet address never changes. This is usually true of Ethernet-based connections—they're often fixed. (In larger organizations they may not be, especially if your TCP/IP control panel is set for DHCP—Dynamic Host Configuration Protocol— connections.) PPP connections, though, are often dynamically assigned. You usually have to pay extra if you want a fixed IP address over a modem connection. If you do, though, then you'll know your address, which can be useful when Web surfing and using FTP.*

Here's how the TCP/IP control panel works:

■ **Connect Via** Use this menu to choose how you'll connect to a TCP/IP network. If you're using a modem, choose PPP; if you're using an Ethernet connection (such as with a university or company), choose Ethernet. If you've installed America Online, then you might also find the option in here to choose AOL Link, which allows you to use AOL's special protocol for a PPP-like connection to the Internet. (AOL Link is discussed in Chapter 19.) If you're using a wireless connection, choose AirPort.

■ **Configure** This option determines the configuration scheme used to log in to your ISP's server. If you're configuring an Ethernet or AirPort connection, you'll choose Manually or Using DHCP Server most of the time; if it's a PPP connection, choose Using PPP Server. (The other configuration schemes will be specified by your ISP or system administrator if they're needed.)

> TIP
>
> *You can choose DHCP server if you are connected to other computers over an Ethernet, and you'd like to network using TCP/IP. If the iBook can't find a DHCP server (like on a small network in your house), it will assign a random IP number, allowing you to use TCP/IP. You can then use Web Sharing to share files between TCP/IP-running computers using Web browsers or FTP programs.*

■ **IP Address** This is your iBook's address on the Internet.

■ **Subnet Mask** This is the numbering scheme required to help your iBook find its way around your local network or ISP.

■ **Router Address** This is the IP address of your Internet router or gateway.

■ **Name server addr.** These are addresses for server computers that can translate between Internet names (like **mac1.mac-upgrade.com**) and numbered addresses (**207.0.129.169**).

■ **Search domains** This is usually left blank. If you enter a domain (like **mycompany.com** or **mysys.net**), it will search those domains for particular computers, in some cases.

Set TCP/IP for an AirPort Connection

If your iBook has an AirPort card installed and you plan to use it for an Internet connection, you'll need to have your AirPort Base Station configured for Internet access. (This is done using the AirPort Setup Assistant, as described in Chapter 24.)

Once the AirPort Base Station is configured for Internet access, you'll need to set up the TCP/IP control panel on your iBook. In the TCP/IP control panel, select AirPort from the Connect Via menu. In the Configure menu, choose either Using DHCP Server or Manually, depending on which method you'd prefer to use. (For a small home network, the Using DHCP Server choice should work fine.)

If you've chosen Using DHCP Server, enter a DHCP client ID (this should be a unique number for each of the Macs on your network) and close the TCP/IP control panel. You're ready to access the Internet. If you've chosen Manually, you'll need to enter an IP address, subnet mask, router address, and name server address. Then, close the TCP/IP control panel.

Now, when you next access an Internet application, the AirPort Base Station will use its modem (if that's how it's configured, as discussed in Chapter 24) to dial your ISP and connect to the Internet. Once connected, your wireless connection will be used for the Internet. Just check your mail or sign on to Web sites—you're online wirelessly!

The Remote Access Control Panel

If you're configuring a PPP connection, you'll need to do that in the Remote Access control panel. Here you're basically setting up the dialing part of your connection—the phone number, user name, password, and other things your iBook needs to know to get you signed on to your ISP's computers. Figure 20-2 shows the Remote Access control panel.

 The Remote Access menu in the Remote Access control panel can be used to switch between related control panels, including TCP/IP, Modem, AppleTalk, and DialAssist.

FIGURE 20-2   The Remote Access control panel

This control panel is a little less intimidating than the TCP/IP control panel. Here's how it works:

- **User Buttons**   Choose whether you're going to connect as a Registered User or as a Guest. In most cases, you'll choose Registered User for a PPP connection.

- **Name**   Enter your user name for your ISP account. This may or may not be the same as your e-mail account name. (For instance, my e-mail address name is **todds** as in todds@shutup101.com, and my account name is also **todds**. With a different account, though, my e-mail name is **publisher** as in publisher@mac-upgrade.com, but I sign in to that account using the name **todd**. So, in this case, the user name goes in the Remote Access control panel, not the e-mail name.)

20

■ **Password**   Enter the password for your ISP account.

■ **Save password**   Check this box if you don't want to enter the password in the future. Remember, this will allow anyone with access to your computer to use your Internet account.

■ **Number**   Enter the phone number that the Remote Access control panel will use to dial the modem and reach your ISP. Usually this will be a seven-digit number (in the U.S.) unless your area uses ten-digit dialing for local numbers.

■ **Status**   Once you're connected to the Internet, you'll see the status of that connection at the bottom of the window. If you're not connected, it'll just say "Idle." Otherwise, it lets you know the current connection rate and whether or not data is being received.

The Remote Access control panel also offers a Connect/Disconnect button that you're probably already familiar with if you've connected successfully. And there are some options behind that Options button. When you click the Options button, you can access the Options dialog box, which offers three different tabs: Redial, Connection, and Protocol. Here's what you can do from each:

■ **Redial**   Select this tab and you'll see the Redial menu. Pull it down and choose an option. You can choose to not redial the connect number, to redial the connect number a certain number of times, or to redial the connect number and alternate number(s). In each case, the text boxes you need in order to fill in the options will appear.

■ **Connection**   In this section you can choose how the log file of connections is kept. (You can view the log by choosing Remote Access | Access Log while you're viewing the Remote Access control panel.) You can also make some other settings decisions, including whether or not Remote Access automatically logs off and how it alerts you when it's still active.

NOTE   *Verbose logging is only necessary if you're trying to troubleshoot a problem with your connection, probably with the help of a tech support person. Otherwise, leave it off—it creates a large log file that isn't necessary if you're not having a problem.*

■ **Protocol**   From the menu you can choose the protocol that Remote
Access should attempt to use. By default it attempts to connect using
both PPP and AppleTalk (ARAP) protocols. If you're reasonably sure you
won't be using Remote Access' AppleTalk features, choose to only use
the PPP protocol from the menu—doing so may speed up connection time
slightly. You can also make some other choices, including TCP header
compression and allowing error correction—both should work fine with
an iBook's modem. Note one interesting choice: Remote Access can start
up automatically whenever a TCP/IP application is started. When Outlook
Express tries to check the mail or Netscape Navigator tries to find a Web
page, for instance, you could have your iBook automatically dial the ISP
and connect on its own.

*There's another feature available under Protocol—you can enter a script
for signing on to a command line host. There are few such hosts these
days, but if you ever need to enter a "dialing script" or "connection script"
using a particular ISP, this is where you'll do it.*

The Modem Control Panel

The Modem control panel is very straightforward—just pick the driver for the
iBook's modem and make some basic settings. Open the Modem control panel by
choosing it from the Control Panels menu in the Apple menu or from the Remote
Access menu in the Remote Access control panel.

```
┌─────────────────────── Modem ───────────────────────┐
│                                                      │
│   Connect via:   Internal Modem                      │
│  ┌─ Setup ──────────────────────────────────────┐    │
│  │                                              │    │
│  │  Modem:     [ Apple Internal 56K Mode... ▼]  │    │
│  │                                              │    │
│  │  Sound:      ● On      ○ Off                 │    │
│  │                                              │    │
│  │  Dialing:    ● Tone    ○ Pulse               │    │
│  │                                              │    │
│  │             □ Ignore dial tone               │    │
│  │                                              │    │
│  └──────────────────────────────────────────────┘    │
│  [?]                                                 │
└──────────────────────────────────────────────────────┘
```

20

Now, pull down the Modem menu and select Apple Internal 56K Modem (v.90) if it's not already chosen. Then decide whether or not the modem's sound will be on (if you'll hear the dialing and screeching) and you can tell the modem whether to dial over your phone line using tones or pulses. Finally, place a check in the Ignore dial tone check box—this is a good idea if you have stutter-tone message notification or some other line conditions that can confuse the modem.

If you're having trouble with your modem connecting, you can choose Apple Internal 56K Modem (v.34) to downgrade the speed of your iBook's modem. This will lower the speed of your connection but may be a little more reliable in certain situations.

DialAssist

If your dialing requirements are more complicated than what Remote Access can handle—one line that offers seven- to ten-digit dialing or so—then use DialAssist to help you set up. Open the control panel and you'll see many different options for choosing how your modem is dialed.

Enter your own stats up top—area code and country. Then, choose your special dialing requirements—Prefix, a Long Distance Access Code, or a Suffix. If you don't see an option that suits your needs, click the associated button in the bottom of the control panel window. The resulting dialog box will allow you to create new dialing combinations to fit your circumstances. In those dialog boxes (each button has its own dialog box), click the Add button to add numbers to dial.

Configure a New Account

If you're adding an entirely new account you'll need to head to the TCP/IP
and Remote Access control panels (assuming both use PPP). Before you begin
changing settings, though, choose File | Configurations in either TCP/IP or
Remote Access. This allows you to create a new, named configuration for your
new account. This way, old settings can be accessed quickly—just change back to
the previous configuration.

To create a new configuration, select one of the existing configurations and
click the Duplicate button. Now, you'll be asked to give the configuration a name.
Type a name and click OK.

To edit the configuration, choose it in the Configuration dialog box and click
Make Active. The TCP/IP control panel switches to reflect that new configuration.
Now you can edit away. When you close the TCP/IP control panel, you'll be asked
if you want to save the changes. Choose Save. To choose another configuration,
select File | Configurations again, select the configuration you want to work with,
and choose Make Active.

20

Remote Access allows you to do the same thing—store different phone numbers, names, passwords, and so on in separate Remote Access configurations. That way each member of your family can dial in individually to his or her account, or you can easily switch between two different dial-up accounts.

I strongly recommend using different configurations if you're changing your setup after moving your iBook or getting a new connection type (like DSL or a new LAN connection). That way you'll be able to revert to the old settings using a simple Make Active command.

> TIP *You can use the Location Manager control panel to automatically switch between your saved configurations so that, for instance, you simply tell your iBook that you're home (instead of at the office or at school) and you can automatically switch all your settings to those necessary for a modem connection. The Location Manager is discussed in Chapter 21.*

Get High-Speed Internet Access

Just hitting full speed on the market are a few technologies that may change the way many households get on the Internet. And most of these new methods use Ethernet connections, which just so happens to be built into your iBook. (In fact, it's high-speed 100Mbps Ethernet.) Here are some of those high-speed technologies:

- **DSL** Digital Subscriber Line technology connects via your regular phone line, using high-frequency signals to transmit data even when you're talking on the phone. The connection uses a special DSL modem that can connect directly to the Ethernet port on your iBook. You can also use a special DSL router, which would allow you to add a DSL connection to a network of iBooks (or other computers on a network). DSL can range in speed from about 128KB per second (twice the iBook's modem speed) to 1.5MB per second, or about the speed of most corporate LAN connections. (Some DSL implementations are even faster, but aren't likely to be used with your iBook.)

■ **Cable Modem**   A cable modem usually splits off from your cable TV line, usually giving you an Ethernet-based Internet connection using the wiring that's already in your home. Cable modems can be very fast—up to 10MB per second—although those speeds usually aren't guaranteed because a cable modem feed may be shared by an entire neighborhood. In peak times, then, speeds may slow down, but they're not likely to dip below modem speeds and should usually be well above the speed of your modem.

■ **Satellite Connections**   You may find that the local satellite TV provider (for the 18-inch dishes) in your area offers Internet access. In this case, you'll usually connect via Ethernet, but make sure they offer Mac compatibility and support. The speeds from the satellite can be four to ten times faster than a modem, although you'll probably need a modem connection and an available phone line to send data back to the ISP, since you can't send data back to a satellite or transmitter.

In any of these cases, all you'll need to do is order the service—a technician will install the service and set up the Internet settings. (If he or she isn't terribly Mac-savvy, you might point out the Configurations option discussed earlier so your existing settings aren't messed up.)

If you need to tell the technician anything, it might be your Ethernet ID number. Fortunately, it's located on a sticker just under the keyboard on your iBook. Just pop open the keyboard (as discussed in Chapter 23) and show the technician the Ethernet ID number.

20

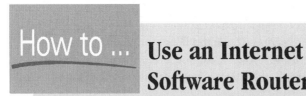

Use an Internet Software Router

What do you do if you have one modem-based Internet connection but more than one computer that you'd like to give access to the Internet? One solution is to use an Internet software router. You'll set up the software on one of your computers, which will act as a router for the other computers to which you want to give Internet access.

If you have an AirPort Base Station, you already have an Internet router for your iBook and other AirPort-enabled Macs. The point of the AirPort Base Station is to give you access to other computers and the Internet from one central point—that Base Station acts as a router for TCP/IP data. To use it for your Internet connection, you'll set it up as discussed in Chapter 24. (In fact, the AirPort Base Station can act as an Internet router for other Macs if the Base Station is connected to your Ethernet network. Just set those Macs to use DHCP in the TCP/IP control panel, and they can use the AirPort's modem to gain Internet access.)

If you have two Airport-enabled Macs, one of them can act as a router as well, using the AirPort Software Base Station, which is a software add-on available from Apple. Again, this configuration is discussed in Chapter 24.

But if you're not using AirPort, you still have some router alternatives. Two popular third-party Internet routers are IPNetRouter by Sustainable Softworks (**http://www.sustworks.com/**) and SurfDoubler from Vicomsoft (**http://www.vicomsoft.com**). Both are commercial products, although you can download demonstration versions that work for a few weeks before you have to pay.

You install the router on a Mac that has a modem connection (or other Internet connection) as well as a network connection to your other Macs. (The best choice is a Mac that stays put—not an iBook, but perhaps an iMac or a desktop Power Macintosh.) With the router application running on the one Mac, other Macs access that Mac for their Internet connection, either using fixed IP addresses or a DHCP addressing scheme. Whenever a TCP/IP request is made by an Internet application on one of your computers, that request is processed by the router that accesses the Internet through the single Internet connection.

Some of the setup can be a bit complicated, but both companies offer documentation and assistants to walk you through the process. Once you've got it up and running, it's pretty painless—just access Internet applications on any of your configured Macs. The Internet connection is made (if necessary) and the data downloaded.

Part IV

Customize Your iBook

Chapter 21

Change iBook's Appearance and Attitude

How to...

- Change the resolution and color depth of your iBook's screen
- Calibrate the screen's colors
- Set basic preferences for the way your iBook looks and acts
- Set the time and date
- Customize the way your iBook uses memory
- Save Energy and automate startup, shutdown, and sleep
- Store your passwords on the keychain
- Change locations easily with Location Manager

In this chapter I discuss the atmospheric and behavioral settings for your iBook—what it looks like and how it operates. You can change these settings using certain control panels. Other control panels are discussed in many other chapters throughout this book—those that govern networking, the Internet, and your modem, for instance. In this chapter, we'll focus on the control panels built into the Mac OS that handle appearance, the monitor, sound, memory, and other basic settings. Plus, you'll learn a little more about some high-end customization technologies that help you automatically store passwords, sign on to servers and change many different settings at once based on your current location.

Adjust Your iBook's Screen

Using the Monitors control panel on your iBook you can change a few characteristics of your iBook's display. Because the iBook's display is integrated into the machine itself, there are only a few settings you need to worry about. In most cases, the iBook's display should already be optimal.

There are two different parts of the Monitors control panel that concern your screen—the Monitor and Color settings. Each will affect how your iBook's screen looks, and each has its own area of responsibility.

Monitor Settings

Click the Monitor button (these buttons work like tabs in a typical tabbed dialog box) and the controls change to show you the monitor settings. There are two sections you'll look at here: Color Depth and Resolution.

Color Depth

Your iBook can display a range of colors from 256 to thousands to millions. This represents the color *palette* available to your iBook—the number of distinct colors that could potentially be shown on the screen. The more colors that appear onscreen, the more photo-realistic the images on your screen. A JPEG photo file displayed at 256 colors will offer less detail than one rendered at millions of colors.

In most cases, leaving this setting at Thousands or Millions of colors is fine. You can change the color depth, though, if you find that you have images that don't look right—they seem less than sharp in places, have too much gray or black in the image, appear too light or dark, or simply seem jagged.

You may sometimes need to change the color depth for games and other highly graphical applications optimized for particular color depths. Many games are optimized for 256 colors, for instance, because the game is able to render more

a.   640 × 480

b.   800 × 600

FIGURE 21-1   At 640 × 480 (top) you see less of the page than at 800 × 600 (bottom).

quickly if it uses fewer colors. Some QuickTime and other digital video applications fare better at thousands of colors.

Resolution

The iBook supports two different screen resolutions: 640 × 480 and 800 × 600. So what does resolution mean? Technically, it means the number of pixels that appear on the screen, expressed in terms of a grid. For instance, 800 × 600 resolution divides the screen into 800 pixel columns and 600 pixel rows. Multiply it all together and you'd get 480,000 pixels on the screen.

The significance of resolution is twofold. First, the more pixels on the screen, the more information you can see—at 800 ×600, you can see a lot more of a given word processing page or Web page, for instance, than at 640 × 480. Second, the more pixels on the screen, the smaller the pixel. In order to see more of the page on your iBook's screen, the elements on the screen will have to get smaller, since the size of your monitor stays the same. Figure 21-1 shows a screen at (a) 640 × 480 and the same screen at (b) 800 × 600.

On the iBook, something else affects the way different resolutions work. Unlike a typical desktop monitor (a CRT), the flat-panel LCD in the iBook isn't capable of resolution switching in the truest sense. Instead, the iBook is able to *simulate* 640 × 480 resolution, which doesn't look quite as good as the 800 × 600 that the iBook's screen is designed for. (You may notice the fuzziness of 640 × 480 if you switch to that resolution on your iBook.)

While you can choose 640 × 480 on the iBook, you'll likely want to keep the display at 800 × 600, which is recommended for two reasons. At 800 × 600, your iBook's screen looks the most crisp. That's because the screen is designed specifically to work best at 800 × 600. At other resolutions, the video driver must do something called *anti-aliasing* to the image, which attempts to smooth the jagged curves on the display using a software trick. Although you could conceivably work this way, it doesn't look nearly as good as 800 × 600.

The second consideration is that many documents—especially Web sites— are designed to work optimally at 800 × 600, since that's the prevailing resolution among Macs and PCs on the Internet. You'll find that 640 × 480 resolution will often make Web pages look a little cramped. In fact, the iBook's ability to work at 640 × 480 is really only for compatibility with some gaming and multimedia titles, which look fine at that resolution.

You can also choose different resolutions and color depths from the control strip, if you have it active. Both control strip modules have icons that look like a display screen; the Color control strip module has an icon color bar on its screen, and the Resolution control strip module's icon has a checkerboard pattern on its screen.

Calibrate the Display

Apple has created a technology, called ColorSync, which makes it possible for you to fine-tune the color, brightness, and other characteristics of your display. This is useful for two reasons—first, it allows you to calibrate the display for different locations, making it easier to view your iBook's screen outside, inside, and under dramatically different lighting. Second, ColorSync allows you to create a color profile for your monitor, so that printing to a color printer looks as true as it can. The more accurate your display, the closer it will be to the final, printed product if you have a color printer.

To begin calibrating, choose the Color button in the Monitors control panel. You can calibrate in one of two ways. The easy way is to simply make sure that "iBook" is chosen in the ColorSync Profile list. This will give you a decent approximation that should cause your display to look fine in average indoor lighting conditions. It should also let your images print okay with your color printer.

The second method takes a little more work. Begin by selecting the iBook entry, then click the Calibrate button. Now you walk through the Calibration Assistant, which guides you through the calibration process.

You may have trouble with the Assistant if you have red-green or similar color vision impairments.

When you're done with the assistant, you'll have a newly calibrated display, and perhaps a more richly colored screen. In the last step of the Assistant you'll give it a unique name—that name is added to the list, and you can switch between it and other standard calibration settings, if desired.

If you're creating different calibrations for different locations, I'd recommend naming them after those locations. For instance, you could call your calibrations "Outdoors," "Campus Library," "Nighttime," and so on.

Sound and Alert Settings

In the Sound control panel you can make some sound adjustments. You're able to adjust the volume, change the input device for recording, and alter the output device for sound. You can also change your system alert and, if you have an external microphone, you can record some alerts of your own.

Sound Settings

You'll use the Sound control panel to make your sound settings. On the left side of the Sound control panel, you'll see entries for the different types of settings. Click one of those and the right side of the control panel changes to show your options.

The Sound control panel lets you choose the input device and output device for sound on your iBook, plus it lets you manage the speakers, volume, and other basics. Most of the time you won't need to play with these too much. By default, the settings will allow you to play audio CDs, listen through headphones, and so on. If you need to get serious about recording audio or outputting audio to different equipment, that's when you'll dive into the Sound control panel. Here's what you can do in each section of the control panel.

Input

Click the Input entry and you'll be able to choose a device for sound input in the top of the control panel. In most cases you'll just have one option, Internal CD. If you install other devices, they'll show up here. Once you've selected one of those devices, you may be able to choose the Input Source from the pop-up menu. Then, if appropriate, you can place a check next to "Play sound through output device" if you'd like to hear the sound from this input source on the output device. (For instance, sound from the Internal CD to your iBook's speaker should play through—that makes sense. If you're using a USB microphone to record your voice, however, you may not want it to play to play through the speaker, since that could cause feedback.)

As discussed in Chapter 23, the iBook has no built-in microphone for recording. If you'd like to record sounds, you'll need to add a USB-based mic.

Output

In the Output section you'll choose the device that the iBook should use for sound sent out of applications. If you don't have any external speakers, receivers, or other devices attached to your iBook, you'll see Built-in as the only option. You can set the volume for output sound using the slider in this window. If you have other output devices attached, you'll select them here.

Speaker Setup

In the Speaker Setup section you can test the arrangement and volume of your speakers. This, obviously, is most useful if you have headphones or external speakers attached to your iBook. Its one small built-in speaker isn't affected much by these settings.

Click the Start Test button and you'll hear a static tone that helps you set the balance of your speakers using the small volume sliders under each speaker. When you're done, click the Stop Test button.

Watch your ears on this test—it uses an annoying static sound.

Alerts

Click the Alert Sounds item in the Sound control panel and choose an alert sound for the Mac OS to let you know that there's a problem, a question, or something else going on. Just select the alert you want to use and adjust the volume using the slider control.

If you have a USB microphone for your iBook, you can also record your own alerts. (Or, you can record alerts from the Internal CD player if that's what you have selected in the Input section of the Sound control panel.) Click Add and you'll see a recording interface that resembles the controls for a cassette recorder.

Click the Record button to record up to ten seconds of sound based on whatever the Input Source is set to in the Input controls. If it's an external microphone, start speaking, singing, or doing whatever you want to record. When you're done, click the Stop button. You can click Play to hear the sound or click Save to save the sound to your list of alerts. Name the sound and click OK. Now you can select it in the Alerts list.

Time and Date Settings

One of the basic settings for your iBook is the time and date. You probably set these when you first turned on your iBook and ran the Setup Assistant. But you may have some reason to revisit them, including a move to another time zone or perhaps recognition that something is set incorrectly. To change the time and date, head to the Apple menu, then choose Control Panels | Date & Time.

There are a number of things you can do in this control panel:

- **Edit Date and Time**   In the Current Date section, click in the Date entry box and either type the date or use the arrows to change the date. You can do the same thing for setting Time in the Current Time section.

- **Format Date and Time**   Under each setting, click the Formats button to change the date and time formats. Each section provides several options for the time or date display.

- **Set the Time Zone**   Click the Set Time Zone button to choose your locale. You can also click the check boxes if you want to automatically track daylight savings or to let the iBook know that daylight savings is currently in effect.

- **Use a Time Server**   When you're connected to the Internet, the Time Server option can synchronize your iBook's clock to an Internet Time Server clock. (Internet Server Time is based on official atomic clocks, making them accurate. Apple provides their Time Servers as a free service.) There's also a Server Options button that checks the clock against the server closest to you.

- **Turn Menu Bar Clock On or Off**   Want a clock on your iBook's menu bar? Click the On radio button. You can set other options (fonts and colors) by clicking the Clock Options button.

General Controls

Once, General Controls was the main control panel for specifying the look of an iBook. These days, it's relegated to a smaller, but still important, role. It has basic controls over how the Finder and menus work. Select Apple | Control Panels | General Controls.

Here's what everything does:

■ **Desktop/Launcher**   These are controls for whether or not the desktop or
the Launcher should appear in the background when you're using other
applications. (The Launcher is a special window that quickly launches
applications. Drop aliases in the Launcher subfolder of the System Folder
to access them through the Launcher.)

■ **Shut Down Warning**   If your iBook is shut down incorrectly (due to
a freeze up, crash, or power failure), you'll get a warning and Disk First
Aid will check your iBook's hard disk. If you don't want this option,
remove the check from the check box.

■ **Protect System Folder/Protect Applications Folder**   If either of these is
checked, then files or folders can't be moved or deleted from the folders.
This is useful for avoiding accidentally deleting important files.

■ **Blinking**   Change the speed and number of times the insertion point and
menus blink.

■ **Documents**   Choose what folder the Open and Save dialog boxes will
display by default.

Memory Settings

The Memory control panel offers an opportunity to manage the RAM in your iBook
and, perhaps, get a little more performance out of your system. Some of the settings are
automatic, but you can make changes. Choose Apple | Control Panels | Memory.

Here's what each setting does:

- **Disk Cache** This area determines how much system RAM is set aside for a disk cache. A disk cache is a special portion of memory where "look-ahead" data is stored to be accessed more quickly than if the Mac OS was forced to load the data straight from the disk. This speeds up hard disk performance and makes your iBook run a little more quickly. Usually, this is set automatically, but if you'd like to enter your own number, click the Custom setting and enter an amount, in kilobytes, for the cache. Setting it lower, however, will likely slow your iBook down a bit.

- **Virtual Memory** Virtual memory allows your iBook to use part of the hard disk to store items that should be in memory, but can temporarily be placed on the hard disk. This makes it possible to run more programs at once. Click the On and Off radio buttons to turn Virtual Memory on and off. (You should always have Virtual Memory turned on unless you have an application or utility that specifically suggests you turn it off.) Choose an amount in the entry box or use the arrows. How much? Add between 1 and 10MB to the current built-in memory.

NOTE *If you only have 32MB of RAM installed in your iBook, you must leave virtual memory on and set higher than the recommendation—between 40–64MB. Otherwise, there simply isn't enough RAM for typical operations. If you find that your iBook runs a little slowly, you should quit some open applications and try, in general, to work with fewer applications open. You should also consider upgrading to at least 64MB (or more) of RAM, as discussed in Chapter 23.*

- **RAM Disk** A RAM disk allows you to create a sort of "virtual" disk that's actually stored in RAM. The advantage of this is that RAM is much faster than a hard disk, so placing data or applications on the RAM disk can make your iBook run a little faster. The disadvantage is that a RAM disk is just as volatile as regular RAM. Don't store important data on a RAM disk since one system freeze or power surge could wipe away all the data. To create a RAM disk, click the On button and choose a size. To get rid of the RAM disk, go to the Finder and delete everything from the RAM disk, then click Off in the Memory control panel.

NOTE *File Sharing needs to be turned off in order to get rid of a RAM disk.*

I don't recommend using more than half of the built-in RAM in your system for a RAM disk, although the more RAM you have, the more you can devote to a RAM disk. If you have 32MB of RAM, then you really can't spare any for a RAM disk—your iBook is using all of that RAM just to function. If you have 64MB of RAM, I'd recommend keeping your RAM disk under 10–15MB or so. With 96 or 128MB of RAM (or more) you're free to have a much larger RAM disk, if you find one useful. Remember, a RAM disk subtracts from the amount of RAM used for running applications.

RAM disks can be particularly useful for iBook owners, since accessing data that's stored on a RAM disk uses less power than accessing the hard disk. In fact, it's possible to run both your applications and data files from a RAM disk (say, AppleWorks and a word processing file you're creating) and hardly access the internal hard disk at all. Avoiding all those spinning parts on the hard disk saves power, making your iBook's battery charge last longer. Unfortunately, you've got to be careful with an arrangement like this, since a crash or a freeze may cause the data on your RAM disk to be lost, since your Save commands, even if you perform them frequently, are saving to the "virtual" RAM disk, not the physical hard disk. So, every so often you should save your document to the hard disk as well.

TIP *What do you put on a RAM disk? Here are a few good options: Place your Web browser's cache storage here by using the Preferences control panel in your Web browser to change the location of stored cache files. Also, store QuickTime movies here so they'll run smoother and be easier to edit. And, as mentioned, you can place applications and data files on RAM disks; just make sure you save to the hard disk fairly frequently and store the files on the hard disk when you're done using them. (Don't store them permanently on the RAM disk.) In fact, there are freeware and shareware utilities available for automatically saving and managing RAM disks. See Chapter 18 for more on shareware.*

In the Memory control panel, check Save On Shut Down to make sure data on the RAM disk is saved when you shut down. The contents saved on a RAM disk can survive a restart, but not a shutdown, unless you choose to save the data.

Don't like the Memory control panel settings you specified? Click the Use Defaults button to return to the original settings.

Save Energy Automatically

Part of your decision to buy an iBook may have been Apple's claims that the iBook can go up to six hours between recharging sessions, a claim that places it ahead of most notebook computers on the market. While impressive, there's quite a bit that goes on behind the scenes to make that long battery life possible. It takes a combination of battery technology and software-based power management, some of which you can control. If you plan to get that six-hour battery life, settings need to be set optimally in the Energy Saver control panel.

The Energy Saver control panel allows you to do some interesting things. You can automate the startup and shutdown of your iBook. You can cause the iBook to blank its screen and go to sleep after a period of inactivity. When your iBook sleeps, the processor, hard disk, and display all consume much less energy, but the power stays on and applications and documents stay open. Tap a key on the keyboard (or the POWER key) and the iBook will spring back to life.

To change Energy Saver settings, choose Apple | Control Panels | Energy Saver.

Sleep Timer

To set how quickly your system goes to sleep and what parts of the iBook power down during periods of inactivity, choose the Idle Sleep button. Now, in the Settings for pop-up menu, choose whether you'd like to alter settings for when the iBook is connected to the Power Adapter (it's plugged in) or when it's running off the Battery.

Now, you can use the Energy Use sliderbar to quickly change the power use characteristics of the iBook. If you're setting Battery energy use, you might want to slide it all the way to the left to choose Better Conservation, which means the iBook sleeps more quickly and may run a bit more slowly in order to save energy.

If you slide it toward Better Performance then the iBook will remain more responsive, but the battery will drain more quickly.

Of course, if you're selecting a setting for the Power Adapter, you might err a bit more toward Better Performance. You probably still want some conservation measures taken, but if the iBook is plugged in you can worry a little less about the slightly greater drain that higher performance takes.

If you'd like to go beyond the basics and tailor the way your iBook conserves energy, click the Show Details button. Now you'll see sliders that allow you to specify when your iBook will sleep, when the display will be put to sleep and how quickly the hard disk will be spun down. You can use the slidebars to change the amount of time that Energy Saver waits before doing these things; you can use the check boxes next to the options to turn them off, if you think that's wise.

Again, you can turn some of these off when you're choosing Power Adapter settings in the Energy Saver control panel, although you should probably leave the basic sleep setting on for both. In the Battery settings, I recommend that you keep all of the sleep timers on and set them as low as you can stand.

Automate Sleep, Startup, and Shutdown

You can schedule your iBook to automatically sleep, start up, and shut down, if you'd like. To do that, click the Scheduled Wakeup & Sleep button. By default, you'll be scheduling an automated time when the iBook will put itself to sleep. If you'd prefer the iBook to shut itself down, place a check mark next to "Scheduled shut down instead of scheduled sleep."

Now, place a check mark next to the option you'd like to automate (they change according to settings, but the options are "Wake up the computer," "Put the computer to sleep," and so on). From the pop-up menu choose the days of the week that this scheduled event should take place. Finally, choose a time when the startup or shutdown should take place.

That's it—close the Energy Saver control panel and the system is armed.

Advanced Settings

The iBook offers some advanced settings that let you determine exactly how the Energy Saver manages sleep so you can get the best performance from your battery-powered machine.

TIP   *The Energy Saver control strip module gives you access to a special command that can help you save energy while you're on battery power. Open the Energy Saver control strip module (it looks like a moon with small stars) and you'll see the option Spin Down Hard Disk. If you plan to use data stored on a RAM disk, listen to an audio CD for a few minutes or stop using the iBook for five minutes, choose this option to spin down the hard disk, which saves energy. Note that you can also put the iBook to sleep or change conservation settings in the Energy Saver control panel.*

Here are the settings:

- *Preserve memory contents on sleep.* Turn this option on and the Mac OS saves the contents of memory to a file called Suspended.image (stored in the System Folder) whenever you put the iBook to sleep. This safeguards your open documents and applications in case the iBook loses battery power while sleeping. This option should be turned on if you attempt to swap iBook batteries while the iBook is asleep, since the iBook has no backup battery. (In general, you should swap batteries with the AC adapter connected, or avoid swapping batteries at all.)

- *Reconnect to Servers.* Turn this option on to have your iBook reconnect to any server computers it was connected to before it was put to sleep. You can also turn on "Remember my passwords" if you'd like the iBook to sign on automatically without asking for your passwords. (Networking is discussed in Chapter 24.)

- *Wake up when modem detects a ring.* Turn on this option if you'd like the iBook to wake from sleep when it detects an incoming call. (You'll probably do this if you're set up to receive faxes with FaxSTF, discussed in Chapter 22.)

- *Allow processor cycling.* This allows the iBook's processor to slow down when the iBook is idle, thus saving power. This one should definitely be active if you plan to get those six hours' worth of battery life.

■ *Turn off the display instead of dimming it.*   This again saves power by turning the display completely off in the amount of time you've set for dimming in the Idle Sleep section of the Energy Saver control panel.

If you have an AirPort card installed in your iBook, the AirPort control strip module allows you to turn off power to the AirPort card. I'd recommend doing so when it's not in use, which will conserve some additional battery power.

Change the Appearance

Another major control panel is the Appearance control panel. This allows you to choose how the Mac's interface looks—the colors, the textures, the behaviors—as well as how the arrows work on the scrollbars and what sort of sounds are made as you're working. To manage all that, it has to have a lot of tabs. Choose Apple | Control Panels | Appearance.

Here's what happens on each tab:

■ **Themes**   Themes are overall, cohesive collections of all the other settings tabs—appearance, color of the desktop, window colors and characteristics, sounds, fonts, and scroll bar settings. Each theme offers a different overall experience. To use a theme, select it from the scrolling list. Close the Appearance control panel and work with that theme, or you can alter it. If you alter it (by visiting the other tabs), return to the Themes tab to name and save your altered creation using the Save Theme button.

■ **Appearance**   Your iBook ships with a default appearance, but theme files (offered by third-party companies) can be stored in the System Folder within the Appearance subfolder. This changes the whole look of the windows, icons, and everything. You can also change the highlight color (the color used when you select text or an icon) and the Variation color (used for the highlight bar in menus and for the scroll boxes in windows).

■ **Fonts**   With the Fonts tab, you can change the font face used for different parts of the Mac OS. Feel free to experiment. You can also experiment with font *smoothing*—this technology causes fonts larger than a certain point size (that you can change with the arrows and Size entry box) to be smoothed or *anti-aliased* onscreen. This makes some fonts look more like printed text than computer screen text, although the overall look varies depending on the fonts used. Text smaller than 14 point can sometimes be too blurry to read when smoothed, so it's probably best to leave this option on for 14 point or higher text.

■ **Desktop**   This tab allows you to place a pattern or picture on the desktop to give your iBook some personality. To place a pattern, use the Patterns list. To place a picture, click the Place Picture button and find the picture in the Open dialog box (there's a folder called Sample Desktop Pictures in the Apple Extras folder that has some sample desktop images), then click Choose. Back in the Appearance control panel, position the image using the Position menu. You can choose Tile On Screen (several copies pasted together to fill the screen), Center On Screen, Scale To Fit the screen while maintaining the correct ratio, or Fill The Screen regardless of dimensions. You can also leave it at the default, Position Automatically, especially if the image is already the same resolution as your desktop. When you've made your choices, click Set Desktop. To remove the picture, click Remove Picture and click Set Desktop again.

TIP   *It's a good idea to match your desktop image's resolution to your screen's resolution—if you're running at 800 × 600, then the desktop picture can also be 800 × 600. Also, you can use any PICT, JPG, or GIF image, and it can be stored anywhere on your hard disk.*

■ **Sound**   Choose a sound track for your theme. The sound track offers preset sounds for many different things you can do in the Mac OS, including selecting from menus, moving icons, scrolling windows, and so on. Choose a soundtrack from the menu, then, by checking or unchecking the different sound effects, choose the sounds you'd like to hear.

■ **Options**   This last tab offers you two check boxes: first, whether or not your scroll arrows appear at just one end of the scrollbar; and second, whether or not you want to be able to double-click a title bar in order to invoke the Windowshade command. Make your choices.

If you've changed the settings extensively, don't forget to return to the Themes tab and give your new theme a name. Otherwise, you're done—click the Close box to exit the Appearance control panel. Your new appearance is now in effect.

Keychain Access

In Mac OS 9, there's a new technology in the OS that allows you to do something interesting. Using your personal keychain, you can store user names and passwords for servers, encrypted files, and, in some cases, Internet sites. Many items that you access on your iBook using a password can be stored on your keychain, just like you can store the keys for your car, house, office, and safety deposit box on a real keychain.

With your Mac OS keychain, you only need to remember one password. The keychain stores the passwords for many other resources, all of which are locked behind a single password that you memorize. Now, instead of looking up passwords on that hidden sheet of paper taped to the bottom of a desk drawer, you can unlock your Mac OS keychain and access passwords automatically.

How does it work? In certain applications, you'll find an option like "Add to Keychain" that allows you to add a user name and password to the keychain automatically. Now, the next time you try to access that user name and password, the application will attempt to retrieve it from your keychain. If your keychain is unlocked, then that password-protected connection (or item) will be opened automatically—you won't have to enter a password! If your keychain is locked, though, you'll have to enter your keychain password before the application can continue. So, as long as you're diligent about locking your keychain, others won't be able to access it and get into your password-protected items.

> **NOTE** *In most cases, applications need to support the keychain in order for it to work. So, it'll take an upgrade in some applications—like Web browsers—before they'll support the keychain. (The "5.0" level of Internet Explorer and Netscape Communicator may support the keychain, but that's not clear yet at the time of writing.) In Mac OS 9, the Network Browser supports the keychain, so you can automatically store your network logins using keychain technology. Likewise, the Apple File Security application supports the keychain, so you can encrypt files on your iBook for secure storage and store the password in your keychain.*

Create Your Keychain

Before you can store your passwords, you'll need to create your keychain. To do that, head to the Keychain Access control panel. If you haven't created a keychain before, you can create one. Here's how:

1. Open the Keychain Access control panel.

2. If you haven't created a keychain, you'll see a dialog box asking if you'd like to create one. Click the Create button.

3. In the Create Keychain dialog box, enter a name for the keychain (for instance, your name) and a password. (You can press TAB to move between entry boxes.) You'll enter the password twice—once in the Password box and once in the Confirm box to ensure that you type it the same way each time. Click Create.

The password you use should be at least six characters long and ideally include a mix of letters and numbers. If you create a password that the Keychain Access control panel determines isn't very secure, you may be asked to reconsider your password. (Click No and change your password.) Also, don't forget your password! There's no way to get into your keychain if you do.

View Your Keychain

Once you've created a keychain, you'll be able to access the keychain in the future by opening the Keychain Access control panel. If the Keychain is locked, you'll see the Unlock Keychain dialog box. Choose your keychain from the Unlock Keychain pop-up menu, then enter your password for the keychain. Click the Unlock button and your keychain will be unlocked.

Once your keychain is unlocked (or if your keychain was already unlocked), Keychain Access opens the keychain's window. Now you'll be able to see the items that are stored on your keychain.

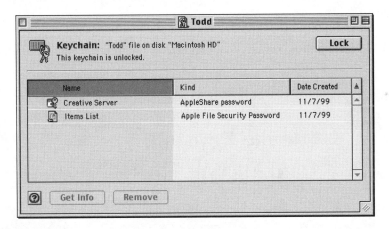

To learn more about an item, select it in the window and click the Get Info button. If you want to remove an item, select it and click Remove. If you'd like to lock your keychain, just click the Lock button. This immediately locks the keychain. The next time an application attempts to access it, the keychain will ask you for your password to ensure that you want the application to have access to your keychain.

You can also set some important preferences for your keychain using the Keychain Access control panel. Select Edit | *Name* Settings (where *Name* is the name you've given to your keychain). You'll be asked to enter your keychain password. Now, in the Change Settings dialog box, you can enter (and confirm) a new password for your keychain. You can also turn on some options:

- *Allow access without warning.*   If this is turned on, applications will be able to immediately access your keychain if it's unlocked. If it's turned off, you'll often see a dialog box that confirms that you want a particular application to have access to your keychain.

- *Lock after minutes of inactivity.*   Turn on this option and enter an amount of minutes of system idle time the control panel should wait before automatically locking your keychain. I'd recommend turning on this option, especially in an office or organizational environment. If you forget to lock your password and you leave your iBook for a few minutes, then the keychain will be locked automatically after the idle time has passed.

- *Lock when the system sleeps.*   Select this option if you'd like your keychain to lock itself whenever the system sleeps. That way anytime you put your iBook to sleep or close its lid your keychain will lock for added security.

Click the Save button to save your changes in the Change Settings dialog box.

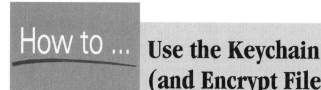

How to ...   Use the Keychain (and Encrypt Files)

You don't really add items to your keychain using the Keychain Access control panel—in some cases you can drag items (like Internet location files) to the Keychain Access control panel. At this point in the implementation of the keychain technology, however, that doesn't often do much good. (At some point in the future, drag-and-drop may work well when many different applications support the keychain.) In the meantime, you'll generally add keychain items using applications. One that supports the keychain is the Network Browser, discussed in Chapter 24.

Another application that supports the keychain is Apple File Security, a new addition in Mac OS 9 that encrypts files in the Finder. *Encryption* is a process that turns the document into a jumble of nonsense, as far as any snooping eyes are concerned. Like an encrypted transmission between nations at war, it'll take the *passphrase* to get into this file. If you don't have the password, you won't be able to open this file.

Drag-and-drop a document or program onto the Apple File Security icon, located in the Applications folder on your iBook. (You can also CTRL-click an item in the Finder and select Encrypt from the pop-up menu.) You'll see a dialog box asking you for a passphrase, which is the same thing as a password. Enter a password twice (press TAB between entries) and make sure the option Add to Keychain is selected.

When you click the Encrypt button, the file is encrypted. At the same time, the password for this item is stored on the keychain. Now, if you double-click the encrypted item in the Finder, you'll be asked for your keychain password if it's locked. Then, once unlocked, the password for this encrypted file is accessed automatically and the file is decrypted!

Get Your iBook to Talk

Text-to-Speech is the technology that allows your Mac to read text out loud. It's as simple as that. You may not have encountered it much unless you have Talking Alerts turned on in the Speech control panel. In that case, you may already be familiar with the clipped female voice that occasionally reads the contents of dialog boxes to you after they've sat on the screen for a while.

Talking Alerts is one basic implementation of Text-to-Speech—you can turn it on or off by opening the Speech control panel and selecting Talking Alerts from the Options pop-up menu. Now, in the Speech control panel, turn off the option "Speak the alert text" and you'll no longer hear items in alert dialog boxes spoken. You can also turn on or off the option "Speak the phrase," which is just a cute way for the iBook to add a little character to its reading—it can say "Alert," "Rats," "Shoot," and many others before it speaks the alert text, if you like. You can also use the slider to determine how long Talking Alerts should wait before it reads the text in alert dialog boxes.

You can also use the Speech control panel to change the voice used for speech. Select Voice from the Options menu and you can choose a different voice (from the Voice pop-up menu) and a Rate of speech using the slider bar. To test the voice, click the small speaker icon. You'll hear a sample of speech at the current settings.

Another way you can use Text-to-Speech is within applications that support it. One such application is SimpleText. In the Sound menu within SimpleText, you can choose the command Speak All to have SimpleText read you the open document, or Speak Selection to speak only text that's been highlighted in the document window. Other applications can speak text or selections, including some that are designed specifically for the task.

Manage Settings by Location

One of the most annoying aspects of portable-computer ownership is being forced to change settings all the time. If you move from an Ethernet network at school or work to a modem connection at home, do you find yourself consulting multiple control panels every time you open your iBook back up? Fortunately, it doesn't have to be that way. If you're diligent with the way you handle your settings, you can switch the settings on many different parts of the Mac OS at once using the Location Manager.

What the Location Manager does is help you create profiles that you can name and save—for home, office, school and so on. Then, it associates particular settings or configurations within your control panels with that saved location profile. It learns, for instance, that your Office location profile uses certain settings in the AppleTalk, TCP/IP, Internet, Sound, Remote Access, and File Sharing control panels, among others. It then stores that profile and automatically switches all of those settings whenever you tell if you've changed locations.

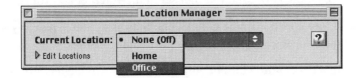

Set Up Location Manager

When you first dig into the Location Manager, you may have some setup tasks to perform. With many control panels, the Location Manager uses that control panel's capability to store multiple configurations. In Chapters 20 and 24, for instance, I discuss the configurations that you can save within a number of networking control panels like the AppleTalk and TCP/IP control panels.

You can also switch between saved Internet sets and Extension sets, if you've created multiple sets in the Internet and Extensions Manager control panels, respectively.

In other cases, though, the Location Manager will simply observe and record the current state of many settings. So, before you create a Location Manager location profile, you'll want to go ahead and set your iBook up exactly as you'd like it for the first location profile. (If you're going to set up Home first, set your iBook up exactly as you'll want it at home, for instance.)

You can set as many of the following as you'd like, but you can also ignore any settings you don't want to store:

■ **AppleTalk and TCP/IP configurations** In this case, you should create a configuration within the control panel itself. For instance, if you're planning to create a location profile for your Office settings, head to the AppleTalk control panel and create a configuration called Office. Make sure it has the appropriate settings and choose Make Active for that configuration. Do the same for TCP/IP.

- **Default printer**   Open the Chooser and select the printer you'd like to use for this location.

- **Extension set**   If you want to, you can dictate a different extension set for each location. You'll need to save the sets using the Extensions Manager, then make this location's set current before closing the Extensions Manager.

- **File Sharing state**   Set file sharing the way you want it recorded (on or off) by the Location Manager.

- **Internet set**   Choose the Internet set in the Internet control panel.

- **QuickTime speed**   In the QuickTime Settings control panel, you can select the connection speed for this particular location.

- **Remote Access and Modem control panels**   Create a configuration (and make it active) in each control panel.

- **Sound level**   Choose a volume for the Output device in the Sound control panel.

- **Time zone**   Choose a time zone in the Date & Time control panel.

Once all or some of these settings have been made, you're ready to create a location profile in the Location Manager. Here's how:

1. Open the Location Manager control panel.

2. From the File menu, choose New Location.

3. You'll see the Location Manager control panel open up to reveal a number of options. Place a check mark next to each setting that you'd like the Location Manager to track for you.

4. If you get any error messages, you may need to open the control panels in question and fix the problem before you can move forward. For instance, the Location Manager won't let you use the Default configuration for AppleTalk, TCP/IP, or Remote Access. If you have the Default configuration selected in one of those control panels, you'll need to create a new configuration and make it active.

5. When you're finished editing the location, choose File | Save Location from the menu. You can then close the Location Manager if you like, or set the Location as the current one as discussed in the next section.

Note two things while you're editing a location. First, you can select a setting by clicking it once. You'll see the current setting state for it in the Values section of the control panel. This makes it easier to see if you need to alter the setting before saving it.

Second, the Auto-Open Items setting is a special case. If you turn this setting on, you'll see another dialog box that allows you to choose items you'd like to have automatically opened whenever you switch to this location. You can select documents, applications, or even folders you'd like opened in the Finder.

Change Your Location

Changing locations is simple. Open the Location Manager and choose the location from the Current Location pop-up menu. Now you'll see a dialog box that reports the progress of the switch.

If everything goes well, all your settings are switched and you're ready to start using the iBook at the new location.

If you change a setting that the Location Manager tracks, you may be asked at some point in the future if you want the Location Manager to save that setting. (For instance, if the Location Manager tracks the Sound Level and you change the volume while you're in the Home location, Location Manager will ask you if you want that new volume saved as part of the Home location profile.)

Chapter 22

Print Your Documents, Manage Fonts, and Send Faxes

How to...

- Decide what type of printer to use with your iBook
- Connect the printer to your iBook (or to your network)
- Use Page Setup and Print dialog boxes to print your documents
- Manage documents with the PrintMonitor or Desktop Printer
- Change the fonts that are installed on your iBook
- Send and receive faxes from your iBook

Y̶ou probably want to print stuff. Whether you already have an iBook-compatible printer, you're wondering if you can make your current printer iBook-compatible, or you're still in the shopping phase, let's take a look at your needs and figure out how to get you up and printing. It's actually pretty easy with an iBook, especially if you're able to buy a USB printer.

To begin, let's talk about the different types of printers you can get and what the advantages are of each. Then, we'll take a look at how you set up a printer and print to it. Finally, we'll end with a discussion of fonts and how to manage them on your iBook.

Choose a Printer

There are two major types of printers that are used in the home, home office, or most businesses and organizations: laser and inkjet. There are also different technologies for setting up the printers. And, the different types of printers can even use different font technologies. So, let's take a closer look at the different types of printers you might be able to buy or use with your iBook.

Laser vs. Inkjet

Inkjet printers tend to be less expensive, more home-oriented machines with fewer bells and whistles. These days, most inkjets can print in color and they print pretty quickly, although higher-quality printing is much slower than it is with a laser printer. Inkjets can be slightly easier to set up, but they rely strongly on their own software drivers, whereas most laser printers use a driver written by Apple that integrates well with the Mac OS.

Laser printers are faster and usually quieter, and offer better print quality. Most inexpensive lasers don't print in color, though, and laser printers are more expensive at the outset. Most laser printers will connect to an iBook using the Ethernet port, making it easy to share the printer with a number of different iBooks, iMacs, or other computers. Laser printers tend to have more professional-level options—paper trays and envelope feeders, for instance. And laser printers that use the PostScript printer language tend to print better quality graphics than inkjet printers that don't use PostScript.

If you're trying to decide between the two, probably the most important considerations are your volume of printing, the need for color, and the desired quality of black-and-white printing. If you expect to print a lot—or if you'll be in situations where you need to quickly print 20- to 100-page documents and send them somewhere—then you'll want a laser printer. You'll also want a laser printer for a lower cost-per-page over the long term. And you'll want a laser if you print many important documents that are mostly text and require no color.

Inkjet technology has improved remarkably, and you can get a good color printer for less than $200 in some cases. These are great if you run a small business and plan to print brochures, signs, menus, thank you notes, invitations, overhead slides and so forth. While not always workhorses for hundreds of pages per month, inkjet printers provide flexible printing with a variety of options. Look for inkjet that accepts a number of different types of paper and transparencies, especially if you plan to make full use of color on business cards, overhead slides, and handbills.

If you want to share one printer between two or more computers, your best choice is a laser printer connected to the Ethernet port. At the time of writing, most printers connected to the USB port can't be shared over a network, although this may change if Apple and/or printer manufacturers write new "printer share" drivers. (For instance, there's a driver for popular Epson USB inkjet printers that allows them to be shared over a network.)

Connection Technologies

Printers also offer a variety of ways that they can be connected to your iBook. There are two ways to directly connect to an iBook—USB and by a network (either Ethernet or wireless). In the case of USB, you'll often find that inkjet printers offer a special cable or adapter for the printer that can be added to give it USB connectivity. The cable can be $50 or more, so factor that in when you're shopping for an inkjet. Other inkjet printers offer USB right from the box, without special add-on cables.

USB to Parallel
Connector

Laser printers will often connect via Ethernet, although how you're connecting dictates the type of Ethernet cable you need. If you're just connecting the laser

22

printer to your iBook, you'll need an Ethernet *crossover* cable, which is designed to allow two Ethernet devices to talk to each other. This is different from a typical Ethernet *patch* cable, which is used to connect a device to an Ethernet hub.

You'll also need an Ethernet hub if you plan to use the laser printer with more than one computer. You can do that easily with all the devices plugged into the hub; all the computers (especially if they're Macs and compatible with the printer) will recognize the printer when you set them up.

NOTE   *You can print from an AirPort-enabled iBook if your AirPort Base Station and Ethernet printer are connected to the same Ethernet hub.*

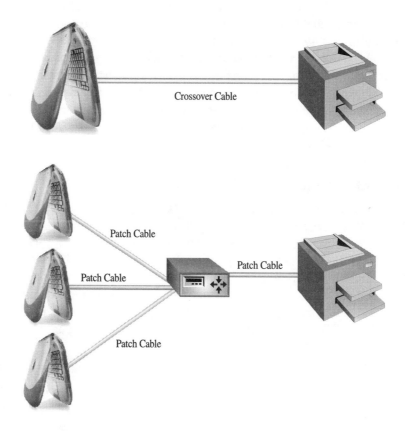

Crossover Cable

Patch Cable

Patch Cable

Patch Cable

Patch Cable

There's a third type of connection—a LocalTalk connection. LocalTalk is an earlier style of Mac networking that allowed older Macs to network to one another without using Ethernet cabling. It's a slow technology that's not as popular anymore, but some printers, especially older Apple laser printers, newer Apple-branded inkjets, and many popular HP inkjet and laser printers for Mac use LocalTalk for their connection. The problem is, the iBook doesn't have a LocalTalk port. (This is the "printer" port on old Macs, if you're familiar with them.)

The solution is a LocalTalk adapter. With one of these adapters, you're able to hook your iBook to a LocalTalk printer through the Ethernet port. The connection is usually seamless—your printer driver is able to find the printer once it's connected, even though you're using an adapter.

The fourth type of connection, a serial connection, is similar. Older Apple StyleWriter inkjets, inkjets from Canon, HP DeskWriters, and some popular Apple Personal LaserWriter printers use serial connections. They don't use LocalTalk, but they do connect to the "printer port" (or the "modem port" in some cases) on older-style Macs. In this case, you need another adapter—a serial adapter. Different companies make different types of adapters—serial-to-USB or serial-to-Ethernet. Which you use is up to you, with one caveat—if you plan to do much networking, I'd go ahead and leave the Ethernet port free and use a USB adapter. If you'll just be using your iBook at home with no other computers in the mix and no major plans for DSL Internet or a cable modem, then a serial-to-Ethernet adapter is fine.

See Table 22-1 for a list of LocalTalk and serial adapter manufacturers.

Printer Languages

Printers can use different languages for describing a page. If your printer uses the PostScript language, then it's generally capable of more graphically complex pages. Professional publishers tend to use PostScript-language printers for their high-end printing needs. A PostScript-language printer includes a special processor, its own RAM, and some PostScript Type 1 fonts built into the printer itself. In this case, a program that wants to print to the printer simply sends a series of PostScript commands to tell the printer how the document should be printed. Then, the printer does all the work using its own processor to create the printed page.

Manufacturer	Adapter(s)	Web Site
Ariston	USB-to-serial	http://www.ariston.com
Entrega	USB-to-serial	http://www.entrega.com
Farallon	Ethernet-to-Localtalk Ethernet-to-serial	http://www.farallon.com
Keyspan	USB-to-serial	http://www.keyspan.com
Momentum	USB-to-serial	http://www.momentuminc.com

TABLE 22-1   Printer Adapter Manufacturers and Their Web Sites

Many inkjet printers use a different language, the Printer Control Language (PCL), a standard originated by Hewlett-Packard Corporation. In this case, the printer requires a special driver so that your iBook can speak the PCL language, create the page, and send it to the printer in the proper format. iBook does all of the processing, which is why inkjet printing can be slower than laser printing; it's also why most inkjet printers are cheaper, since they don't have their own processor, RAM, and so on—they rely on the iBook for all that.

This situation is also why inkjet printers need to have special driver software written for them, while PostScript-language printers, even if they aren't specifically designed to be Mac-compatible, often work just fine using the LaserWriter 8 driver discussed later in this chapter.

Earlier non-PostScript printers were made specifically for Macs using the QuickDraw printer language. For instance, HP's DeskWriter series, although nearly identical to the DeskJet series, used QuickDraw instead of PCL for the Mac version. These days that's much less common, especially for USB-based printers.

Using PC Printers

Some of the newer PC printers can be used with either Windows-based PCs or Macs, depending on the software driver you use, since both use USB.

With a product called Infowave's PowerPrint USB (**http://www.infowave.com/**), it's possible to connect a parallel-port PC printer—either an inkjet or a non-PostScript laser printer—to your iBook, using the USB-to-PC parallel port adapter and special driver software.

PowerPrint works with Canon, Epson, Lexmark, and NEC printers as well as HP's LaserJet and DeskJet series. During the installation process choose the type of printer drivers you want to install, or a generic set of drivers, if appropriate.

Both HP and Epson have USB-to-parallel kits that also work with their own brands of printers. The Infowave kit is specifically designed for older printers that don't have iBook-specific driver software.

After the installation is complete, simply access the printer's driver in the Chooser as discussed later in this chapter. The printer is treated the same as if it were a regular Mac-compatible printer.

Set Up Your Printer and iBook

You've seen a number of different ways to attach an iBook and a printer, including special adapters and cables. In most of those cases, you'll have a particular adapter cable that plugs directly between the printer and iBook.

It so happens that the type of cabling you use generally dictates the type of software driver you'll use, too. All printer drivers are selected in the Chooser, which you open from the Apple menu. The Chooser allows you to select printers and determine certain characteristics about how that printer will conduct itself, including how it's connected. If you have a USB or serial-adapted printer, you'll use an individual printer driver from the manufacturer. If you have a laser printer that's connected via Ethernet, you'll likely use the LaserWriter driver.

 If your laser printer offers a special driver written for Macintosh, you should use that driver. If the driver comes on a floppy diskette, contact the company to see if they have a downloadable or CD-ROM version; you might also examine the discussion of creating disk images in Chapter 18.

Choose a USB or Serial-Adapted Printer

If your printer is an inkjet or a laser printer that's been adapted to your iBook via a serial-to-USB or serial-to-Ethernet adapter, then choose the individual printer driver for that device. The driver will say DeskJet 880, USB LaserJet, Epson 740, or something similar. If your particular printer's driver doesn't appear in the Chooser, then you may not have installed it.

DESKJET 880C

Check the CD that came with the printer for a Mac driver installer program. If you don't find Mac drivers, try the manufacturer's support Web site or contact customer support to get the drivers. The easiest way to get the driver software is to download it from the manufacturer's Web site.

 Printer drivers are installed right in the Extensions folder within your iBook's System Folder, just in case you want to look for them. Your printer may also require some other support files in the Extensions or Control Panels folder.

Once you've installed the printer drivers, select the printer from the Chooser. Hopefully, the connection will be found (by your iBook) on the right side, where you'll see the USB symbol and the printer's name. (It's also possible you'll see a Printer Port symbol if you're using an adapter.) When you've selected the connection, choose the Setup button (if one appears) to set basic printer preferences. Otherwise, just click the close box and your printer is set. In some instances, a desktop printer icon will appear.

Choose an Ethernet Printer

If your printer is connected via Ethernet, either using a crossover cable or plugged directly into an Ethernet hub, setting up the printer is usually very simple. In the Chooser, select the LaserWriter 8 printer driver (or the driver you specially installed for your laser printer). Now, on the right side of the Chooser window, select the printer you want to use. In cases where your iBook resides on a large network, you may see more than one choice.

NOTE   *Not all networks will have the AppleTalk zones pictured here. If yours doesn't, you'll simply see all available PostScript printers when you click the LaserWriter 8 driver. If your network does have zones, you may need to select the appropriate zone for the printer you want to print to. Ask your system administrator for details.*

Select the PostScript printer and click the Create button. This allows you to create (or use) a PostScript Printer Description (PPD) file that can be used to control this printer.

If you believe you have a PPD installed for this printer (PPD files are stored in the Extensions folder inside the System Folder), then you can choose Select PPD and search for it. If not, then you're best off choosing Auto Setup where the LaserWriter driver will help you decide what the printer is capable of. You can get information about the printer by clicking the Get Info button. If you have your printer manual around and you want to set some options for your particular printer, click the Configure button. Otherwise, click OK.

Now, close the Chooser. When you do, your desktop printer icon for this printer will appear.

NOTE   *If you don't see your printer when you select the LaserWriter 8 driver in the Chooser on an AirPort-enabled iBook, the printer may not be configured correctly. Ethernet printers that use IP (instead of AppleTalk) can be used by AirPort-enabled iBooks and Macs. If you have such a printer, you may need to use the Desktop Printer Utility (located in the Apple Extras folder in the Apple Laserwriter Software folder) to configure a desktop printer. Consult your AirPort documentation or system administrator for details.*

Print Stuff and Manage Print Jobs

Once you have your printer set up, you're ready to print. If you've changed printers recently, you may have been asked to open the Page Setup item in your applications. Or you may want to explore the options in Page Setup before printing, so that you know everything is set up correctly.

Once you've invoked the Print command and sent the print job to the printer, it's passed to either the print spooler or the desktop printer. In the case of a spooler, you'll simply see its entry in the Application menu—you can switch to it if desired to see your progress. If your print driver uses a desktop printer, you can manage the print job from there.

Page Setup

Once you've created a document and you're ready to print it, begin by choosing
File | Page Setup. That brings up the Page Setup dialog box.

Actually, you don't need to visit this dialog box every time you plan to
print—only when you need to change a major option for your printer or when
you've recently changed printers (while the application was open) and you need
the application to recognize the new printer. The Page Setup dialog box is most
significant because it introduces you to Clarus the DogCow, one of Apple's
official mascots. But it's also where you set some important options:

- ■ **Page Size**   Choose what size paper the application should plan on printing
  to. (The default is 8.5 × 11-inch paper.)

- ■ **Scaling**   Enter a percentage if you'd like the document to be printed at
  anything other than 100 percent.

- ■ **Orientation**   Choose whether the document should be printed in Portrait
  mode (regular orientation on the page) or in Landscape mode (lengthwise,
  as with ledger sheets).

- ■ **Options**   The Options button provides options unique to your particular
  printer model.

Changes in the Page Setup dialog box are noted with Clarus. Change the page
size and you'll see the page change relative to Clarus; change the orientation and
you'll see the image change to reflect that, too. When you're done setting up the
page, click OK.

Clarus, a DogCow, says "Moof," according to Apple's technical information library.

The PrintMonitor

Once the print job is sent, you'll probably hear the printer come to life and prepare to feed paper and print. You may also see a new entry in the Applications menu called the PrintMonitor (or something similar, like Epson Monitor). The PrintMonitor works in the background to allow your iBook to print while you continue to work on other things. You can also use the PrintMonitor to manage your print jobs.

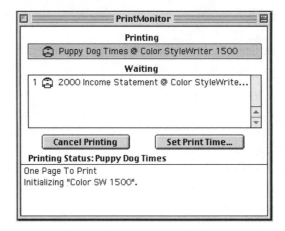

Using the PrintMonitor, you can view the print jobs that have been sent to the printer; if you've sent more than one document to the printer, each appears in the PrintMonitor queue, with the current job at the top. Select a print job and click Cancel Printing to clear the job from the print queue, or click Set Print Time to schedule the print job to print sometime in the future.

While the PrintMonitor is open you can also select File | Stop Printing to suspend printing for the moment. If you'd like to continue printing, select File | Resume Printing.

The Desktop Printer

Many Mac-compatible inkjet printers and Ethernet laser printers will create a desktop printer icon that you can use to manage your print jobs. It works a lot like the PrintMonitor, but is a little friendlier and a little more powerful.

Once you've sent a print job to the printer, you should see your desktop printer icon change to reflect the fact that it has a document that's ready to be printed.

If you need to, you can manage that print job by double-clicking the desktop icon to open the print queue window, where you can see the scheduled print jobs.

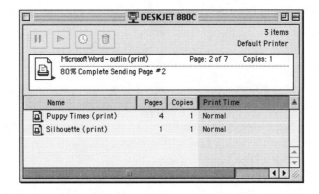

Select a print job in this window, then use the controls at the top of the window to control it—you can pause a job, start it again, give it higher priority, schedule the print job, or delete it.

TIP *Dragging a print job from the queue list to the current print job window will change its priority to urgent, moving it to the top of the queue.*

You'll also notice that while the desktop printer queue is open, there's another command menu in the Finder's menu bar—the Printing menu. Pull it down and select Stop Print Queue to halt all printing; choose Start Print Queue to continue printing. Click the Close box to close the queue window and the printer will continue printing in the background.

SHORTCUT *If you have more than one desktop printer, then you don't have to return to the Chooser to switch between them. A small printer icon appears on the menu bar, very near the Application menu in the top-right corner. Click that icon and you'll get a menu where you can change the active printer.*

Understand and Add Fonts to Your iBook

A *font* is a collection of letters, numbers, and punctuation marks with a particular typeface, weight (bold or not bold), and size in plain or italic. However, the word "font" is also frequently used to mean a typeface with a particular design, such as Courier or Arial. I'll use the term "font" loosely.

When you select a font the application passes that information to the Mac OS, which helps the application render that font. Fonts are stored in a subfolder of your System Folder called the Fonts folder. The font files serve two purposes. First, font files tell your printer how printed text should appear. Second, they tell your Mac how to display text on the screen.

Add Fonts

You can buy both TrueType and PostScript Type 1 fonts from computer stores or online computer sales outlets—any such fonts should work fine with your iBook. To add a font for your iBook's applications, just drag-and-drop the font file onto the System Folder icon. A dialog box will appear telling you that this file will automatically be added to the Fonts folder. Click OK.

> **NOTE**   *If you're using PostScript Type 1 fonts, you should have Adobe Type Manager (ATM) installed and working on your iBook. ATM is a control panel that's installed along with Adobe Acrobat Reader, so by default, your iBook should have it active. If you have Mac OS 9 installed on your iBook, you'll need ATM 5.4.2 or higher; older versions are incompatible.*

Fonts can either be stored loose in the Fonts folder, or they can be saved in a special kind of folder called a *suitcase*. Because there's a limit of 128 items in the Font folder, a suitcase can be used to get around that minimum by, for instance, grouping all the Times New Roman fonts (TrueType and bitmap versions) in the same suitcase.

You can also use suitcases for organization—drag as many fonts as you want to into a suitcase and name it "Special Design Fonts" or something similar. Now, drag this suitcase into the Fonts folder before you launch QuarkXPress, GraphicConverter, or another application that you use with these fonts. At other times when you're working in regular applications, you can store the font suitcase in a different folder on your iBook, so that those fonts aren't used. The fewer fonts you have active, the faster your applications will run. If you open the Fonts folder, you'll see that many of the fonts are already stored in suitcases.

Arial Black

Double-click a suitcase and you can drag-and-drop fonts in and out of the suitcase. The best way to create your own suitcase is to create a duplicate of an existing suitcase and rename it. (You'll also want to delete the fonts in your duplicate suitcase by dragging them to the Trash.)

 If you'll deal with fonts a lot, you might clean out a duplicate suitcase and save it as your "master" suitcase. You can duplicate your master suitcase whenever you need a new suitcase. This way, you won't have to clean out the fonts every time.

The renamed suitcase can now store font files. Just drag all fonts for that suitcase—both bitmap and TrueType fonts, if you've got them—onto the suitcase icon.

Delete Fonts

To delete a font, just open the Fonts folder and drag the font (or suitcase) to the Trash.

It's a good idea to think carefully before deleting a font file, because you can't always anticipate when an application or document might need that particular font. If you want to simply deactivate a font, drag it to a folder outside of the System Folder. (Create a "Disabled Fonts" folder on your hard disk, for instance.) Now that font won't appear in the Font menu of any of your applications. If you get error messages requiring the use of a disabled font, you can still drag the font back into the Fonts folder if it's needed.

Remember, too, that many of the files in the Fonts folder are actually suitcases that have more than one font inside of them (usually, but not always, in the same typeface family). If you don't want to delete the entire suitcase, you can double-click the suitcase to open it, then drag the font files to the Trash individually.

Fax with Your iBook

Your iBook comes bundled with a program called FaxSTF that makes it possible—perhaps even easy—to send and receive faxes. All you have to do is have your modem plugged into the telephone line and make some basic preference settings. The rest of it should be set up and ready to use.

Send a Fax

Obviously, your iBook, right out of the box, doesn't offer the full functionality of a fax machine, since it doesn't have a mechanism for getting pages to fax into your iBook so you can send them along. If you have a scanner (see Chapter 23), you can replace your fax machine. Without one, you're relegated to sending documents that you create—in AppleWorks, Microsoft Word, QuarkXPress, Adobe PhotoDeluxe, or other programs—to distant fax machines. In that sense, faxing is just a substitute for printing.

In fact, that's how it works on your iBook. While you're viewing a document you want to fax, hold down the ⌘-OPTION keys while selecting the File menu. If your fax software is working, you won't find a Print command on the menu. Instead, you'll see a Fax command. Select it and you'll see the FaxPrint dialog box.

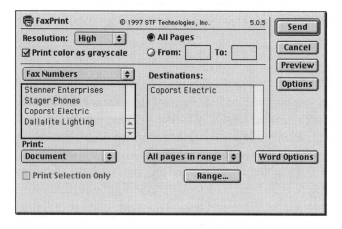

In the dialog box, choose the resolution of the fax, which pages to send, and so on. (A low-resolution fax will send a bit quicker but look worse at the other end.) Then, select your recipient from the list of names and drag it to the Destinations window pane. If your recipient isn't listed, add him or her through the FaxSTF browser (discussed in the next section). You can add a temporary fax number by selecting Temporary Address from the Fax Numbers pull-down menu. Then, fill out the dialog box and click ENTER.

With your addressee chosen, click Send. (You can click Preview, first, if you'd like to see what your fax will look like.) After you click Send, your modem will dial the number for the distant fax machine and transmit the fax. You'll see the Fax Status window, apprising you of the success or failure of the connection.

22

Receive a Fax

FaxSTF, unfortunately, doesn't have an option that allows you to manually accept a fax. In order to have your iBook receive a fax, you'll need to configure the FaxSTF Browser application to listen for the phone ringing. Here's how:

1. First, launch the FaxSTF Browser, which is located in the FaxSTF folder inside the Applications folder.

2. With the browser open, select Edit | Preferences.

3. Select the Fax Modem icon on the left side of the dialog box.

4. On the right side of the dialog box, pull down the Answer On menu and choose the number of rings the fax software should wait before it picks up the phone line.

5. Click OK.

Now the iBook will answer after the designated number of rings and attempt to receive a fax, if one is incoming. When the iBook detects a call on the line, you'll see the Fax Status window appear to tell you if a fax has connected and is being transmitted. The Fax Status window includes a Stop button, which will allow you to stop an attempted connection, just in case you decide it's a person on the line that you need to speak with.

How to ... Read the Fax

Received faxes appear in the FaxSTF Browser window. First, launch the FaxSTF Browser, which is located in the FaxSTF folder inside the Applications folder. On the left side of the window, select the Fax In folder and a list of received faxes will appear on the right side of the window.

To view a fax, double-click it. It'll appear in its own window. From there, you can print the fax using the File | Print command. You can also use the Action menu to alter the fax somewhat, making it look better, print faster, or align correctly.

Chapter 23

Upgrade Your iBook

How to...

- Add USB peripherals to your iBook
- Add a removable drive
- Add a CD-R or CD-RW drive
- Add speakers or a USB microphone
- Upgrade the RAM in your iBook
- Install the AirPort card in your iBook
- Change the battery

23

The Universal Serial Bus (USB) has done wonders for Apple's entire line of computers, in terms of ease of use and convenience. USB is easy to use—it offers hot-swappable technology, it's a snap to set up, and, in most cases, it simply works when you plug something in.

USB is convenient because the iBook relies on it for upgrading nearly all peripherals from keyboards and mice to printers and removable drives. That means all the peripherals for the iBook are reasonably new, fast, and easy to configure. This is an important distinction among some of the latest Apple computers (the iMac, iBook, Power Macintosh G3 and G4) and nearly every other computer made—because it primarily uses USB, the iBook is only compatible with the latest and most modern peripherals.

If you absolutely must connect older peripherals, that's possible, too. You simply need the right adapter for the job. You'll see all those options in this chapter.

 This chapter doesn't cover printers, although many of them use the USB port on your iBook. See Chapter 22 for information on installing and configuring a printer.

The Universal Serial Bus

USB is a technology designed to allow other technologies that have traditionally been connected to Macs via "serial" ports to connect to a faster, more modern equivalent. The connector, the speeds, and the methods of connection have all been updated. USB offers three major improvements over the serial ports that have been used in both Windows-based PCs and older Macintosh computers for nearly two decades:

■ **Speed** The USB port on an iBook can transfer data up to 12 megabits per second or over 12,000 kilobits per second. In fact, this speed makes it possible to connect devices—such as removable drives, hard disks, and scanners—that have traditionally relied on an external SCSI connector. While USB isn't as fast as SCSI, it's fast enough for these peripherals, and it offers some other advantages over SCSI, like easier configuration.

■ **Ease of Use** Aside from being *hot-swappable* (meaning you can plug and unplug devices without damaging them or your iBook), the USB port can also provide power to some peripherals, meaning fewer of them require their own power cords and adapters.

■ **Device Support**   Old serial ports offered one peripheral per port; USB can support up to 127 devices, as long as those devices don't mind sharing the connection. That means you can easily hook up a scanner, joystick, printer, Zip drive, digital camera, mouse, keyboard, and most anything else without much trouble.

With these improvements you can see why USB is a boon for the iBook—not only is it quick and extensible, but it's also simple to use. Aside from the Ethernet networking port, you really only have USB to worry about on an iBook—one type of connection, one type of configuration.

USB Ports and Hubs

Your iBook has one USB port that supports up to 12 megabits per second. That'll make it tough to plug in the other 126 devices USB supports, eh?

To use more than one device, you need to get a device called a *USB hub*. This device will probably have its own AC adapter. The USB hub also has four, eight, or more USB ports you can use for additional devices (see Figure 23-1).

FIGURE 23-1   A USB hub enables you to connect more than one USB device to your iBook.

If one of the peripherals you're adding is a keyboard, it likely has another USB port you can use to connect a second device. Otherwise, you need a hub if you want to connect more than one device. A number of vendors sell hubs. Here's a partial list of the vendors and their Web sites:

Ariston Technologies	**http://www.ariston.com/**
Belkin Components	**http://www.belkin.com/**
Entrega Corporation	**http://www.entrega.com/**
Interex	**http://www.interex.com/**
MacAlly	**http://www.macally.com/**
Newer Technology	**http://www.newertech.com/**

Install a USB Device

Some USB devices require drivers that are placed in the Extensions folder and used whenever the device is recognized on the USB bus. These drivers vary from specific for a particular device to more generic that use Game Sprocket technology, for instance. (Game Sprockets are drivers that are included with your iBook; you don't need to install them.) Keyboards and mice don't necessarily require drivers (plug them in and they should work) although they will require special drivers in some cases—for example, to program more than one mouse button or to remap the Windows key to the ⌘ key. All these require special driver software.

The normal game plan is to install the USB driver and then plug in your USB device. If all goes well, your USB device will be recognized and the driver will be properly loaded and used with the device. (This can sometimes appear to freeze the iBook while the driver gets situated. You should always wait a few seconds after you plugged in a USB device before you panic.) In other cases, you may need to restart your iBook for the USB device to be recognized. If the device is a game controller that uses Game Sprockets drivers, you won't be able to use the device until you're playing a game that supports Game Sprockets. (See Chapter 15.)

Add a Mouse, Keyboard, or Controller

Mice and keyboards are generally the easiest devices to add. In many cases, they don't even require special drivers. Apple's USB software has built into it some generic drivers that can recognize nearly any USB mouse or keyboard that's been plugged into an available USB port on your iBook or hub.

In other cases, though, you do need a driver. The Contour Unimouse, for instance, from Contour Design, offers three-button support. Because the Mac OS is designed for a one-button mouse, a special driver is required to define what the other two buttons do. Fortunately, they can do a lot. For instance, the buttons can be programmed to simulate a double-click, a CTRL-click (for contextual menus), or even a drag-lock, where clicking the mouse button once simulates clicking and holding down the mouse button so you can drag items.

In the case of the Contour mouse, individual drivers have been designed for many different scenarios. To activate one, drag the driver to the System Folder, drop the driver, and it's automatically placed in the Extensions folder. Now, plug the mouse into the USB port (or unplug and re-plug the mouse) to activate the driver.

In other cases, the mouse or pointing device (trackball, graphics tablet) comes with a special control panel that enables you to customize the behavior of the mouse buttons.

Keyboards usually require even less customization, unless the keyboard has special features like a built-in pointing device. Some keyboards originally designed for Windows require a special driver that allows the Windows keys and other keys to be used as Mac OS equivalents. Although the keyboards are basically the same, the Mac OS recognizes the ⌘ and POWER keys, which are unique compared to many Windows-oriented keyboards.

A number of companies offer unique pointing devices and keyboards for the iBook. Here are a few of those companies and what they offer:

Ariston Technologies	**http://www.ariston.com/**	Mouse
Belkin	**http://www.belkin.com/**	Mouse, keyboard
CompuCable	**http://www.compucable.com/**	Mouse
Contour Design	**http://www.contourdesign.com/**	Mouse
iMaccessories	**http://www.iMaccessories.com/**	Mouse, trackball, keyboard
Interex	**http://www.interex.com/**	Mouse
Kensington	**http://www.kensington.com/**	Mouse, trackball
MacAlly	**http://www.macally.com/**	Mouse, keyboard, trackball, joystick
Microsoft	**http://www.microsoft.com/**	Mouse
Wacom	**http://www.wacom.com/**	Pen tablet

NOTE   *What's a pen tablet? A pen tablet is a flat surface that enables you to use a pen for moving the mouse pointer—great for drawing, touch-ups, or just for a familiar interface for moving the mouse pointer.*

23

Add a Removable Drive

A removable drive can be an important addition because the iBook lacks a floppy drive, and many users aren't connected to local area networks. Online backup and file transfer is certainly one option, especially if you have a higher-speed connection. (Online backup is discussed in Chapter 18.) But if you want to back up on physical disks, then a removable drive is a good idea.

Two basic approaches exist to removable media—removable disks and writeable CD technology. Removable disks include Iomega's Zip drive, Imation's SuperDisk, and the Castlewood Orb drive. All these are designed to use compact floppy-like disks that can store between 100MB and 2.2GB, depending on the drive used. Here's a look at each:

- **Iomega Zip (http://www.iomega.com/)**   The Zip drive is a popular choice for removable storage offering between 100-250MB of storage space. (For 250MB, you need the special Zip250 drive.) It's reasonably quick, and Zip disks are popular with Mac and PC users alike. If you plan to share media among different computers, this may be the best solution.

- **Imation SuperDisk (http://www.superdisk.com/)**   The SuperDisk offers the unique capability to read traditional 1.4MB floppy disks as well as the special 120MB LS120 disks. The SuperDisk is a touch slow compared to other removables, but very flexible. This is a good solution if you need to read floppy disks, but you also want extra capacity.

- **Castlewood Orb (http://www.castlewood.com/)**   The Castlewood Orb drive offers 2.2GB of storage on reasonably inexpensive media, making it easy to back up nearly your entire iBook to a single disk.

You'll also find some external drives on the market that don't quite fit the "removable" mold, but they are, nonetheless, popular ways to extend your iBook. A few companies make floppy drives for iBooks, enabling you to use a typical 1.4MB floppy disk. Other companies make actual external hard disks in large (4-10GB) capacities.

Be warned, USB is a little slow for use with an external hard disk drive—the external disk is never going to be as fast as the iBook's internal disk. That doesn't mean it won't be useful, though, because having such a large capacity for backup—along with the option of unplugging the drive and using it with another computer—is a convenient touch. Here are some manufacturers of floppy and hard disks for iBooks:

iDrive	**http://www.idrives.com/**	Floppy drive, hard disk
LaCie	**http://www.lacie.com/**	Hard disk
Newer Technology	**http://www.newertech.com/**	Floppy drive
VST Technologies	**http://www.vsttech.com/**	Floppy drive

Install a Removable Drive

Removable drives require special software for installation on an iBook because each has its own unique USB driver. Once the driver is installed, hooking up the drive should be simple. Just plug the USB cable into the drive and then into the port on the side of the iBook, or into an available hub on your USB port. Right after you plug in the drive, you either have success, or you see a message that suggests you haven't correctly installed the drive's software.

You want to be careful with your removable drives because some of them don't react well in certain configurations. Make sure you're using the most up-to-date Mac OS, Mac updates, and iBook firmware (see Chapter 26). You should also avoid plugging and unplugging USB devices while a removable disk is being written to, and you may have to stop using some external devices (like a scanner) while you're copying data to certain removable drives.

Once you have the removable drive connected with the drivers correctly installed, pop in a disk. It should appear on the desktop, like any other disk.

Zip 100

Currently, it isn't possible to boot from USB-based disks and drives, even if the disk has a System Folder on it. With past Mac models it has been possible to boot from removable media, making them good diagnostic tools. With the iBook, you can still boot from a CD in the internal CD-ROM drive, but not from Zip disks or similar media.

NOTE *Macintosh models with dual-channel USB, like the slot-loading iMac, iMac DV, and most Power Macintosh G4 models, can boot the Mac OS from a USB disk. Others, however, including the iBook, must boot from an internal disk or the CD-ROM drive.*

23

Back Up to the Removable

The Iomega Zip drive comes with special software to help you manage backing up to the drive—other removable drives may include the same. Whether you use that same software or backup application like Retrospect or Retrospect Express, you can use the removable drive to back up your important files automatically to the removable disk.

You've already seen (in Chapter 18) that online backup can be automated in this way and with great success. When you're dealing with disks, though, consider these things:

- **Rotate Media** If you can, rotate backups between three or more different disks. If you need to back up often, you can back up Mondays, Wednesdays, and Fridays. Then, the next week, you can use your software to do an incremental backup, which simply adds files that have changed since the last backup. If you don't want to back up that often, back up once a week and rotate new media in each week for three or four weeks, and then start over.

- **Archive** This is important: Every so often (say, once a week in a business situation, once a month at home) archive one of your removable disks—that is, drop it out of the rotation and store it somewhere safe. This does two things. It gives you a reasonably up-to-date and emergency copy of your data. It also gives you a copy of your data that's fixed in time. If your iBook subsequently gets infected with a virus or if you accidentally delete or change a file, you still have the older copy to use.

- **Test** Especially in a business situation (or even with your thesis, business plan, novel, or personal investment portfolio), test the backup media occasionally to make sure they're working OK.

Once you get into the swing of things, you should find it's easy to automate the backup process. In many cases, it's just a question of telling the backup software when to schedule the backup, and then leaving the right disk in the drive when it's time for the backup (see Figure 23-2).

Retrospect or a similar product can be used to schedule a backup session automatically using your removable drive.

CD-R Drives

You might also want to consider a CD-R (CD-Recordable) or CD-RW (CD-Rewritable) drive for your iBook. These drives work a lot like other removable drives, although they tend to be a little slower for saving data and a little pricier for the drive itself. The disks, on the other hand, can often be cheaper.

A CD-R drive can write once to a CD-R disc, which can then be read by nearly any CD-ROM drive. This is a convenient way to transfer files or send files great distances. Because CD-R discs are cheap, they can hold up to 650MB of data and they're pretty resilient. CD-R discs are also a great medium for archiving important documents from your hard disk because the CD-R disks store well, don't take up a lot of space, and can be popped in to any Mac if there's trouble with your iBook.

CD-RW disks are slightly more expensive, but enable you to erase information on the disc and write to it again. In this way, a CD-RW is much like a Zip or similar removable drive. CD-RW drives tend to be capable of writing to CD-R media, too, so you can have the best of both worlds. Companies making CD-R and CD-RW drives for the iBook (via USB) include:

Fantom Drives	http://www.fantomdrives.com/
Freecom	http://www.freecom.de/
LaCie	http://www.lacie.com/
QPS, Inc.	http://www.qps-inc.com/
Sony	http://www.sony.com/
WinStation	http://www.winstation.com/

CD-R technologies sometimes require special software, the most popular being Adaptec Toast, a program that enables you to "burn" an entire CD at once. You can also write to CDs in *sessions,* meaning you can write to the disc at different times, storing data sequentially on the disc. This process usually necessitates two things. You have to set up the software to copy over a number of different files, and then you have to leave it to its task. This is because CD-R works more slowly than other removables, which are often closer to hard disk speeds. Toast also lets you create audio CDs and CDs designed to use the file format that Windows computers generally read.

If Toast doesn't sound right to you, another popular Adaptec software tool is DirectCD, which enables you to mount the CD on your desktop and copy files to it, just as if it were simply another disk attached to your iBook. That means you can drag-and-drop files onto your CD-R disc or save directly from applications to the disc, instead of taking the time to set up all your files and burn them to the CD-R.

Scanners and Digital Cameras

Scanners and digital cameras are also being designed to support USB these days, offering an easy way to get digital images into your iBook for use in newsletters, reports, and Web sites. Scanners enable you to place an image or document flat on the glass bed of the scanner's top—like a copy machine—and digitize the image or document so it can be used on your iBook's screen. In fact, some scanners include special Optical Character Recognition (OCR) software that allows a scanned document to be turned into a regular word processing document, enabling you to edit and store the document in an application like AppleWorks.

Add a Scanner

Scanners for the iBook tend to be inexpensive, and they include decent bells and whistles. If you're comparison shopping, look for high-end color support (32-bit color or better), high *true* resolution (600 × 600 or better), and extras like

Photoshop plug-ins and OCR software. Here are some scanner manufacturers with iBook-compatible products:

AGFA	**http://www.agfa.com/**
Artec	**http://www.artecusa.com/**
Microtek	**http://www.microtek.com/**
Umax	**http://www.umax.com/**

Generally, you simply install the scanner's software, plug in the scanner, and start scanning. Some models offer buttons on the scanner that can be used to activate the scanner and start up its software. Other models are software-driven only, using either a special program or a Photoshop plug-in to acquire images from the scanner. Most scanners include a copy of Adobe PhotoDeluxe, for instance, that supports the plug-in and enables you to scan images directly from the scanner into PhotoDeluxe, so you can then manipulate the images.

Many scanners are TWAIN-compatible, enabling you to scan images directly from applications that offer a TWAIN acquisition command.

Add a Digital Camera

Two different types of iBook-compatible digital cameras exist. One is a *still* camera, designed to be carried around and used just like a typical 35mm point-and-shoot camera. The difference with a digital still camera is, instead of taking pictures on film, it takes pictures that are stored in a computer-compatible format, often JPEG. These images can be downloaded from the camera and used immediately in a photo-editing program, in a desktop layout, or for Web pages.

NOTE
Some digital still cameras can connect to your iBook using USB to transfer pictures. Others use standard memory cards—the SmartMedia or CompactFlash cards to store images. You can buy USB devices that let you plug a SmartMedia or CompactFlash card into your iBook, enabling you to copy the images directly off the memory card.

The other type of digital camera is a video camera. You can get small cameras that are attached via USB and create a video of you and your immediate surroundings. These cameras offer lower resolution and picture quality than your typical video camera, but they're useful for Internet conferencing and similar applications.

You can also get video capture devices that enable you to hook up a typical camcorder and digitize video via the USB port.

Most of these USB cameras have their own software and drivers that must be installed. In the case of a digital still camera, you acquire images much the same way as you do from a scanner—using PhotoDeluxe, Photoshop, or the camera's own software to download images from the camera to your iBook.

For the live feed from a digital video camera, install the camera's software, hook it up to a USB port, and run the digital video application—some are probably included with the camera, others (like those designed for Internet video) will be available elsewhere. Once you have the camera's software running, you should be able to record the video, capture images from it, and so on.

Here's a list of current digital camera manufacturers. (Note, many digital still cameras also use USB as an interface. If you buy one of these cameras, make sure it includes Macintosh driver software.)

Ariston Technologies	**http://www.ariston.com/**	Video camera, video capture device
Belkin Components	**http://www.belkin.com/**	Video capture device
Epson	**http://www.epson.com/**	Still cameras
Kensington	**http://www.kensington.com/**	Video camera
Kodak	**http://www.kodak.com/**	Still cameras
Logitech	**http://www.logitech.com/**	Video cameras
Newer Technologies	**http://www.newertech.com/**	Video capture device
Ricoh	**http://www.ricoh.com/**	Still cameras
XLR8	**http://www.xlr8.com/**	Video capture device

Digital video, like removable drives, can be demanding on the USB bus, so it's recommended you use digital video cameras and similar devices while the removable disk isn't operating. You get better performance that way.

Special USB Adapters

Because USB is a newer technology, not all devices designed to work with Macs in the past will work with an iBook. In a sense, this is a good thing because it means only the latest technology works with an iBook, and that technology is more likely to be fast enough and advanced enough to integrate well with the iBook. At the same time, though, this means you can't hook up older peripherals you may already own.

Fortunately, a number of companies are making adapters for the USB port on the iBook that enable you to connect other sorts of devices that don't natively support USB. We already saw some adapters for hooking up printers in Chapter 22. Here's a list of adapter manufacturers and the types of adapter products they offer:

Ariston Technologies	http://www.ariston.com/	USB-to-serial, USB-to-SCSI, USB-to-parallel
Belkin	http://www.belkin.com/	USB-to-serial, USB-to-parallel, USB-to-SCSI
Compucable	http://www.compucable.com/	USB-to-serial, USB-to-parallel, USB-to-ADB
Entrega	http://www.entrega.com/	USB-to-serial
Griffin Technologies	http://www.griffintechnology.com/	USB-to-ADB, USB-to-serial
iMaccessories	http://www.iMaccessories.com/	USB-to-parallel
Keyspan	http://www.keyspan.com/	USB-to-serial
Microtech	http://www.microtechint.com/	USB-to-SCSI
MidiMan	http://www.midiman.net/	USB-to-MIDI
Momentum	http://www.momentuminc.net/	USB-to-serial
Newer Technologies	http://www.newertech.com/	USB-to-SCSI
Opcode	http://www.opcode.com/	USB-to-S/PDIF, USB-to-MIDI
Second Wave	http://www.2ndwave.com/	USB-to-SCSI

What are these technologies that can be adapted to work with USB? Here's a quick look:

- ◼ **Serial**   Older Macs use serial ports for many connections, including external modems, some digital cameras, PDA synchronize cables, and non-Postscript printers.

- ◼ **ADB**   Apple Desktop Bus is used to connect keyboard, mice, and other pointing devices for older Mac computers.

- ◼ **SCSI**   Used by Macs and PCs to connect external drives and scanners to the computer. SCSI is a faster technology than USB, so a USB-to-SCSI connector isn't recommended for daily use. It's a great way to hook up an existing scanner or hard disk occasionally, if only to get a few files or images transferred to your iBook.

- ■ **Parallel**   Used on Intel-compatible PCs to connect to many printers (and some other devices). These adapters can be used to connect PC printers to your iBook, as long as you have a driver that allows your iBook to print to that printer.

- ■ **MIDI**   The Musical Instrument Digital Interface enables you to connect MIDI keyboard synthesizers and other devices to your iBook to edit music and play back songs.

- ■ **S/PDIF**   This is a technology used to transfer digital audio from specialized equipment. It can be connected to an iBook, so you can edit multitrack audio and other digital audio files.

Add Microphones and Speakers

Although not reliant on USB, your iBook can support external speakers through the sound out port on the side of the iBook. For speakers, choose powered, computer-shielded speakers. This is important because speakers not designed specifically for a computer can affect your iBook's display.

The output for speakers is actually a line-level output, which means you can plug your iBook directly into a stereo amplifier, if you like, and, if you have the right audio cable adapter, listen to iBook sounds through your stereo system. (And, obviously, you can use headphones.) To connect, you need an adapter from the iBook's 1/8" RCA stereo mini-plug connector to the inputs on your stereo system.

The iBook has neither a microphone port nor a built-in microphone like the iMac, so you need to add a microphone that supports USB. Currently, the iMic adapter from Griffin Technology (**http://www.griffintechnology.com/**) is one of the few solutions on the market. No doubt others will follow.

Install RAM or the AirPort Card

The iBook makes it easy to install RAM or to install the AirPort card, a special networking card designed to be installed inside your iBook. You need to get inside your iBook to make these upgrades, but it's not tough to do.

 Whenever you go inside a computer, you need to guard against static electricity discharge, which can damage computer components. The best way to do this is to buy and wear a wrist strap, which grounds you and discharges static. You can get a wrist strap from most computer and electronics stores.

Open Your iBook for Upgrading

To install additional RAM or an AirPort networking card, you need to get inside your iBook. You do that by flipping up the keyboard (you install these upgrades under the keyboard).

The iBook User's Guide that shipped with your iBook includes additional instructions and diagrams for installing RAM and the AirPort card.

Here's how to get under the keyboard:

1. Shut down the iBook (choose Special | Shut Down in the Finder).

2. Unplug the iBook's AC adapter from the iBook, if it's plugged in.

3. Close the iBook's lid and turn the iBook over.

4. Remove the iBook's battery, as detailed later in this chapter in the section "Remove the Battery."

5. Turn the iBook right side up and open its lid again.

6. At the top of the keyboard, between the ESC and F1 keys, and the F8 and F9 keys, you'll find two small catches. Using a fingernail, lightly pull back on each catch (toward the keys and away from the keyboard housing). They should come back easily. When you have them pulled back, lift the top of the keyboard (see Figure 23-3).

7. The keyboard should come away easily. Place it (with keys facing down, preferably on a soft, lint-free towel) on the wrist rest of the iBook. Be careful with the ribbon that connects the keyboard to the iBook—don't unplug, tear, or twist it.

That's it. You're inside the iBook. Now, depending on what sort of upgrade you're planning, you may have a little more digging to do.

FIGURE 23-3   Opening the iBook for upgrading

Install the AirPort CardTwo

Different steps are actually involved in installing the AirPort card. First, you install the card. Then, you need to install the software that comes with the card. Here's how to install the AirPort card:

NOTE   *The AirPort card comes with an adapter attached to it that allows it to be installed in an iMac DV or a Power Macintosh G4 computer. You'll need to remove this circuit board adapter—there's small metal guard that you pry off, then you unplug the card from the adapter. See the instructions that came with the AirPort card for details (as well as for diagrams of the installation process.)*

1. Open the iBook as instructed in the previous section.

2. Touch a metal surface inside the iBook. This should discharge any built-up static electricity.

3. Flip up the wire bracket. You see the end of the AirPort antenna. Plug it into the AirPort card.

4. Place the card in its space with the ID number facing up and then slide it into its slot, which is toward the bottom of the keyboard housing.

5. Press the wire bracket back down to lock the card in.

6. Replace the keyboard and the battery, and start up the iBook.

Install the AirPort Software

Once you've installed the AirPort card and started up your iBook, you're ready to install the AirPort software. Insert the CD-ROM included with the AirPort, then double-click the Apple SW Install icon and follow the instructions in the installer. After installation, your iBook will be restarted.

 Once it's configured, you'll use the AirPort control strip or the AirPort application (in the Apple menu) to manage your iBook's AirPort connection. These are discussed in Chapter 24.

Join an Existing Network

When your iBook has restarted, you'll see the AirPort Setup Assistant. This Assistant does two things. If you already have a wireless network configured (that is, if you already have a Base Station configured and the iBook is in the vicinity of that Base Station), then you can use the Assistant to join that wireless network. If your wireless network is already configured, the option "Set up your computer to join an existing wireless network" will be enabled. Select it and click the right arrow at the bottom of the screen. On the next screen you'll enter the password for that network and click the right arrow again. Then you'll click Go Ahead to configure your iBook to access that network.

Configure a Base Station

If you have an AirPort Base Station that has not been completely configured (or if you want to reconfigure the Base Station), you can configure it from the AirPort Setup Assistant. This gives the Base Station a network name, a password, and tells it how you want it to connect to the Internet.

In order for this to work properly, you'll need to set up your iBook's TCP/IP control panel (for any Internet connection) and Remote Access control panel (only for a modem connection) with the settings you'll want the Base Station to use. The

Assistant is going to copy those settings from your iBook to the Base Station. So, if your iBook isn't already configured in this way, you'll want to do so before continuing. (You don't have to quit the Assistant; just switch to the TCP/IP and/or Remote Access control panels. If you need help, consult Chapter 20.)

Now you're ready to configure the Base Station.

1. Choose "Set up an AirPort Base Station" in the assistant and click the right arrow.

2. Your iBook will need to be set up with the Internet settings that the AirPort Base Station is going to use for its Internet connection. If your TCP/IP and/or Remote Access settings are set for Internet access (as described earlier in this section), click Yes in the Assistant. If they aren't, you can switch to TCP/IP and Remote Access to set them up, then switch back to the Assistant and click Yes.

3. Enter a password that will be assigned to this Base Station and click the right arrow.

4. Next, you can choose whether to simply copy your iBook's active Internet settings to the Base Station or to use different settings. Make your selection and click the right arrow. (If you choose to use different settings, you'll see a screen that allows you to change the configuration that will be used. You can't enter a new configuration, you can simply switch between saved configurations on your iBook.)

5. On the next screen, tell the Assistant what type of Internet connection you'll be using with the Base Station and click the right arrow.

6. Now you'll give the wireless network you're creating a name and a password. Enter those, then click the right arrow to move on.

7. Next, you can choose to give the Base Station a different password. This password is used to administer and change settings on the Base Station. It's a good idea to give it a different password if you want to keep your network users from changing the Base Station's configuration. Make your choice and click the right arrow. (If you choose to assign a different password, you'll see another screen allowing you to enter that password. Do so, then click the right arrow to move on.)

8. If you want your iBook to join the network being created, click Yes on this next screen.

9. Now the Assistant is prepared to set up the AirPort Base Station. Click Go Ahead and the Base Station will be configured.

Your Base Station will now be configured, and your iBook will be set up to connect to it. You can see this setting by opening the AirPort application in the Apple menu. You can also return to the AirPort Setup Assistant (it's stored in the Assistants folder on your hard disk) if you need to change settings on the Base Station.

Install an AirPort Base Station

If your iBook has an AirPort card installed and configured, it doesn't necessarily need an AirPort Base Station to network wirelessly; it can network computer-to-computer with another AirPort-enabled Mac, if you'd like (this is covered in Chapter 24). An AirPort Base Station, however, makes it easy to wirelessly network your iBook to an existing Ethernet network. The Base Station also makes it possible to give your iBook wireless Internet access.

The AirPort Base Station is an add-on product ($299) available from Apple. It's a small rounded device that looks a little like a UFO. On the back of it, you'll find two ports—one for an Ethernet connection and one for a phone line. (Although it's not available at the time of writing, Apple is also planning to release the AirPort Software Base Station, a software add-on that allows an individual AirPort-enabled Mac to act as a base station.)

If you have a modem connection to the Internet, you can plug your phone line into the Base Station. The Base Station's built-in modem can then be used to give Internet access wirelessly to any AirPort-enabled iBooks or other Macs that are in the vicinity of the Base Station (its range is about 150 feet and it can support 10 Macs). Once configured, the Base Station will dial its modem whenever a connected device requests Internet access (for instance, whenever you launch an Internet application on your iBook.)

Using the Ethernet port, you can connect the Base Station to an Ethernet network (plug it into your Ethernet hub) for AppleTalk or TCP/IP file sharing. That way wireless Macs can connect with wired Macs in order to share files. You can also use the Base Station to connect to an Ethernet-based

Internet-access device, like a DSL modem or cable modem. In that case, you can provide high-speed Internet access to all your AirPort-enabled Macs.

Finally, the Base Station can also act as an Internet router for your Ethernet-based Macs. If you have a small Ethernet network, you plug the Base Station into your Ethernet hub, and configure *all* of your Macs to use DHCP or a fixed IP address, using the Base Station's address as the Router address. Now, whenever you access an Internet application on any of your connected Macs—wireless or wired—the Base Station will connect to the Internet using its modem and start transmitting Internet data.

How do you configure the Base Station? Use the AirPort Setup Assistant, as described in this chapter. Or, you can use the AirPort Utility (in the AirPort folder inside Apple Extras on your hard disk) to see more advanced settings for the Base Station. Don't forget that you'll need to have your iBook (or another AirPort-enabled Mac) close enough to the Base Station to talk to it, and you'll need the administrative password if one has been set up for this Base Station.

Install RAM

Your iBook can accept one SO-DIMM memory module in capacities of 32, 64, or 128MB or RAM. (The module should be 1.25-inches or shorter, 144-pin SO-DIMM RAM.) To install the RAM, you need to get under the AirPort's slot inside the iBook. Here's how:

 The iBook User's Guide *includes drawings that will help you see exactly how to install RAM in your iBook.*

1. Open the iBook as instructed in the previous section, "Open Your iBook for Upgrading."

2. Touch a metal surface inside the iBook. This should discharge any built-up static electricity.

3. Flip up the wire bracket. If you have an AirPort card, you need to remove it. Slide it out of its connector slot (away from the trackpad and toward the screen) and place it to the side (you can leave the wire connected and rest the card on the iBook's plastic case, if you like).

4. Remove the two screws on the right side of the metal shield (called the *RAM shield*), and then lift the shield out of the iBook.

5. Insert the RAM into its slot at about a 45-degree angle. Then, press down on the module to lock it in place.

6. Replace the RAM shield, re-install the AirPort card (if you have one), and close up your iBook.

Once you have the RAM installed, replace your battery and/or plug the iBook in to its AC adapter (and plug the adapter into a surge protector or wall socket). Now, start up the iBook by pressing the POWER key. Once the desktop appears, choose About This Computer from the Apple menu. If your RAM was installed successfully, you should see a new total amount of RAM in the Built-in Memory entry of the About This Computer dialog box.

Close Your iBook

Once you're done installing RAM or the AirPort card, you need to close your iBook. For the most part, it's simply the reverse of opening it:

1. Make sure you have the wire bracket locked down on the RAM guard or the AirPort card, if one is installed.

2. Lift the keyboard and slowly flip it back over, so the keys are facing up. Remember the ribbon cable—don't snap, bend, or fold that cable..

3. Place the bottom lip of the keyboard under keyboard housing.

4. With the plastic tabs pulled back, replace the top of the keyboard in the keyboard housing. Press down lightly on the tabs to make sure they're in all the way.

That should be it. If you notice any odd bulging or other issues with the keyboard, try tilting it back up and securing it again. The tabs can be a little tricky.

Remove the Battery

With most portable computers, the battery slides out easily. This is generally done because portable computer batteries traditionally don't last longer than a few hours and it can be convenient to swap batteries when the installed battery starts getting low on power.

With the iBook, Apple doesn't encourage this behavior. Because the iBook is rated as six hours of battery life, the suggestion is you won't need to swap the battery. Instead, you should recharge the battery in your iBook whenever you're near an AC adapter and use Sleep mode and other low-power options in the Energy Saver control panel to manage power consumption.

That doesn't mean you can't remove the battery and swap it, if you like, or change the battery if you notice your iBook's battery isn't accepting a charge or is losing power too quickly. In those cases, you want to remove and re-install the battery.

> **NOTE**   *If you plan to put your iBook to sleep to remove and/or swap the battery, you should turn on the option "Preserve memory contents on sleep" in the Advanced Settings section of the Energy Saver control panel. Otherwise, any open documents or items on a RAM disk will be lost.*

Here's how:

1. Plug in the AC adapter. If you don't have access to the AC adapter (or you don't have access to a wall socket), you can still change the battery if you like, but you'll only have about 15 seconds before the iBook's clock loses its setting.

2. Put the iBook to sleep (Special | Sleep) or shut down the iBook (Special | Shut Down).

3. Shut the iBook's lid (note, you can do this in lieu of choosing Special | Sleep).

4. Turn the iBook over.

5. Using a coin, turn the two screws on the battery enclosure about one-quarter turn to the left (counter-clockwise).

6. Using the small plastic tab, lift the battery out of its bay.

That's it. If you're swapping batteries, you simply reverse the process:

1. Line up the battery's connector with the connector port in the battery bay. Slide the battery gently into the port until the entry battery can rest in the bay.

2. Replace the battery cover by placing the small tabs in the battery bay first and then swinging the rest of the battery cover over the iBook's rubber feet.

3. Using a coin, turn both screws one-quarter turn clockwise.

4. Turn the iBook back over and open the lid.

Now, depending on whether the iBook was sleeping or shut down and what sort of power the iBook had connected, one of four things will happen:

- If the iBook was shut down, it needs to be restarted. Press the POWER button.

- If the iBook was put in sleep mode and the AC adapter was connected, the iBook should wake from sleep mode as it normally would.

- If the iBook was put in sleep mode, the AC adapter was not connected, and the option "Preserve memory contents on sleep" was not turned on in the Energy Saver control panel, then the iBook will need to be restarted. Press the POWER button. The iBook will likely run Disk First Aid automatically on start up and may need to have its Date & Time control panel reset.

- If the iBook was put in sleep mode, the AC adapter was not connected, but the "Preserve memory contents on sleep" was turned on in the Energy Saver control panel, then the iBook will not wake up normally. Instead, you need to press the Power button on the iBook. Instead of a typical startup process, however, you'll see a small dialog box appear with a bar indicator. The indicator shows RAM contents being restored from disk. Once restored, your desktop, all open applications, and documents will reappear.

NOTE   *Again, this special wake from sleep will only work if the battery is removed and replaced in about 15 seconds. Otherwise, it's best to change the battery while the iBook is plugged in, if at all possible.*

Chapter 24

Network iBook and Transfer Files

How to...

- Set up an Ethernet network
- Enable AirPort, AppleTalk, TCP/IP, and file sharing
- Set up users, groups, and privileges
- Connect to your network
- Create a server
- Connect to remote file-sharing networks

Oﾠne of the nice things about Macs in general is their capability to network easily with one another. They can share files and resources like printers without special software, without much special hardware, and, usually, without you needing a master's degree in information systems.

Networking an iBook is actually simpler, if that's possible. The iBook has two basic ways to network—through the Ethernet port or without wires at all, using AirPort technology. From there it takes just a few control panel settings to get you up and running with connected machines.

Let's look at what's required to get on an existing Mac network—the type you'd find at school, work, or perhaps in your dorm.

NOTE
If you plan to use AirPort equipment for a wireless network, consult Chapter 25 to learn more about the setup and configuration of AirPort. Then you can return to this chapter to see how to set up file sharing, Web sharing, and other technologies for use with AirPort.

Get Connected to a Network

A *network* is two or more computers connected by special cabling (or, these days, wirelessly) to one another for the purpose of sharing files and resources like printers. With a file-sharing network established, you can place files on other computers that are attached to yours. Likewise, other computers can access your computer, if you think that's a good idea.

The Internet is a network by this definition—it just happens to be a large one. Using either your modem, AirPort connection, or Ethernet cabling, you can connect to the Internet. Then you can *log on* to different computers on the Internet and download data. If you set your computer up for Web sharing, then others can access files on to your iBook, too.

For a regular network, there's a similar control panel called *File Sharing* that enables you to turn your iBook into a file server, enabling others to sign onto your iBook and access certain files. This sort of a network is called a *peer-to-peer network*.

The other type of network is a *client-server network*, where one central computer acts as the server and all the other computers—the clients—log in to the central server. This is the type of system you'd use in a larger organization or campus where having many machines all accessing files on one another would be chaotic.

Ethernet Connections

In either a peer-to-peer or a client-server network, your iBook gets connected the same way. First, you need to wire up your Ethernet connection so it connects your iBook to the other machine(s) in your network. If you're connecting the iBook to one other machine, you can use a *10baseT crossover* cable. If you're connecting to more than one machine, you use a regular Ethernet *patch* cable to connect your iBook to an Ethernet hub, which then enables you to connect to many other machines (see Figure 24-1). Once you've got the Ethernet all wired up, you configure the networking protocol.

Notice the connector on the end of an Ethernet cable looks a lot like a phone cable connector, only it's larger. When you're connecting it to your iBook, make sure you've chosen the Ethernet port, not the modem port. (The connector won't fit in the modem port, but you could create trouble by trying to squeeze it in.)

To remove the Ethernet connector, press the small tab on the connector in toward the connector, and then pull the cable out. This works just like removing a phone cable connector from a wall jack.

FIGURE 24-1   An Ethernet hub allows many computers to connect one another using Ethernet cables.

24

AirPort Connections

If your iBook has an AirPort card installed, you can use the AirPort application
(in the Apple menu) to turn the card on and off and to select a network. (You can also
use the AirPort control strip to switch between networks and turn the card on and off.)

If the AirPort card is turned on, select the name of the network base station
you'd like to connect to from the Choose Network menu in the AirPort application
window. Once you've made your pick, you'll be able to choose AirPort in the
AppleTalk and/or TCP/IP control panels in order to use those protocols for
wireless networking.

> NOTE   *You can also set up AirPort for a computer-to-computer connection.
> That's detailed later in the special box called "How to...Connect Two
> Macs Wirelessly."*

Choose Your Protocol

Once you have the network set up between your iBook and other Macs (or other
computers), you need to choose the protocol you're going to use to pass data between
them. Two major protocols are in use today by Macs: AppleTalk and TCP/IP.
AppleTalk is the traditional favorite of Mac users—it tends to be easier to configure
on smaller networks and can allow newer Macs to network with much older (ten
years or more) Macs.

TCP/IP, the protocol used over the Internet, is quickly becoming a popular
option, however. In Mac OS 9, it's now possible to set up a small network that
includes file sharing over TCP/IP. Likewise, larger Mac networks can also use
TCP/IP to share files. And you can use TCP/IP as the basis for a connection to
UNIX, Microsoft Windows, and other computers over a network.

Which do you use? Your protocol choice is dictated somewhat by circumstances.
If you're connecting to a lab of Macs in an educational or organizational setting, you
need to be configured to use the protocol the system administrator has chosen. That
may be AppleTalk or TCP/IP. If you're setting up your own LAN, you can choose
either, keeping in mind that AppleTalk is best for communicating with older Macs
and peripherals, while TCP/IP is faster and may be necessary for tasks like
multiplayer gaming.

You can only have one TCP/IP configuration at a time, so if you decide to use it for creating a LAN, you may be unable to use your iBook's modem for Internet access. If you don't have a special *router* (either hardware or software) or *gateway* for accessing the Internet over your LAN, then you probably want to use AppleTalk to connect your Macs and TCP/IP, as discussed in Chapter 20, for your Internet access.

The AppleTalk Control Panel

In many educational and organizational settings, the protocol of choice is AppleTalk. AppleTalk is by far the most popular way to network Macs, and it's easy enough to accomplish—you don't need all the identifying numbers and codes that are required, in many cases, for a TCP/IP connection. (TCP/IP, however, is gaining, especially due to improvements in Mac OS 9 and higher versions of the Mac OS.)

In the AppleTalk control panel, you choose the connection you're going to use for your network. If you choose Ethernet or AirPort, you might also see another menu, the Zones menu. This menu enables you to determine which AppleTalk zone your iBook will appear in. (You'll only see this if you're connected to a large network.)

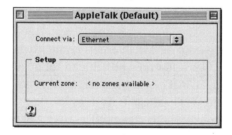

NOTE
Zones are designations network administrators use to separate Macs artificially from one another. For instance, you can separate Accounting computers and Human Resources computers in different zones, so users are less likely to access a hard disk or printer not in their AppleTalk zone. If you're at home setting up your own network, you won't see zones because they require hardware—either a router or a server computer that acts as a router.

The AppleTalk control panel has another feature you may find handy—Configurations. Choose File | Configurations to save different AppleTalk configurations, giving each its own name. This can be useful if you move your iBook back and forth between different places where you have a network and you'd like to set different AppleTalk settings quickly.

TIP   *You can use different AppleTalk configurations to make automatic adjustments to your settings in conjunction with the Location Manager, discussed in Chapter 21.*

To create a new configuration:

1. Select an existing configuration and click Duplicate.

2. Give the duplicate configuration a name in the dialog box and click OK.

3. Select the new configuration's name and click Make Active.

Now you can use the AppleTalk control panel to change the settings for this configuration. The original configuration keeps its original settings and you can switch back to it by opening the Configurations dialog box again, selecting the original configuration, and choosing Make Active.

Connect to a Windows Network

You may find your iBook is better off using a different protocol if you're not connecting primarily to other Macs. For instance, MacIPX is a control panel that adds Novell Netware to your iBook so you can log in to a Netware server. This is only a likely scenario if your office uses Netware to network its PCs or if you're using the IPX protocol specifically for multiplayer games. If your office or organization uses Windows NT Server as a server operating system, you probably still sign in using AppleTalk because Windows NT can enable you to share files and access printers over AppleTalk.

If you're simply trying to connect your iBook to a Windows 95/98 peer-to-peer network, you can use a program called *Dave* from Thursby Software (**http://www.thursby.com/**). Dave enables your iBook to log in to a network of Windows machines running the basic Windows file-sharing protocols.

Still another solution is TCP/IP. If you enable TCP/IP on both your iMac and on Windows machines, you can share files using the Web Sharing control panel, as described later in this chapter. This is a convenient way to share files quickly between computers that use two different operating systems.

The TCP/IP Control Panel

In some cases, you want to use TCP/IP as your networking protocol instead of AppleTalk. TCP/IP configuration is discussed in detail in Chapter 20, and configuring for a local network instead of the Internet isn't all that different.

For most local networks, you set the TCP/IP control panel's Connect Via pop-up menu to Ethernet or AirPort. Now, in the Configure menu, you choose either Manually or DHCP. Which you choose, again, depends on circumstances and your network administrator. If you have a fixed IP address on your network (which can be used for both Internet and LAN access, for instance), then you enter that IP address, a subnet mask, router address, and name server, if appropriate. In most cases, you need to consult your network administrator to learn the correct numbers for this entry.

If you're setting up a LAN for your home or organization, and Internet access isn't a factor, you can set your TCP/IP control panel to DHCP and forget about it.

Now, in Mac OS 9, file-sharing and Web-sharing servers appear in your Network Browser, as discussed in the next section.

NOTE   *If your iBook has Mac OS 8.6, you can use it to connect to TCP/IP file servers, but not to create one yourself. Mac OS 9 is the first Mac OS version to support file sharing over TCP/IP. You can, however, set up Web sharing over TCP/IP, as discussed later in this chapter.*

If you want to use TCP/IP for both LAN networking and a modem-based Internet connection, then you likely need to set up an Internet router. If you have an Internet router, then you can probably set all your networked Macs to the DHCP protocol. Internet routers are discussed in Chapter 20.

Browse the Network

Once you've got your Ethernet cable plugged in, AirPort card set up and AppleTalk or TCP/IP configured for Ethernet or AirPort, you're ready to log in to any Appleshare-compatible server computers on the network with your user name and password. Open the Network Browser located in the Apple menu. With the Network Browser active, you see all the different network neighborhoods your iBook can access.

NOTE   *If your iBook has Mac OS 8.6, you won't see network neighborhoods – you'll either see the computer names or AppleTalk zones if your network has zones active. Then, you can double-click a particular zone to find the computer you want to access.*

Network neighborhoods represent the different types of servers you find on your network. You may encounter a few basic neighborhoods. If you use AppleTalk for your networking, you see an AppleTalk neighborhood. You can click the disclosure triangle next to the AppleTalk neighborhood to see the computers accessible via AppleTalk. (If your LAN has AppleTalk zones active, you see the zones inside the neighborhood, which you can then open to reveal the computers associated with each zone.)

You may also see a Local Services neighborhood, which represents your iBook's own Web server, if you've turned on Web Sharing. In addition, if your network has an assigned domain name, you may also see that name in the Network Browser as a neighborhood (such as my domain, "mac-upgrade.com").

When you find the computer you want to log in to, double-click it in the Network Browser to bring up the login screen. If you don't see the TCP/IP computer you want to log in to, click the Shortcuts button (the hand with a pointing finger icon) and choose Connect to Server. This enables you to enter an IP address for the TCP/IP server.

Now, enter your name and your password, and then click Connect to connect to the server. Note the password is case-sensitive, so don't use uppercase if your original password used lowercase.

 If you want to change your password, click the Change Password button. Enter your old password, your new password, then click OK.

If you entered your user name and password correctly, you're shown the different disks or folders available to you from the server computer. Pick a disk and double-click the disk to mount it on your desktop. That's it: You've logged in and you're able to access files on the network drive as if they were on your own iBook. The disk is mounted on your desktop, just like a removable disk or a floppy disk image.

SHORTCUT *You can create aliases to server volumes by dragging them out of the Network Browser to the Finder. Using the alias, you can sign back on to that server quickly. Just double-click the alias and, if you're connected to the network and the server is available, you'll see the login screen.*

When you're done with a disk, either drag it to the Trash can, or select it and choose File | Put Away. That will un-mount the disk. Once you've put away all disks and files you've logged in to for a particular server, you're logged out of the server computer automatically.

Store Connections on Your Keychain

In Mac OS 9, there's a new feature called the *keychain,* which enables you to store often-used login names and password in one central place. This way, you don't have to remember all your user names and passwords for different servers. Connecting to servers using the Network Browser is one place where this comes in handy.

If you'd like to use the keychain, you should first set it up, as described in Chapter 21. Then, you can add a login to the keychain using the Network Browser. Here's how:

1. Locate the computer you want to log in to and double-click it as you normally do.

2. Now, in the Connect dialog box, enter your user name and password, and then click the check box to turn on the option Add to Keychain. Click Connect.

3. If your keychain is locked, you see a dialog box that asks you to enter your keychain password. If your keychain is unlocked, then your user name and password are added to the keychain automatically.

Now, whenever you log in to the server using the Network Browser, you won't see the Connect dialog box. Instead, your keychain is consulted and, if it's unlocked, the password is given automatically. If your keychain is locked, you're asked to enter your keychain password and then you may see a dialog box asking whether you want to give the Network Browser access to the keychain. Once you've set it up, you never have to remember your server password again!

 The Network Browser offers the same menus for shortcuts, favorites, and recent servers available in the newer Navigation Services Open dialog box that appears in updated applications. Those menus are discussed in Chapter 5.

Use the Chooser

If you don't like the Network Browser, you can use the Chooser to log in to servers. Open the Chooser and click the AppleShare button. If you have AppleTalk zones, click the zone you want to access in the AppleTalk Zones menu. In the "Select a file server" area, double-click the server you want to log on to.

If you're going to connect to a TCP/IP-based server, click the button Server IP Address, and then enter the IP address for that remote computer. Click Connect and the Chooser will attempt to access the server.

From here, in either case, it's the same as using the Network Browser—enter a name and password, and then double-click the disk you want to mount. To log out, put away all open disks.

Set Up Your Own Network

Once you have your network connections in place and AppleTalk and/or TCP/IP up and running, you're ready to set up file sharing and share folders from your iBook on the network.

24

Set Up File Sharing

When you set up file sharing, you're actually turning your iBook into a server computer. Other users attached to your network can sign into your iBook, access any folders you make available to them, and copy files to and from your iBook. If that's what you want to do, then you can enable file sharing in the File Sharing control panel.

The File Sharing control panel requires you to enter an Owner Name, Password, and Computer Name in the top of the control panel. If you've completed the Mac OS Setup Assistant (after you turned on your iBook for the first time or after you installed or upgraded the Mac OS), then you should already have entries here. You can change them, if you like. To start up file sharing, click the Start button under the File Sharing Off heading. This begins the process of file sharing. If you have AppleTalk configured and your Ethernet cables properly connected, you're in business—your iBook becomes a server.

In Mac OS 9, you have the additional option of turning on file sharing over TCP/IP. If you want to share your files over your TCP/IP network (and you configured the TCP/IP control panel as discussed earlier in this chapter) you can click the check box next to the option "Enable File Sharing clients to connect over TCP/IP." This enables anyone who knows your iBook's IP address to connect to your iBook and share files.

NOTE   *For file sharing over TCP/IP to be useful, you probably want to have a static IP address–one that doesn't change, which you enter manually. If you have a LAN of Macs running Mac OS 9 or higher, you can also set your iBook to use DHCP and your file server should appear in those Macs' Network Browser.*

Create Users and Groups

Of course, before you can get serious about file sharing, you have to decide who can access your computer and what they can access. By default, you can already access your iBook from another computer—using the Owner name and password. (This gives you special access, by the way, enabling you to see every folder and file on the iBook, regardless of what other security measures you put in place.)

For other users, you need to create user accounts for individuals accessing your iBook over a network. Do that by selecting the Users & Groups tab in the File Sharing control panel. (If you're running Mac OS 8.6, you use the separate Users & Groups control panel.)

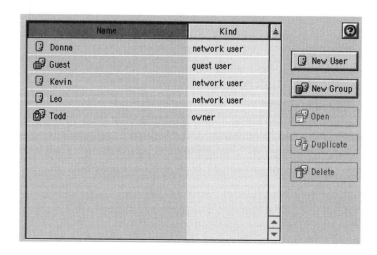

Actually, you don't have to create users if you give Guests and/or Everyone privileges to your Macs. (See "Set Sharing Privileges" later in this chapter.) Going through the motions of creating users is good, though, so you can specify privileges and make sure no one snoops around your network while you're connected to the Internet or connected via Remote Access. Too much security is better than too little.

CAUTION *If you're using file sharing over IP, you should be especially vigilant about your guest access. Because people can potentially access your iBook over the Internet (depending on your configuration), you should only allow users with a user name and password to sign on.*

To create a new user in Users & Groups:

1. Click the New User button.

2. You see a dialog box that enables you to enter a name and an initial password for this person. If you want the user to be able to change his or her own password, leave the check in the Allow User To Change Password check box.

3. Click the close box to add the person to your list of users.

If you have more than one user (aside from yourself and the Guest account) you need to create a new group. A group accepts some or all of your users, so you can set file-sharing privileges for the entire group. For instance, if you want people to have access to a folder you created on your disk called Accounting Files, then create a group that has everyone in it who should be able to access that folder. Alternatively, if you have a special folder called Assistant Files which only your assistant, Rick, is allowed to access, you can set up Rick individually for that particular folder.

Here's how to create a group:

1. Click the New Group button.

2. Give the group a name.

3. Drag names from the Users & Groups window to the window for that group.

4. Click the close box when you finish.

Now, with your users and groups created, you can set the privileges for those users. Do that by accessing the Sharing settings for each individual folder.

Set Sharing Privileges

Select a folder you want to share with a particular user or group and choose File | Get Info. In the Get Info window, choose Sharing from the Show menu. Now you're ready to set privileges for this particular folder.

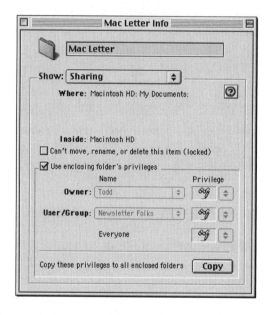

What does it mean to *set privileges*? You get to decide which user or group can access this particular folder and what he, she, or they can do with it. Here's what the settings do.

- **Can't Move, Rename, or Delete This Item (Locked)**   Click this box to deny users permission to alter the folder itself. This locks the folder.

- **Use Enclosing Folder's Privileges**   If clicked, the folder should use the same sharing settings as its parent folder. If the Mac Letter folder is in the Documents folder, then checking the check box means the sharing privileges for Mac Letter are the same as those for the Documents folder. If you uncheck this box, you can set the privileges separately.

- **Owner**   Choose which user is owner of this folder. That's usually you.

- **User/Group**   Choose which user or group has access to this folder. If you want more than one user to have access, you need to place those users in a group. If you want more than one group to have access, you need to place users from all those groups in one larger group.

- **Everyone**   If you want to give all users—regardless of their user and group status—certain privileges for the folder, choose from this menu.

Consider granting access only to the Owner and a particular user or group, not to Everyone. That helps you manage the security of your files.

Next to the Owner, User/Group, and Everyone entries, a little icon appears showing the privileges assigned to each.

You can assign to a particular user or group one of four access levels:

- **Read and Write Access**   The user or group can both save files and access existing files.

- **Read Access**   The user or group can read (open or duplicate) files from a folder, but can't save files to that folder.

- **Write Access**   The user or group can save files, but can't access other files in that folder.

- **None**   The user or group has no access to the files in that folder.

Finally, click the Copy button if you want these privileges copied to all subfolders.

Set Up Web Sharing

You've already seen that setting up TCP/IP enables you to transmit files between various types of computers—Macs, UNIX machines, Windows computers—without adding special software. But we've used that TCP/IP network so far only for file sharing over TCP/IP. If you don't have Mac OS 9, then you can't turn on this option. Likewise, if your goal is to allow other computers (like Windows, UNIX, and so on) to connect to your iBook, those computers probably don't have an Apple File Services client, which would be necessary for them to log in to your iBook.

Using the Web-sharing capability built into the Mac OS, you can share files with other computers using just TCP/IP. Web sharing works a little like file sharing, but it enables you to share a specific folder with users who don't have

Macs (or Mac users to whom you don't want to grant full file-sharing access). Open the Web Sharing control panel, select a folder to share, and click Start.

Select the folder you'd like to share.

Click Start.

If you select the Use File Sharing To Control User Access option, you can force users to enter a user name and password to access the folder (see the section "Create Users and Groups," earlier in this chapter). Now, using a Web browser or FTP program, any sort of computer can log in to your iBook and transfer files. (See Chapter 18 for more on FTP.)

 If your iBook is connected to the Internet and you have Web sharing active, anyone who knows your IP address can access your Web-sharing folder. The additional security of turning on Use File Sharing to Control User Access helps mitigate this threat, especially if you disallow guest access and make sure you have set sharing privileges for the folder you've selected as the Web-sharing folder. Otherwise, the most secure way to handle this is not to turn on Web sharing while you're otherwise connected to the Internet.

Network Two Macs Together

If you have one Mac you want to connect to your iBook, you can use an Ethernet crossover cable to connect them without an Ethernet hub. Then set up AppleTalk and the File Sharing control panel and you're ready to sign on.

NOTE

You can also connect these two machines using TCP/IP and File Sharing over IP if you have Mac OS 9 on at least one of them. You won't be able to simultaneously use the modem on those machines to access the Internet, however, unless you have a software Internet router, as described in Chapter 20. If you're creating a quick little network to swap files, I recommend using AppleTalk. Likewise, if you have two AirPort-enabled Macs, you can connect them together quickly, as discussed later in the chapter in the special box called "How to...Network Two Macs Wirelessly."

Here's the procedure:

1. Connect the two computers' Ethernet ports using an Ethernet crossover cable—a special cable that needs to be bought specifically for this purpose. (Ask for an *Ethernet crossover cable* from the salesperson at a computer shop. This is assuming, of course, you can actually find a salesperson in a computer shop, especially if it's a "megastore.")

2. On each computer, open the AppleTalk control panel. If AppleTalk warns you it's not currently turned on, click Yes to make sure AppleTalk will be turned on after you set up the control panel.

3. In the AppleTalk control panel, choose Ethernet built-in from the Connect Via menu. Do this for both computers. (You'll likely choose the same setting for your other computer, unless it has an Ethernet card instead of Ethernet built in. In that case, it'll say Ethernet Slot A1 or something like that.)

4. Close the AppleTalk control panel on both computers. Choose Save when asked if you want to save the settings. This will set AppleTalk. (You may receive an error if the Ethernet crossover cable is incorrectly installed or if you're not using a crossover cable.)

5. Make sure your Sharing privileges settings are the way you want them for the particular user who's going to sign in. (If it's just you, then you want to log in to the other computer as Owner, so you can get the most privileges available.)

6. On one of the computers, open the File Sharing control panel. Turn on File Sharing.

Connect Two Macs Wirelessly

If you have an AirPort card installed in your iBook, you can use that card to connect directly to another AirPort-enabled Mac without a base station. To do so, open the AirPort application on each Mac and select Computer to Computer from the Choose Network pop-up menu. Close the AirPort application. Now, you can set each Mac's AppleTalk or TCP/IP control panel to AirPort, and share files as discussed in the section "Network Two Macs Together."

7. Once file sharing has started up, use the Chooser or the Network Browser to access the server and see if it's available.

8. When you find the server, double-click it to log on. Enter your name and password and click Connect.

9. Finally, choose the disk you want to mount—double-click it and it'll appear on your desktop.

To log out of the server, choose all the disks you've mounted and drag them to the Trash, or select them and choose File | Put Away from the Finder menu.

Chapter 25

Work with DOS and Windows Files and Programs

How to...

- Read DOS and Windows disks with your iBook
- Exchange files and documents with Microsoft Windows users
- Use the File Exchange control panel to launch Windows documents
- Run Windows and DOS programs with emulation software

The Mac OS has built into it the ability to deal with a wide range of files, including files that were originally created for Microsoft Windows. Part of that capability comes thanks to the File Exchange control panel, which, along with other system extensions, allows the iBook to read disks that were originally created in Windows' native format (or that of the predecessor to Windows, DOS).

There are three different types of Windows compatibility that we're concerned with. Out of the box, the iBook can handle two of those—the third requires an extra application purchase. They are

- **Disks**   Your iBook can mount, display, and manipulate files on many different types of disks, even if they weren't originally designed for the Mac OS. This is true of CD-ROMs as well as removable disk drives—Zip, LS120, floppy disks—that you might connect via USB.

- **Documents**   Your iBook can also store and work with Windows documents on two different levels. First, you can easily store Windows documents in folders using the Finder or move them around as e-mail attachments, via FTP, and so on. Second, you can translate many document types using nothing more than AppleWorks and its included translators.

- **Applications**   Running actual Windows programs on your iBook is a little tougher—it can't be done right out of the box. It is possible to run Windows programs if you've installed either SoftWindows or Virtual PC, both of which are Mac applications designed to emulate Windows. They're not perfect, but they'll get the job done in a pinch.

Mount and Use PC Disks

A disk originally created for a PC usually won't pose a problem, as long as you have a removable drive that can read the disk attached to your iBook. A CD-ROM is a great example. A CD designed exclusively for PCs can still be read by an iBook—just pop it in the drive and take a look. It should appear right on the desktop.

Once it's mounted, you can treat a PC disk like any other—you can move files from it into the Finder. If the disk is a removable disk like a PC-formatted Zip disk, you can copy files to it from the Finder, too. Copy a PC file onto your hard disk or the desktop, and you're also able to rename the file, duplicate it, create an alias, and so on.

It isn't always a good idea to rename a Windows file, especially a document. The three-letter code at the end of the original name is important for both the iBook and most Windows computers. Your computer identifies the document with this code—.doc indicates a Microsoft Word document, while .bmp indicates a Windows bitmap graphic. If you don't leave the names intact, the documents can become harder to use.

You can get rid of the disk the same way you would any other. Drag it to the Trash or select the disk and choose File | Put Away.

Load and Save PC Documents

Certain documents created on your iBook can be read by applications in Windows. For instance, Microsoft Word 2000 for Windows (and other Word versions) can read Microsoft Word 98 documents that have been created on a Mac. ClarisWorks for Windows can read a file created in AppleWorks (if you save it in ClarisWorks 4.0 format).

And there are certain types of files that are universal. Many of the graphics file formats can be read on any platform—GIF, JPEG, and TIFF. Text files (TXT) and Rich Text Format (RTF) documents—those that include some formatting—can be read by nearly any word processor, and Adobe PDF documents can be created on nearly any computer and sent to another type of computer to be viewed.

Translate a Document

With some documents that started life on a Windows machine, it's possible to simply double-click the icon and launch an associated application on your iBook. It usually works better, however, if you open the application first and use the File | Open command to open the document. That makes it easier for the application to recognize that it needs to translate the document before using it.

If you're working with graphics files, see Chapters 13 for a discussion of translating graphic file formats.

Use AppleWorks

If the document is the sort that could conceivably be edited in AppleWorks (for instance, it's a word processing document or a spreadsheet), then fire up AppleWorks and choose File | Open from the menu. In the Open dialog box, find the file you'd like to open. Now, here's the trick: Pull down the File Type menu in the Open dialog box and take a look at the options—these are all of the files that can be translated into AppleWorks format.

Actually, in many cases, files that can be translated will simply appear in the window—this may be tougher with files that don't have the correct filename extension or that have been transmitted over the Internet. In any case, if the file can be translated by AppleWorks, you'll likely be able to select it in the window and choose the Open command. The file will be translated and it'll appear in AppleWorks. You should then be able to edit it.

The best results always come from using the same program. If you're dealing with a Word for Windows document, Word for Macintosh is the best way to open and edit the file. You don't lose formatting, which can happen when you translate between formats.

Communicate the Format Type

One of the most important ways to exchange Windows documents is to discuss the document format with the person who is sending you the file. Usually, if they save the file in the most compatible way possible, you'll have better luck translating it into AppleWorks.

For instance, AppleWorks works well with Microsoft Word 6.0 (Word 95 for Windows) documents, as long as they don't have special header and footer formatting. And things like annotation commands or colorful text may not show up at all. Rich Text Format is even better, although the formatting tends to be rudimentary. Translation generally won't work for very complex documents like those created in QuarkXPress or Adobe PageMaker, especially if you're trying to translate into AppleWorks. (You'll have better luck translating directly between the two high-end applications, if you own one of them, but even that doesn't always work well.)

If you find that your work dictates that you use a particular file format and you can't find a happy translation medium, then your best bet may be to break down and buy the same application that's being used on the PC side. Often these applications are file-format compatible, so you can use the Mac version of WordPerfect, for instance, to read WordPerfect for Windows documents.

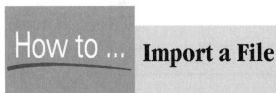

How to ... Import a File

If you're dealing with a file that isn't a common file format like a word processing document or an image file—or if you simply want to use a different application that you've added to your iBook—then you should look around for an Import command, probably in the File menu of that application. Often you'll be able to import some common file formats into different applications.

For instance, I have FileMaker Pro, the high-end version of AppleWorks' database module, on my iBook. FileMaker Pro can import a number of different types of documents—from dBase database documents to text files that use a comma or a tab between each field entry—directly into a FileMaker Pro database. To do that, I simply choose the Import/Export command in FileMaker Pro.

Actually, AppleWorks can import some of these same types of files into the database module. Choose File | Open to load a DBF or comma-separated text file into a database. Remember to choose Database from the Document Type menu so that the file is imported into the database module. (Otherwise, it'll appear as a word processing document.)

Save a File for Use on a PC

If you're working with a document that you'd like to send to a PC user, many of the same considerations apply. You should ask the person which applications he or she uses that might work for the translation. If it's a word processing document, most applications can read Word 6.0 or, if not, they can almost certainly read RTF documents. If you're sending a spreadsheet, it's probably best translated into Excel, then sent on its way.

To do this, choose File | Save As, then find a place to save the file. When you're ready to translate, choose the type of file you want to create from the Save As menu. Then, click Save to save the file.

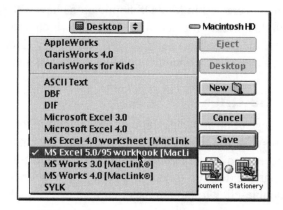

You may want to note that the translators in AppleWorks don't actually append a filename extension to a file as it's being saved. It's a good idea to name the file with the correct extension before sending the file. (In fact, the most compatible filenames are up to eight characters long with a three-letter extension and no spaces, like *filename.doc*.) Here's a quick look at common filename extensions for DOS and Windows computers:

Microsoft Word	.doc
Microsoft Excel	.xls
WordPerfect	.wp
Rich Text Format	.rtf
Plain text, ASCII text (no formatting)	.txt
HTML	.htm
dBase (standard PC database format)	.dbf

Note that ASCII text and "Plain" text mean the same thing—it's the very common text format that allows you to send text characters in a document without *any* formatting (no bold, italics, and so on). In a worst-case scenario, if you're having trouble exchanging word processing documents with a Windows (or Unix) user and you want to send just the bare-bones text, you can do it with a document saved in ASCII text format.

The File Exchange Settings

The filename extension system is pretty important to PCs, since it's really the only way that Windows can tell one type of file from another. The Mac OS works differently—documents created in Mac OS applications have a special creator code built into them that makes it clear to the Mac OS which application created the document even if the name has been changed completely. That's why it's usually so easy to double-click a document and launch the associated application.

PC Exchange Settings

With the File Exchange control panel, some of this functionality is translated to Windows documents that you open on your iBook. File Exchange sits in the background and takes a look at any DOS documents that you copy to your iBook. When it sees a filename extension it recognizes, it gives that document a creator code, so you can double-click to launch the document.

TIP   *If File Exchange doesn't seem to be recognizing files that it should, open the File Exchange control panel and make sure the Open Unmapped Files on Any Disk Using Mappings Below option has a check mark next to it. If it doesn't, click it to activate the option.*

You might find it useful to edit the way File Exchange manages filename extensions. To do so, open File Exchange and click the PC Exchange tab. Now, notice that you're seeing the Windows filename extensions and their relationships to Mac OS applications.

You can select a particular entry and click Change to edit that entry. You'll see a dialog box that allows you to choose which Mac application should be associated with a particular filename extension. (If you don't see the application you want associated with a file type, click the Select button to search for the application's icon on your hard disk.) Scroll to find the application you want associated with the file, then choose the exact type of file it is from the list of types that application recognizes. Then click the Change button to make your alterations.

If you're encountering a filename extension that isn't already entered in the File Exchange control panel, click the Add button. You'll see a dialog box that helps you enter the new filename extension and associate it with a Mac application.

File Translation

Usually, if you double-click a Windows document that isn't directly associated with a Mac application, you'll get a dialog box that allows you to choose which application you'd like to use to open the document.

This doesn't necessarily translate the document; if the application can't read the document, you'll probably get an error message. If you'd like to translate that document before it's opened by the application, look for an option in the dialog box like Open in SimpleText Using QuickTime Translation or Open in AppleWorks Using MacLinksPro Translation. These options will allow you to translate a document, then open it up to edit it.

If you'd like to automatically translate certain files from a Windows format into the format of one of your Mac applications, you can click the File Translation tab in the File Exchange control panel to control translation behavior. To create a new translation scheme, click the Add button. You'll then search (in a typical Open dialog box) for the type of document you'd like to translate. Once you've found it, click Open. You'll then page through a list of applications and choose the one that you want associated with this sort of file.

This works, by the way, with regular Mac documents and applications, too, making it easy to change an association even if you're not working with Windows documents.

Run DOS and Windows Programs

Want to actually run DOS and Windows programs on your Macintosh? You'll need an emulation application—a Macintosh application that simulates the Windows operating system or a Pentium computer environment. These are very sophisticated applications that allow you to re-create a whole computer environment within your iBook—you're literally running Windows and DOS applications within an application that, in turn, runs within the Mac OS.

The sophistication of these applications reaches out to the printer, your hard disk, and even your modem. In most cases, it's easy to use all of these things within the Windows environment, even though the peripherals may actually be designed for a Macintosh.

There are two different emulation packages available for the iBook. Both emulators actually emulate a Pentium MMX computer, but SoftWindows from Insignia Corporation (**http://www.insignia.com/**) uses special drivers to communicate between the Windows environment and your iBook. Performance tends to be optimized for Windows applications and is a great choice if you're running business or productivity applications in the Windows environment. Windows games work well, too.

Connectix Virtual PC (**http://www.connectix.com/**) is the other emulator. As shown in Figure 25-1, it emulates a Pentium MMX computer, but it also emulates other popular PC hardware, making it possible to use standard PC drivers. This offers a little more flexibility—you can run other PC operating systems like Windows NT and Linux, and it is upgradable to new versions of Windows. While more flexible, Virtual PC runs a little slower than SoftWindows because it has to emulate all that other hardware, too.

Both SoftWindows and Virtual PC can generally be purchased for between $100 and $200, depending on rebates, bundling deals, and similar promotions. Both work well with an iBook, but they can require a lot of RAM; if you don't have at least 64MB of RAM in your iBook, you may experience these emulators at slower speeds than you would with more RAM.

> TIP   *Both companies offer a less expensive version of their emulators that doesn't include Microsoft Windows as part of the standard package. This can be useful if you already own Microsoft Windows or if you simply plan to play DOS games, which is the target market for these products. Prices are about $50–$75 for RealPC from Insignia and Virtual PC with DOS from Connectix.*

25

FIGURE 25-1   Connectix Virtual PC allows you to run PC applications on your iBook.

Chapter 26

Troubleshoot, Update, and Maintain Your iBook

How to...

- ■ Find technical support resources
- ■ Troubleshoot your iBook's hardware
- ■ Troubleshoot software
- ■ Deal with errors
- ■ Fix freezes and hangs
- ■ Reinstall, restore, or update your iBook's software
- ■ Maintain your iBook for long life

It's never good when your iBook starts giving you serious trouble. Hopefully, you won't encounter this much, although the likelihood is that, eventually, you'll have to troubleshoot something. The nature of today's computing is that it isn't all flawless.

Not that it has to be an intolerable experience, either. One of the tricks is adhering to a good maintenance schedule. If you do that, you'll probably have fewer instances of trouble. Better yet, if you do have trouble, a solid backup routine will help you minimize that trouble, allowing you to get back to work as quickly as possible.

So, let's take a look at the three different aspects of keeping your iBook healthy and happy: troubleshooting, updating, and maintenance. Using these three different steps, you can keep your iBook running well, or get it up and running again after you've had some trouble.

Find Tech Support Online

Since this is the Internet-savvy iBook we're talking about, I recommend that you get to know online resources for troubleshooting your iBook right at the outset. Apple's iBook-specific support pages are very useful and offer some great features, including online message areas for iBook users. These sites offer a great way to learn more about your iBook, identify potential problems, and do what is probably the most important step in keeping your iBook tuned—stay up on the latest news and information.

Enter **http://www.apple.com/support/** in a browser, then look around for the link to iBook Support. (There's currently an iBook graphic with a menu—pull down that menu and choose iBook Support. Apple likes to change the design of their pages every once in a while, though.) Once you select iBook Support, you'll be taken directly to Apple's special support Web site for the iBook. It's here that you'll find all sorts of information about the iBook, including the latest news, articles on different technologies related to the iBook, and pointers to any software updates that have been released for the iBook.

I won't harp specifically on certain parts of the iBook Support site because the site is likely to change. You'll probably always find a link to the Tech Exchange or a similar message area that allows you to exchange messages with other iBook users and Apple Tech Support specialists. You'll probably also find links to the latest update, including updates to the iBook's firmware, to the Mac OS, to the applications that came with your iBook, and to the modem's firmware, among others. (*Firmware* is a type of software/hardware driver combination that can be

26

installed to update your iBook. The firmware updates usually fix bugs or add new features and capabilities to hardware like your iBook's modem or the iBook itself.)

While you're online, you might also want to check out some of the popular Mac-oriented sites, where you'll find news and help on various issues affecting your iBook as well as the entire Macintosh industry. Here's a sampling of them:

Macintouch	**http://www.macintouch.com/**
Macworld	**http://www.macworld.com/**
Mac News Network	**http://www.macnn.com/**
MacCentral	**http://www.maccentral.com/**
MacAddict	**http://www.macaddict.com/**
iMacToday	**http://www.imactoday.com/**
MacFixIt	**http://www.macfixit.com/**
Mac-Upgrade.com (my site)	**http://www.mac-upgrade.com/**

All of these sites can help you find new peripherals, follow the news regarding Apple, discuss Mac and iBook troubleshooting issues, and so on. Many of them also have user forums, where you can post questions and read archives of questions and responses between Mac users.

Troubleshoot Your iBook

The first signs of trouble will probably be that something goes wrong onscreen. The key, as with actual health problems, is to observe the symptoms and look for anything that might be related. To begin, then, let's take a look at the symptoms of iBook trauma and see what should be done as a first-aid measure.

There are two basic types of problems you can have with your iBook—hardware and software. With an iBook, most hardware problems are going to require a look from a service technician, since there aren't many moving parts, and the iBook can be difficult to service yourself.

You can try troubleshooting software problems, but those problems are more varied and can sometimes be tough to track down. We'll try, though.

Hardware Symptoms

There are a couple tell-tale signs that something has gone wrong with your iBook. Here's what they are, what might cause them, and a few things to try before sending your iBook off to the repair shop.

Blank Screen or Tones

If you've just tried to turn on your iBook and you've gotten no response, you're seeing a blank screen, and/or you're hearing tones, it's possible there's something wrong with the internals of your iBook, like a RAM module that's not properly installed or something that has come loose. Before you send it to the shop, though, test a few things:

- Wait a few minutes to make sure it's not just taking a long time for the iBook to start up. If you have the startup disk set to Network Disk (in the Startup Disk control panel), it can take a few minutes before your iBook starts up from its internal disk. Change this setting in the Startup Disk control panel once your iBook has started up. (The Network Disk setting is only used when you're using NetBoot, a technology built into Mac OS X Server that allows iBooks and other newer Macs to boot over an Ethernet network.)

- It's possible the battery has drained. Plug in the AC adapter and try again. (Make sure you're using the AC adapter that came with your iBook or an approved replacement AC adapter from Apple. Other AC adapters may not work correctly or at all.)

- Check for signs that your surge protector (a surge protector is a power strip that's designed to protect against power surges—I recommend one when your iBook is plugged in) is working correctly and that it hasn't absorbed a power surge, which might cause a fuse to blow on the power strip.

- Restart the iBook by pressing CTRL-⌘-POWER (on the keyboard).

- Unplug all USB peripherals. Try restarting.

- If you've recently installed an AirPort card or additional RAM, open up your iBook (as discussed in Chapter 23) and remove the RAM and/or card. Then, close up your iBook, plug it into the AC adapter, and try to start up again. If the iBook starts up, you may have incorrectly installed the RAM and/or card the first time. Try again, being careful that the card or RAM is seated properly. If, once it's reinstalled, you still can't get your iBook to start up, the card and/or RAM may be defective.

- If other types of restarting fail, restart the iBook with the POWER key or a paperclip as shown in Chapter 1.

26

If it doesn't start up with a paperclip and with no devices attached, reset with a paperclip again, this time holding the reset button in for five seconds. This resets the Power Manager. Now try to start up with the POWER key.

Apple notes a special problem on iBooks that have Preserve Memory Contents On Sleep selected in the Memory control panel. If the iBook fails to start up properly, the preserved RAM memory contents may be corrupt. To get around this, restart and immediately hold down the ESC key. This erases the preserved memory contents and starts up the iBook normally. Obviously, it's a last resort since you may lose data (anything that was in RAM memory at the time and hadn't been saved to the hard disk) by doing this. You'll also lose the contents of a RAM disk, if you were using one.

If none of that works, you may need to take your iBook in for service.

How to ... **Troubleshoot Display Problems**

Sometimes the problem with your iBook's display may not be a software issue, but an actual problem with the display. Although the iBook is a ruggedized version of a typical notebook computer, it's still possible that you'll run into display problems.

One common symptom is a screen that suddenly goes black or seems filled with "static" like a TV not connected to an antenna. This can indicate damaged cabling or circuitry inside the iBook. Try changing the angle of the screen to see if that improves things. This problem can occur by dropping the iBook or by repeatedly picking up the iBook by the display portion of the case. Have the iBook serviced immediately (after all, it may still be under warranty) if such display problems crop up.

Blinking Question Mark

If a question mark is blinking in the middle of your screen, it's a sign that the iBook can't find a disk with a working System Folder on it. Here's what you can do:

- Wait a minute or so. It may resolve itself. (If it does, check your Startup Disk control panel and make sure you have your iBook's internal hard disk selected as the startup disk.)

- Restart with CTRL-⌘-POWER.

- Reset the iBook using the POWER key or a paperclip.

26

If none of the previous steps does away with the blinking question mark, consider performing a step called "zapping the PRAM" to see if that gets your iBook to notice the drive and boot from it. Do that by restarting the iBook. After the startup tone, hold down ⌘-OPTION-P-R until you hear the startup chime two more times. Then, release the keys. That may cause iBook to find the internal hard disk and start up normally.

If these things don't work, start from the iBook Software Install or Software Restore CD and run Disk First Aid. Here's how:

1. Restart. (You can press CTRL-⌘-POWER, use the paperclip method described in Chapter 1, or restart with a paperclip.)

2. As the iBook starts, place the iBook Software Install or Software Restore CD in the drive tray. The iBook should start up from the CD. (If it doesn't, you should restart the iBook, this time holding down the C key right after the iBook plays its startup tones.)

3. Once the iBook has started, double-click Disk First Aid, which is located in the Utilities folder on the Install or Restore CD.

4. Run Disk First Aid as instructed later in this chapter in the section "Disk Doctors."

5. If Disk First Aid is able to fix the problem, try restarting again (this time, without holding the C key down). Your iBook may start right up from its

hard disk, signifying that the problem is fixed. If not, you may need to try commercial disk-doctor programs like Norton Utilities or Micromat TechTool (also described in the section "Disk Doctors").

The last resort is to reinstall the entire Mac OS, since it's possible that your System file or parts of the Mac OS are corrupted. Reinstalling the Mac OS is covered later in the section "Reinstall, Restore, and Update."

Peripheral Doesn't Work

If a USB device isn't working, check to make sure any required driver software is installed correctly and the device is correctly connected to the iBook. Also check to see if the device's power cable (if it has one) is plugged into the wall socket or surge protector. And make sure the surge protector is turned on and check to see that the AC wall socket is getting power. (It doesn't have a light switch that turns it on, does it?)

If everything is plugged in correctly, reset the device by turning it on and off. Also, unplug and replug the device's USB connector (which will often reset its USB driver) and follow the manual's instructions for resetting the device.

If the non-working device is connected to a hub, turn the hub on and off to reset it. If the USB device still doesn't work after unplugging and replugging it in, plug it directly into the iBook's USB port (instead of a hub). If it works, it could be that you have the wrong type of hub. Your USB peripheral may require a "powered hub," that is, a hub that supplies power to devices via the USB connection. Not all hubs are powered hubs.

If you're having trouble with your printer, check to make sure it's selected (highlighted) in the Chooser. Turn it on and off again (if it doesn't have a switch, unplug and replug the printer's cable), or check the printer's manual for a command that allows you to restart the printer.

If none of these work, unplug the device from the USB port and restart your iBook. Now, with the desktop up, plug the device back into the USB port. Hopefully, the cause will be detected, and the device will begin working again.

Get iBook's Battery to Work

If you're having trouble getting your iBook to run from its battery (that is, it'll run fine with the AC adapter, but unplug it and it goes dead) you should check the following:

- Make sure the battery is charging by plugging in your iBook's AC adapter (the one that shipped with it or an Apple-approved alternative).

  Remember that the iBook's power connector glows amber if the battery is charging and green if the battery has reached full charge. If the power connector is not glowing, you may have a problem with the AC adapter or your wall outlet. Try a different outlet or a different power strip. If you have access to one, try another adapter, too.

- Remove and reinstall the battery to make sure it's properly seated.

- Reset the power manager by pressing the reset button with a paperclip for a full five seconds.

- Try a different battery.

Software Problems

There are three basic causes of software problems. Let's define those quickly, then we'll take a look at the symptoms your iBook may be experiencing. Here are the problems that software can encounter on your iBook:

- **Bugs**   Bugs are the result of mistakes or oversights by programmers who created applications for the Mac OS. Usually, the only fix is to stop using the program (or stop using the problematic command) and update it.

- **Conflicts** Conflicts occur when two pieces of software—two applications, an application and a Mac OS extension, or two extensions—don't get along. Conflicts cause crashes and freezes and are usually solved by finding the culprits and updating or disabling them. Extension conflicts (conflicts between Mac OS extensions that load as the iBook starts up) are discussed later in "Troubleshoot the System Folder."

> TIP
> *Read the Read Me file that accompanies any applications causing you trouble. The Read Me file might tell you that the software is known to conflict with other software on your iBook.*

- **Corruption** Corruption occurs when data is overwritten with either bad or nonsensical information. This can cause all sorts of trouble, but typically causes crashes and freezes. This is solved by finding the corrupt data file and fixing it with a disk doctor program, replacing the corrupt data file with a new copy from a CD or installer program, or deleting the corrupt file.

Software Symptoms

These are the common symptoms and the first aid you should perform for the problem:

- **Error** This is an error message in the form of an alert dialog box (outlined in red) that includes an OK button. It tells you the last command you attempted could not be executed because something went wrong. *First Aid: Click OK and save your work. If the error sounds data-threatening—you're out of memory or disk space, a disk couldn't be found, or an error number is reported—it's a good idea to quit the program and restart your iBook.*

- **Crash** In this case, you get an error message and the application shuts down. Sometimes the application itself tells you about the problem; sometimes the Finder tells you there was an "Unexpected Quit." *First Aid: Save data in other open applications and restart your iBook.*

- **Freeze** Sometimes you'll get an error message, but typically the mouse pointer won't move, the clock isn't ticking, and nothing seems to be happening. *First Aid: Wait. See if anything happens. If you're using an external keyboard and/or mouse, check the trackpad and iBook's keyboard to see* *if they work. (You may have worked the external keyboard loose.) Check for any activity, such as the CD-ROM spinning or clicking sounds from the hard disk. Move on to the section "Freezes and Hangs."*

■ **Hang** This is similar to a freeze, but the mouse pointer still moves and you might see the clock change or the application menu blink (if it was blinking before). In other words, there's activity.
First Aid: Wait. Note if any activity in the front-most application occurs. If your data is important (and not recently saved) you should wait at least ten minutes before forcing the application to quit, as described later in "Freezes and Hangs."

Once you've gotten past the immediate first aid, you can move on to diagnose the cause of the problem and attempt a long-term solution.

Error Messages

These are the best sorts of errors to encounter, since they give you some indication of what's going on. If the error didn't crash the application, you'll likely already have some idea what's wrong. A printing error means you should check out your printer or the Chooser; an error loading a Web site or getting your e-mail might have something to do with your Internet connection (Remote Access, PPP, or TCP/IP control panels).

Some of the time, the error message is your guide. (Not every message is helpful, though, since some of them are designed exclusively for programmers to troubleshoot their applications.) Read the error message, then consult the rest of this section or check out the part of this book where that application or issue is discussed—something may be wrong with your iBook's settings or hardware configuration.

Some of the errors aren't as specific—let's take a quick look at those.

Out of Memory Error

Many times, an error message will tell you that you don't have enough memory or "not enough memory to complete task." This can happen for a variety of reasons.

If the error occurs in the Finder, quit some of the open applications that you have running. If the problem continues, quit all applications and attempt to restart your iBook. If that doesn't work (or if it freezes your iBook) see the section "Freezes and Hangs."

If the Out of Memory error occurs in the application you're using, do the following:

1. Save your data.

2. Switch to the Finder and choose About This Computer from the Apple menu.

3. Look to see how much of the application's memory allocation is being used (does it fill the entire allotted space?) and how much is left in the "Largest Unused Block." If the memory's allocation is filled or nearly filled, you'll want to assign the application more RAM through its Get Info dialog box, as discussed later in this section.

4. If the Largest Unused Block is less than 2MB or so, you might need to quit some of your other applications. You should also check the Memory control panel and make sure Virtual Memory is turned on. If Virtual Memory isn't turned on, your applications will require more RAM, and you'll be able to run fewer programs before errors occur. In nearly all cases, it should be turned on. (See Chapter 21 for more on the Memory control panel.)

If the problem is with the application's memory allocation, make these changes:

1. Quit the application.

2. Find the application's original icon. Select the icon and choose File | Get Info.

3. In the Get Info box, select Memory from the pull-down menu. You'll see entries for the Minimum Size and Preferred Size of the application. This is the amount of memory, in kilobytes, that the Mac OS allocates for the program. You might add about 512KB to the minimum and about 2000KB (or more) to the preferred.

4. Click the Get Info box's close box to close the window and register the change.

26

Now you should quit all applications, restart, and see if the error recurs. (You don't have to restart, but it's best to do so since restarting clears out memory and starts over fresh.)

If you get memory errors even though you've increased the allocation and you've shut down some applications, it's possible that memory has become fragmented. This is a temporary condition where memory is filled with unattached bits of data that haven't been properly disposed of after you've opened and closed many applications and/or documents. (It's sort of like application litter.) If memory gets too cluttered by fragmentation, you need to restart the iBook to get it working properly again.

TIP   *If Out of Memory errors happen often, consider upgrading the RAM in your iBook. Many iBooks shipped with 32MB of RAM, which is a little skimpy, especially if you're running Mac OS 9 and trying to work with graphics applications and games. Consult Chapter 23 for more on upgrading RAM.*

Disk Is Full Error

If your hard disk gets full or close to full, you'll start to see all sorts of error messages, including "Disk is Full." Most applications, Internet programs, and games write temporary files, preferences files, and other sorts of data to your hard disk, even when you're not actively saving a document. If your hard disk gets full, it will cause applications and the Mac OS to have trouble.

If it happens to you, the best plan is to delete any old documents (especially after you've backed them up to removable media or an external disk) and uninstall any applications or games that you don't immediately need. (You'll find that most application installers also have a Remove or Uninstall choice in their Custom Install menu.) You should also consider getting rid of image files and QuickTime movies—these are culprits that can take up a lot of disk space, as can games and educational software.

Crashes

There are a couple different kinds of crashes you'll encounter. Often they'll include an error message or an alert, but sometimes they just happen. Here's a look at what could occur:

- ■ **Error Message or Code** When an error message appears within the application itself, it means the application noticed the error. This can lead you to the source of the problem. It may be a bug in the document or corruption of the document.

- ■ **Unexpected Quitting** The program disappears, followed by a message in the Finder. This sort of crash often happens because there's a bug in the program or the program encountered a corrupt data file. This can also be a conflict, although corruption is the most likely culprit.

- ■ **No Message** In this case, the program just quits or disappears. You might notice more error messages in the Finder regarding memory. This could be corruption, but it's likely a conflict.

Test for Crashing

So what can you do about a crash? The most important thing is to get data saved in your applications and restart your iBook. After that, your priority is isolating the crash—figuring out when the crash occurs and any factors that contribute to it. Here are some questions to consider when it comes to crashes:

- ■ **Has your iBook been on for quite a while without restarting, or have you been running many different programs?** If so, it might just be that your iBook needed to be restarted.

- ■ **Have you added anything recently?** If you've recently installed a new application or utility program, it's possible it installed a new extension that's causing trouble. You can always try disabling any new extensions (see the section "Troubleshoot the System Folder" later in this chapter for information on how to do this).

- ■ **Is the crashing consistent?** If your iBook crashes every time you do something in particular—load a QuickTime movie, check your e-mail, load a particular game—then you may be closer to a solution.

If you can reproduce the error fairly consistently, then there are a few things you can try to test for the error and isolate it further. Here's what to try:

- **Test Different Documents**   It's possible that a particular document is corrupt, especially if the crash occurs as you're opening a document, as you're saving a document, as you're printing, or when you move to a particular page in a document. Find a similar document or two and test the application with those to see if the same crash occurs. If it doesn't, you can try running a disk doctor utility (or a special file-fixer utility) or just avoid using that document.

- **Remove the Preferences File**   Most applications have a Preferences file that's stored in the Preferences subfolder of the System Folder. Quit the application, move the Preferences file to the desktop or another folder, and restart the application. Some of its default behavior may change, and the crashing may also stop. If it does, throw away the Preferences file and reset your preferences within the application.

- **Restart Without Extensions**   As your iBook starts up, hold down the SHIFT key all the way until the desktop appears. This starts your iBook without extensions. Now, run the application and see if the error recurs. If it doesn't, there might be an extension conflict. See "Troubleshoot the System Folder," later in this chapter.

Fix Internet Crashing

Did the crash happen while you were browsing the Web? There may be a corrupt preferences file or a corrupt file in your browser's cache. You can delete the cache in Internet Explorer by choosing Edit | Preferences, then choosing Advanced. Click the Empty Cache Now button to empty the cache. In Netscape Communicator, choose Edit | Preferences. In the Preferences window, select the Cache category, then click the button Clear Disk Cache Now. Click OK to close the Preferences dialog box.

There is a special Internet Preferences file that's created by the Internet control panel. That Internet Preferences file gets changed and saved often by different applications, which can lead to corruption after a while. If you are crashing in many different Internet applications, try opening the Preferences folder and dragging the Internet Preferences file onto the desktop. Restart your iBook, reset your Internet Preferences in the Internet control panel, and try out your applications. If the crashing has gotten better, toss the old Internet Preferences file in the Trash. After doing so, you may have to reconfigure the Internet control panel and your Internet applications.

Freezes and Hangs

A *freeze* will bring the mouse pointer to a halt and nothing else will happen on the screen. A *hang* is a little different—the mouse pointer moves, even though things otherwise seem frozen. Why the difference? A hang results when an application has gone into an endless loop of some sort and can't break out to give control back to the Mac OS. A freeze occurs when an application goes bad and causes the Mac OS itself to seize up.

Freezes are odd symptoms, because they can be attributed to all the types of problems we've discussed: bugs, conflicts, or corruption. Freezes can also be caused by other applications that are running in the background, or even by trouble with printing or networking.

If it's really a freeze, you probably can't recover from it—the best you can do is restart. But, that doesn't mean you shouldn't try some stuff. After all, it's important to know if your iBook has actually frozen, or if it's just a hang. Here's what to do:

- If you have an external mouse and keyboard, make sure they haven't been unplugged accidentally. Try the iBook's keyboard and trackpad to make sure things are really frozen.

- Check the screen carefully for any activity.

- Wait. Get up and grab a cup of coffee or check to see if the mail has come. Five minutes or more might be a good idea.

- Press ⌘-. (period) to see if you can interrupt the program. Press ESC. If those don't work, try ⌘-Q to quit. If none of them are working, you can try a force quit—press ⌘-SHIFT-ESC. If the Force Quit dialog box appears, click the Force Quit button. The application may quit forcefully and return to the Finder without saving data.

- As a last resort, press ⌘-POWER (the POWER key on the keyboard). If a dialog box appears, type **G F** (include the space) and press RETURN. You'll either quit the program, you'll completely freeze up, or you'll get a crash requiring an immediate restart.

If none of those suggestions work, the iBook has frozen. Try to restart using CTRL-⌘-POWER to force the iBook to restart, or hold down the POWER button on the iBook's keyboard for five seconds or longer. If that doesn't work, you'll need to use the POWER key or a paperclip to restart the iBook. (See Chapter 1, which details the location of the reset hole.)

If the force quit does work, save work in other applications and restart immediately. After a force quit, your iBook is likely to crash or freeze again pretty soon.

Now, after you've restarted your iBook, you should test to see if the freezing recurs. Here are some possibilities:

- If the freeze recurs after you've restarted and launched the application again, check the application's Read Me file for known conflicts with other applications or Mac OS extensions.

- Try removing the application's preferences file from the Preferences folder in the System Folder and launch the application again to see if the freeze recurs.

- Start with extensions off (hold down the SHIFT key through the startup process) and see if the freeze recurs.

- Check with the software publisher's Web site to see if there are any bug fixes or other suggestions. Contact the publisher's technical support folks to see if they have any suggestions.

Fix Problems with Icons and Aliases

If your iBook begins to lose its unique icons—for instance, AppleWorks document icons become just plain white pieces of paper—or aliases begin to fail, that's a sign that the desktop database is corrupt. The desktop database is comprised of some special, hidden files that track the data you store using the Finder.

Other symptoms of desktop database problems include the Finder slowing way down, your iBook taking a long time to start up, and applications taking a long time to load and save documents.

The solution is to rebuild your desktop. You can do that with TechTool (described in the "Disk Doctors" section, later in this chapter), or you can do it the old-fashioned way that's built into the Mac OS. Hold down the ⌘-OPTION keys as the iBook starts up and keep holding them until you see the dialog box asking if you want to rebuild the desktop.

26

If you haven't run Disk First Aid in a while, it's probably a good idea to do that, just in case other parts of your disk have encountered trouble. (You can run it from the Utilities folder on your iBook.) You could even run a disk doctor tool like Norton Utilities if you have one handy.

Troubleshoot the System Folder

Occasionally, your problems will arise from within the System Folder, usually in the shape of an extension conflict. The extensions, stored in the Extensions folder, are small bits of computer code designed to patch or add themselves to the Mac OS as it starts up. For instance, Apple ships extensions that add QuickTime capability—the ability, at the Mac OS level, to identify and play back digital movies. If you started up your iBook with extensions off, you'd find that it's unable to play QuickTime movies because the proper extensions haven't been loaded.

In most cases, an application that's designed to work with the Mac OS has been tested fairly thoroughly and shouldn't experience a conflict. (This isn't always the case, and many applications have to be updated slightly when a new Mac OS update is created by Apple since small inconsistencies can affect programs.) But application authors, no matter how diligent, can't test their application with every conceivable extension available for the Mac OS—there are thousands of them. So, you'll sometimes experience a conflict or similar problem, thanks to an extension.

One of the solutions that some folks follow is to simply try not to install too many extensions. If you're the type who wants minimal trouble from your iBook, I'd recommend that you avoid most utilities, shareware, and other add-ons. If you're looking for no fuss, you should certainly look for software that specifically mentions the iBook or that has clearly been tested to work well with your version of the Mac OS—Mac OS 8.6, 9.0, or higher.

The best way to troubleshoot an extension problem is to hope someone has already figured it out and all you have to do is read about the conflict. If that doesn't work, though, then it's up to you to root out the conflict using the Extensions Manager. Let's take a look.

TIP *Want to track future installations to see if they add items to the Extensions folder? Go open it right now. Select every file in the folder—just click somewhere in the folder and press ⌘-A. Now, choose File | Label and give the files a label. Now, when a new extension is added, it won't have a label and the original extensions will. You can check every time you install a new application.*

Is the Conflict a "Known Issue"?

The Read Me file for the application that seems to be suffering a conflict, as well as any other Read Me files you can come across (especially those for applications or utilities you've recently installed), is the first place you should look when you suspect a conflict. If you've recently installed extensions or control panels, you should look into them as well. It's possible that the conflict is actually a known issue, and that the software publisher recommends you not use the program in combination with certain extensions or particular applications.

You should also check the technical support Web site for the troubled application and call the application publisher's customer support number. If there really is a conflict, you're probably not the first person to ever encounter it and tech support might be able to point you in the right direction.

Don't forget about the Mac OS Read Me files, which can help you determine conflicts and known problems.

Extensions Manager: Test for Conflicts

When a conflict occurs between an extension and an application—or an extension and another extension—it's tough to diagnose on your own. But if you can't find information from any of the software publishers that seem to be involved, then testing yourself becomes necessary.

You won't enjoy, this, though. Set aside a few hours one afternoon and grab a book or magazine, because this can take a while. You'll want to use the Extensions Manager—it's a control panel that allows you to selectively activate and deactivate extensions and other control panels that are installed on your iBook.

TIP   *Conflict Catcher from Casady and Greene (**http://www.casadyg.com/**) does a nice job of automating this process, making it a bit more bearable. Casady and Greene also has a time-limited demo that you can download to test for trouble.*

Here's how conflict troubleshooting works:

1. Select Control Panels | Extensions Manager from the Apple menu to open the Extensions Manager.

26

2. In the Extensions Manager, pull down the Selected Set menu and choose Mac OS 8.6 All. (If you have Mac OS 9, choose Mac OS 9 All.) This selects only the extensions that Apple originally designed to work with the iBook.

3. Click the Restart button. After your iBook restarts, launch the application that was giving you trouble and see if the same error persists. If it does, then your application may have a conflict with the Mac OS itself. Contact the application publisher.

4. If you get a different error after restarting, it's possible that you disabled an extension required by the application—if the application gives you some indication of which extension it is, go into the Extensions Manager and re-enable that extension. (Click to place a check mark next to any extension that you want to have installed.) Now restart and test again.

5. If you're not having trouble anymore, that's a sign that you're having a bona fide extension conflict. Open the Extensions Manager again, and choose View | As Folders. This allows you to see everything that's in the Extensions folder at one time.

6. Make sure you're viewing extensions—the Extensions folder is revealed and a list of extensions appears below it. Now, place a check mark next to three or four extensions at the top of the list. (The first time you do this, you'll be asked to create a new extensions set. Click Duplicate Set, then enter a name like "Test Set" and click Duplicate.) Once you've added three to five extensions in alphabetical order, click the Restart button.

7. Test again for the conflict. If things seem to be working OK, go back to step 6 and keep adding extensions.

> TIP
>
> *It's often handy to print out the Mac OS All Sets and the Test Sets you create. This way you can compare what's different, crossing out what is similar on each page. I find this speeds up extension troubleshooting. In the Extensions Manager's File menu you can choose "Save Set as Text," which allows you to save the set as a text file. You can then open that file in SimpleText and print a list of all the items in that set.*

8. If the conflict does recur, stop what you're doing, go back and re-disable the last batch of extensions you enabled. (Here's why it's a good idea to write down the extensions you're adding each time.) Now, enable the *first* of those extensions and Restart.

9. After the restart, open your application and test for the conflict. If the conflict doesn't occur, go back, enable the next extension, and restart again. Repeat until the conflict does occur. When it does, you've figured out which extension is causing the conflict! Actually, you only know one of the extensions causing a conflict. You still need to do a little more testing.

10. In the Extensions Manager again, pull down the Selected Set menu and choose the Mac OS 8.6 All or Mac OS 9 All entry again. Now, find the extension you've identified as a problem and place a check mark next to it. (When you do, you'll be asked to create another extension set. Call this one "Test 2 Set" or something similar, and save it.) Click the Restart button.

11. Test to see if the conflict problem recurs. If it does, then you can pop down to the section below called Resolve the Conflict. If the conflict *doesn't* recur, then you'll need to start the conflict test again—it looks like your conflict may involve two extensions.

12. Add three or more extensions to the Test 2 Set and restart. Test for the problem. Add more extensions if it doesn't recur. If you do encounter the problem, then disable the last set of added extensions and add them back in one at a time, restarting and testing each time. Finally, when you identify the second extension that's causing trouble, you're getting very close.

13. From the Selected Sets menu, choose Mac OS All once more. Place a check mark next to the two extensions you've identified as the problem. (You'll be asked to create a third set—call it "Test 3 Set.") Now, with just the Mac OS extensions and the two potential problem extensions enabled, restart.

14. Test again. If you get the conflict, you've found your problem. If you don't get the conflict, you may be in the absolutely rare situation of a three-way conflict. Pop some popcorn and keep testing.

Resolve the Conflict

Now that you know what's causing the problem, the best way to resolve the conflict is to visit the makers of the conflicting software and see if any of them have a work-around, an admission of guilt, or an upgrade posted that deals with this problem. You might also want to call their customer support line and see if you can get any help that way.

If those things don't work out, you might want to select one of the extensions and leave it disabled if it's not absolutely vital to your daily iBook experience. At least then you won't have to deal with the conflict.

You can try one other thing, too. Sometimes extensions conflict because of the *order* in which they're being loaded. Extensions load alphabetically, so you can change the order by opening the Extensions folder in the System Folder and editing the name. Put a space in front of the name to move it to the top of the alphabetical list. If you want the extension to load at the bottom of the extensions list, place a bullet point (OPTION-8) in front of the name. Now, restart with your edited extension names and see if the conflict recurs.

Reinstall, Restore, and Update

Eventually, you may get to the point that you need to reinstall your applications, reinstall the Mac OS, or even update the iBook or Mac OS. As far as reinstalling and restoring go, you can do those things easily using the software CDs that came with your iBook. You can also update your iBook using the updates posted by Apple on the iBook Support Web site.

Uninstall and Reinstall Applications

If you want to get rid of an application, the best way to do it is usually to launch the applications installer program and choose Uninstall or Remove from the Custom Install menu. That's the best way because, with most applications, it removes any special extensions or control panels the application added to your iBook.

If you need to manually uninstall an application, that shouldn't be too much harder. Just drag the application's folder to the Trash. Now, open the System Folder, then the Preferences folder, and drag the application's Preferences file to the Trash, too.

Before doing this, it's a good idea to check the application folder and make sure you didn't store any important documents in that folder—you can reinstall the application, if necessary, but you can't recover the documents you delete accidentally. You should also stop to consider whether or not you have another application that can read documents created in the uninstalled application. If you don't have one and you think you may need to read those documents at some point, then you might want to translate them to another document format before tossing the application for good.

If you've uninstalled an application in this way, then it's usually pretty simple to reinstall the application—just run the installation program. Before reinstalling, you should probably make sure that the old Preferences file has been deleted, and that there isn't another version of the application already on your hard disk. (Two versions of the same application could cause trouble, and will definitely cause confusion.) Other than that, reinstalling is pretty easy to do.

Software Restore

If you ever get in real trouble with your iBook, you have an out that can save you, get things up and running again, and hopefully go a long way to solving your problems. It's called the Software Restore, and it allows you to reinstall the Mac OS and your applications to the state they were when you first pulled your iBook out of the box and set it up.

Even if that sounds enticing, realize that this is a recourse of last resort. Doing this can wipe out any changes you've made to the Mac OS, settings you made in various control panels, updates you've made to your applications, and so on. It's important that you not perform a Software Restore lightly, since you're in for some extra work—reconfiguring and reinstalling extras—once you've performed the Restore. Still, it's there if you need it.

To perform the Software Restore, you'll be restarting your iBook and booting off the Software Restore CD. Here's how the Software Restore works:

1. If your iBook is on, insert the Software Restore CD in your iBook's CD-ROM drive and restart the iBook. If your iBook is off, start it up, then quickly press the CD-ROM drive's button to open it. Place the Software Restore CD in the drive and close it back up.

2. If your iBook doesn't automatically start up from the CD, restart the iBook and hold down the C key after you hear the startup tone.

3. Once the iBook has started up from the CD, double-click the Apple Software Restore icon on the CD.

4. Now choose between the three basic ways to perform a Software Restore. Click the Restore In Place check box if you'd like the iBook to restore the Mac OS and applications to their original state. Choose Erase Mac HD Before Restoring if you'd like the hard disk to be erased before the restoration takes place. If you choose Restore, Saving Original Items, then the existing contents of your hard disk will be moved to a folder called Original Items, and your applications and Mac OS will be restored.

NOTE *Choosing Restore In Place won't erase your Documents folder or most of the other folders on your hard disk. It will, however, change settings in the Mac OS and may erase any updates you've added to the software originally bundled with your iBook. Choosing Erase Mac HD Before Restoring will wipe out everything on the disk, including documents, games, and so on. If you've installed a newer version of the Mac OS or any of its components, you'll need to reinstall it after the Software Restore. Choosing Restore, Saving Original Items will require quite a bit of additional hard disk space.*

5. If you've chosen Erase Mac HD Before Restoring, you can also choose how you want your hard disk formatted—with Standard or Extended Mac OS format. The Extended Mac OS format gives you more efficient use of the hard disk so that you can pack more files onto the drive. (Extended is the best choice, but you might have some reason to choose Standard that you're not willing to share with the rest of the class.) Make your choice from the menu.

6. Once you've made all your decisions, click Restore to begin the process.

Your iBook starts the process of erasing your hard disk (if you chose that option) and restoring the original Mac OS and applications to your hard disk. After this process is over, your iBook is restarted and, hopefully, starts up from its internal hard disk again in all its splendid, restored glory.

Now it's up to you to go through the process of configuring the iBook again and copying over documents from your backups. You may also need to reinstall applications, reapply updates, and basically spend an afternoon getting everything back into shape.

Update Your iBook's System Software

Early in this chapter we discussed the fact that you can update the firmware in your iBook. You can also update applications and, occasionally, the Mac OS. In most cases, those software updates use an interface that's exactly like the typical software installer—you choose the installation and tell the installer which drive you want to install on. They aren't tough to use. Check Apple's iBook Support Web site for details on the various updates available for iBook software and the Mac OS.

SHORTCUT   *If you have Mac OS 9, you may be able to skip all this searching if you use the Software Update control panel. That's discussed in the sidebar "How to...Use Software Update," later in this chapter.*

A firmware update is a slightly different story. You'll also find these on the Apple Support site, but they're installed slightly differently. First, you'll want to download the update from the Web. Then, once the update has been processed by StuffIt Expander, it appears as a disk image. Double-click it to mount the disk. Once the disk appears on the desktop, double-click the Firmware Updater icon.

NOTE   *It's also possible that you'll find updaters for other firmware inside your iBook, like the modem's firmware. In these cases, the instructions may be slightly different. See the Read Me file that comes with those firmware updates for instructions.*

Here's how the process goes:

1. If your firmware is up to date already, you'll immediately see a dialog box letting you know that. If it's not, all applications are quit in the background and the updater continues.

2. You'll see a dialog box explaining the process. When you click Update, your iBook restarts.

3. Now, after the iBook has restarted, you'll see a small indicator bar that tells you that the update is progressing.

4. When the update is finished, PRAM is automatically zapped (you'll hear a series of startup tones), then the iBook starts up.

5. When you get to the desktop, the iBook should tell you that the firmware was updated successfully.

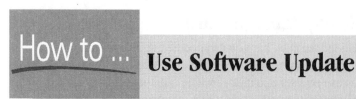 **Use Software Update**

Mac OS 9 comes with a new utility that's specially designed to help you maintain your iBook. The Software Update control panel, new in this version, uses the Internet and a special database maintained by Apple to help ensure that your system software is as up to date as possible. It's also very easy to use. Choose Software Update from the control panels and you'll see the Software Update control panel appear.

Now, to update immediately, click the Update Now button. If your iBook is designed to connect automatically to the Internet—or if you have an Ethernet or wireless Internet connection—Software Update will jump on the Internet, check Apple's servers, and see if anything important has been updated. (Note: If you use Remote Access to connect, you may need to have your connection running before Software Update can work its magic.)

If Software Update finds anything, it will notify you with a dialog box, asking if you're interested in downloading the update. If it doesn't find anything, you'll see a dialog box to that effect, too.

If you'd like, you can schedule Software Update to check on its own for updates to the Mac OS. Here's how:

1. Turn on the Update Software Automatically option.

2. Click the Set Schedule button.

3. In the Set Schedule dialog box, you can choose the time of day and which days of the week you want Software Update to check for updates. Click OK.

4. Back in the Software Update dialog box, turn on the Ask Me Before Downloading New Software option if you don't want Software Update to automatically download any updates in the background.

Upgrade to Mac OS 9

If your iBook came with Mac OS 8.6, you may wish to update to Mac OS 9, which is available as a commercial package in stores, or, if you qualify, through the low-cost Mac OS Up-to-Date program (**http://www.apple.com/macos/ uptodate/**). Mac OS 9 adds a number of different features to your iBook, many of which are discussed throughout this book.

NOTE *If you already have Mac OS 9, incremental updates can be accomplished using the Software Update control panel, which is discussed in the previous sidebar "How to...Use Software Update."*

The Mac OS 9 installer works pretty much like the Mac OS 8.6 installer—you run the installation program and read the instructions on screen. Here's how it goes:

1. Double-click the Mac OS Install icon. This launches the installer.

2. After you've read the introductory screen, click the Continue button.

3. You'll see another screen in the Installer that tells you whether or not you have enough disk space for the installation. (If you have more than one disk connected to your iBook, you can select the disk where you'll install the Mac OS from the Destination Disk pop-up menu. You're not likely to

have a disk to select, however, since the Mac OS can't start up from USB disks connected to an iBook.) If you don't have enough disk space, you should switch back to the Finder and delete files you don't need. If you have enough disk space, you can consider performing a Clean Install by selecting the Options button and selecting Perform Clean Installation. Then, click the Select button.

NOTE   *A Clean Install creates a new System Folder on your iBook's hard disk and installs Mac OS 9 into that System Folder. It then makes it the active System Folder, turning your current System Folder into a folder called "Previous System Folder." This has the advantage of starting you off with a clean, perfect new installation of Mac OS 9. It has the disadvantage of not including your Preferences files, any new extensions you've installed, or anything else that's changed in the System Folder. If you have a good backup of your current System Folder and you're not having any trouble with it, you can perform a regular installation that installs over the existing System Folder. If it works, it's a lot easier.*

4. Now you'll see the Before You Install document, which is simply a Read Me file that tells you last-minute information about Mac OS 9 and its known issues and conflicts. Click Continue when you're done reading.

5. Now you'll read the Software License Agreement. After dissecting it and running it by your attorney for approval, click Continue. In the box that pops up, click Agree if you agree with the license. If you click Disagree, the Installer reverts to the Welcome screen.

6. Otherwise, you're at the Installation screen. Here you can do two things. To begin a standard installation of the Mac OS, click the Start button. To customize your installation, click the Customize button. This brings up a list of components to be installed by the Mac OS installer. Place a check mark next to items you want to install and click to remove the check mark next to items you don't want to install. Then, click the Start button to begin the installation.

NOTE *You can customize even further, if you like. If you want to customize what each component installs, select the pop-up menu next to that component in the Installation Mode column. Choose Customized Installation from the menu, and you'll see more options for customizing what, exactly, the component installs. Click OK once you've customized the component, then click Start to begin the overall installation.*

The installer checks your hard disk for errors, installs new hard disk driver software if it is needed, then begins installing the Mac OS. When it's done, you'll see a dialog box that asks you to restart your iBook. Click the Restart button. When the Mac OS starts back up, it should be the new version!

26

Maintain Your iBook

One of the best ways I know to help you get the most out of your iBook is a maintenance schedule. It's important to any iBook that some basic steps take place every week, every few weeks, or once every couple of months.

Here, then, are some of the things you do in the course of iBook maintenance. Let's begin with a schedule for the maintenance, then we'll take a close look at what each schedule item entails.

The iBook Maintenance Schedule

A lot of the problems that occur with your iBook's hard disk, Mac OS system files, and other arcana occur slowly—a little file corruption starts to sneak in, causing more problems. Pretty soon things cascade.

What are the things you should do? There are two lists: the occasional stuff (every few days) and the time-based issues. As you work, you should regularly do the following when you're working with your iBook:

■ **Restart occasionally.**   After starting and quitting many programs, your iBook's memory can become fragmented, which leads to errors. If you restart (using the Special menu) after lunch or before a major Internet surfing session, you'll get better performance with fewer errors.

■ **Check your hard disk space regularly.** If your hard disk ever fills up or comes close to it, you'll start to see errors in your applications. Make a point of throwing away documents that you're done with and basically keeping things tidy. That way you won't fill up your drive, plus you won't have to commit to major purging sessions every few months to regain disk space. Check disk space by opening your Macintosh HD icon and looking at the top of the window to see how much space is available. You can also select your hard disk icon in the Finder and choose File | Get Info. Check the Available entry.

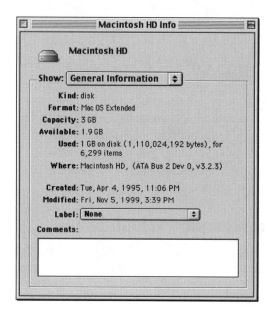

That's just the stuff you should do occasionally while working on your iBook. Here, then, are some issues you should look into on a regular basis:

■ **Once or a Few Times a Week** Back up your hard disk to an online site or to a removable disk. Online backup is discussed in Chapter 18; removable disks and backups are discussed in Chapter 23.

■ **Every Week** Since your iBook is designed to live on the Internet, chances are that you're downloading and working with many different files from different sources. This is a great way to catch a computer virus, as discussed later in this chapter. Every week you should run a virus-checking program.

- **Every Month** Rebuild the desktop file and run Disk First Aid. Do this by holding down the ⌘ and OPTION keys and restarting your iBook. Hold down the keys all the way through the startup sequence until you see the Rebuilding the Desktop dialog box. Disk First Aid can be found in the Utilities folder on your iBook's hard disk.

- **Every One to Three Months** Head out to the Apple iBook Support site, **http://www.apple.com/support/**, the SoftWatcher Mac site, **http://www.softwatcher.com/mac/**, and the Version Tracker site, **http://www.versiontracker.com/** to see if there are updates to your iBook's system software or applications. These updates will often fix bugs and sometimes include new features that you'll want to add. You should also check to see if Apple has posted a new version of the iBook's hard disk driver or an update to the Mac OS that you should consider installing.

26

NOTE *If you have Mac OS 9, you can set the Software Update feature to automatically check for updates, making it unnecessary to check for updates to your Apple software. You'll still want to search for other software updates, however.*

- **Every Three Months** With a program like Norton Utilities, MicroMat's TechTool Pro, or Alsoft's DiskExpress Pro, you should check your hard disk for problems with corrupt directories or files. You can also, at this point, run a defragmentation utility to determine if your disk has become fragmented and in need of repair. See the section "Disk Doctors," later in this chapter.

That checklist should keep your iBook out of trouble, most of the time. If you follow this sort of schedule, then it's much less likely that problems will fester and grow on your iBook. You'll experience less trouble and more carefree computing.

Check for Viruses

A computer virus is a program that attaches itself to other programs and attempts to replicate itself as much as it can, usually by being transferred via disks, network connections, and the Internet. Not all viruses are designed to cause harm, although they can, anyway, by accident. Others really are designed to infect your files, rendering them useless or sometimes deleting or destroying them.

In one sense, viruses on computers work the same way that physical viruses work. The more you're exposed to high-risk situations—the Internet, swapping

Zip disks, and using a large computer network—the more likely you are to be infected. And with your iBook, you're probably spending enough time online to be high-risk.

 In case you're curious, viruses are computer programs written by people. Virus authors are usually interested in causing consternation and fear around the world. Sometimes that's enough—other times, it's important to the virus author that they also cause trouble and loss.

Viral Symptoms

By definition, viruses are hidden. There are sometimes some symptoms that can tell you when a virus has struck or is present. While these symptoms might be caused by other problems, too, it's a good idea to run your virus-checking program when you encounter issues like these:

- Long, unexpected disk activity occurs, especially when no applications are running.

- The system unexpectedly restarts after running or downloading a program or mounting a removable media disk.

- Apparently automatic behavior occurs that can't be attributed to a program or AppleScript—such as files moving on their own, the mouse pointer doing odd things, or dialog boxes appearing.

- A launched application doesn't appear or appears after a long delay.

- Files and folders disappear suddenly or can't be opened.

- File details, the amount of space on a drive, or similar statistics change on their own.

There are also viruses that work within particular applications instead of within the Mac OS. Viruses appear especially frequently in Microsoft Word, where documents can be automatically turned into templates, making it impossible to access parts of the document or to save the document as a regular Word file. If you notice odd behavior in a Microsoft Office application, that might be time to look for a Word (or Excel) Macro virus.

Detect and Clean Viruses

If you're online a lot with your iBook, consider getting yourself a virus-protection program. These programs generally run in the background, checking files as they appear on your hard disk or from a removable disk. You can also schedule them to check while you're not using your iBook—late at night or on the weekends, for instance.

There are two major virus packages for the Mac OS—Norton AntiVirus (**http://www.norton.com/**) and Dr. Solomon's Virex (**http://www.drsolomon.com/**). Both of these are available from online Mac stores as well as in computer stores and superstores that carry Mac OS products.

Most of the time the scans take place in the background. When the virus program detects a file that it thinks may be infected, it'll let you know. Sometimes the detector will automatically move infected files to a particular folder. Other times, it may be able to clean the virus from the file after it's been isolated.

I wouldn't even try to clean a file unless you absolutely need access to its data and you don't have a good backup. (Remember, the backup might be infected as well—you should check). If the infected file is a document that you need, you can try to clean the virus from it.

Both of the major virus protection utilities give you the choice of scheduling scans, scanning files as they're added to your iBook (from the Internet or from removable media), or only scanning when you actively ask the program to scan. For maximum protection you should leave the scanner on all the time to check programs as they're downloaded. If you find this is annoying, then I'd recommend scheduling regular scans for when you're away from the computer.

One thing you should definitely do is update your virus definitions. The virus-protection publishers come out with updates, usually every month, that allow the software to detect more viruses, fight them better, and protect against new types of infections. You should surf to the publisher's site or to **http://www.download.com/**, **http://www.macdownload.com/**, or **http://www.versiontracker.com/** to see what new virus definitions have been uploaded for your checker.

The QuickTime AutoStart Virus

One particularly vicious strain of virus has cropped up in the past few years. It's called the AutoStart virus, and it infects Macs and iBooks through a loophole in QuickTime. When QuickTime CD-ROM AutoPlay is enabled, it allows a CD to be automatically started up when it's inserted in the CD-ROM drive.

26

Unfortunately, that same feature allows this virus to be launched, copying itself to your System Folder and potentially causing damage throughout your files.

One way to avoid the virus is to open the QuickTime control panel and choose AutoPlay from the pull-down menu. Now make sure that neither of the AutoPlay options is selected. That will keep the virus from copying itself on your hard disk.

The major virus programs can detect most strains of the AutoStart virus, so run the checker regularly.

When a Virus Isn't a Virus

Viruses are a popular topic for e-mail hoaxes—e-mail messages distributed in chain-letter form, telling you to "pass it on" and "spread the word." These messages offer spurious information about some dire problem. The e-mail warnings generally show up in the form of a virus alert that's been released by "the U.S. government," "Microsoft," "a university lab," or some other organization that seems credible. A dead giveaway is misspellings or grammatical errors in the message.

Most of them also claim that reading a particular e-mail message or loading a particular Web page causes a virus to spread to your iBook. This really isn't the case—a virus can't be spread through the text of a message, so simply reading an e-mail message will not give your iBook a virus. If you *execute an attached document or program*, then it's possible to get a virus, so don't use attachments from people you don't know.

The "open an e-mail" virus alerts are hoaxes, though. Read carefully and you'll see that they probably even have misspellings or bizarre grammatical constructs, considering their supposed source. For the official word on viruses (and many virus hoaxes) the best place to turn is the Symantec Anti-Virus Research Center at **http://www.symantec.com/avcenter/index.html** on the Web.

Disk Doctors

Part of your maintenance routine will require the use of special utility programs designed to help you find corruption, fix disks, and so on. A few of those utilities are free, but others will cost some money. Let's take a look at both.

Disk First Aid

Disk First Aid (see Figure 26-1) is included with your iBook and is designed to find problems with the directory structure of your iBook. Run it every month or so because it enables you to find directory problems before they crop up. To run Disk First Aid, find it in the Utilities folder and double-click its icon.

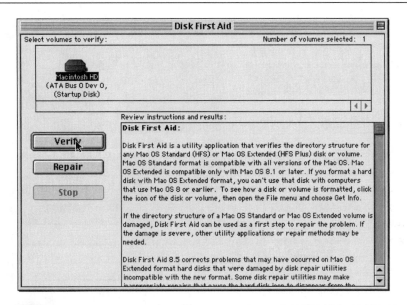

FIGURE 26-1   Disk First Aid can solve many basic problems with your iBook's disk.

In the top window, select the disk you want to verify—most likely it's the Macintosh HD volume. You can now click Verify to simply have Disk First Aid take a look at the drive and see how everything is doing. If you want to repair the disk while it's being verified, click Repair. This accomplishes two steps in one click.

Now Disk First Aid runs through the disk looking for corruption in the directory structure. If it finds a problem, it'll alert you, asking if you want to fix the problem. (This is true in some cases; in others, it just goes ahead and fixes things.) Otherwise, you'll get through your session and, hopefully, receive a clean bill of health.

MicroMat TechTool

MicroMat makes two versions of TechTool. The first is a freeware version you can download from their Web site at **http://www.micromat.com/**. TechTool Freeware (see Figure 26-2) is a program that makes it easy to do two things—rebuild your desktop and zap PRAM. Zapping PRAM is a technique used when you're troubleshooting a Mac. Rebuilding your desktop is something you should do regularly, and TechTool Freeware makes it easier and does it more thoroughly than the OPTION-⌘ method.

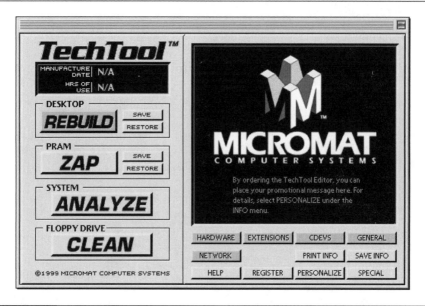

FIGURE 26-2 TechTool Freeware can perform a few basic tasks like rebuilding the desktop and zapping PRAM.

You'll want to get TechTool 1.1.9 or higher for use with your iBook. Version 1.1.9 was still in development at the time of writing, but should be available by the time you read this.

TechTool can also be used to save the PRAM and Desktop Database before they're zapped and rebuilt, respectively, just in case any trouble arises. And it can be used to analyze your system for some basic troubles, as well as offering information about your iBook (just click the buttons in the lower-right portion of the window).

Along with TechTool Freeware, MicroMat also makes a version called TechTool Pro, which is commercial software. It adds the ability to analyze your iBook in depth and fix disk problems and file issues, including accidentally deleted files. It's very useful to have around.

Norton Utilities

MicroMat's major competitor is Symantec Corporation, maker of Norton Utilities (**http://www.norton.com/**). Norton Utilities offers a number of different programs that help you keep your iBook running smoothly, including:

- **Norton Disk Doctor**   Analyzes and fixes all sorts of trouble with your hard disk.

- **Volume Recover and FileSaver**   Allows you to track and save data from files or entire disks, including removable disks.

- **Speed Disk**   Defragments and optimizes your hard disk for better performance.

- **CrashGuard**   Recovers from some errors in your applications before they freeze or crash your iBook.

- **UnErase**   Tracks and retrieves files you've deleted accidentally.

Norton is a great way to keep your iBook in good shape, guard against trouble, and if you make an occasional mistake, it'll try to bail you out.

26

Index